Biblical Interpretation for Laypeople and Other Martyrs

Biblical Interpretation for Laypeople and Other Martyrs

A SANE STUDY IN HERMENEUTICS FOR CONTEMPORARY LIFE

David W. Melber

Copyright © 2019 by David W. Melber.

Library of Congress Control Number:		2018915275
ISBN:	Hardcover	978-1-9845-7443-5
	Softcover	978-1-9845-7442-8
	eBook	978-1-9845-7441-1

All rights reserved. No part of this book may be reproduced or transmitted in any form or by any means, electronic or mechanical, including photocopying, recording, or by any information storage and retrieval system, without permission in writing from the copyright owner.

Any people depicted in stock imagery provided by Getty Images are models, and such images are being used for illustrative purposes only.
Certain stock imagery © Getty Images.

NIV
Scripture quotations marked NIV are taken from the Holy Bible, New International Version®. NIV®. Copyright © 1973, 1978, 1984 by International Bible Society. Used by permission of Zondervan. All rights reserved. [Biblica]

KJV
Scripture quotations marked KJV are from the Holy Bible, King James Version (Authorized Version). First published in 1611. Quoted from the KJV Classic Reference Bible, Copyright © 1983 by The Zondervan Corporation.

NKJV
Scripture quotations marked NKJV are taken from the New King James Version. Copyright © 1982 by Thomas Nelson, Inc. Used by permission. All rights reserved.

RSV
Scripture quotations marked RSV are taken from the Revised Standard Version of the Bible, copyright © 1946, 1952, 1971 by the Division of Christian Education of the National Council of the Churches of Christ in the USA. Used by permission.

NRSV
Scripture quotations marked NRSV are taken from the New Revised Standard Version of the Bible, Copyright © 1989, by the Division of Christian Education of the National Council of the Churches of Christ in the United States of America. Used by permission. All rights reserved. Website

Print information available on the last page.

Rev. date: 01/02/2019

To order additional copies of this book, contact:
Xlibris
1-888-795-4274
www.Xlibris.com
Orders@Xlibris.com
788823

Contents

PREFACE.. ix
ACKNOWLEDGMENTS.. xi
INTRODUCTION xiii

CHAPTER 1   HISTORICAL BACKGROUND 1
CHAPTER 2   SUMMARY OF BOOKS OF THE BIBLE 21
CHAPTER 3   TOOLS OF INTERPRETATION 50
CHAPTER 4   THE PROCESS OF HERMENEUTICS 55
CHAPTER 5   METHODS OF INTERPRETATION 85
CHAPTER 6   SHORT FIGURES OF SPEECH 110
CHAPTER 7   LONG FIGURES OF SPEECH........................... 121
CHAPTER 8   PROPHECY AND TYPOLOGY 131
CHAPTER 9   SYMBOLISM AND APOCALYPTIC
             LITERATURE 146
CHAPTER 10 THE CANON OF SCRIPTURE 156
CHAPTER 11 THE INSPIRATION AND AUTHORITY 184
CHAPTER 12 PURPOSE OF SCRIPTURE 199
CHAPTER 13 APPLICATION OF BIBLE TO MODERN
             ISSUES.. 220

CONCLUSION 341
APPENDIX A: THE TOOLS 345
APPENDIX B: DEFINITIONS 351
BIBLIOGRAPHY 355

Dedicated to Ann,

whose love was the embodiment

of Christ's love and whose loss has diminished my life

PREFACE

Flaws in some citations have to do with the development of the book. I originally wrote this series as a topic for a summer youth camp in the early 1970s. The reception from the kids was positive enough that I rewrote it and adapted it for adults. I have used it for adult Sunday schools over the years. Each time I presented it, I made minor modifications and additions. The topic was merely in outline form. I had my own notes to illustrate each point before having the class members do the assignments. In the mid-1980s, the notes on the outline were so cluttered I put it in text form. For the first decade or two, I made no notice of where I got my information. Citations were irrelevant. Now I am sorry that I paid no attention to my sources. I have forgotten numerous resources.

This study will not go into the nuances of scholars for several reasons. First, the clarity of scripture is sufficient to communicate without one having to be a scholar.

Another reason for not going so deep is that I don't have the academic ability to dig deeply into scholarly issues. This book is meant to be fairly simple, but it is not meant to be the pabulum that most laywomen and laymen are used to getting. I intend to challenge the reader to push the envelope beyond the Sunday school children's level of understanding and develop the ability to interpret the Bible in such a way that they can grapple with the complicated and challenging moral issues of our day—to interpret and apply scripture like an adult. I tried to write in such a way that a layperson with average intelligence would understand 95 percent of this writing. St. Paul said it very well: "When I was a child, I talked like a child, I thought like a child, I reasoned like a child. When I became a man, I put the ways of childhood behind me" (1 Cor. 13:11). While it may be challenging, I have attempted to write it on a level that a layperson with average intelligence can understand virtually all of it.

Chapters 9 and 10 are chapters I believe laypersons desperately need to study. Chapter 9, on canon, deals with the issue of what belongs in the canon of scripture and how the books got there, something of which most laypeople have little knowledge. It is not that they cannot understand— it is just that no one ever shared it with them. Chapter 10 deals with inspiration, an issue that has divided many denominations. And it is an issue that many of us have been dishonest or schizophrenic about or have played like the three little monkeys about—choosing to close our eyes, ears, and mouths. Years after writing this last statement, I came across this statement by Peter Berger: "Honest, sustained reflection recoils from cognitive schizophrenia."[1]

Chapter 11, perhaps one of the most important chapters, is on epistemology (how do we know?), ontology (what is our purpose?), and ethics (what *should* we do?). Finally, chapter 12 deals with the application of biblical principles to actual life situations based on sociological and journalistic research rather than strongly held fallacious perceptions that people have that may have little to do with reality.

This study of hermeneutics is oriented toward the laity. I hope it will provide a playing field in which understanding scripture from a nonschizophrenic point of view will be nonthreatening and thoughtfully Christian rather than wild-eyed speculation and ignoring context. It is my hope that this book will be a breakthrough for some laity and that it will be a springboard to unleashing the power of the Holy Spirit in their lives through their biblical studies.

---

[1]   Peter L. Berger, *A Rumor of Angels: Modern Society and the Rediscovery of the Supernatural* (Garden City, New York: Anchor Books, 1970), 29.

ACKNOWLEDGMENTS

When one puts anything into print, it's like having a child. He wants to believe his baby is perfect. But then it comes under the influence of others—friends, teachers, etc. The child begins to express ideas that are no longer just reflecting the mother's or father's ideas. But it may be better. Because of that, I am grateful for all those who have read my manuscript and found the flaws in the baby I created and have made it better. My gratitude goes to Tom Egan, a former Roman Catholic priest, a fellow senior softball player, and a retired adjunct professor of philosophy at Loyola University.

However, the text is not aimed at people with his academic acumen, but at the laity. Therefore, I also acknowledge the ordinary, intelligent, but nonacademic Christians who honored me by critiquing the book. I am indebted to others who made significant contributions to making the book applicable to laypeople: Merle Zimmermann, Jonathan Hoyle, Lil Boyle, John Berry, Cheryl Nuwash, and Judi Rockman. The remaining flaws are mine.

INTRODUCTION

In 1961, in his little book *Your God Is Too Small,* J. B. Phillips attempted to address the immature, and therefore dysfunctional, concepts that Christians have of God. He pointed out that

> while their experience of life has grown in a score of directions, and their mental horizons have been expanded to the point of bewilderment by world events and by scientific discoveries, their ideas of God have remained largely static. It is obviously impossible for an adult to worship the conception of God that exists in the mind of a child of Sunday-school age, unless he is prepared to deny his own experience of life. If, by a great effort of will, he does do this, he will always be secretly afraid lest some new truth may expose the juvenility of his faith.[2]

He further says that the outsider sees joining the church, therefore, as being "a party to a piece of mass-hypocrisy and to buy a sense of security at the price of the sense of truth."[3] I propose that the same thing is done with the Bible. I have known numerous Christians with this approach to

---

[2]   J.B. Phillips. *Your God Is Too Small* (New York: Macmillan Publishing Co., 1961), 7.

[3]   *Ibid.*

the Bible and to God, operating with a concept of the Bible as being written by people whom God "zapped" to get their attention and then sent them a previously spell-checked email that they then shared with the world.

Forty-five years after Phillips's complaint, Marcus Borg argued the same point, citing his own growth in understanding of the faith. "As the twentieth century and the second Christian millennium draw to a close, an older way of understanding Christianity that nourished . . . the lives of millions of people for over a thousand years has ceased to be persuasive to many in our time."[4] In talking about his own faith experience, he further says, "Internalization of the modern worldview began to create doubts about my childhood faith."[5]

There are numerous reasons for the crises of faith, which Phillips and Borg address. I propose that one of the reasons for that crisis is our method of biblical interpretation. We often find ourselves operating with a five-year-old's understanding of the Bible.

Christians who care at all about their faith literacy spend some time studying the Bible. But little or nothing is done to seriously delve into hermeneutics—*how* one interprets the Bible. I believe the chasm between the laity and the clergy has developed largely because clergy are afraid to be honest with the laity regarding what they know or believe about the Bible. Pastors often believe it is too dangerous for the laity, or they are afraid of the laity, fearing that the laity may be suspicious of their theology. And when the clergy's understanding is discussed with the laity, it is often *not* discussed in a way that makes sense to adults or an approach that the Bible *itself* suggests. Roy A. Harrisville and Walter Sundberg reiterate, "Leaders in the church are often afraid of the consequences of introducing historical-critical method into Bible study."[6]

I also confess that I have relied heavily on secondary sources. For those who may not be acquainted with the distinction between primary and secondary sources, a primary source is the original document quoted

---

[4]   Marcus J. Borg. *The God We Never Knew: Beyond Dogmatic Religion to a More Authentic Contemporary Faith* (San Francisco: Harper, SanFrancisco, 1998), 2.
       See also, Marcus J. Borg. *Meeting Jesus Again for the First Time* (San Francisco: HarperSanFrancisco, 1995), 3–15.

[5]   *Ibid.*, 21.

[6]   Roy A. Harrisville and Walter Sundberg. *The Bible in Modern Culture: Baruch Spinoza to Brevard Childs* (Grand Rapids: William B. Eerdmans Publishing Company, 2002), 12.

or referred to. For example, if I refer to something C. S. Lewis says in *Mere Christianity* directly from the book, I am using a primary source. If, however, I refer to what Walter Brueggemann says that C. S. Lewis says, I am using a secondary source.

Chapter 1

HISTORICAL BACKGROUND

In earlier times, one could make biblical references, and most people would know what you were talking about. Unfortunately, one can no longer assume that Christians have studied the Bible enough to have a grasp of the historical context of references. Therefore, I will begin with a very brief historical overview of biblical content and immediate postbiblical history.

Exodus records the slavery in Egypt and the Exodus, Sinai, and the giving of the law. Leviticus focuses on regulations of sacrifice, priesthood, and ritual obligations. Numbers focuses mainly on the organization of the people and a census. Deuteronomy is portrayed as a long sermon by Moses just before Israel enters the Promised Land, reminding them of "the importance of the covenant law as a guide for Israel's life in the promised land."[7]

The history of Israel begins in the Middle or Late Bronze Age. Movement of humans from a hunting and gathering nomadic life to agricultural life occurred in the last part of the Stone Age. This was the beginning of civilization, which began about 9000 BCE to the beginning of the Bronze Age about 3500

---

[7] Lawrence Boadt. *Reading the Old Testament: An Introduction* (New York: Paulist Press, 1984), 90.

1

BCE.[8] "The earliest city-state rulers in the Near East, the Sumerians, are of the language family quite distinct from any known today . . ."[9]

In Egypt, around 3000 BCE, Menes conquered the Upper Egypt, the area nearest to the Mediterranean Sea. Although African in race, these Egyptians were Semitic in outlook. That is, culturally, they were more like Arabians. From 1750 to 1550 BCE, foreign invaders from Asia, the Hyksos, dominated northern Egypt. Amenhotep IV, the "heretic king," began radical reform in 1378 BCE, attempting to change from polytheism to the worship of a single god, as the sun disk Aton. He named himself Akhenaton, "the beloved of Aton," and moved his capital to El Amarna. It was probably during the Nineteenth Dynasty (about 1300 BCE), under Seti I and Ramesses II, that Israel was reduced to slavery. Lawrence Boadt says, "It has become widely accepted that Seti I was the pharaoh who enslaved Israel, and Ramesses II was the pharaoh during the actual Exodus."[10] Of course, there is not a 100 percent agreement to this conclusion.

BEFORE THE COVENANT PEOPLE

The Beginnings: Primeval Period (Genesis 1–11)

Prehistorical Period (Stone Age to before 4000 BCE)

The domestication of plants and animals took place during the Neolithic Revolution (ca. 8000–4500 BCE in eastern Upper Mesopotamia and spread to Anatolia (Turkey) and the Levant (Lebanon and Syria).

Genesis begins with two stories of creation (Gen. 1–2:4a and Gen. 2:4b–3:24). Genesis 3 attempts to explain why people do bad things to one another and why people die.

Protohistoric Period (4000–3000 BCE)

The protohistoric period (4000–3000 BCE) of the Middle East was a time of incredible development. Genesis 4–11 try to explain the author's belief that based on the fall of humanity into sin, things went from bad

---

[8] *Ibid.*, 30.

[9] *Ibid.*, 32.

[10] *Ibid.*, 39. Yes, but there is no consensus regarding the issue of the time of the Exodus. Some scholars do not believe the Exodus actually happened. Others believed it happened by numerous small immigrations into Canaan.

to worse. It covers the prehistorical (before about 4000 BCE) Stone Age period, attempting to explain the reason people suffer and hurt one another, the development of technology and civilization, and the reason for ethnic and linguistic diversity. I conceive of a father or mother sitting around the campfire and the child asking, "Daddy, why do people treat each other so bad?" or "Daddy, why do those other people talk so funny?" The parent satisfies the child's curiosity by telling a story to explain the reality. During this period of time, writing came into use, and the Egyptian and Sumerian (Mesopotamian) empires developed.

About 3500 BCE, Sumerians appeared in Lower Mesopotamia, coming perhaps from the mountains of Iran. Centers developed at Eridu, Uruk, Nippur, and Ur.[11] Writing also originated in Mesopotamia at least by the middle of the fourth millennium BCE. The cuneiform of the Sumerians and Akkadians is the earliest writing of which we are aware.[12] The potter's wheel was invented, and a system of laws was developed. They originally governed their city-states by an assembly of citizens.

Historical Period (3000 BCE to the beginning of Bronze Age)

Between 3000 and 2400 BCE, the Sumerians were ruled by divinely appointed kings. In 2400, the Akkadians, under Sargon, broke Sumerian power. Akkad fell to Babylonia under Hammurabi and his successors for two hundred years (1750–1550 BCE). The Kassites came to rule from 1550 to 1500 BCE.[13]

ISRAEL AS A TRIBE

Patriarchs: The Rule of Sheikhs
(Genesis 12–50), 2000–1700 BCE

Abraham (2000–1850 BCE)

Genesis 12–50 focus on the traditions about the patriarchs of Israel— Abraham, Isaac, and Jacob (Israel) and his twelve sons. It doesn't take

---

[11] *Ibid.*, 40.

[12] "Cuneiform script," *History of Writing*, en.m.wikipedia.org.; "History of Writing," *History World*, www.historyworld.net/wrldhis/PlainTextHistories. asp?historyid=ab33.

[13] Boadt, *op. cit.*, 40-42.

much imagination to see that the period of the patriarchs, between about 2000 and 1700 BCE, is a much more historically reliable period than Genesis 1–11; but it is also highly legendary. The period begins with Terah leaving Ur of the Chaldees (southern Iraq) for Haran (in modern southeast Turkey) with his sons, one of whom is Abram. While there, God promised Abram to make him father of nations.

Abram (2000–1850 BCE) immigrates to Canaan (where Israelis and Palestinians now fight each other). Abram and Sarai, his wife, are unable to have a child. Therefore, Sarai (whose new name is changed to Sarah) gives her slave girl, Hagar, to Abram (whose name is changed to Abraham) so that they have social security in their old age as well as ensuring the future of their people (Gen. 16). Ishmael (1900–1750 BCE) is born to Hagar but is not to be the one who carries on the promise. During this period, the Babylonian creation myth (*Enuma Elish*) and the Babylonian flood story (*The Epic of Gilgamesh*) were written.

Isaac, Jacob, and Esau (1900–1700 BCE)

Isaac married an in-law, Rebekah, who delivered twins, Jacob and Esau (Gen. 25). Not much is recorded about Isaac except the record of Abraham's near sacrifice of him and the sibling rivalry between Isaac's and Rebekah's sons.

From the time of their birth, the two boys could not have been more different. Jacob was a sedentary, responsible homebody, who raised sheep and goats, endearing himself to his mother. But Esau was a fast-living, hard-drinking, three-sport-letterman, captain-of-the-football-team, butt-kicking hunter, who fulfilled his father's aspirations. Mom and Dad practiced poor parenting, showing favoritism and causing resentment and conflict.

Because of Esau's irresponsibility and Jacob's deviousness, Jacob defrauded his brother out of his birthright (Gen. 25) and his blessing (Gen. 27). However, when their father died, Jacob escaped to Paddan Aram (in southeast Turkey), where his uncle lived. Ironically, Jacob was swindled by his father-in-law, whose daughters, Leah and Rachel, Jacob married. He escaped back to his homeland and reconciled with his brother. During this time, the Babylonian Code of Hammurabi (1700 BCE) was written.

The Twelve Patriarchs (1750–1650 BCE)

A second generation of favoritism led to family problems. Jacob's favoritism toward his son Joseph resulted in such hatred that his brothers sold him to Ishmaelites, who sold him to an Egyptian. Because of his faithfulness to God, Joseph lived through adversity and became vizier of Egypt, saving both Egypt and his own family, who, because of a drought, immigrated to Egypt. During this period, northern Egypt was ruled by the Hyksos (1720–1560), who had invaded from the Mediterranean Sea, driving the Egyptians far south down the Nile Valley.

Exodus under Moses and Joshua: Liberation and Land (1650–1200 BCE)

Exodus and Wandering (1250–1230 BCE)

In the meantime, the Egyptians overthrew the Hyksos, and the people of Israel were enslaved. Under Moses, another Israelite vizier of Egypt who had given up his claim to fame, led Israel out of slavery and led them in the desert of Sinai and east of the Jordan River for forty years before preparing to invade Canaan, what is now Palestine.[14] During their time of wandering, Moses received the Decalogue (Ten Commandments). They worshipped a golden calf, were often rebellious, built the Tabernacle, and conquered tribes east of the Dead Sea and Jordan River.

Invasion of Canaan under Joshua (1220–1200 BCE)

With the invasion of the land of Canaan, Israel began to make the transition from nomadic herders to an agricultural society, developing the concept of land ownership. The new economic situation required new laws regarding property ownership, many of which are reflected in Exodus and Deuteronomy. The land was only partially conquered (mainly the uplands) under Joshua. This situation would become a problem over the next couple of centuries.

---

14 How much of the story is historical is difficult to determine. It is obvious that millions of Israelites did not escape from Egypt as Exodus says (Exod. 12:37), either from the standpoint of time frames, logistics, or the desert's ability to sustain that many. There is a wide range of scholarly ideas regarding whether there was an exodus and, if so, how many there were. Some believe that Israel was just a small tribe among the Canaanites, and some believe that only some of the Israelites escaped from Egypt. There is also considerable doubt among scholars that there was a leader named Moses and, if so, whether he had the high status in the Egyptian government. However, considering there is no way to really know to what extent the story is historical, I will present the story as it is in the Bible.

The Philistines controlled much of the coastline, establishing city-states at Gaza, Ashkelon, Ashdod, Ekron, and Gath. The Philistines' origin may have been southern Russia. They were part of the Sea Peoples who invaded from the north about 1200 BCE. They brought iron weapons, the smelting of which they learned from the Hittites of Turkey, and carefully guarded the secret of their technological superiority.[15]

Under the Judges: The Confederacy (1200–1030 BCE)

Early Problems

For about the next two hundred years, Israel tenuously held on to the ground they had conquered. A cycle of apostasy, defeat by local alien powers, dependence on God, and rescue by a local hero, or "judge," was repeated over and over. As tribes in a given area of Israel were harassed and invaded by local kingdoms, they repeatedly found someone to lead them in battle (Judg. 3:9, 15, 31; 24:14; 7:1–25; 12:4; 16:30–31). The leader, or "judge," was usually successful in throwing off the opposition. Othniel threw off Edom, which later, Ehud, the southpaw, also had to do. Deborah and Barak pushed back the Canaanites, and Gideon defeated Midian. Jephthah defeated Ammon, and Samson crippled the Philistines' hold on Israel. But the cycle of harassment never seemed to end. Their form of government—an amphictyony, a loose confederation of family-related tribes worshipping a common god—was not working. The "local heroes" were obviously not the solution. They saw that kingships seemed to work pretty effectively. Therefore, some began to call for a king "like the other nations." There were also stories of enormous depravity during that period (Judg. 19–21). They were tired of "every man doing what was right in his own eyes" (Judg. 17:6), suggesting the need for a centralized government to call the depraved to be accountable for their behavior.

Movement toward a Centralized Government

Their first attempt at kingship was disastrous. Abimelech, a son of the national hero Gideon, made the first attempt at becoming king. First, he murdered seventy of his brothers to eliminate the competition. The city of Shechem made him their king but became disenchanted and rebelled, ending in his death.

---

[15]   Boadt, *op. cit.*, 46.

BIBLICAL INTERPRETATION FOR LAYPEOPLE AND OTHER MARTYRS 7

Samuel: Last Judge

For over two centuries, Israel had no official leader. And the problem was not *only* international. There were domestic problems as well. If "every man does what is right in his own eyes," then the potential for evil would stagger the imagination. And it did occur (Judg. 17–21), resulting in blood feud, lawlessness, unspeakable crimes, and chaos. Out of this chaos, there arose a spiritual leader, but no political leader (1 Sam. 3:19–20). Samuel was a circuit rider, between Bethel, Gilgal, Mizpah, and Ramah (1 Sam. 7:16–17). Samuel's sons were unscrupulous men, taking bribes (1 Sam. 8:3). The people's representatives, sheikhs from each tribe, asked, "We want a king like the other nations" (1 Sam. 8:4–5). Now all Israel acknowledged Samuel, who served at Shiloh as a "prophet" (1 Sam. 3:20). But Samuel was not a warrior. When the Ark of the Covenant was captured by the Philistines, the call for a central warrior-leader increased. So they asked Samuel, in his declining years, to "appoint a king for us to judge like all the nations" (1 Sam. 8:5). Samuel was basically anti-king, interpreting the desire for a king as rejection of their God, Yahweh (1 Sam. 12:12). He tried to warn them of the cost of having a king, but they would not listen (1 Sam. 8:10–21), so he acquiesced.

Saul: Kingdom in Name Only (1030–1010 BCE)

Samuel found the biggest, toughest (and most handsome) young man around, Saul, a forty-year-old Benjamite (1 Sam. 9–10), to lead them in battle and anointed him king. But deciding on a new type of government does not imply knowing how to administer it. Since they had only seen kingships from a distance, they did not have a clue how to do it. Therefore, Samuel seemed to have written some kind of constitution (1 Sam. 10:25–27). But apparently, he gave no thought about the problem of succession, which would lead to problems later. There seemed to have been an expectation that Jonathan would succeed his father. But Jonathan was killed in battle.

Although Saul was chosen (1 Sam. 10:1), there was nothing to do until a call to arms occurred. One could call Saul a king, but no one would know he was a king by his daily activities. And good fighters don't necessarily make good kings. Although Saul seemed to have begun well, he lost much support after making a number of serious bungles, assuming the priestly office (1 Sam. 13:11–14), making an unwise oath that could have lost a battle, and preparing to kill his son Jonathan for his own mistake. But the people would not allow him to execute the one who had been most responsible for their victory in battle (1 Sam. 14:45). Saul, terrorized by an evil spirit (paranoia) (1 Sam. 16:14), was jealous of one of his subordinates, David (1 Sam. 18:7–9), who had gained notoriety by defeating the Philistine champion Goliath. Probably because of his heroics and the fact that David behaved wisely (1 Sam. 18:30), "all Judah and Israel loved David" (1 Sam. 18:16). Although this was an overstatement, because of David's popularity, Saul tried to kill him (1 Sam. 18:20–29, 19:10). In his paranoia, Saul put eighty-five priests to death because he suspected them of complicity with David (1 Sam. 22). The more paranoid he became, the more he contributed to this self-fulfilling destruction.

ISRAEL AS A KINGDOM

The United Kingdom: Consolidation, Power, and Glory (931–722 BCE)

David (1010–970 BCE): Transition to a True Kingdom

Discontentment with Saul led Samuel, in a private ceremony, to declare David king while Saul was still on the throne (2 Sam. 2:4). After Saul's death, Israel chose David, at age thirty (2 Sam. 5:1–4), to be their king. Often, when people get power, they are corrupted by it (18:30). But David never really got the idea of what a monarchy was and therefore was only partially successful in setting up a kingdom.

But David did make some astute moves to consolidate power. He moved his capital to Jerusalem, a more centralized city. He brought the Ark of the Covenant to Jerusalem, making Jerusalem the focal point of worship and government. He personally showed great devotion to the ark (2 Sam. 6:12–23) and made plans to build a temple to house the ark (7:1-2). He also made some strategic diplomatic maneuvers. Although Saul tried to kill David, when *he* had the opportunity, he did not kill Saul because Saul was "the LORD's anointed" (1 Sam. 24, 26). He publicly honored Saul and his family after Saul's death, thus gaining the devotion of many Benjamites, the tribe of Saul.

There was still some opposition to David among the northern tribes, resulting in civil war (2 Sam. 3:1), but David administered justice (2 Sam. 8:15), basically solidifying his support.

BIBLICAL INTERPRETATION FOR LAYPEOPLE AND OTHER MARTYRS   9

Rudimentary Bureaucracy

David built a palace (2 Sam. 5:11). This required a growing bureaucracy and tax money to pay for it. His military expanded. Administration and records were required. The beginning of bureaucracy is recorded in 2 Samuel 8:16–18. Later in his reign, because of his advanced age, David did not appear on the field of battle (2 Sam. 21:17).

Family Problems

But David was a lousy husband and father. Problems within his own household led to the destruction of David's hold on Israel. A rift developed between David and his wife, Michel (2 Sam. 6). David's son Amnon raped his half sister Tamar. David did nothing, so Absalom, Tamar's blood brother, did—murdering Amnon, his half brother (2 Sam. 13:1–39). Absalom was exiled by David but was later allowed to return to Jerusalem. However, for two years, David refused to see him. When Absalom burned General Joab's field for not interceding on his behalf, Joab interceded, and Absalom was allowed to see his father (2 Sam. 14:1–13).

Political Problems

Absalom began to make campaign promises to be more just than David, which many of the people accepted (2 Sam. 15:1–6). He conspired against David, having himself declared king of Hebron (2 Sam. 15:10).

He was killed for his effort. But there was still some resentment in the family of Saul (2 Sam. 15:10). There was a rebellion under Sheba, a Benjamite. Many of those outside the tribe of Judah followed him (2 Sam. 20:1). There was no clear-cut way of deciding who should succeed David as king or *how* to determine who would succeed him. So his son Adonijah prepared to become king (1 Kings 1:5-27). To his embarrassment, David's arm was twisted by Bathsheba, and he (perhaps because of senility) was convinced that he had promised to make Solomon king. So David designated Solomon as his successor.

Solomon (970–931 BCE)

Lives like a Real King

When Solomon came to the throne, he had his half brother Adonijah killed (1 Kings 2:25). He took revenge on Joab, fired the high priest Abiathar, and put Shimei (who had cursed Solomon's father) under house arrest[16] for supporting Adonijah (1 Kings 2:32–38). Solomon established a marriage alliance with the Egyptian pharaoh, building Pharaoh's daughter a house, as well as one for himself. He built the magnificent temple that David had planned (1 Kings 3:1). This required a greatly expanded bureaucracy (1 Kings 4:1–19). There was a great deal of literary activity—proverbs and historiography. His military had many horses and chariots (1 Kings 4:26). The cost of the temple was exorbitant (1 Kings 5:1–12). Solomon's palace was so lavish that accountants gave up on keeping records (1 Kings 7:1–47), an open invitation for corruption. His opulence was becoming legendary (1 Kings 8:62–9:28, 10:14–29). Besides Pharaoh's daughter, other treaties of alliance were negotiated through marriages, resulting in seven hundred wives and three hundred concubines (1 Kings 11:2). There were also palaces required for his harem and building programs, requiring a forced labor tax (1 Kings 4:13–18, 11:28). His military increased to a standing army of 1,400 chariots and twelve thousand horsemen (1 Kings 10:14–29) and who knows how many infantry.

Solomon's Lifestyle Leads to High Taxes

A disgruntled general under Solomon, Jeroboam had escaped to Egypt (1 Kings 11:26). Apparently, Solomon had developed a process for transfer of power, for upon his death, his son Rehoboam ascended to the throne. However, there were problems. Samuel had warned of the financial burden of having a king. Solomon's opulent lifestyle and the expenses from his marriage treaties laid a heavy tax burden on Israel.

Divided Kingdoms: Brothers at War (931–722 BCE)

Rehoboam's Failure

At the beginning of Rehoboam's administration, representatives from the tribes requested a reduction of taxes. Instead, wanting to show who was in charge, he threatened much heavier taxes. That was the blunder that Jeroboam needed. Returning from exile, he led a rebellion against the tyrant. He became head of all tribes except for Judah (Rehoboam's tribe) and part of Benjamin.

---

[16] He was eventually executed when he left his place of refuge (1 Kings 2:46).

Rebellion and Division

Jeroboam established his capital at Samaria and set up temples in the north at Dan and Bethel (1 Kings 12) to siphon devotion from Jerusalem, where Solomon's temple was. The northern kingdom, which followed Jeroboam, became known as Israel. The southern kingdom, which followed the dynasty of David and Solomon, became known as Judah. The record of spiritual and moral corruption in the northern kingdom was consistently poor. Their apostasy from the faith of the covenant resulted in numerous assassinations and political chaos. The record of Judah, the southern kingdom, was spotty.

Corruption Produces Prophets

During this period, prophets came forth to call both kingdoms back to the roots of their faith. Elijah and Elisha challenged the apostasy and injustice of the Ahab-Jezebel administration during the early ninth century BCE. The failed policies of Rehoboam were followed in Judah by the successful reigns of Asa and Jehoshaphat in the late tenth century and early ninth century BCE. During the early eighth-century reign of Jeroboam II, Israel experienced great prosperity among the rich. But from the records of the prophets Amos and Hosea, it is easy to see that their riches came at the expense of the poor, whom they manipulated and cheated (e.g., Hosea 12, Amos 8).

Israel Disappears

To the east, the Assyrians began to expand from the Mesopotamian river valley westward. Hoshea, king of Israel, allied with Egypt against Assyria (724 BCE). Sargon II (722–705 BCE) of Assyria defeated them, conquered Israel; and Samaria, its capital, fell in 722 BCE. Israel's inhabitants were deported to various parts of the expansive Assyrian Empire. They were absorbed into the countries to which they were exiled, intermarried, lost their ethnic and religious identity, and were never heard of again. The Assyrians, under Sennacherib, also beleaguered Judah but could never quite destroy Jerusalem (2 Kings 18).

The Kingdom of Judah Alone: No Vestiges of Glory (722–586 BCE)

(2 Kings 18–25, 2 Chronicles 29–36, Zephaniah, Nahum, Habakkuk, Jeremiah, Ezekiel)

Under Hezekiah (2 Kings 18–20; Isaiah 36–39; 2 Chronicles 29–33)

Hezekiah, with the counsel of the prophet Isaiah, who served as something equivalent to the secretary of state, set probably the best example of faithfulness to God of all the kings of Judah. However, politically, his reign was difficult. He had been a vassal of Sargon II. Upon Sargon's death in 705, Hezekiah and other vassal states rebelled. Most of Judah was conquered by Sennacherib of Assyria, and Jerusalem was surrounded. According to the annals of Sennacherib, he had Hezekiah confined in Jerusalem "like a bird in a cage."[17] Hezekiah agreed to pay a large tribute (2 Kings 18:14–16). It is also recorded in 2 Kings that God intervened and destroyed the Assyrian army with a plague (2 Kings 19:32ff.). Hezekiah was also helped by a rebellion of a city in southern Mesopotamia, Babylon.

Josiah's Reform

In the late seventh century BCE, under King Josiah, Jeremiah felt the call to be a prophet (627 BCE). Josiah instituted major religious reforms (620 BCE). According to 2 Kings, the reform was motivated by discovery of "the book of the law" (chapter 23), usually considered to be Deuteronomy. But 2 Chronicles says that "Book of the Law" was discovered in the temple *during* his religious reform (chapter 34). Josiah was killed during the battle with Pharaoh Neco (609 BCE), who was supporting the declining Assyrian Empire against the rising Babylonians.

Destruction of Judah and Exile (2 Kings 24–25, 2 Chronicles 36, Jeremiah, Esther, Daniel 1–5)

The Babylonian Empire, under Nebuchadnezzar II (604–562 BCE), conquered Assyria and spread west, invading Judah. In 609 BCE, Pharaoh Necho installed Jehoiakim (609–598 BCE) as his vassal king of Judah

---

[17] Grant Fram, ed. 2011-2014. *Royal Inscriptions of the Neo-Assyrian Period Project (RINA)*. Winona Lake, IL: Eisenbrauns. <http://oracc.museum.upenn.edu/rinap/corpus/.> Sennacherib 015, Cylinda4 C, Iv 20.

(which, since the northern kingdom no longer existed, had again adopted the name Israel). However, in 605 BCE, the Babylonians defeated Egypt at the Battle of Carchemish (Jer. 46:2, 2 Kings 24:7) and overran Israel.[18] Jehoiakim, king of Judah, became a vassal of Nebuchadnezzar for three years but rebelled (2 Kings 24) in about 602 BCE. He had Jeremiah put on trial because of his treasonous prophecies. Jeremiah's prophecies about Jehoiakim (Jer. 22:17–19, 2 Kings 24:4) did not come true, but Jehoiakim did die during the siege. Jehoiachin came to the throne in 597 BCE. After three months, he surrendered and was exiled with ten thousand leading citizens. Nebuchadnezzar placed Zedekiah on Israel's throne. Zedekiah (598–587 BCE) revolted against Babylonia in 589 BCE. Nebuchadnezzar invaded, and Jerusalem fell in 587 BCE. The people of Israel, now called Jews, were exiled to various places in the Babylonian Empire. The prophet Jeremiah was taken with the exiles to Egypt in the deportation of 587 BCE.

ISRAEL AS AN ETHNIC GROUP

Exile and Restoration: From Nation to Ethnic Group (586–333 BCE) (Ezra, Nehemiah, Haggai, Zechariah, Malachi)

Exile (586 BCE)

Actually, three deportations of Judah are recorded: 597, 587, and 582 BCE. The Assyrians, more than a century before, had deported people from elsewhere in the empire to Samaria (2 Kings 17). After the third deportation by the Babylonians, only the poorest of the land of Judah (Israel) were left (2 Kings 24:14, 25:12). They were exiled to various places in the Babylonian Empire, including Babylon and the city that would later become Alexandria, Egypt. The condition of the exiles may have become better than those left in Israel. With their temple burned to the ground, the Jews[19] developed a new institution, the synagogue. However, after three generations in foreign lands, they learned the local languages, and their children began to lose the Hebrew language.

---

[18]   After the northern kingdom of Israel fell, the southern kingdom of Judah is sometimes called Judah and sometimes now called Israel in contemporary Biblical texts.

[19]   During the intertestamental period, they became known as Jews.

Change of Political Fortunes

But the seemingly invincible Babylonian Empire was not to last long. Nothing could have looked bleaker for God's people. But God was not finished with Judah. Cyrus the Great of Persia, in what is now Iran, revolted against the Medes (Babylonians) (555 BCE). The Persians soon overcame the Babylonians (539 BCE). The policies of the Persians were much more open than those of other nations. They honored local gods.

Benefit of Persian Foreign Policy

So seventy years after their exile (538 BCE), Cyrus decreed the return of those Jews who wanted to do so. The second temple was begun in 537 BCE. Zerubbabel returned as administrator and Joshua as priest (520–515 BCE). A second immigration to Israel occurred with Ezra as priest (458 BCE), and Nehemiah returned as administrator (445–443 BCE) and restored the walls of Jerusalem. Although harassed by Sanballat, governor of Samaria, and others (Neh. 2:10–19; 4:1–7; 6:1–14), the walls of Jerusalem were repaired. A temple was constructed, but it was much less magnificent than Solomon's temple. Under Nehemiah and Ezra, reforms were inspired by Deuteronomy (Neh. 13:6–22), including requiring Jewish men to divorce their non-Jewish wives.

Nothing Lasts Forever: Alexander Overthrows Persian Empire[20]

Persia was spreading like wildfire. It looked like no one could stop them. But in Macedonia, Philip II came to power (359 BCE). He conquered Greece, but before he could invade Asia Minor (Turkey), he was assassinated. His son Alexander the Great (336–323 BCE) moved on the Persian Empire, performing a blitzkrieg across Asia Minor (334 BCE), Syria, Palestine, Egypt (332 BCE), and Babylon (331 BCE), crossing the Indus River in Pakistan (326), where his generals refused to go farther. But history is so fickle. Alexander expanded into India, creating the most expansive empire in the history of the world to that time. And just at the time of his greatest triumph, at the age of thirty-two, Alexander died in Babylon (323 BCE).

---

[20] "Alexander the Great," History.com; www.history.com/topics/ancient-history/alexander-the-great.

Under Hellenistic Rule: Caught in the Middle (333–63 BCE)

Alexander's Empire Disintegrates

Alexander's empire was divided into four parts among his generals. Ptolemy ruled Egypt, and Seleucid ruled Syria. The generals and their descendants competed for hegemony (control) of Palestine. Most of the time, they were ruled by the Ptolemys; and generally, they supported the Ptolemys. But there were Seleucid parties in Israel.

Maccabean Revolt (1 and 2 Maccabees)

Antiochus II the Great (223–187 BCE) conquered Judea, bringing Israel under the rule of the Seleucids. He introduced Greek religion and customs in Jerusalem. During the Great Persecution (167–164 BCE) under Antiochus IV Epiphanes, Jewish practices were abolished; and the cult of Olympian Zeus was introduced in the temple, an abomination to the Jews.

Antiochus Epiphanes instituted a policy of requiring the elder of each town to sacrifice to the Greek gods. Mattathias, priest in Modein,[21] led a revolt with his five sons. Judas Maccabeus, "the Hammer," (166–160 BCE) was the first. He had considerable success. Jerusalem was taken, and the purification of the temple occurred (164 BCE). The Jewish holiday Hanukkah is the commemoration of the rededication of the temple. Judas made a treaty of friendship and mutual support with a growing power in the west, Rome, but was killed in battle in 161 BCE. His brother, Jonathan Maccabeus (160–142 BCE), with Rome's help, defeated the Seleucids. Upon the death of Jonathan, Simon Maccabeus became high priest and ethnarch[22] (143–134 BCE). The Jews became autonomous (142 BCE) for a time. Following Simon, his son, John Hyrcanus I (134–104 BCE) became both high priest and ethnarch. Upon his death, his son Judah Aristobulus I (104–103 BCE) even took the title of king of Israel. But in order to maintain his rule, he appealed for help to his ally, Rome. The Roman general Pompey deposed Philip II, the last Seleucid of Syria (64 BCE). During this time, political parties—the Pharisees, Sadducees, and Essenes—began to develop.

---

[21] Sometimes spelled "Modin."

[22] Not king, but leader of his ethnic people.

Roman Rule: Liberator Becomes Oppressor (64–6 BCE)

Rome's Benevolence Turns Sour: Pompey Takes Jerusalem (63 BCE)

The problem is that the liberating army stayed. Rome came to rule Palestine. But Rome was on the verge of irreversible trouble. Cleopatra VII, queen of Egypt (51–30 BCE) came to power, challenging Roman authority. Rome was temporarily distracted by a civil war, which ended when Julius Caesar defeated Pompey. Caesar allied with Cleopatra and became dictator of Rome but was assassinated in 44 BCE. Civil war again broke out. Marc Antony and Octavian defeated Caesar's senatorial assassins. But when Antony allied with Cleopatra, Octavian moved against the forces of Antony and Cleopatra, defeating them in 31 BCE.

Herod Becomes King

Herod the Great from Idumea, a small kingdom south of Judah, was appointed king of Israel by the Romans and ruled from 37 to 4 BCE. Although he married a Jewess, he was resented by Jews. Although he was a good administrator and added great splendor to the temple, he could never satisfy the Jews. Herod was also a paranoid, murderous maniac. The Pharisees Hillel and Shammai established opposing theological schools in Jerusalem during this period.

THE NEW ISRAEL: MISSION TO THE WORLD

The Kingdom among Us: Coming of the Messiah (6 BCE–30 CE)

Birth of Jesus (6 BCE)

Jesus was probably born between 6 and 4 BCE. Herod died in 4 BCE. His son Archelaus squelched a rebellion in Jerusalem (4 BCE). But Rome removed him, and Judea became a procuratorial Roman province in 4 CE. This time saw the origin of the Zealots, militants whose assassinations made life miserable for Rome and the Herodian party. Although the history of Jesus is very hard to nail down, it seems that he ministered from one to three years and was executed in about 30 CE, during the reign of Tiberius Caesar (14–37 CE). Just before Jesus's ministry, Procurator Valerius Gratus (15–26 CE) deposed Annas,

BIBLICAL INTERPRETATION FOR LAYPEOPLE AND OTHER MARTYRS   17

considered by the Jews to be the legitimate high priest, and elevated Annas's son-in-law, Joseph Caiaphas, to high priest. In 26 CE, Pontius Pilate replaced Gratus as governor of Judah.

Ministry of Jesus

Herod Antipas, the son of Herod the Great, married Herodias (his brother Philip's wife) at about the time of the beginning of Jesus's ministry (27 CE). John the Baptist was beheaded (29 CE) for calling Antipas's sin to the attention of the public. Jesus, who may have been a disciple of John, took the mantle of John and refocused the emphasis of John's preaching. Through his preaching of love, integrity, caring for the poor, and the kingdom of God, he attracted many of the common people to himself, especially the outcasts. But this was a challenge to both the entrenched establishment of the Jews and the Romans. As a threat to the status quo, he had to be dealt with.

Death and Resurrection of Jesus

The time of the crucifixion of Jesus can be narrowed to the time when Herod Antipas was tetrarch of Galilee, Pontius Pilate was governor of Syria, and Caiaphas was high priest. Jesus's crucifixion occurred in about 30 CE. One might have expected that this was the end of the movement, but the rumors of his resurrection changed the course of history.

The New Testament Church: From Ethnic Group to World People (Acts of the Apostles)

The Coming of the Advocate (Acts 2)

Approximately fifty days after the report of Jesus's resurrection, on Pentecost (30 CE), the disciples were infused with spiritual power and courage (Acts 2). The Jesus movement began to grow at a phenomenal pace, so much so that they were not able to keep up with the care of their poor. Seven deacons were chosen to administer social care (Acts 6).

The Ministry of Peter (Acts 1–5, 9:32–12:19)

Most of the earlier chapters of Acts of the Apostles deal with the ministry of Peter. A major development under Peter was a break with the ethnic character of Judaism by the embracing of a non-Jewish Roman soldier, Cornelius. One of the deacons, Stephen, was stoned to death because of his proclamation of Jesus's resurrection. A man who participated in the killing of Stephen was a zealous Pharisee named Saul of Tarsus. This traditionalist led a campaign to exterminate the Jewish-Christian heretics. Saul's conversion on the road to Damascus in 36 or 37 CE became a major change in the direction of the church. Because of his previous opposition to the church, there was suspicion of him. Saul visited the elders of the church (39 CE) and was accepted. In the meantime, James, the brother of John, was executed (44 CE) by Herod Antipas.

Paul's Missionary Journeys

Saul's persecution of the church caused many followers of Jesus to become religious refugees. A number of them fled and sought asylum in Antioch in Syria (now Lebanon). It is from Antioch that Saul launched his first missionary journey (45–49 CE) (Acts 13–14), which he shared with Barnabas and Mark, taking him to Cyprus and Asia Minor (now Turkey) and back to Antioch. On this journey, Saul took the name Paul (probably his Roman name). After Paul's success, not only among Jews, but among Gentiles, problems arose in the church between the two cultures. The problem was dealt with by the first church council (Acts 15) by representatives of the congregations in Antioch and Jerusalem (48–49 CE). They decided that the Gentiles did not have to abide by Jewish practices, such as circumcision, in order to become disciples of Jesus.

When Paul and Barnabas made plans for a second journey (Acts 15:36–19:41), they had such a contentious disagreement over whether to take Mark that they split the sheets. Barnabas took Mark and sailed for Cyprus. Paul took Silas on his second missionary journey (50–52 CE) and headed back to Asia Minor. From there, he took Luke with him and headed for Greece. Generally speaking, they first went to synagogues to witness to Jews. In each place, contention over Jesus resulted in animosity. In Corinth, Paul met Priscilla and Aquila, who had, with other Christians and Jews, been driven out of Rome by Emperor Claudius (50 CE). From there, he went to Ephesus in Asia Minor. After three years there, they returned to Antioch.

On his third journey (53–58 CE), Paul went to Asia Minor (Acts 20), spending most of his time in Ephesus (54–57 CE). It became one of the new centers of the church. From there, he made a quick trip through Greece, back through Asia Minor, and then to Jerusalem.

BIBLICAL INTERPRETATION FOR LAYPEOPLE AND OTHER MARTYRS   19

Paul Sent to Rome (58–63 CE)

Paul was arrested in Jerusalem and sent to Caesarea under protective custody. From there, he was sent to Rome. The trip was very eventful, including a storm and shipwreck. Paul spent two years under house arrest in Rome (Acts 21–28). The Acts of the Apostles ends with Paul in custody. It is believed by many that Paul was released and perhaps continued his ministry in the west, including Spain. But Rome burned in 64 CE, and Emperor Nero blamed the Christians, initiating the first local Roman persecution of Christians. Paul is thought to have been imprisoned during this persecution of Christians, and he and Peter were executed in about 67 CE.

Post–New Testament Developments: A Ferment in the World

Christians Persecuted

Some of the leading apostles were imprisoned and beaten by the Sanhedrin (Acts 5), but this was no full-fledged persecution. The first persecution broke out with the stoning of Stephen (Acts 7) in Jerusalem. Saul's persecution of Christians caused them to become refugees to other parts of Judea and Samaria. Saul had expanded his persecution toward Damascus. But it was cut short by his conversion (Acts 9). Paul was ill-treated by both Jewish and Gentile opposition in various places because of his message about Jesus, but it was never a persecution. In about 51 CE, Jews were expelled from Rome (and Christians with them). No other real persecution occurred until 64 CE, under the Roman emperor Nero. Under Emperor Titus, Ignatius, bishop of Antioch and perhaps a student of Peter, was martyred in 110 CE. Persecutions of Christians under Emperor Trajan began in Bithynia, part of what is now Turkey in about 111 to 113 CE.

Jewish Uprisings

A Jewish rebellion in Palestine brought Vespasian (69–70 CE), who had to leave to become emperor before he finished off Jerusalem. His son Titus conquered Jerusalem and burned the temple in 70 CE. Some rebels escaped to Masada. The siege of Masada ended with mass suicide of the Jews in 73 CE. Because of the chaos, Rabbi Johanan ben Zakkai founded the academy at Jamnia, establishing the Jewish biblical canon (70 CE or later). Under Emperor Hadrian (117–138 CE), the temple was dedicated to

Jupiter in 130 CE, resulting in a second Jewish rebellion under Bar Kokhba (132–135 CE). Jerusalem fell to the Romans in 134 CE and was renamed Aelia Capitolina. It retained that name until Constantine became emperor in 313 CE. Captives were sold. Polycarp, bishop of Smyrna and disciple of John, was martyred (156 CE).

Chapter 2

SUMMARY OF BOOKS OF THE BIBLE

Until about the advent of television, many people who were in pews on Sunday morning would also read their Bible at home. And for those who used the daily devotion booklets supplied by their denomination, in addition to the short little text that was the basis for the short devotion, many would also read a chapter or two that were suggested at the end of the devotion. Others simply set goals of reading a chapter or two each night until they read the entire Bible, even including Leviticus's incredibly boring descriptions of the colors of the curtains and the number of rings on which they hung in the Tabernacle. And they would ask their pastor about the confusing parts for which they had no background, requiring their pastor to do a little additional research himself (and in recent years, herself). But the interest level for reading the Bible has fallen dramatically.

And a part of the problem may be the churches and pastors. The pericopes are the scriptural lessons for each Sunday. Many churches use the Revised Common Lectionary, used by many mainline denominations, as well as the Roman Catholic Church (with some revisions). The texts are arranged in a three-year cycle to cover a whole range of topics so that pastors do not become Johnny-one-notes, emphasizing the same thing

21

every Sunday. Each Sunday, there is (generally) an Old Testament lesson, a psalm, an epistle lesson, and a gospel lesson. One year is based on Matthew, another on Mark, and another on Luke, with John scattered throughout all three years. This exposes the congregations to a lot of different texts. However, there are also a lot of significant texts left out.

And in some denominations (or local churches), Bible class lessons are produced for the pericopes. This means that the pastor does not have to prepare anything additional for adult Bible class, which sometimes becomes a rehashing of what will be discussed in the sermon and therefore not very stimulating. It is also a boon for lazy pastors who don't want to spend the time doing additional study for Bible class.

Therefore, even (I would venture) *most* of the people who are in the pews every Sunday are woefully biblically ignorant. They don't know what's in the Bible. Few even know where to find epistles, much less Habakkuk or Haggai. Therefore, pastors often cannot assume that the allusions they make to events and people will be understood. So they have to go back and give the background. I was almost finished with writing this book when it occurred to me that people reading the book would very likely be biblically illiterate. Therefore, I inserted this chapter to give a thumbnail sketch of the contents of the books of the Bible. For those who are well acquainted with the contents of the books of the Bible, this chapter can be skipped.

The Hebrew Bible

Genesis
Since I addressed the basic content of Genesis in chapter 1, I will simply say it addresses the Creation, the development of civilization, the flood, the call of Abraham, the patriarchs, and how Israel ended up in Egypt.

Exodus
Exodus tackles the Egyptian enslavement of Israel, the Exodus, the giving of the Ten Commandments, the legal system of Israel, and their sojourn in the wilderness.

Leviticus
Leviticus focuses on religious and ritual law of Israel.

BIBLICAL INTERPRETATION FOR LAYPEOPLE AND OTHER MARTYRS   23

Numbers

Numbers deals with a census taken of Israel, the law of the Nazirites, complaints against Moses and Aaron, spies sent to Canaan, Israel's conflicts with kingdoms east of the Jordan River, and the transfer of leadership to Joshua.

Deuteronomy

Deuteronomy is portrayed as a sermon by Moses that recaps the Exodus and wandering in the wilderness, as well as the death of Moses. It is largely a recap of the law in Exodus (chapter 20), including the giving of the Ten Commandments (chapter 5).

Joshua

This book discusses Joshua leading Israel in taking parts of Canaan (beginning with the battle of Jericho), the allocation of land to the twelve tribes, and a sermon by Joshua (chapters 23–24) calling on the new settlers to "choose this day whom you will serve, whether the gods your forefathers serve beyond the River, or the gods of the Amorites, in whose land you are living. But as for me and my household, we will serve the LORD" (verse 15). It closes with Joshua's death.

Judges

The confederation of Israel has no centralized government. As they are pressed by nations around them, leaders called judges arise to defeat their enemies. A recurring theme is that Israel turns from Yahweh, God sends a kingdom to oppress them, they cry to Yahweh, and he sends a judge to save them. As they feel oppressed by the threat of other nations and experience some of the most despicable behavior by Israelites (chapters 17–21), many are offended and call for a king "like the other nations."

Ruth

Ruth, a Moabite woman and the widow of an Israelite man, returns to Canaan with her mother-in-law, Naomi. She seduces an Israelite man, Boaz, who willingly marries her; and they become the ancestors of David.

1 Samuel

Samuel becomes the spiritual leader of Israel, taking the mantle of Eli, but they still have no political unifier. Because of Israel's demand for a king, Samuel anoints Saul, a Benjamite, king of Israel. He turns out to be unstable. David, who defeats the Gathite Goliath, becomes a hero and is more respected than Saul. Saul's jealousy of David leads him to attempt to kill David, who escapes Saul. Samuel anoints David while Saul is still on the throne. Saul is killed in battle against the Philistines.

2 Samuel

David becomes king, consolidating his power through wise political decisions regarding the treatment of Saul's family (chapters 4 and 9). He makes his capital in a centralized place at Jerusalem (chapter 5) and brings the Ark of the Covenant to Jerusalem (chapter 6), unifying religious devotion to Jerusalem as well as the political center. David commits adultery with Bathsheba, the wife of one of his mercenary generals, Uriah the Hittite, whom he has killed to cover up his sin (chapter 11). The prophet Nathan gets wind of the travesty and confronts him; he confesses and is assured of forgiveness (chapter 12). One of his sons rapes his half sister; her brother murders the offender. Absalom, a son, attempts a coup but is killed (chapters 13–14). Although David was a good politician, he was a lousy husband and father.

1 Kings

The old king David is convinced by Bathsheba that he has promised to turn over the crown to her son Solomon (chapter 1). Upon David's death, Solomon becomes king (chapter 2). He begins his rule in humility and wisdom (chapters 3–4). But over the years, he begins to live an opulent lifestyle. He builds a magnificent temple (chapters 5–6) and cements treaties with wives (chapter 11), whom he has to support. Because of high taxation, dissent and even rebellion occur (chapter 11). Upon Solomon's death, his son Rehoboam ascends the throne (chapter 12).

His arrogance results in a rebellion under Jeroboam, one of Solomon's former generals. The nation of Israel splits—the northern kingdom claiming the name Israel and the southern kingdom, which follows the dynasty of Rehoboam, taking the name Judah (chapter 12). The two kingdoms commit internecion, their bloodletting making them vulnerable to outside forces. The kings of Israel are consistently bad kings. The kings of Judah have a spotty record. Nonwriting prophets Elijah and Elisha (chapters 17–19) speak out against the cruel tyranny and apostasy of Ahab and his Syrian wife, Jezebel (1 Kings 16:29; 22:53).

BIBLICAL INTERPRETATION FOR LAYPEOPLE AND OTHER MARTYRS   25

2 Kings

The prophetic office passes from Elijah to Elisha (chapters 1–7). Ahab and Jezebel are killed (chapters 9–10). Hezekiah's rule over Judah is the apex of its justice, supported by the prophet Isaiah (chapters 18–20). Under Josiah, the book of the law is discovered (chapters 22–23), initiating reform. The northern kingdom is destroyed by the Assyrians in 722 BCE and is exiled all over the Assyrian Empire, thus losing their identity as a people (chapter 17). Assyria attacks Judah, but because Jerusalem holds out under King Hezekiah, it is unsuccessful in its attempt to destroy Judah in 586 BCE (chapter 25). Babylon defeats Assyria and invades Judah, destroying Judah, burning the temple to the ground, and exiling Judah to various parts of the empire (chapter 25).

1 Chronicles

The beginning of the book begins with the genealogy from Adam until David (chapters 1–9). It recaps the reign of Saul and David, making David look much better as a king than the books of 2 Samuel and Kings does, ending with the death of David.

2 Chronicles

It recaps the reigns of Solomon and Rehoboam, the civil war, the division of the kingdoms, and the recap of the civil war, the division of the united Kingdom of Israel into the Kingdoms of Judah and Israel, and their fall. It ends with Persia defeating Babylon and King Cyrus I allowing the exiled Judahites to return to their homeland.

Ezra

Ezra and Nehemiah were originally a single book, written around 400 BCE, covering the history of Judah from about 538 to 457 BCE. Cyrus permits the Israelites (Judah retakes its original name) to return home (chapters 1–2). Between 538 and 515 BCE, a couple of waves of Jews return to their homeland. Adversaries make their resettlement difficult, so in about 458 BCE, King Artaxerxes of Persia sends Ezra to govern Israel and provides finances to rebuild the temple (Ezra 5–7). Ezra instructs the people in the Old Testament law (Ezra 6–7). In order to maintain religious, cultural, and ethnic identity, Ezra forces Israelite men to give up their non-Israelite wives (Ezra 9:10–10:15).

Nehemiah

Because of Nehemiah's grief for the returning exiles, in about 445 BCE, Artaxerxes sends him to rebuild the walls of Jerusalem. But opposition by their neighbors to the north mounts. So as the workers on the walls do their jobs, they have to carry weapons (chapter 4). Once the walls are finished, Ezra reads the law to the people (Nehemiah 8:1–11), and they celebrate the Feast of Booths (Nehemiah 8:12–18). Their officials are chosen (chapter 10), and a census is taken (Nehemiah 11:1–12:39), probably to establish racial purity. The temple is restored, the Sabbath kept (13:1–22), and men were punished for marrying foreign wives (Nehemiah 13:23–27).

Esther

When the Persian king Ahasuerus (Xerxes I) removed his queen, Vashti, the Jewess Esther is chosen queen. Mordecai, who had saved the king by exposing a plot against his life, is hated by Haman, to whom he would not kneel. Haman plots to have all Jews killed in order to have Mordecai killed. Having been convinced by Haman that the Jews are traitors, the king authorizes the killing of Jews. Mordecai and Esther learn of the plot. Esther takes her life in her hands to come before the king without being summoned and pleads for the Jews. Because Persian kings could not rescind their edicts, Ahasuerus arms the Jews to defend themselves. At a banquet hosted by Esther, Haman's plot is exposed; and in an ironic turn of events, Haman is impaled on the stake that he had built for Mordecai. The story is one of major irony and is the basis for the Jewish celebration of the festival of Purim. Despite the wonderful story, the book's most notable attribute is the fact that the name of God is not mentioned even once.

Job

The book of Job is an example of wisdom literature, exploring the issue of the problem of suffering. It comes with a prologue and epilogue in story form, bracketing a series of dialogues. The book begins with a bet between God and the adversary (Satan) that Job, an extremely rich and successful man and who is a "person of absolute integrity" (Job 1:1), would not remain faithful to God if all his wealth, his children, and his health were taken away from him (chapters 1–2). God takes the bet (or bait) and accepts the challenge, allowing the adversary to do everything but take Job's life.

BIBLICAL INTERPRETATION FOR LAYPEOPLE AND OTHER MARTYRS   27

In Job 3:1–37:24, Job's friends Eliphaz, Bildad, and Zophar encourage him to confess the sin that had caused God to withdraw from him. Job responds with a defense of his behavior (Job 29:1–31:40), followed by Elihu also trying to convince him to confess. The focus is on the nature of God's care of creation and how to interpret the natural order (Job 31:4–37).

In Job 38:1–42:6, there is a dialogue between God and Job in which Job questions God's integrity. God allows him to speak his mind but responds that in spite of appearances, God is faithful (Job 38–41). God's response is about how creation works, informing Job that in order to criticize God, he needs greater knowledge of the world than he has (Job 38–41). God claims that he is the creator and that Job has no right to question his behavior. Suffering may occur because of the natural order of the world as God created it. The book finishes with the epilogue in which, because of his faithfulness, Job's wealth is restored even greater than before, and he has other children (Job 42:7–17).

Psalms

The book is a collection of 150 songs, many of which are used in worship, ranging from soup to nuts in their content and concerns. There are prayers for help (Pss. 44, 74), songs of praise (Pss. 29, 47, 93), songs of thanks (Pss. 30, 116), songs of trust (Pss. 16, 23), wisdom psalms (Pss. 37, 49, 73), instructional psalms (Pss. 1, 19, 119), royal psalms (Pss. 2, 18, 20, 21, 45), songs of Zion (Pss. 46, 48, 76, 84), entrance liturgies (Pss. 15, 24), and historical psalms (Pss. 78, 105, 106, 136). Psalm 119, an instructional psalm of 176 verses, is an acrostic[23] psalm, divided into twenty-two sections, in which each line in each section begins with the same letter of the Hebrew alphabet. "Each poetic line in the first section begins with the letter *Aleph* (א), each line in the second section begins with *Beth* (ב) and so on,"[24] making it easier for Hebrew children to remember.

---

[23] "A composition in verse or an arrangement of words in which the first, last, or certain other letters in each line, taken in order, spell a word or phrase," Clarence L. Barnhart and Robert K. Barnhart (Eds.), *The World Book Dictionary* (Volume one A–K). Chicago: *World Book-Childcraft International, Inc., 1982.* In this case, the pattern is the Hebrew alphabet, from *A* to *Z*, so to speak (i.e., alpha to tau).

[24] McCann Jr., J. Clinton. "The Book of Psalms," *The New Interpreter's Bible* (Vol. IV) (Nashville: Abingdon Press, 1996), 1166.

Proverbs

The Proverbs are a collection of popular sayings of wisdom literature, including oracles, riddles, allegories, and dark sayings. Some are framed in contrast and comparison. They deal with relationships, the meaning of life, the passing on of wisdom from one generation to another, and cause and effect. Since they are written by different people with different perspectives, many contradict one another.[25]

Ecclesiastes

Ecclesiastes, written by the Qoheleth (teacher), is largely a pessimistic book, divided into two units. The teacher complains that the people of long ago are not remembered (Eccles. 1:11) and that the search for wisdom is chasing after the wind (Eccles. 1:12). An increase in knowledge increases sorrow (Eccles. 1:18). So he encourages to "enjoy yourself" (Eccles. 2:1).

And the wise are no better off than the fool because the same fate befalls all of them (Eccles. 2:14). So despite the pleasures, he hates life (Eccles. 2:17). Part of his frustration is that he must leave his wealth to those who come after him, who might use it foolishly (Eccles. 2:18–19).

His basic points are the pointlessness of human endeavors, the mysterious nature of God, and the inevitability of death. He even sees God as indifferent to humans (Eccles. 7:13, 8:11, 9:2, 10:5). But the only proper response is to worship God (Eccles. 5:1–7).

Song of Songs

This R-rated expression of love between a husband and wife has often been called the Song of Solomon. Although Solomon is referred to, the man speaking his poetry speaks in the first person, whereas Solomon is spoken of in the third person. In fact, at the end, he says that Solomon can keep his "thousand" wives, but he is content with his one and only love (Song of Sol. 8:11–12). Because it is so risqué, it was interpreted as representing God's love for his people. Otherwise, it would probably not have made the cut when the Old Testament canon was adopted.

Isaiah

Most scholars believe Isaiah was written in three different eras. The first thirty-nine chapters of the book record the ministry of the prophet Isaiah during the reigns of Uzziah, Jotham, Ahaz, and Hezekiah, as well

---

[25] Examples are mentioned in chapter 13.

BIBLICAL INTERPRETATION FOR LAYPEOPLE AND OTHER MARTYRS   29

as during the threats from Assyria, including Sennacherib's near defeat of Judah. Isaiah was something like the secretary of state or at least a foreign affairs advisor to Hezekiah. Isaiah said that worship of God required consistent behavior regarding God's plan, including condemning the wealthy who are cheating the needy (Isa. 10:1–2).

Beginning with chapter 40, the book looks at the era of Babylonian captivity from the point of view of one of Isaiah's disciples, including condemnation of the oppression of the poor by the rich and the hope of return and resettlement, including the prophecy of the suffering servant in Isaiah 52:13–53:12. Chapters 55–66 cover the Persian period, including the prospect of the new creation and a new Jerusalem (Isa. 65:17–25), and conclude with the prospect of all nations streaming to Zion to worship Israel's God (Isa. 66:18–24).

Jeremiah

This prophecy is about the ministry of the prophet Jeremiah during the reign of Josiah, king of Judah. It also deals with the issue of whether Judah would fall to the Babylonians and the question of where God is during Israel's suffering. Jeremiah informs Judah that because of the leaders' treatment of the poor and their unfaithfulness to God, they are responsible for their own disaster. The theme is established in the first chapter. God "digs up and pulls down, destroys and demolishes," but also "builds up and plants" to accomplish God's purposes in the world (Jer. 1:10). Chapters 1–25 cover the deterioration of Judah's beliefs and institutions as the nation collapses. In Jeremiah 30–33, there is a collection of oracles of restoration and hope. Chapters 36–45 deal with the story of Jeremiah's prophecy, rejection, and courage during his persecution, which even includes an attempt on his life. But he also promises a new covenant and relationship between God and his people (Jer. 31:3134). When Jerusalem falls, Jeremiah is taken to Egypt with the exiles and ministers among them.

Lamentations

The book is a lament, describing the brutal situation during the attack on and destruction of Jerusalem in 586 BCE. Tradition says that it was written by Jeremiah due to the misery caused him because of the message he had to proclaim to Judah (Israel) and the hatred he suffered because of that message. However, it is divided into five poems that are so different that they are thought to be a separate compilation of laments, perhaps by different people.

Ezekiel

The prophecy of Ezekiel is proclaimed from Babylon, where he was exiled in 586 BCE. He holds out hope for the restoration of Jerusalem and a return of the Israelites to their homeland in the vision of the Dry Bones (Ezek. 37:1–14). His prophecy is portrayed with outrageous behavior and fantastic visions such as the Valley of the Dry Bones (Ezek. 37:1–14). He proclaims that Israel's suffering is caused by their apostasy. Unlike previous thinking, in which the sin of the nation is emphasized, he focuses on the responsibility of individuals for their own sins. Ezekiel's prophecies are delivered in the form of oracles judging Israel (Judah's new name) (chapters 1–24), oracles against foreign nations (chapters 25–32), and messages promising restoration of Israel (chapters 33–48). In my mind, one of the most beautiful expressions of God's love is Ezekiel 16. A sheikh finds a newborn baby girl dying in the desert. He takes her home, raises her, and gives her the ultimate honor of marrying him. But she turns to adultery. Nevertheless, he loves her so much he cannot give her up and calls her back home. That level of forgiveness expresses the inexhaustive and unquenchable love of God for his flawed creation.

Daniel

Daniel is apocalyptic literature that deals with conflicts between good and evil and God's final plans for earth and humanity, calling them to be ready for the end of time.

Part 1 contains folktales about Jews working in foreign courts during their exile in Babylon and after Babylon's defeat by the Persians between 606–536 BCE (chapters 1–6), including the young men in the fiery furnace (Dan. 3:1–30), Daniel in the lion's den (Dan. 6:1–28), everyone who refused to compromise with idols and were completely faithful to God, and the writing on the wall at Belshazzar's feast (Dan. 5:1–31). These are examples of how Jews should be faithful to their God. Daniel and his friends learn wisdom and can interpret signs and dreams.

Part 2 gives reports of visions (chapters 7–12). Although written later, it was written in Daniel's name. The writers' visions encourage God's people to commit themselves to fearless and total commitment to Israel's God, whose reign won't come without suffering. God will destroy empires that crush God's people, including that of Antiochus IV of Syria, who commits the "desolating abomination" (Dan. 9:27). But the visions reveal God's ultimate triumph over evil and a heavenly world at the end of history,

BIBLICAL INTERPRETATION FOR LAYPEOPLE AND OTHER MARTYRS   31

including the vision of the "ancient of days" seated for final judgment, delivering all authority to "one like a son of man" (Dan. 7:9–14). One of the latest books in the Old Testament, it is the first to refer to the resurrection of the dead (Dan. 12:2–3).

Hosea

This book was written during the reign of Jeroboam II in the northern kingdom; because of their manipulation of others (Hosea 12:7–8) during a time of rapid economic growth, the rich are getting richer, and the poor are getting poorer (Hosea 12:8; Amos 3:15, 6:3–7). The book portrays the life of Hosea, who marries Gomer, an adulterous woman whose unfaithfulness breaks his heart and whom he continually calls to be faithful, an illustration of Israel's spiritual unfaithfulness to Israel's God, Yahweh (Hosea 1:2, 2:2–20). The prophecy is neatly divided into three sections: Hosea's family as a sign of God's faithful love of Israel (Hosea 1:2–3:5), God and his people in conflict (Hosea 4:1–13:16), and God's judgment continues but is not the final word (Hosea 11:11, 12–14:8)—each including both judgment and promise.

Joel

Although impossible to assign a time of writing, it may have been carried out in Judah. It portrays the invasion of a swarm of locusts (Joel 1:1–12, 2:1–11), perhaps representing an invasion of Assyrians or Babylonians or an actual infestation of locusts but assuring God's people that he would protect them. Joel calls on them to "tear your hearts [in repentance] and not your clothing [an outward expression of grief]" (Joel 2:13) and return to Yahweh (Joel 2:12–17). Judgment will not be just local, but cosmic—shaking the sun, moon, and stars (Joel 2:10–11). But ultimately, the hills will drip with wine and flow with milk in the restoration of Judah (Joel 3:18).

Amos

Amos's prophecy, written during the reigns of King Uzziah of Judah and Jeroboam II of Israel (and sometime thereafter), is directed toward Israel in the early eighth century BCE. He rails against the social extremes of prosperity and abject poverty caused by the greed of the rich, exploitation, and their cheating of the poor (Amos 2:6–8, 5:10–13, 8:4–6). In their arrogance and duplicity, the rich continue to attend worship while defiling God by their exploitation of the poor (Amos 4:4–5, 5:21–23) while also worshipping idols (Amos 5:26-27, 8:14). Amos concludes that God "despises their solemn assemblies" because of their treatment of the poor. Although this is reasonable speculation because it is so out of character with the book, a brief section of hope of restoration placed at the end (Amos 9:11–15) has led some to suggest this section was added later by someone other than Amos.

Obadiah

The shortest book in the Old Testament, Obadiah, was written sometime after 587 BCE. It has one focus—a visionary condemnation of Edom, a nation southeast of the Dead Sea, traditionally descended from Jacob's brother, Esau.

Jonah

This writing is portrayed as a call to Jonah to pronounce condemnation of Nineveh. But Jonah tries to escape his call by fleeing by ship to Tarshish but is thrown overboard, swallowed by a large fish, and vomited out. Finally, he reluctantly proclaims his message to Nineveh. However, Nineveh repents and is forgiven, and Jonah is angered by God's forgiving Nineveh. It ends with a rhetorical question: "Shouldn't God forgive a large city that repents?" It is a highly evangelistic book, demonstrating the incredible forgiving nature of God.

Micah

Micah—who prophesied during the reigns of Jotham, Ahaz, and Hezekiah—condemns the rich of both Judah and Israel for oppressing the poor. Merchants cheat their customers, and religious and judicial leaders are corrupt (chapters 2–3). The author of the book complains that prophets are told to keep quiet. Both nations believe that because they are "God's people," they will be protected. He uses the destruction of Israel's capital, Samaria, as a warning to Jerusalem (Mic. 1:5–7) but concludes with oracles of hope (chapters 4–5) with a future Messiah being born in Bethlehem (Mic. 5:2). Chapter 7 concludes with hope, forgiveness, and restoration (verses 8–20).

Nahum

Nahum begins with a hymn regarding the divine power of the creator (Nah. 1:2–8), which is bad news for Nineveh (Nah. 1:9–13), but beneficial to Judah (Nah. 1:4–15). It poses the question as to why God's people suffer while evil

BIBLICAL INTERPRETATION FOR LAYPEOPLE AND OTHER MARTYRS   33

nations such as Assyria prosper. In great detail, the prophet Nahum proclaims that God will destroy the evil Nineveh (contrasted to Jonah's portrayal of Nineveh's repentance), and God's people will prosper (Nah. 2:1–3:19).

Habakkuk

The first part is portrayed as a disagreement between Habakkuk, who doesn't understand why God allows the wicked to swallow up the righteous, and God himself (Hab. 1:2–2:5). Like Nahum, Habakkuk questions why God allows violence and injustice to go unpunished. God assures him that patience will show him the vindication of God's justice. It includes the statement "the righteous will live by his faith" (Hab. 2:4). The last part of the book promises the coming of the Babylonians to destroy Judah, but who will also themselves be ultimately punished.

Zephaniah

The prophet Zephaniah, who may have spoken just before Josiah's reform (who ruled about 640–609 BCE), proclaims that the people of Israel are worshipping the gods of other countries rather than Yahweh, believing Yahweh is not active in history. He proclaims that "the Day of the LORD" will bring terrible punishment (Zeph. 1:9–10) but also a time of cleansing and restoration for Jerusalem (Zeph. 3:11–13) and all nations will ultimately come (Zeph. 3:9).

Haggai

During the time of the prophet Haggai's ministry, Israel had been returned to its native land, but work on the temple had stalled. However, the prophet, who spoke in the second year of King Darius I of Persia (about 520 BCE), says that the reason they are not doing well is that they had neglected the rebuilding of the temple. So apparently as a result of his message, they finish the project in about 515 BCE.

Zechariah

Also, speaking to the first generation of the Jews who had returned from exile in Babylonian captivity, Zechariah speaks in apocalyptic language regarding the messianic age. Chapters 1–8 and 9–14 are so different that some believe they were written by two different people. Chapters 1–8 contain mostly visions with the rebuilding of the temple as a primary concern, and Judah is called to turn from sin. There is a hope of restoration of Israel's people to their homeland. Besides the temple, there is a concern for the restoration of the priesthood, ritual practices, and the monarchy under Zerubbabel. In chapters 9–14, the king is expected to come any moment (Zech. 9:1–10); but before that, the people, priests, and prophets must be cleansed (Zech. 12:10–13:1, 12:13–14, 13:3–6). The reunion of the northern and southern kingdoms will not occur until their leaders turn from their sin and reform their ways (Zech. 11:7–11).

Malachi

Israel experiences conflict within the priesthood (Mal. 1:6–2:9), mixed marriages and divorce (Mal. 2:10–16), offenses regarding tithes (Mal. 3:7–15), and sorcery, perjury, and social injustices (Mal. 3:5). The prophet Malachi focuses on reforming abuses in worship practices (Mal. 2:10–17) and the consequences of not remaining in a right relationship with God and with one another (Mal. 3:1–6, 7–18, 4:1–6).

The New Testament

The Gospel according to Matthew

Written perhaps around 80 or 90 CE, probably aimed at Jewish Christians, it portrays Jesus as the new Moses. It includes Jesus's Hebrew genealogy (Matt. 1:1–17), birth narratives that focus on Joseph (Matt. 1:18–25), the coming of the magi (Matt. 2:1–12), the flight to Egypt (Matt. 2:13–18), the Sermon on the Mount (chapters 5–7), dealing with the sin of the brother (Matt. 18:15–20), the parable of the unmerciful servant (Matt. 18:21–35), the workers in the vineyard (Matt. 20:1–16), the sheep and the goats ("whenever you did it to one of these, you did it to me") (Matt. 25:21–46), and the Great Commission (Matt. 28:18–19).

The Gospel according to Mark

Perhaps written in around 70 CE, Mark portrays Jesus as the Messiah, son of God, which is a secret during Jesus's lifetime, known as the "messianic secret." He is "the Way" (Mark 1:2–3). The coming of the kingdom of God is proclaimed by John the Baptizer (Mark 1:14–15), who is arrested by Herod Antipas, the son of the king who wanted to kill Jesus when he was born. With his mentor John the Baptizer imprisoned, Jesus begins his ministry, teaching "with authority" in Galilee (chapters 1–8). He comes into conflict with the religious leadership almost immediately. Toward the end of his ministry in Galilee, Peter confesses Jesus as the Messiah (Mark 8:27–30), followed by Jesus informing his disciples that he will be executed (Mark 9:30–32, 10:32–34). Chapters 11–16 are a narration of his final week. In Mark 16:1–8, he turns up missing from his tomb. Women are informed by a young man that he has gone to Galilee, where they will see him. Although the versions we have had in the past (notably the King James Version, or KJV) end Mark at chapter 16 verse 20, with Jesus commissioning the disciples, the earliest manuscripts end with chapter 16 verse 8, suggesting that the last twelve verses were added somewhat later.

The Gospel according to Luke

Luke is the first of a two-volume set, which includes the Acts of the Apostles, written to a person named Theophilus, perhaps a person with that name or just someone (or anyone) who is a "lover of God." Luke puts great emphasis on "the Spirit" (Luke 1:15, 35, 41, 67; 2:25–27). Like the Old Testament books of Samuel, Chronicles, Kings, and Ezra-Nehemiah, it is divided into two scrolls because of its length. The maximum length of a scroll was about thirty feet. Anything longer was too heavy and cumbersome. Finding text one was looking for meant the scroll had to be unrolled to the appropriate place. In fact, the word "volume" comes from the Latin word for "scroll."[26]

Some scholars believe it was written in the 80s or 90s while others believe it was the first or second decade of the second century. Like Matthew, the basic skeleton of the book is based on Mark's gospel. Assuming there was a Q[27] document with sayings of Jesus, Luke puts some of them together with Mark and adds information of his own that he has gotten from his own research (Luke 1:1–4). It includes the story of the road to Emmaus (Luke 24:13–35), his own resurrection story (Luke 28:1–15), and his ascension story, which happens not on a mountain in Galilee, as in Matthew 28:16–20, but outside of Jerusalem (Luke 24:50–53). He has his own birth narrative about Jesus, which focuses more on Mary (Luke 1:18–25). It includes the story of the young Jesus in the temple (Luke 2:41–52) and emphasizes his complete humanity (Luke 2:52).

---

26   Borg, Marcus J. *Evolution of the Word: The New Testament in the Order the Books Were Written* (New York: HarperCollins, 2012), 424.

27   Many scholars believe that there was a document containing Jesus's sayings, which they called *Quelle* ("source" in German), which is referred to as Q.

It has three early hymns in the first chapters: the Benedictus (Luke 1:67–79), the Magnificat (Luke 1:46–55), and the Nunc Dimittis (Luke 2:29–32). But the reason I love Luke more than the other gospels is that in his gospel, he focuses on Jesus's care of the poor, the marginalized, and the discriminated against. In Luke, Jesus is born in a humble setting (Luke 2:6–7); and the good news of his birth comes to despised shepherds (Luke 2:8–20), people who, because of their nomadic profession, cannot fastidiously observe the Mosaic ceremonial law. He shows concern for Samaritans, who are fanatically hated by the Jews (Luke 9:52, 10:33, 17:16); hated tax collectors, who are considered to be traitors to their own people (Luke 5:27–31; 7:29, 34; 15:1; 18:9-10; 19:1-10); criminals (Luke 23:32–43); and women (Luke 10:38–42; 7:36–50; 13:12; 23:27, 55). It includes the best-known and best-loved parables: the lost sheep (Luke 15:1–7), the lost coin (Luke 15:8–10), the prodigal son (Luke 15:11–32), the rich fool (Luke 12:51–21), the good Samaritan (Luke 10:25–37), the rich man and Lazarus (Luke 16:19–31), the Pharisee and the tax collector (Luke 18:9–14), the ten lepers (Luke 17:11–19), the sower (Luke 8:1–15), and the wise and foolish builders (Luke 6:46–49).

The Gospel according to John

Written in about 90 CE or later, this gospel portrays Jesus as the "Word of God," who was from the beginning of creation the incarnation of God in the flesh. It includes the "I am" statements ("I am the way, the truth, and the life" and others) (John 6:35; 8:12; 9:5; 10:7, 9; 10:11, 14; 11:25–26; 14:6; 15:1, 5), the Samaritan woman at the well (John 4:1–39), Mary Magdalene seeing Jesus on Easter morning (John 20:1–18), doubting Thomas (John 20:24–28), and Nicodemus's evening conversation with Jesus, which includes John 3:16 (known as the gospel in a nutshell). It portrays Jesus completely differently from the other three gospels, making Jesus speak like the author of the gospel rather than the way he speaks in the other gospels.

Acts of the Apostles

The second tome of the Lukan work, which was written to Theophilus, records the life and expansion of the early church, which provides its basic outline. Chapters 1–7 record the life of the church in Jerusalem, ending with the first persecution. This results in Jesus's followers becoming refugees and the expansion of the church into Judea and Samaria (chapter

BIBLICAL INTERPRETATION FOR LAYPEOPLE AND OTHER MARTYRS   37

8) and to Damascus in Syria (chapter 9). Chapter 10 deals with the bringing of the gospel to the Gentiles, beginning with Peter's ministry to Cornelius. Chapter 11 covers Peter's defense of his decision to baptize a Gentile and relates the growth of the church in Antioch. In chapter 12, James, the brother of John, is executed. Peter is imprisoned, and Herod Antipas dies.

Beginning with chapters 13–14, Acts makes a transition to the ministry of Saul of Tarsus (later called Paul). His first missionary journey records the evangelization of Cyprus and east central Turkey. Chapter 15 records the first church council in Jerusalem, which deals with the issue of what is required of Gentile Christians.

Saul's second missionary journey begins in Turkey, then expands to Macedonia, Greece, and Ephesus (in southwest Turkey) (chapters 16–19). His return to Jerusalem and arrest are recorded in Acts 20:1–23:22. From there, he is sent to Caesarea under protective custody, defends himself to two Syrian governors and Herod Agrippa (Acts 23:23–26:32), and is sent to Rome for trial, where he ministers for two years under house arrest (chapters 27–28). That is where it abruptly ends.

Romans

The epistle to the Romans was possibly Paul's first letter, perhaps from Corinth around 58 CE. Others believe that because it is such a coherently written Christian theology, it probably was written much later. But like the guesswork on many books, it is mere speculation. There is nothing to anchor Romans to a specific time in history. It is the most theologically oriented of Paul's letters, including an affirmation that the gospel is for both Jews and Gentiles (Rom. 1:16–3:20), who are justified by grace through faith (Rom. 3:21–4:25) not just to get to heaven, but for their relationships with others in this life. Since chapter 5 begins with the word "therefore," you know that conclusions about the Christian life begin, which continue through chapter 8. Chapters 9–15 deal with God's sovereignty, Israel's salvation, the importance of Christian love, a method of dealing with weak Christians, and his plan to visit Rome for the first time.

1 Corinthians

This letter was written to the congregation that Paul had established in 49 or 50 CE. It was a multiethnic and multiclass congregation, unlike our congregations (and denominations) today, which are largely segregated by race as well as by class. However, because of that inclusiveness, problems appear.

Paul had previously written them a letter (1 Cor. 5:9), probably from Ephesus, and had received a letter from them (1 Cor. 7:1). Apparently, members of the congregation have written Paul regarding problems in the church.

There are divisions in the church in which members claim to follow different leaders, including Paul. He responds that Christ is not divided (1 Cor. 1:12–23). Another problem is that a man is living with his father's wife. Paul orders excommunication (1 Cor. 5:1–13).

A third problem is that members are suing one another in court. Paul says it is a shameful denial of the unity of the church, arguing that the congregation should be able to mediate the problem (1 Cor. 6:1–11). So many of them had previously been Gentiles who worshipped other gods and lived depraved lives, so it is not surprising that they still have problems with sexual immorality. Paul says that their bodies are the "temple of the Holy Spirit" that should not be abused (1 Cor. 6:12–20).

Some wonder whether Christians should be celibate. Paul says that if they are not married, it might be a good idea for them to remain unmarried. But if they cannot control their sexual desires, they should marry. However, if they are married to non-Christians, they should not divorce them because they may be of benefit to their non-Christian spouse (1 Cor. 7:1–40).

They have also written him regarding whether it is okay or not to eat meat sacrificed to idols. Paul says since idols are nothing, it is okay to eat it. But if eating this meat causes a brother or sister to violate their conscience, they should refrain (1 Cor. 8:1–13, 10:23–11:1).

Further, the congregation is divided over who has the best spiritual gifts. Paul responds that the church is like a body and that each part of the body needs the others. He further argues that some of the best gifts are those that seem to be the least important (chapters 12–14). Within this context, he expounds on the "love chapter" (1 Cor. 13:1–13), in which he says the three greatest gifts are "faith, hope, and love," the greatest being "love" (verse 13).

Another problem is that the rich members in the congregation arrive early to the worship service, which includes a full meal, and start to eat and drink before those who have jobs can get there. And by the time the poorer members arrive, the richer ones have eaten most of the food and are already getting drunk. Paul says by doing this, they are violating the "body of Christ" (i.e., the church) and are eating and drinking unworthily (1 Cor. 11:21–27).

BIBLICAL INTERPRETATION FOR LAYPEOPLE AND OTHER MARTYRS   39

Then there are those who deny the resurrection of Jesus. He argues that after his death, many people have seen Jesus, concluding that if Christ is not risen, their faith is futile and they were still in their sins (1 Cor. 15:1–58).

Finally, chapter 16 encourages the Corinthian congregation not to slack off in their raising money to feed the Christians in Palestine.

2 Corinthians

There are three natural divisions in 2 Corinthians: chapters 1–7, 8–9, and 10–13. These seemingly natural divisions seem to be separate letters, which were combined into one scroll when others copied them. After all, paper was very expensive.

But *when* the letters were written is the big question. In 1 Corinthians, Paul had sent Timothy to Corinth and said he planned to come soon to talk to them regarding their conflicts (1 Cor. 4:17–19). Apparently, he had made the visit, for in 2 Corinthians 2:1, Paul refers to a "painful visit" and refers to a letter for which he partially apologizes (2 Cor. 2:4, 7:8). Some scholars believe that this letter was chapters 10–13, in which Paul's anger is quite evident. But chapters 1–7 are of a considerably different tone, with no hostility at all, suggesting that it may have been another letter—maybe the next letter. Chapters 8–9 look like they may have been another letter that is all about the collection being taken up for the Christians suffering privation in Palestine. Some scholars even believe chapters 8–9 could be two letters.

In chapters 8–9, Paul angrily defends his teaching against whoever has attacked him, saying they are "false apostles, deceitful workers" (2 Cor. 11:13), and boasts about his superiority (2 Cor. 1:22–23), even boasting about the suffering he has done for the gospel (2 Cor. 11:23–28) and about his ecstatic experiences (2 Cor. 12:1–4). He acknowledges that he has a "thorn in the flesh" but argues that it is his strength because he does not depend on himself, but upon God's grace (2 Cor. 12:7–10). He concludes by saying he will make a third visit and expresses his concern over their quarreling and slandering (2 Cor. 12:20–21).

Because chapters 8–9 have such a different tone, perhaps Paul had made his third visit, and the situation had been rectified. He merely appeals to them to go finish the collection for the saints in Palestine, encouraging them by bragging on the generosity of the Macedonian churches and telling them how he has been bragging to the Macedonians about the generosity of the Corinthians.

This section also has a different tone, suggesting that the conflicts had been rectified. However, the man who has been living with his father's wife has apparently repented but has not been forgiven by the community. Paul asks what they are waiting for. They should forgive him and return him to the bosom of the church (2 Cor. 2:5–11).

He reminds them that the ministry of the Spirit is superior to legalism (2 Cor. 3:2–8), for it enlightens (2 Cor. 3:12–18) rather than perpetuates darkness and blindness (2 Cor. 4:1–6). Finally, he acknowledges that we are "earthen vessels" (breakable) (2 Cor. 4:7–12) and that we are a new creation in Christ. He continues by saying that Christians do not lose heart because although we are physically wasting away, we fix our eyes on what is unseen because "what is seen is temporal, but what is unseen is eternal" (2 Cor. 4:16–18). Therefore, we no longer look at things from a merely human point of view (2 Cor. 5:16–18).

Galatians

Most scholars believe that Galatians was written sometime during the early 50s while Paul was in Ephesus. There are some obvious similarities to the emphasis in Romans. However, it is not nearly as organized or temperate as Romans. Paul writes this letter in anger. It is written not to one congregation, but to the "churches of Galatia" (north central Turkey).

Apparently, Christians who have been called Judaizers have made the circuit of Lystra, Derbe, Pisidian Antioch, and perhaps other churches, convincing many in the churches that in order to be a Christian, a person must observe the Jewish ceremonial laws. Paul says that by listening to such nonsense, they are foolish and have been "bewitched" (Gal. 3:1). He is so angry that he says he hopes those who require circumcision "would castrate themselves" (Gal. 5:12). This is not temperate language. He says that requiring circumcision will perpetuate division between Jewish and Gentile Christians (Gal. 3:26–28), using Hagar and Sarah as an allegory of the difference between constrictive law and the refreshing freedom of the gospel (Gal. 4:21–5:1). If the Gentile Christians want to follow the Jewish ceremonial laws (including circumcision) voluntarily, that is fine. But it cannot be legalistically required.

Since those Judaizers have challenged Paul's authority, he has to defend his apostleship, arguing that the apostles James, Cephas (Peter), and John recognize the grace given him to evangelize the Gentiles as Peter was evangelizing the Jews (Gal. 2:7–10). He says that he even has the temerity to rebuke Peter when Peter is pressured to withdraw fellowship with the uncircumcised Christians (Gal. 2:11–14). Both Jews and Gentiles are saved by faith (Gal. 2:15–21), not rituals. And within the church, "there is no longer Jew or Greek, there is no longer slave or free, there is no longer male and female; for all of you are one in Christ Jesus" (Gal. 3:28). Even Abraham, the ancestral father of the Jews, was not saved by works, but by faith (Gal. 3:6–9, 15–18). The law was added to point out our transgressions (Gal. 3:19–4:7).

Freedom is a major theme. Our relationship with God as a result of faith in the gospel has freed us from the oppression of the law (Gal. 5:2–15). And the fruits of the spirit (Gal. 5:22–25) are contrasted with the works of the "flesh"[28] (Gal. 5:16–21). He concludes with the instruction that if anyone is caught in a transgression, he should be restored in the spirit of gentleness, always remembering that any of us can be tempted (Gal. 9:1–5). By the time he gets to chapter 6, his anger seems to have cooled down. So he is presumably also referring to restoring the Judaizers.

Ephesians

Unlike the previous epistles, this epistle is a "disputed" letter of Paul, which means it may have been written by a follower of Paul's teachings, but not by Paul himself. And since the words "in Ephesus" are not in the earliest manuscripts from the fourth and fifth centuries,[29] it is also disputed that it was originally addressed to the Ephesians. Further, despite the fact that Paul ministered in Ephesus for three years, there are no personal greetings as there are in his authentic letters. Nor are there any references to the circumstances in the church. The central theme is the unity of the church between Jews and Gentiles "built upon the foundation of the apostles and prophets, with Christ Jesus himself as the cornerstone" (Eph. 2:11–20).

And the one body was "called to the one hope of your calling, one Lord, one faith, one baptism, one God and Father of all, who is above all and through all and in all" (Eph. 4:4–6). The writer calls on them to put on the whole armor of God in order to resist temptation (Eph. 6:13–17). And like Colossians, it has a "household code" that subordinates women

---

[28] "Flesh" (*sarx* in Greek) does not mean "body," but man's inclination to evil, what the fathers of the church called "original sin."

[29] Codices Vaticanus, Sinaiticus, and Alexandrinus.

(Eph. 5:22–25) and reinforces slavery (Eph. 6:5–8), which has a completely different tone from Galatians 3:28. However, it does encourage husbands to "love their wives as Christ loved the church" (Eph. 5:25) and masters to treat their slaves well (Eph. 6:9). So much of it is so similar to Colossians that some believe that both were written by the same person, perhaps as late as 90 CE. The earlier winsomeness of the equality of all Christians was being replaced a bit with a conservative trend toward the issue of female and slave equality.

Philippians

Philippi was the first city Paul went to in Europe in about 47 or 48 CE. His letter to them, perhaps written in the late 40s, is the warmest and most personal letter of all. The word "joy" is repeated so often that only a few examples can be noted (Phil. 1:3–4, 18; 2:2, 17–18, 28; 3:1, etc.). One of the most beautiful hymns in the Bible is found in Philippians 2, where Paul encourages members of the church to think just like Christ.

At the end of the letter, he thanks the congregation for their financial support of his ministry (Phil. 4:10–20).

Colossians

Although the epistle claims to be from Paul, it may have developed later because it is so different from the letters consistently considered to be authentically Pauline in both terminology and ideas. Many or perhaps most scholars believe it was written later by a disciple of Paul in the 80s or 90s. It claims to be written to the churches in Colossae (Col. 1:2) and Laodicea (Col. 4:16), whom he has not yet met.

Like Ephesians, the "household codes" emphasize the subordination of women (Col. 3:18) and slaves (Col. 3:22), which is contrary to the emphasis of either Jesus or Paul. In Colossians 3:11, he seems to be saying the same thing that Paul said in Galatians 3:28 but leaves out "male and female."

The emphasis of the book is that Jesus is "the image of the invisible God, the firstborn of all creation . . . For in him all the fullness of God was pleased to dwell" (Col. 1:15–20). And regarding the response of faith, he encourages the following of Christians: "As God's chosen ones, holy and beloved, clothe yourselves with compassion, kindness, humility, meekness, and patience . . . forgive each other; just as the Lord has forgiven you . . . clothe yourselves with love. . . . And whatever you do, in word or deed, do

BIBLICAL INTERPRETATION FOR LAYPEOPLE AND OTHER MARTYRS   43

everything in the name of the Lord Jesus, giving thanks to God the Father through him" (Col. 3:12–17).

1 Thessalonians

Thessalonica was the capital of Macedonia, where Paul ministered soon after crossing the Aegean Sea into Macedonia on his second missionary journey. After going to Athens, he sends Timothy back to check on them (1 Thess. 2:17–3:6). It may be that this is the first document of the canonical New Testament, written in about 49 CE. Apparently, some Christians have died (maybe martyred) since Paul left, and members are wondering if they will miss the Rapture. Paul says that when Jesus returns, he will bring with him those who have died (1 Thess. 4:14). They will rise first (1 Thess. 4:16). Only after that will those who are still alive be "caught up in the clouds together with them to meet the Lord in the air" (1 Thess. 4:17).

2 Thessalonians

It seems obvious in 1 Thessalonians that Paul thinks Jesus's second coming will be very soon, during their lifetime. There is apparently concern in the church regarding the delay. Apparently, some think the Second Coming will be soon, so they see no reason to work any longer. Without funds, they become freeloaders on the rest of the congregation. So Paul writes the congregation, speculating that there will be signs before his coming. There will be a "rebellion" and the coming of the "lawless one . . . who takes his seat in the temple of God, declaring himself to be God" (2 Thess. 2:3–4). Second, he warns the freeloaders against idleness, for they become busybodies and a burden to the faith community (2 Thess. 3:6, 11). He concludes, "Anyone unwilling to work should not eat" (2 Thess. 3:10). This verse has been abused by people who want to justify their lack of concern for those who are unable to get a job or do not make enough to support their families and need financial assistance. Paul concludes by calling for peace in the congregation (2 Thess. 3:16).

1 Timothy

The first of the three pastoral epistles is considered an authentic letter of Paul by very few scholars. The reasons are as follows: the vocabulary and style are different from Paul's letters, the passion in Paul's letters is absent, and the level of the institutionalization (1 Tim. 3:1–7) of the church is much more developed than the ragtag churches to which Paul ministered.

Further, the role of women has deteriorated from the time of Jesus and Paul (1 Tim. 2:8–15), slavery is reinforced (1 Tim. 6:1–2), and they are told to determine who is worthy and who is not worthy to receive financial help (1 Tim. 6:7–10). Finally, Paul does not condemn the rich but encourages them to be generous and share (1 Tim. 6:17–18).

2 Timothy

It is claimed that 2 Timothy was written while Paul was in prison. It does refer to Eunice and Lois, Timothy's mother and grandmother, respectively. The author warns Timothy that there will be characteristic behaviors "in the last days" (2 Tim. 3:2–5). Timothy is urged to be faithful to his ministry, listing things that need to be done (2 Tim. 4:1–5). He reminds Timothy that all scripture (the Old Testament) is "God-breathed" and "is useful for teaching, for reproof, for correction, and for training in righteous, so that everyone who belongs to God may be proficient, equipped for every good work" (2 Tim. 3:14–16).

Titus

In the third pastoral epistle, the church has apparently spread from the cities where Paul has originally made inroads to villages because Titus is encouraged to "appoint elders" (*presbyteroi*) in every town (Titus 1:5). Apparently, over them are "bishops" (*episcopoi*) who need to have certain qualifications (1:5–9) for teaching older men and women, younger men and women, and slaves (Titus 2:1–10). Unlike Paul's attitude toward slavery, in Titus, slaves are directed to be submissive to their masters (Titus 2:9–10); but the letter gives no directions to masters regarding the treatment of their slaves. It may be that Christian slaves of Christian masters are becoming restive because of what Paul has written in Galatians regarding the equality of all Christians. The members of the church are encouraged to be submissive to rulers and authorities (Titus 3:1). Finally, he lists numerous behaviors that they should avoid as reborn people (Titus 3:2–11).

Philemon

This is the only Pauline epistle that was written to an individual, although he wanted it shared with the church. Paul may have been in prison in Ephesus. A slave of Philemon's, Onesimus, has escaped and come to Paul. Under Paul's influence, he has apparently become a Christian. Paul sends Onesimus back to Philemon with this letter. Paul uses some

BIBLICAL INTERPRETATION FOR LAYPEOPLE AND OTHER MARTYRS   45

coercive psychology on Philemon to get him to free Onesimus. He has heard of Philemon's love and says that "for that reason" (verse 8), he is bold to ask on the basis of love (not command) for an "old man" who is a "prisoner" for the faith, to release Onesimus, whom he calls his "child." He argues that Onesimus can now be "useful"[30] to Philemon. As he sends Onesimus back, he is sending his own heart, asking that Philemon release him "voluntarily." He offers to pay any damages that Onesimus might have caused. So if Philemon considers Paul a partner, he will welcome Onesimus back as he will welcome Paul, reminding Philemon that he "owes his very self" to Paul. With that kind of hitting below the psychological belt, I wonder how Philemon could refuse. I couldn't.

Hebrews

The theme is stated in Hebrews 1:1–2: "In many and various ways, in times past, God spoke to the father through prophets, but in these last days has spoken to us through His Son, whom he appointed heir of all things through whom also he made the world." Written probably sometime between 60 and 90 CE, Hebrews emphasizes Jesus's humanity so he can identify with us (Heb. 2:5–18), portraying him as greater than Moses (Heb. 3:1–6), as the great high priest (Heb. 4:14–5:10), as a priest like Melchizedek (Heb. 7:1–17), and as the sacrifice for sin. Rather than offering his sacrifice every year like the Jewish priests do, Jesus offers his life "once for all" (Heb. 9:11–10:18).

Regarding Christians' response to what Jesus has done, the book says, "Faith is the assurance of things hoped for, the conviction of things not seen. For by it the men of old gained approval. By faith we understand that the worlds were prepared by the word of God, so that what is seen was not made out of things which are seen" (Heb. 11:1–3). The author follows up with numerous examples of people of faith, beginning with Abel (Heb. 1:4–40). Then the writer concludes, "Therefore, since we are surrounded with such a cloud of witnesses, let us also lay aside every encumbrance, and the sin which so easily entangles us, and let us run with endurance the race that is set before us, fixing our eyes on Jesus, the author and perfecter of faith, who for the joy set before Him endured the cross, despising the shame and has sat down at the right hand of the throne of God" (Heb. 12:1–2). Finally, he concludes that God disciplines his children for their benefit (Heb. 12:4–12).

---

[30]   The meaning of the word "onesimus."

James

This document was written by someone named James. Some believe it was written in the 40s or 50s. Others believe it was written later in response to an abuse of Paul's letter to the Galatians that emphasized justification by faith. Borg believes that the author was acquainted with the oral tradition spread about Jesus or the hypothetical Q document, which will be discussed later in chapter 10.[31] His emphasis is to be "doers of the word and not hearers only" (James 1:22–25), for "faith without works is dead" (James 2:14–26). He encourages total commitment to Christ, contrasting loyalty to Christ with "friendship with the world" (James 4:1–10), castigating them for buddying up to the rich while ignoring the poor (James 1:10–11, 2:1–6, 5:1–5). It is certainly a document that balances the faith that overemphasizes "justification by faith" in Romans and Galatians (i.e., reveling in "I'm saved") to the exclusion of Jesus's emphasis on discipleship of those who are truly his people.

1 Peter

Although claimed to have been written by Peter, it was written in a time when the gospel had spread all over what is now Turkey (1 Pet. 1:1). The document is a cyclical letter to the churches in Pontus, Galatia, Cappadocia, Asia, and Bithynia. Since it ends with greetings from those in Babylon, an early cryptic name for Rome, it was apparently written from that city (1 Pet. 6:13), perhaps around 80 or 90 CE. The author refers to himself as "elder" (1 Pet. 5:1). The term "Christian" seems to already be in common use (1 Pet. 4:6), and he uses the expression "born again" (1 Pet. 1:23), which is also only used in John's gospel, a late writing.

He says that God has given us a "new birth into a living hope through the resurrection of Jesus . . . into an inheritance that is imperishable" (1 Pet. 1:3–4). The trials that Christians are suffering are to test the genuineness of their faith, which is "more precious than gold" (1 Pet. 1:6–7). He says that although the recipients of his letter have not seen Jesus, they love him (1 Pet. 1:8), for they know that they have been ransomed "not with perishable things like silver or gold, but with the precious blood of Christ like that of a lamb without defect or blemish" (1 Pet. 1:18–19).

Despite referring to Rome as Babylon, the book endorses the Roman government, encouraging the recipients to "accept the authority over every

---

[31] Borg, 2012, *op. cit.*, 193.

BIBLICAL INTERPRETATION FOR LAYPEOPLE AND OTHER MARTYRS   47

human institution" (1 Pet. 2:13–14), reflecting "the growing accommodation of early Christianity to conventional cultural values, a movement away from the radicalism of Jesus and Paul."[32] It affirms the legitimacy of slavery (1 Pet. 2:18–21) and the authority of husbands over their wives, who should honor their husbands as the weaker sex (1 Pet. 3:1–7).

He encourages them not to be "conformed to the desires that you formerly had in ignorance" (1 Pet. 1:13–14); to rid themselves of "malice, guile, insincerity, envy, and slander (1 Pet. 2:1), and to express "unity of spirit" (1 Pet. 3:8). That unity is expressed in temple imagery, calling on the recipients to be "living stones" and Jesus being the cornerstone (1 Pet. 2:4–7). In addition, he uses the concept of priesthood for Christians, paraphrasing Exodus 19:6: "But you are a chosen race, a royal priesthood, a holy nation, God's own people, in order that you may proclaim the mighty acts of him who called you out of darkness into his marvelous light" (1 Pet. 3:9). He closes by encouraging Christians not to fear, but to cast their cares on God (1 Pet. 5:7).

There are some mystifying expressions in 1 Peter. The text says that after his death, Jesus preached in the spirit "to the spirits in prison" who were disobedient in the time of Noah, which prefigured baptism that now saves (1 Pet. 3:18–21). And the gospel is "proclaimed even to the dead, so that, though they had been judged in the flesh as everyone is judged, they might live in the spirit as God does" (1 Pet. 4:6).

2 Peter

Written between 120 and 150 CE, 2 Peter could be the last New Testament document. The writer is acquainted with the letters of Paul (2 Pet. 3:15–16), which by then had been proliferated among the churches. He tries to explain the delay of the second coming of Jesus (2 Pet. 3:3–13). Because their ancestors have already died, he tries to explain the delay by arguing that God's timing is not like ours: "With the Lord one day is like a thousand years, and a thousand years are like one day" (2 Pet. 3:8). Time is relative. Besides that, he is giving time for people to repent (2 Pet. 3:9). He warns against false prophets (2 Pet. 2:1–22) and various kinds of sin (2 Pet. 2:3–14).

---

[32]   *Ibid.*, 555.

1 John

Probably written around 100 CE, the author encourages Christians to love one another, for "whoever does not love does not know God, because God is love . . . This is love: not that we loved God, but that he loved us and sent his Son as an atoning sacrifice for our sins" (1 John 4:8, 10). It condemns those who deny that Jesus came "in the flesh" (1 John 4:1–3).

2 John

Thirteen verses, written by someone who calls himself "the elder," condemn "antichrists," or those who "do not confess that Jesus Christ has come in the flesh" (verse 7)—a denial condemned in 1 John.

3 John

Also written by "the elder," it is sent to someone named Gaius. He commands Gaius to show hospitality to Christians because they are brothers and sisters, even to the ones who are strangers.

Jude

Written perhaps around 100 CE, it is a judgmental document that warns against intruders who have sneaked in to pervert the grace of God.

Revelation

This was written by John of Patmos, probably sometime between the late 60s and the mid-90s CE. Although there have been localized persecutions beginning with Saul's persecution of the church (Acts 7–8), there have been no serious attempt to irradiate the church until the reign of Emperor Domitian (81–96 CE), which could be the time of this book. Or it could have been written in response to the local persecution in Rome by Emperor Nero in 64 CE. But the fact that John is writing from the island of Patmos suggests that it is a more pervasive persecution.

The book is an example of apocalyptic literature in which the writer assures suffering Christians that despite the persecutions, Jesus is in control and that if they remain faithful, he will return "soon" to take them to his kingdom. He expresses his revelation in a series of ecstatic visions.

Chapter 1 is an inaugural vision, followed by an addresses to seven churches[33] in Asia (southwestern Turkey)—Ephesus, Laodicea, Thyatira, Smyrna, Philadelphia, Pergamum, and Sardis—calling on them to be

---

[33] The number 7 symbolizes "completeness" in the Hebrew culture.

BIBLICAL INTERPRETATION FOR LAYPEOPLE AND OTHER MARTYRS   49

faithful. From that point on, the book is made up of visions filled with symbolic numbers, colors, creatures, and events. Chapter 6 portrays heaven's worship of the Lamb with a scroll (Rev. 4:1–5:14). The opening of seven seals unleashes war, famine, plague, death, earthquakes, and the blackening of the sun. The moon becomes bloodred, and the stars fall from the sky. Seven angels blow seven trumpets. A third of the earth burns, a third of the sea monsters and ships are destroyed, a third of the rivers become poisonous, and a third of the sun, moon, and stars are darkened. Giant locusts ascend from the "bottomless pit."

A third of humankind is killed (Rev. 8:6–11:19). A pregnant woman clothed with the sun and with the moon under her feet is attacked by the dragon with seven heads and ten horns, but she escapes as the dragon knocks down stars with his tail (chapter 12). Chapter 14 is the vision of the Lamb standing on Mount Zion with 144,000 who have the Lamb's name on their heads. Chapter 17 is a vision of a woman "drunk with the blood of the saints"—apparently Babylon (Rome), a city (or empire) destined to fall (chapter 18). Satan will be confined, the saints will rule with Christ during the final judgment (chapter 20), and a new heaven and new earth will be established (chapter 21).

Chapter 3

TOOLS OF INTERPRETATION

It is difficult enough to understand English writings that are four hundred years old, much less Greek and Hebrew writings that date from two thousand to three thousand years ago. The people for whom the writings were originally intended had little problem understanding them. Readers forty to fifty years later also had little trouble. But as the years wore on, people who became Christians did not understand Jewish culture, so help was required in order to understand the original intent of scriptural texts. There are numerous tools that can assist in our understanding of biblical meaning. A brief list of reference books is listed in appendix A.

Bible atlas. Like any atlas, a Bible atlas is a bound collection of tables, charts, and maps. Atlases are helpful by geographically locating an event. It helps anchor biblical events in geography and history instead of them being "out there somewhere." Most Bibles have some maps; and many of them will have a list of geographical places, such as cities, with references to their coordinate locations on a specific map. Coordinates are horizontal and vertical lines on a map that help locate a place. In most maps, the point at which the lines intersect is the coordinate. Coordinates on many maps

50

are the longitude (or meridian) and latitude (or parallel) lines. But in Bible atlases, they are usually found in squares made by east–west and north–south parallel lines, designated by references like A-6 and G-4.

Bible dictionary. A Bible dictionary is an encyclopedic study of names, places, and concepts in the Bible. If you want to make an overview study of David's life or find out something about Jericho, you can turn to these names and read about them. The dictionary will usually give biblical references in parentheses when it talks about some specific incident. If you are reading about David and it refers to his showdown with Goliath, the reference will tell you where the incident can be found in the Bible. Many Bibles have a brief Bible dictionary in the reference section in the back of the Bible. Some will have it at the bottom of the page or in an insert that discusses the topic. Of course, a Bible dictionary goes into much more detail and covers many more topics.

center column reference. Virtually all reference Bibles used to have a center column reference, located between the two columns. Some still do. Now some have these references at the bottom of the page, included in the commentary. It can be used to cross-reference passages or concepts. For example, if we read 1 Peter 2:9, it may occur that we have seen these words somewhere else. The passage reads, "But you are a chosen race, a royal priesthood, a holy nation, God's own people, that you may declare the wonderful deeds of him who called you out of darkness into his marvelous light." Checking the center column reference under 1 Peter 2:9, we find Deuteronomy 10:15, Isaiah 43:20–21, Exodus 19:6, Deuteronomy 7:6, Exodus 23:22, Titus 2:14, etc. All the texts have something to do with the "calling" of God's people. But we find that Exodus 19:6 says, "And you shall be to me a kingdom of priests and a holy nation. These are the words which you shall speak to the children of Israel." These words are the exact words that Peter chose from the Old Testament to apply to the Christian Church.

For laypersons really interested in biblical study, a good Bible dictionary, concordance, commentary, and Bible atlas can provide a good foundation for study. Since they can be expensive, I would recommend checking Half Price Books, Goodwill Industries stores, Salvation Army stores, Craigslist, and other Internet resources. The Text This Week[34] has

---

34   www.textweek.com.

numerous commentaries on the readings (or pericopes) for each Sunday used by numerous denominations. Commentaries range from fathers of the early church to those of the Middle Ages to those of more recent centuries, such as Luther, John Wesley, and Matthew Henry. It also has the texts of several English translations and the original languages. Bible Gateway[35] has many different versions in several languages, including the original languages and audio Bibles. By entering a keyword or topic, it can also function as a concordance. It also has a store from which one can buy Bibles and other resources at quite reasonable prices. Working Preacher[36] has studies of the texts for the readings from each Sunday of the church year, including a Spanish study of the gospel. For those who want to study in somewhat less detail and are limited financially, a very good study Bible may be the answer. They usually run about $40 to $60. Again, a secondhand purchase might be found at one of the sources mentioned.

commentary. A commentary is a book or series of books explaining the meaning of specific sections of the Bible. Bible commentaries range from very brief volumes that only comment briefly on major sections of a biblical book to commentaries of fifty or sixty volumes that go into great detail on specific words. There are many study Bibles that have brief commentaries at the bottom of the page.

concordance. A concordance is a book containing words of the Bible in an alphabetical sequence with the word in the text or part of the text, with reference to chapter and verse. A concordance is useful in two ways. If you want to refer to a specific passage that you know, you can find it. All you have to do is choose a major word from the passage and look it up in the concordance. Let's say you want to look up Jesus's words: "Ask and it shall be given you, seek and you will find, knock and it will be opened to you." You choose one of the main words, such as "knock," and go down the list under the word "knock" until you find "*k* . . . and it shall be given." You will find that it is located in Matthew 7:7.

Another way to use a concordance is to find out how a word is used by a specific person or in a specific book of the Old or New Testament. For example, if you wanted to see how Paul used the term "righteousness" or

---

[35]   www.biblegateway.com.

[36]   www.workingpreacher.org.

BIBLICAL INTERPRETATION FOR LAYPEOPLE AND OTHER MARTYRS   53

"righteous" in Romans, you look up these words, go down to the Romans references, note the references, and then look them up in the Bible. It is a very helpful reference book. Many Bibles, except for the very cheapest ones, will have a small concordance in the reference section in the back of the Bible. However, an entire concordance book is a hundred times more helpful.

contemporary and near-contemporary writings.
Archaeologists are providing us with more texts that are contemporary to and near contemporary to the Bible. Books such as the Babylonian flood story (*The Epic of Gilgamesh*), the Babylonian creation story (*Enuma Elish*), the Dead Sea Scrolls, the writings of Josephus, the pseudepigrapha, and the Nag Hammadi collection are writings that occurred contemporaneously to the Bible and help shed light on the cultures in which the Bible was written and the way people thought in biblical times. In many instances, they help us understand social behaviors that were taken for granted by the people who first received the oral roots or written texts of the Bible, but which are otherwise less understandable to us.

gospel parallels. Many Bibles, especially study Bibles, have gospel parallels. Gospel parallels have the names of the gospels at the top of columns, the name of the event to the left of the columns, and the reference where the description of the event and the name of the gospel intersect. In books of gospel parallels, the text of the event is actually written out. An example is the parable of the fig tree:

Mark 24:32–33	**Mark 13:28–31**	**Luke 19:29–31**
[32]From the fig tree: learn its lesson: as soon as it's a branch becomes tender and puts forth its leaves, you know that summer is near. [33]So also, when you see all these things you know that he is near, at the very gates.	[28]From the fig tree learn its lesson: as soon as its branch becomes tender and puts forth its leaves, you know that summer is near. [29]So also, when you see these things taking place, you know that he is near, at the very gates.	[29]And he told them a parable: "Look at the fig tree, and all the trees; [30] as soon as they come out in leaf, you see for yourselves and know that the summer is already near. [31]So also, when you see these things taking place, you know that the Kingdom of God is near."

historical novels. Historical novels are books that set the story in a particular historical period and, while not necessarily historical, may give the flavor of a specific time and culture in which the event is to have taken place. *The Blue and the Gray, Centennial, Lonesome Dove,* and *Pearl Harbor* are such books that were made into TV series. Books like *The Robe* and *Spartacus* are historical novels. James Michener's *The Source* is a wonderful series vignette about the prehistory and history of Palestine and a good source to put oneself into the historical situation. Anne Rice's *Christ the Lord: Out of Egypt* and *Christ the Lord: The Road to Cana* and my own *The Making of a Messiah: Influences on Jesus' Childhood and Youth* are examples of historical novels about the life of Jesus.

lexicon. A lexicon is a cross-language dictionary. A lexicon gives the meaning of a word of another language and usually the specific form (like first person present passive). Unless one has some familiarity with the original language, this kind of text will be of little use.

word study books. A word study book is a book that traces the meaning of biblical words. The Hebrew words *qadosh* (in various forms) and *chasid* and the Greek words *hagios, hieros,* and *hosios* are all translated "holy" in English. With a word study book, one can trace the use of the words, who uses the various words, and the specific meaning of the words conveyed by various authors. This can also be done with an exhaustive concordance, such as *Young's Analytical Concordance to the Bible.*

Chapter 4

THE PROCESS OF HERMENEUTICS

When I was a seminary student, Richard Jungkuntz wrote an expression on the board that at first baffled the class: "Stan Wore Horse Collar in Nightcap." I have enjoyed using this one ever since. Some people know what a "horse collar" is. And most people know that a "nightcap" is a "late evening drink (usually alcoholic)." In "'*Twas the Night before Christmas*," the author says "I in my *cap* had just settled down for a long winter's nap." "Cap" is short for "nightcap," wearing apparel to keep one's head warm—before central heating. But Dr. Jungkuntz pointed out that there is another meaning for "nightcap." When Jungkuntz informed us that the expression had been a headline on the sports page in the late 1940s or early 1950s, eyes immediately lit up. Since Stan "the Man" Musial had been my favorite baseball player, I knew that the expression meant that Stan Musial had gone hitless in the second game of a doubleheader. These kinds of figures of speech may be easily understood by contemporaries but can be baffling to people in later generations. This brings us to the point of the book—interpretation.

Definition of "Hermeneutics"

The Greek word "hermeneutics" comes from Hermes, the messenger of the gods, the patron of eloquence and learning, and the son of Jupiter and Maia. The word *hermēneuein* can mean "to expound, explain, interpret, or translate," depending on the prefix.

In Luke 24:27, on the road to Emmaus, Jesus joined some disciples on the road. "Beginning with Moses and with all the prophets, He *explained* (*diermēneuein*) to them the things concerning Himself in all the Scriptures."

In John 1:41–42, Andrew came to his brother, Simon, and said, "We have found the Messiah (which *means* (*methermēneuein*) 'the Christ')." Here, the word means "is translated."

In John 1:38, John the Baptist directed his disciples to Jesus with the words "Behold the Lamb of God." Two disciples caught up with him and said, "'Rabbi' (which *means* (*methermēneuein*) 'Teacher'), where are you going?" Here, it means "translated." Luke, writing for non-Jews, was not sure they would know what "rabbi" means; so he translated the word for them.

In John 9:7, Jesus told the blind man, "Go wash in the Pool of Siloam (which means (*hermēneuein*) 'Sent')."

In Acts 9:36, the text says, "In Joppa there was a disciple named Tabitha (*hermēneuein*) translated Dorcas, meaning gazelle) . . ."

In 1 Corinthians 14:13, Paul tells the congregation in Corinth that if someone speaks in tongues, someone should be able to (*diermēneuō*) give the meaning. Here, the word could mean "translate," "interpret," or "explain."

A Mental Process

In the old movie *The Affairs of Dobie Gillis*,[37] Dobie's English professor is a woman with her snoot in the air. Dobie said that he believed that the rules of interpretation were determined by the way people used the language. The teacher answered, "Certainly not. Rules of language are made up by scholars." Dobie understood the process. The professor was deluded.

Hermeneutics has been called "rules of interpretation." However, it is not a set of mechanical rules, but inferences drawn from observing the way language works. It is reflecting on patterns of what we are doing when we speak or write. In the "horse collar" statement, the person who wrote the headline probably did not spend a lot of time analyzing how it

---

[37] Weis, Don, dir. MGM, 1953. Film.

BIBLICAL INTERPRETATION FOR LAYPEOPLE AND OTHER MARTYRS   57

was that he put the expression together or the process people would use to interpret it. He simply thought it was "catchy" and used it. If I had read that headline the next day, I would not have focused on the figures of speech or the process I went through to understand the statement. I would have looked at it and turned cold inside because my hero had been hamstrung by the pitchers in one game. Hamstrung? Well, I just used another figure of speech to say the same thing.

Factors Affecting Interpretation

Even with people we know well, communication is not always clean and neat. Misunderstandings occur. There *are* times when we have difficulty interpreting the Bible. That should not be too surprising since there are times when we have difficulty interpreting the meaning of what is said by people we know very well. We talk to each other using words both of us know, but still, we have misunderstandings.

Once I called on a member of a congregation I was serving. We began with the obligatory polite preliminaries. "How are you, Peggy?" I asked. Rather than the usual "Fine, how are you?" she told me how things were actually going. It was not terrible, but something negative had happened. Then after telling me her problem, she asked, "And how are you?" I answered, "About the same," meaning "I am about the same as usual" (that is, "I am fine"). She sympathetically answered, "Oh, I'm sorry to hear that. What is the matter?" She thought that when I said "About the same," I meant about the same as *she* was doing. Well, we had a laugh over the miscommunication, but there are times when the miscommunication can cause problems. Married people experience it. Wars have started because of miscommunication. My guess is you can think of numerous times when taking the meaning of someone's words the wrong way has led to hard feelings. Well, if we have some difficulty communicating with someone we know well and with whom we share pretty much the same meaning of words, it is small wonder we have some difficulty with the Bible. So let's look at some of the factors that contribute to our misunderstanding of the Bible.

Cultural-Historical Factors

"Culture" can be defined as the total way of life shared by members of a society, including thinking, feeling, ways of acting, values, belief, education, type of housing, clothing, and technology. Sociologists have studied the values of American culture. American values are considerably different from the values of the culture of the Bible. Brinkerhoff and White concluded that Americans believe in achievements and success, activity and work, humanitarianism, efficiency and practicality, progress, material comfort, equality, freedom, conformity, science and rationality, nationalism, patriotism, democracy, individualism, and racial superiority.[38] Robin Williams added these values: education, religiosity, male supremacy, romantic love, monogamy, and heterosexuality.[39] I would add religious (but not political) pluralism. But values also change over time. Within the last decade, the attitude toward homosexuality has radically changed in the United States. In our culture, we expect and like change. Other cultures hate change like the plague.

Dennis Bratcher pointed out that we tend to be ethnocentric in our thinking in that we "tend to view the world and life as if everyone sees it the same way that we do," representing a cultural imperialism.[40] In *Star Trek II: The Wrath of Khan*, Spock says to Kirk, "The needs of the many outweigh the needs of the few." Kirk responds, "Or of the one." Bratcher points out that this thinking "runs counter to our basic western, and especially American, cultural values. . . . most western culture is permeated with a concern with self-interest." But in much of the world, especially in Africa, Latin American, and the Far East, "the primary concern is not the individual but the family or the wider community. In such cultures an individual is not defined by who she is or what she has achieved as an individual, but in terms of what they contribute to the group, to which family they belong, and how well they have fulfilled obligations to other family, tribal, or community members."[41] If you've seen many cowboy and Indian movies, at some point, you must have been exposed to the idea that among many Native American tribes, there was no such concept as ownership of real estate. It could only be used, not owned, because it was

---

[38]   David B. Brinkerhoff and Lynn K. White. *Sociology* (St. Paul: West Publishing Company, 1991), 58.

[39]   James M. Henslin. *Introducing sociology: selected readings* (NY: Free Press, 1975).

[40]   Dennis Bratcher. *Community and Testimony: Cultural Influence in Biblical Studies.* http://www.crivoice.org/historyculture.html.

[41]   *Ibid.*

BIBLICAL INTERPRETATION FOR LAYPEOPLE AND OTHER MARTYRS   59

"given by the Great Spirit to provide for the needs of those in his care. . . . To them, [buying land] was a violation of the sacredness of the land."[42]

Ancient Israelites believed in honor, extreme hospitality, tribes, maintaining traditions, the total power of the sheikh, male superiority, polygamy, slavery, marriage determined by the father, magic, and polytheism (later changing to henotheism and even later by absolute monotheism).

History

People describe things in terms of what they know. For example, Jesus is seen as a king. If he had been born in 2018 in the United States, it is unlikely that he would have been referred to as a king. We are confronted with history in the Bible. Some people would understand history as "what happened in the past." However, nobody can repeat everything that happened. So one must select which happenings they want to report on. The very decision to choose one happening or data and not another is a different history from the history told by someone else who selects a different set of happenings. So "history" is a selection and therefore an interpretation of the available data. It is unlikely that if Paul lived among us now, he would call himself the "slave" of Christ. In fact, the Greek word for "Christ," *christos*, means "anointed one." Since people are not anointed for office today, he would not be called *christos* (the anointed one), but something more contemporary like "installed."

Geography

Geography is the stage on which history is played out. It puts us within certain limits of experience. In tropical areas, women wore nothing to cover their breasts. Missionaries who believed that there was something intrinsically wrong about exposing women's breasts considered as part of their mission to get these women to wear brassieres. If Eskimos were to describe "heaven," their description would be different from the way it would be described by Iboes in Nigeria. Therefore, it makes sense that the ultimate *shalom* in the Old Testament would be described in terms of every man having his own fig tree and his own grapevine and a cool wind coming in from the Mediterranean Sea rather than the hot sirocco from the Transjordan desert area.

---

42   *Ibid.*

Oriental-Occidental Ways of Thinking

Harley Swiggum, who wrote *The Bethel Series*,[43] liked to point out the difference between the Occidental and Oriental thinking. From their Oriental point of view, to honor God, one takes his shoes off in God's presence and covers the head. Most Americans would think it scandalous for someone to come into church barefooted and wearing a hat. For many Orientals, it is very important for them to wear a beard. Indeed, to shave the beard might have been a disgrace. For the Occidental, it is not. There was even a point during the 1960s and 1970s when many Americans saw beards as a sign of protest. (As a pastor, I got into some minor hot water over my beard). For Orientals, cross-eyed people are desirable. For Occidentals, they are not. Fat wives are desirable for Orientals, but not for Occidentals. Oriental parents arrange marriages because it is considered too important a decision to be made by mere children, and being in love to marry is neither required nor necessarily expected. For modern Occidentals, being "in love" seems absolutely essential and none of the parents' business.

We live in an urban twenty-first-century Occidental (Western) culture. The Bible was written between about 1200 BCE and 100 CE under mostly Oriental influence. Some of the material came from oral traditions that go back hundreds (maybe thousands) of years earlier. Westerners tend to ask questions of process (*how* did something happen) and think in more abstract terms. The Oriental mind is more inclined to address questions of purpose (asking *why*) and thinking in more concrete terms. The biblical writers not only spoke "to," but "out of'" a specific cultural context. Our thinking is always influenced to a major extent by the culture in which we live. Even within the same society, thinking can be different because of different circumstances. Farmers—who realize that despite their best efforts, the weather, to some extent, determines the success of the crops—tend to be more fatalistic than the urbanite with a job in which he knows how much his after-deduction net income will be.

The culture out of which scripture came was at times nomadic, sometimes rural, at times urban (but not at all like ours), and sometimes Oriental in outlook. Later, the Israelites saw things from the perspective of the people of a nation united under a king. Finally, they saw things from

---

[43] Madison, Wis.: Adult Christian Education Foundation, 1960. Swiggum addressed this issue when discussing page 3 in the first book, which addressed the Old Testament.

BIBLICAL INTERPRETATION FOR LAYPEOPLE AND OTHER MARTYRS   61

the point of view of an ethnic group who lived and worked in a nation in which they had no political power at all.

They had no copyright laws, no concept of plagiarism, and no publishing for monetary gain. I'm not sure we think anything should be published without a monetary motivation. (After all, why did I write this book? Would I have written it if I had lived in the culture of Paul? Well, maybe so). The more people who read this paragraph, the better off I will be financially. And we are well aware of the seriousness with which we take copyright issues when the first thing we see on a videotape is a threat of prosecution if we break a copyright law. "Without the expressed consent of the NBA" is probably not even noticed by most listeners, but in reality, it is very serious for someone videotaping a game.

The people of the Bible thought in terms of unchangeable laws of nature (natural orders), whereas we think in terms of evolutionary change. When disaster hit them, they asked, "Whose sin brought down God's wrath on us?" We ask, "What were the natural cause-and-effect factors that brought this on?" For them, if one was born blind, they asked whose fault or whose sin caused it. So if we impose our way of thinking on them, we will *inevitably* skew the interpretation and thus change the meaning of the original text.

In Exodus 21:17, the son who curses his parents is subject to death. This is not the same as saying a "bad word" or merely expressing disrespect. Unfortunately, one can hardly get through a conversation without hearing "goddamn" used thoughtlessly several times. But for the Hebrews, words had power and were agents for good or evil. So the spoken word was an active agent for hurt. They believed in the power of the curse. A curse could bring about death, maybe even eternal ruin to the person's soul. Our concept of cursing is not at all the same as what Exodus was dealing with. So if we do not understand *their* concept of the "curse," we will understand that passage as a despicable, contemptible law. If a slave girl had a baby by her owner on the knees of the legal wife, it belonged to the wife. We believe that if a woman is pregnant, the baby is hers.

They saw slavery from a completely different perspective. They saw it from an Old Testament perspective, which was originally indentured servanthood to pay off debts. An indentured slave was free after a certain time frame or when the high priest died. Slavery of the kind we think of resulted from the capture of enemies in battle. They had no professional slave trade that captured people specifically for the purpose of enslaving them. But in the New Testament, the Roman meaning of slaves as disposable property surely changed the Jews' understanding of slavery.

Paul and Culture

Paul has been vilified for his attitude toward women. But Virginia Mollenkott argued that those who criticize Paul's attitudes have not been realistic regarding the power of culture. She argued that in Galatians, he *revolutionized* human orders, arguing that there is no distinction between the sexes (Gal. 3:28).[44] Paul ascribed high status to Nympha (Col. 4:15), Junia (Rom. 16:7), Phoebe (Rom. 16:1–2), and Priscilla (1 Cor. 16:16). He (or a disciple) encouraged both male and female Christians to submit to one another (Eph. 5:21–22), that *all* Christians are to behave in the same way (Col. 3:18–29), and argued for no distinction between the sexes (Gal. 5:13).[45] This goes against the grain of Paul's upbringing, which had formed his whole habit of thought.[46]

Mollenkott believed that Paul was confused over the issue, torn between the paternalistic attitude of the culture and the gospel. When one criticizes Paul, he has to ignore the fact that Paul had to overcome two thousand years of history that affected his understanding.[47]

The same is true of the Pauline attitude toward slavery (Philemon, Col. 3:22–4:1, Eph. 6:5–9). He lived with the background of two cultures. In the Hebrew culture, it had been common to sell oneself into slavery for a specific, limited time to pay debts. He also was a part of an entire cultural region in which the taking of slaves as booty in war was so common that if one would suggest that there was something wrong with it, everyone would have looked at him as if he should be put away in a padded cell. Finally, he had been exposed to the extreme brutality of the system of Roman slavery in which slaves were at the total mercy of their owners. So when Paul says that slaves should obey their masters and then add that masters had an obligation toward their slaves, who were pieces of cheap property, that was mind-blowing in the Roman world. It was so revolutionary that it was almost unthinkable to say that a master had obligations toward his slave.

---

[44]   Virginia Ramey Mollenkott. *Women Men & the Bible* (Nashville: Abingdon, 1977), 102, 84.

[45]   *Ibid.*, 21–25.

[46]   *Ibid.*, 102, 84, 96–100, 21–25.

[47]   *Ibid.*, 96–105.

BIBLICAL INTERPRETATION FOR LAYPEOPLE AND OTHER MARTYRS   63

Mollenkott also asserted that the Old Testament authors and rabbinical teaching reflect a culture that, like the Taliban in our day, "assume[s] that patriarchy is the will of God."[48] She saw vestiges of Paul's rabbinic conditioning when he says in 1 Corinthians 14 that "women are not allowed to speak, but must be in submission" (verses 34–35). But in 1 Corinthians 11, she observed that Paul had no problem with women prophesying and praying in public as long as they have their heads covered (verses 7–9), appealing to "nature" and "practice" (verses 13–16), which are also expressions of cultural thinking.[49] In one place, Paul supported cultural conditioning of his patriarchal background; and in one place, he did not. Mollenkott believed that Paul was torn between culture and the gospel.

Jesus and Culture

Luke comments, "Jesus grew in wisdom and stature, and favor with God and man" (Luke 2:52). That is an expression of the fact that Jesus was a part of his culture. He learned his times tables and spelling from his parents. He learned to understand the faith in the way his parents and his rabbi did. He may have been influenced by John the Baptist. But because of the teaching he had received, he also was under the influence of God's Spirit and could put the will of God over the values he had learned from his culture.

The culture into which Jesus was born was a highly patriarchal society. The birth of a boy child was met with joy. The birth of a girl was met with disappointment. In their prayers, Jewish men thanked God that they were not born a woman. Women were relegated to the fringes of society.

But Jesus did something absolutely unthinkable, breaking many taboos against women (Matt. 9:22),[50] refusing to support a double standard in divorce (Matt. 19:3, 5:32), and affirming the right of women to study theology when he informed Martha that Mary's listening to his teaching was preferable to providing hospitality, an extremely important activity in their culture (Luke 10:41–42).[51]

---

[48]   *Ibid.*, 91–92.

[49]   *Ibid.*, 96–100.

[50]   *Ibid.*, 13–21, 122.

[51]   Mary was a proto-Yentl. In case you are too young to remember, *Yentl* was a movie in which Barbara Streisand played the daughter of a rabbi who taught her secretly; and after his death, she dressed like a male in order to attend *yeshiva* school. Barbra Streisand, dir. MGM, 1983. Film.

And Peter, who studied under Jesus, after talking about women's submission to husbands, says husbands were to treat their wives "in the same way," suggesting no difference in the way they treat each other (1 Pet. 2:18–25).[52] So the pages of the New Testament record a revolutionary way of treating others that was mind-boggling to conservative traditionalists.

Archeology

Generally, people of that time understood basically what was meant by the biblical writings. Soon afterward, however, especially as people of different cultures became Christian, difficulty in interpretation set in. For us, archeology illuminates many of the texts that we would not understand otherwise.

In the last two centuries, significant archeological discoveries have shed light on the meaning of words, events, and the culture of the Bible. The discovery of the Ugaritic library in what is now Lebanon and letters and texts at Tell el-Amarna in Egypt have shed light on the times of the patriarchs. The Dead Sea Scrolls have shed light on the first century BCE and Jesus's time, and the Nag Hammadi library has shed light on Christians' understanding of the Christian faith in the second century CE, right after the time of Jesus. The Code of Hammurabi of Babylonia, just before or about the time of Abraham, and the Ashurbanipal library of Assyria give light on the seventh century BCE. These are some of the most significant archeological discoveries that shed some light on the Bible. If you are interested in learning some specifics about these discoveries, you can find articles online, including *Wikipedia*.

Selectivity of the Message

A second factor contributing to misunderstanding is selectivity of the message. When one's mind is already made up, he looks for passages that will support his views and ignores those that will seem to oppose his point of view. In one episode of *The Waltons*, John-Boy had a girlfriend who wanted to get married. He did not want to make the leap. So they quoted Bible passages at each other. As I recall, she quoted Proverbs: "He who finds a wife finds what is good and receives favor from the LORD" (Prov. 18:22). John-Boy quoted Paul: "I wish that all men were as I am [single]" (1 Cor. 17). They went back and forth until they ran out of Bible passages,

---

[52]   Mollenkott, 1977, *op. cit.*, 25.

BIBLICAL INTERPRETATION FOR LAYPEOPLE AND OTHER MARTYRS   65

so they began with other slogans. He said, "Haste makes waste." She answered, "He who hesitates is lost." He: "Look before you lead." She: ". . .etc.," he: ". . .etc.," until they run out of proverbs. The point is they were not listening to the Bible speak but wanted the Bible to support what they had already decided.

In fact, entire church bodies emphasize different things depending on which books they focus on. Those who focus on Acts, especially the first few chapters, will likely have a heavy emphasis on "charismata," gifts of the Spirit, such as healing and speaking in tongues. Those who focus on Revelation and Ezekiel are liable to take a dim view of the world, see it as ominous and persecuting, and focus on signs of the end of times with a heavy emphasis on "getting to heaven." Those who focus on Romans and Galatians are liable to emphasize personal trust and faith and tend to be more quietistic in their faith. Those emphasizing the gospels, especially Matthew and Luke, and the epistle of James may be more emphatic on personal caring for the poor, needy, and disenfranchised. It is not at all difficult to determine what the Bible *should* say and then make it serve our beliefs.

Only a short time ago, it was common for racists within the church to use selectivity of the message in interpreting the Curse of Ham (Gen. 9:18–27) to justify slavery. When one is not honest about letting scripture speak but wants to use the Bible to justify his way of thinking, this kind of skewing can occur. To use Noah's curse of Canaan (not Ham) to justify slavery, one must ignore the fact that Noah was in a drunken state when he pronounced it—that the curse was *not* on Ham, but on Canaan (who was not African, but was a Semitic nemesis of the Israelites)—and impose an anthropology on Shem, Ham, and Japheth, which literally everyone knows is fallacious. What we want to be true is so emotionally controlled that it caused Jerome to completely mistranslate Genesis 3:15 in the Vulgate, using the word "she" rather than "he" shall crush the serpent's head.

And of course, there are people like Bill Maher, television host of the HBO talk show *Real Time with Bill Maher*[53] and previously with the ABC show *Politically Incorrect*, who quote the Bible for their own purposes. Maher is usually rational and quite nuanced when he looks at political and economic situations. I may disagree with him on specific issues but usually acknowledge that he has done his homework and has good intentions. However, when it comes to the Bible, he loses his perspective and interprets

---

[53]   HBO. Television.

the Bible like a five-year-old. Now if someone pointed that out to him, he might answer, "Well, that is the way Christians interpret it." And some Christians do interpret the Bible the way he does. They do it for security. He does it to debunk the faith.

Now when I wanted to do something and my mother would not let me, I would make the following appeal: "Everybody else is doing it" (which, of course, was rank hyperbole). Her answer was always, "If so-and-so (or everybody) jumped off a cliff, does that mean you have to?" Now ignoring the fact that she ended her sentence with a preposition, I didn't like her answer. But I did understand the rationale. "Everybody else is doing it" is never an adequate reason for anything. But Bill Maher seems to think that everybody interprets the Bible like a five-year-old (which, of course, is also hyperbole), and therefore, he must interpret it that way also.

Of course, his fundamentalist interpretation of the Bible is meant not to support the Bible but to demean it and the faith it represents. I doubt, however, that Maher interprets Uncle Remus or Aesop that way. If he interpreted Aesop and Uncle Remus the way he interprets the Bible, he would probably belittle Aesop and say something like "Gee whiz,[54] Uncle Remus! Are you so ignorant that you don't know that rabbits and foxes cannot talk to each other? Each has his own language, neither of which is English. Don't you know they have totally different languages since that Tower of Babel incident? And if they did, don't you know they wouldn't talk like an uneducated Southern black dialect? They would talk like a Midwesterner."

But unfortunately, Maher has a lot of good ammunition. He has people like Hal Lindsey, whose book *The Late Great Planet Earth*[55] turned out to be a spurious prediction of the end of the world, but he continues to write equally strange books that some people still take seriously. Or John Hagee of Cornerstone Church in San Antonio, who spews forth a continuous hateful barrage, including his private biblical interpretation that Hurricane Katrina hit New Orleans because of a "homosexual rally."[56] I doubt that the infants who died in the hurricane were homosexual—but I could be

---

[54] Of course, he would use a sleazier expression.

[55] Grand Rapids: Zondervan, 1970.

[56] Matt Corley. "Hagee Says Hurricane Katrina Struck New Orleans Because It Was 'Planning A Sinful' 'Homosexual Rally." *ThinkProgress.* Apr 23, 2008. https://thinkprogress.org/hagee-says-hurricane-katrina-struck-new-orleans-because-it-was-planning-a-sinful-homosexual-rally-55b392a04322.

BIBLICAL INTERPRETATION FOR LAYPEOPLE AND OTHER MARTYRS   67

wrong. And if God were so outraged with New Orleans that he aimed Katrina at the city, one would think if God were consistent, he would have wiped San Francisco off the face of the earth long ago. But maybe God is not consistent. Well, that shows how inconsistent ideologists can be when they want to prove their point.

Or Pat Robertson, who claimed the children of Haiti, a nation of ten million that is 96 percent Christian (an astronomically higher percentage than the United States), died in the Haitian earthquake because of the Bois Caïman vodou ceremony during the Haitian Revolution way back in 1791 that may have involved a few hundred people.[57]

Of course, Bill Maher has plenty of ammunition because he doesn't focus on the interpretation of Christians and Jews who interpret the Bible like adults. In order to pursue his faith that says there is no God, *he must* interpret the Bible like a five-year-old. He, of course, can justify his method of interpretation because he can say, "I see Christians interpret it that way!" So people who claim to be Christian but spew out hate-filled rhetoric that is the opposite of what Jesus taught unfortunately give people like Maher plenty of ammunition.

Maybe rather than focusing on some religious kooks, Maher should focus on people like Jesus, Francis of Assisi, Dietrich Bonhoeffer, Maya Angelou, Martin Luther King Jr., Bishop Desmond Tutu, Bishop Oscar Romero, Mother Teresa, Bill Moyers, and Harriet Tubman.

And look at the way the Taliban, al Qaeda, and ISIS pervert the mostly peaceful teachings of the Quran. They support their own cultural agenda by claiming it is Allah's will. Allah becomes their servant by manipulating the teachings of Islam to support their cruelty. When it comes to war, Muhammad's teaching of a just war was much like that of St. Augustine. My guess is because of the way they blaspheme Allah with their attempt to make him serve their cultural beliefs, Allah vomits when he hears their name, and Muhammad rolls over in his grave.

The selection of facts *gives* meaning to what is observed. Biblical writers were part of the culture in which they grew up. They did not explain their cultural perspective. Indeed, most of the time, they were not aware of the way it shaped their thinking.

---

[57]   Ryan Smith. "Pat Robertson: Haiti 'Cursed' After 'Pact to the Devil.'" CBSNEWS.com, Jan. 13, 2010, 1:58 pm. http://www.cbsnews.com/news/pat-robertson-haiti-cursed-after-pact-to-the-devil/.

Personal Differences in Receivers: *Sitz im Leben*

Sitz im Leben is a German expression that means "the place where one sits in life" or one's social location. The position that one occupies in a society has a strong influence on the way that person understands social situations and how he experiences a message.

Compare, for example, the attitude of a man on the Ford assembly line with the attitude of the same man who becomes a supervisor and whose new social location enables him all at once to see the point of view of management—and perhaps later on, that perspective is all he can see. In the Old Testament, compare the dangerous position of Amos, Elisha, and Elijah with the position of Isaiah, who was something like secretary of state in Judah or at least a foreign affairs advisor. In the present, middle-aged white people often consider the 1950s to be a more "innocent age" than now. Only white people with psychological blinders on could say that. African Americans, who suffered under the cruelty of segregation, who knew they could be murdered by whites who would not be prosecuted (much less convicted), and who were prevented from voting by the most ingenuous de jure and de facto means, would see that time not at all innocent, but much more cruel than the present.

There was a great chasm in the way different groups heard Jesus's words. The Pharisees, who were seen as very upright and had a tendency toward pride in their personal religion, received Jesus's message much differently from those who were outcasts in the first-century Jewish society. Considering the different way receptors receive the message, how would a message condemning drunkenness be received by different people? If a pastor preaches a "hellfire and brimstone" sermon on drunkenness, a social drinker might say to herself, "This message has nothing to do with me. I am not a drunk like that scum that falls down drunk in the street and tries to get welfare from the rest of us." A teetotaler might gleefully respond, "Give 'em hell, preacher. Drinking is a major sin!" An alcoholic might respond with despair, saying, "I am not worth anything. I am no good. God hates me!" A youth who takes speed or marijuana but does not drink alcoholic beverages might think, "Yeah, alcohol is a middle-aged hang-up."

Religious Pluralism

In America, where there is every variety of church, if one's pastor expresses views that are contrary to one's own preconceived views, the

BIBLICAL INTERPRETATION FOR LAYPEOPLE AND OTHER MARTYRS   69

member does not have to listen and put his preconceived beliefs to the test. He can go across the street to a church where the pastor will say what he wants to hear or what he already believes. When there is only one church, divided along parish lines, one had no such choices. If he did not like what the priest was saying, he simply had to listen and perhaps learn something.

Frontier Christianity

On the eastern seaboard, the clergy tended to be educated. But as Americans pressed on to the frontier, they were often without benefit of educated clergy. They had their Bible, and as they read, they gained ideas about the meaning of the texts that may not have been in the minds of the original authors at all. During the Second Great Awakening (ca. 1780–1820), learning was even belittled, and ignorance was considered a virtue by many.[58] The Second Great Awakening made major inroads on the frontier. This period of history resulted in a plethora of new denominations, including the Seventh-Day Adventists, Advent Christians, Churches of Christ, Christian Church (Disciples of Christ), African Methodist Episcopal, Millerites, and African Methodist Episcopal Zion Church, while stimulating growth of the Baptists, Methodists, Shakers, and Mormons. But with its serious emphasis on Christian morality, it gave impetus to the abolition, temperance, and suffragist movements.[59] So there was much good that came out of this rebellion against entrenched, socially conservative mainline denominations. But some strange interpretations resulted in the proliferation of new denominations, further undermining the overt unity of Jesus's church.

Deductive Use of the Bible

Deductive reasoning involves going from the general to the specifics. One makes a general statement about belief and then finds specific proof texts that will support or not support one's notion. Inductive reasoning goes from the specifics to the general. For a Christian or Jew, inductive reasoning means that he would search the scriptures for texts that address an issue based on the centrality of the gospel and draw a general conclusion

---

58   Nathan O. Hatch. *The Democratization of American Christianity* New Haven, Conn. (Yale University Press, 1989).

59   *Ibid.*; *Second Great Awakening*, en.m.wikipedia.org.

70 DAVID W. MELBER

based on the specifics. Unfortunately, deductive interpretations seem to be more common.

Random Selection

Some people believe that they can open the Bible, put their finger on a passage, and get direction from God regarding their problems or concerns at a particular time. It may have worked for John Wayne, Harry Carey Jr., and Pedro Armendáriz in the 1948 movie *3 Godfathers*,[60] who found their way across the desert to save their orphaned godchild; but it doesn't work that way in real life. In real life, it is not necessarily so funny.

Perhaps a depressed person believes he can get guidance from scripture by simply opening it, putting his finger down, and letting the text guide him. He first opens to Ezekiel 13:2 and reads, "Hear the word of the LORD." Well, there is proof. Now we are getting somewhere. Then opening to another place, the finger falls on the words of Matthew 27:5: "Judas went out and hanged himself." Finally, another text is chosen at random. The finger falls on the words from Luke 10:37: "Go and do likewise." For a person despairing of life, this may not result in a happy conclusion.

For a person wrestling with the question of their "purpose" in life, randomly opening the Bible, placing a finger down at Ecclesiastes 1:1–2, and finding the words "The words of the Teacher, the son of David, king in Jerusalem, 'Vanity of vanities,' says the Teacher, 'vanity of vanities! All is vanity'" could push a person over the edge into suicide.

Presuppositions

Much of the meaning for the receptors of a message depends upon the cultural presuppositions, the underlying assumptions, beliefs, and ides that are generally shared by people in a culture. But they are rarely described or even noticed because they seem so basic and so obvious. In John 9:3, when the disciples saw blind man, they asked Jesus, "Whose sin was it that caused this man to be born blind?" In their way of thinking, it was obvious that if someone was born blind, there had to be an underlying cause having to do with moral failing, and "Jesus' response must have been quite a

---

[60] John Ford, dir. Argosy Pictures, 1948. (Also known as *Three Godfathers*). Film.

BIBLICAL INTERPRETATION FOR LAYPEOPLE AND OTHER MARTYRS   71

shock."[61] That is still true. For example, the interpretation of a passage by a Jehovah's Witness and a Baptist may be completely different because of their different backgrounds.[62]

Ignoring the Context

Many of the previous reasons for misinterpretation can be boiled down to ignoring the context. When writing, people do not just throw out random statements. They develop trains of thought. Ignoring the context will almost certainly result in missing the point. Skewed or messed-up interpretations are most often caused by two things: One is ignoring the context. The other is ignoring the foundation, the gospel, God's love for the world—a love that is *not* a euphemism for selfishness or self-interest.

Conclusion

So with all these stumbling blocks, can we learn anything from scripture? Well, Luther said that the Bible is perspicuous (clear) so that the simplest peasant can understand it.[63] So in order to learn from scripture, one must come to scripture as free of preconceived notions as he or she can.

The Hermeneutical Process (Eugene Nida)[64]

Illustration

Eugene Nida and William Reyburn assert the following: "In any message there are two important elements that carry meaning: form and

---

61   Eugene A. Nida and William D. Reyburn. "Meaning Across Cultures," *American Society of Missiology Series*, No. 4. (Maryknoll, New York: Orbis Books, 1981), 14.

62   *Ibid.*, 9–10.

63   *The Bondage of the Will* (J. I. Packer and O. R. Johnston, Tr.) (Grand Rapids: Fleming H. Revell, 1957), 71–74.

64   Oral presentation made to the faculty and students at Concordia Theological Seminary, Springfield, Illinois, in about 1963 or 1964. See also Eugene A. Nida and Charles R. Taber. *The Theory and Practice of Translation* (Leiden, Netherlands: E. J. Brill, 1969), 12–32, in a more developed and somewhat altered form.

content."[65] But the content is conveyed by the form. As Marshall McLuhan pointed out, "the medium *is* the message."[66] Eugene Nida, once head of the translation department of the American Bible Society, illustrated what we do when we interpret the Bible and try to apply it to our present circumstances.

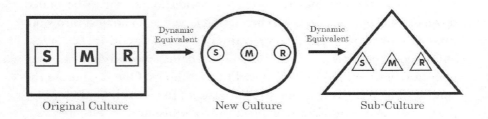

    Original Culture   New Culture   Sub-Culture

Scripture's Cultural   Modern Man's   Subculture
       Context   Cultural Context   Context (e.g., Youth)

S = source, situation to which the word speaks
M = message, human messenger speaks *to* and *out of* a cultural context
R = Receptors, background affects the understanding of the message

Nida says that a situation originally presents itself to which God's Word needs to speak. So a message is proclaimed by an individual who speaks to the situation within that cultural context. However, that person is also a part of the cultural context and therefore is limited in what he can even *see* about the situation to which he addresses the Word. This is such an important concept that it needs to be repeated: *However, that person is also a part of the cultural context and therefore is limited in what he can even see about the situation to which he addresses the Word.*

But two thousand years later, we have a situation to which the Word of God needs to speak. So someone in the modern context attempts to apply that previous biblical message to the present receptors in a somewhat different situation. The receptors' backgrounds affect the way in which they receive the message.

---

[65] Nida and Reyburn, *op. cit.*, 33.

[66] *Mechanical Bride: Folklore of Industrial Man, The* (New York: The Vanguard Press, 1951); *Understanding Media: The Extensions of Men* (New York: McGraw Hill, 1964); *The Medium Is the Message: An Inventory of Effects* (New York: Random House, 1967).

BIBLICAL INTERPRETATION FOR LAYPEOPLE AND OTHER MARTYRS   73

In many instances, translators are secondary receptors of the message[67] who may have a considerably different understanding of the world than the writers of the Hebrew Bible and the New Testament. The culture of the Bible, especially the Old Testament, has more in common with African and Middle Eastern tribes than with Western civilization.

But historians will argue that we can learn from the past because throughout history, our problems are basically the same. And according to Nida and Reyburn,

> as anthropologists have frequently pointed out, there is far more that unites different peoples in a common humanity than that which separates them into distinct groups. Such cultural universals as the recognition of reciprocity and equity in interpersonal relations, response to human kindness and love, the desire for meaning in life, the acknowledgement of human nature's inordinate capacity for evil and self-deception (or rationalization of sin), and its need for something greater and more important than itself—all these universals are constantly recurring themes in the Bible.[68]

Therefore, in the present day, "the preacher's task is to lead the congregation in finding relevant parallels in modern life, and in discovering how persons can meaningfully live out the Good News in worship of God and the service of others."[69]

The third step occurs when a situation occurs in a subculture, such as youth, or another culture (e.g., an American missionary ministering to the bushmen of Papua New Guinea). The message is framed in that second culture, speaking *out* of that second culture *to* another culture or (sub) culture. But the receptors of the message in the third culture or subculture will be influenced by their own preunderstanding.

---

[67]   Nida and Reyburn, *op. cit.*, 20.

[68]   *Ibid.*, 28.

[69]   *Ibid.*, 32.

Indigenization

Nida and Taber argue that "correctness must be determined by the extent to which the average reader for which a translation is intended will be likely to understand correctly."[70] My belief in the truth of this statement is the reason for my writing this book. Despite the challenge of the book, I believe the average reader can handle the ideas herein. And Nida and Taber believe that despite the difficulties, this is even true in communication across language and cultural barriers. They argue that because the receptors of the second and third stages, are influenced by their own culture, Nida says that in order to communicate from one culture to another and then to another (sub)culture, one must use a process of indigenization. One must attempt to make a foreign text indigenous to the new culture to which it is being addressed.

They further point out that it is impossible to communicate the message in a precise way. The best one can do at each level is to express it in a "dynamic equivalent." So "translating consists in reproducing in the receptor language the closest natural equivalent of the source-language message, first in terms of meaning and secondly in terms of style."[71] For example, "terrier" is more specific than "dog," but a dog is a mammal. "To use the word 'mammal' would not be technically incorrect, it would not really communicate."[72]

Dynamic Equivalent

Nida and Reyburn argue that "basically a translation should be the closest natural equivalent of the message in the source language,"[73] and "dynamic equivalence is therefore to be defined in terms of the degree to which the receptors of the message in the receptor language respond to it in substantially the same manner as the receptors in the course language."[74]

We need to be careful how we communicate the Word. There is a story of a Sunday school teacher who was waxing eloquent about the blessings

---

[70]   Nida and Taber, 1969, *op. cit.*, 1.

[71]   *Ibid.*, 12.

[72]   *Ibid.*, 20.

[73]   Nida and Reyburn, *op. cit.*, 70.

[74]   Nida and Taber, *op. cit.*, 24.

of heaven. She said, among other things, that in heaven, "we will sing God's praises forever." One boy in the class vociferously objected to going to heaven because "I hate to sing." I do not know if this is a true story or not, but it doesn't take too much imagination to believe it could happen in a class of middle school boys. But surely, if we "overphotographize" scriptural concepts, we can miss some people. Nida and Taber in *The Theory and Practice of Translation* argue that "no communication, even within a single language, is ever absolute."[75] The Sunday school teacher found that out the hard way.

Where misunderstanding is possible, it is necessary to clarify the misunderstanding, perhaps by including marginal notes. The greater the cultural distance of the languages, the greater the need to make extreme modifications to communicate the concept. For example, English and German are culturally similar, even having cognate words (house and *Haus*, mother and *Mutter*, father and *Vater*), as are Hausa and Fulani. However, English and Zulu are of completely different language families and require more extreme modifications.[76]

If the term "God the Father" is spoken to someone for whom "father" is someone who has been a wonderful, caring person, then one has communicated, generally speaking, what was intended. If, however, "father" is an abuser or simply someone who impregnated the mother and then took off, leaving the family to fend for itself, and if "mother" is someone who "busts her butt" to keep the family together and care for her children, then perhaps "mother" would better communicate the concept that we want to communicate.

The process required is to determine what the text says, what it means, and then what it means to us today. In Matthew 18:21, Jesus tells Peter that we are not to forgive seven times but seventy times seven (or perhaps seventy-seven times). If one does not understand that in Jesus's culture, seven was a symbolic number meaning "completeness" or "fullness" and that multiplying a number by ten or squaring it intensifies the concept, he may miss the point. If one multiples seventy times seven and comes up with 490, then he *has* missed the point. The point is that we should forgive infinitely, as God has done for us.

---

[75]   *Ibid.*, 4.

[76]   *Ibid.*, 5–6.

Translating from One Language/Culture to Another

Eugene A. Nida and William D. Reyburn point out that "communication of meaning across cultures always requires certain adjustments in the form of the message if the content is to be accurately and faithfully transmitted, for strictly word-for-word renderings inevitably tends to distort the meaning of the source-language message."[77] So a number of problems must be addressed.

Idiomatic Expressions

Idioms are a good example of how word-for-word translations may make no sense. An idiom is a phrase or a fixed expression that has a figurative or sometimes literal meaning. The figurative meaning is different from the literal meaning.[78] Idioms make no sense when translated literally (or rather literalistically). "When pigs fly" (meaning something that will never ever happen) or "wild and woolly" (meaning uncultured and without laws) would mean nothing to someone who was not part of the culture in which it was stated. In German, *est tut mir aber leid* literally says "It does me but sorry." A little confusing? It means "I'm sorry."

If I asked you to name an idiomatic expression, you might be hard-pressed (I just used one) to think of one. There are thousands of them, but we don't notice them because they are such a part of our speech. Here are a few (actually *a lot*): you can't judge a book by its cover, wear your heart on your sleeve, water under the bridge, wag the dog,[79] an axe to grind, backseat driver, barking up the wrong tree, beating around the bush,

---

[77]   Nida and Reyburn, *op. cit.*, 1–2.

[78]   https://en.wikipedia.org/w/index.php?title=Idiom&oldid=727716105, last modified June 30, 2016, at 20:21.

[79]   In 1997, a terrific spoof movie by this title was made, in which the president of the United States, in order to divert focus on a sex scandal just weeks before the election, hires a movie producer who convinces him to go to war against Albania and manufactures a hero left behind enemy lines (who is actually criminally insane). The "hero" is rescued but then is killed trying to rape a farmer's daughter. The producer covers up the death by claiming his injury occurred during the war. The producer decides he wants credit for his greatest production, and he must be killed by the CIA in order to prevent him from spilling the beans. I laughed through the entire movie. Barry Levinson, ed. *Wag the Dog*. Baltimore Pictures. TriBeCa Productions, Dec. 25, 1997. Movie.

BIBLICAL INTERPRETATION FOR LAYPEOPLE AND OTHER MARTYRS   77

between a rock and a hard place, bite your tongue, can't cut the mustard, chew someone out, close but no cigar, come hell or high water, crack someone up, cross your fingers, cry wolf, cup of joe.

I realize that I went overboard with giving examples, but it was just too much fun. Now you probably didn't have any difficulty understanding the point of each idiom; but for someone from another culture, except for a few, it would be almost impossible to get the point.

Since we've read the New Testament for two thousand years, we understand the expression "They lifted up their voices" (Luke 17:13). But if we heard it for the first time, we might assume it would not be difficult because voices are not heavy, but we might wonder how one would get hold of it. Or in hearing that "his countenance fell" (Mark 10:22), we might have wondered whether it was injured in the fall. And if we did not have the background, "to gird up the loins of the mind" (2 Pet. 1:13), we would not understand that it means "to get ready in one's thinking."[80]

Few idioms of a source language can be translated into a receptor language with meaning. The tax collector "beat his breast" would be confusing for West Africans because it was a sign of repentance in the Bible, whereas in West Africa, people "beat their breast" as a sign of pride. For repentance, they beat their heads.[81] So adjustments must be made, perhaps by introducing nonfigurative substitutes for figurative language.[82]

Problems of Tense, Number, and Sentence Structure

Differences in tense, mood, voice, number, and sentence structure can also be a problem. For example, Greek makes a distinction between the first and second personal pronoun "you," whereas in English, you cannot tell whether the word "you" refers to one "you" or several "yous." Once in Greek class, my professor, Ray Martens, called on me to translate a part of the gospel according to John (or maybe one of the Johannine letters). Being from Texas, I translated a second person plural with the word "y'all." Dr. Martens, who always sat on his desk with his legs crossed and the Greek New Testament in hand, slowly uncrossed his legs, got up, and began to pace back and forth. I should tell you that he was from Giddings, Texas.

---

[80]   Nida and Taber, *op. cit.*, 106.

[81]   Nida and Reyburn, *op. cit.*, 1981, 2.

[82]   *Ibid.*, 41.

"Gentlemen," he said, "I want you to notice the preciseness of Dave's translation of that second person plural with 'y'all.'" All the Yankees in the class rolled their eyes back in their heads.

Another problem is tense. English has seven tenses. Although modern Hebrew does, ancient Hebrew did not have "strictly defined past, present, or future tenses, but merely perfective and imperfective aspects, with past, present, or future connotation depending on context,"[83] closer to the concept of completed or uncompleted action.[84] There is no progressive tense in German. I remember that at the beginning of my high school German class, it was not uncommon for someone just learning German to say or translate "Ich bin gehen," which in English would mean "I *am* going." But this makes no sense to the German, which would mean "I *exist* going." Germans simply say, "Ich gehe," or "I go."

Cultural Difference in Values

The difference in values between the transmitter culture and the receptor culture makes translation a challenge. In the Garden of Gethsemane, Jesus didn't put up a fight or flee (Luke 22:52–54). The meaning of the message would not be understood by the Guaica of Venezuela, who would consider Jesus a coward or out of his mind. Among Hindus, Jesus's healing of blind Bartimaeus (Mark 10:46) would not be a blessing, but a curse because the receiving of his sight enabled him to see the ugliness and misery of the world. Jesus being circumcised on the eighth day is considered cruel in some cultures. And unlike Judaism, many cultures consider menstruation a sign of fertility rather than uncleanness. In India, the problem with killing a fattened calf in the parable of the good Samaritan is that cows are considered sacred. Nida and Reyburn have argued that in India, it would be better to translate the waiting father as killing a sheep rather than a fattened calf. In the Balinese culture, the viper is regarded to be a snake of paradise. So for them, the expression "generation of vipers" (Matt. 3:7, 12:34, 23:33; Luke 3:7) would not be a denunciation, but praise. Therefore, they believe it

---

[83] "Modern Hebrew verb conjugation," https://en.wikipedia.org/w/index. php?title=Modern Hebrew verb conjugation&oldid=727096289, last modified on 26 June 2016, at 17:05.

[84] Iclnet.org; Yaron, "Heblish-Hebrew lessons: Day 36," Sept. 2, 2010, free-hebrew.com.

BIBLICAL INTERPRETATION FOR LAYPEOPLE AND OTHER MARTYRS   79

may communicate the meaning better by substituting a more generic term like "vermin."[85]

The expression "upon Edom I cast my shoe" (Ps. 60:8) may not have meant much in the West[86]—that is, until at a press conference in Baghdad on December 14, 2008, when Muntadhar al-Zaidi threw a shoe at President George W. Bush. For Westerners, it had to be explained that in the Arab culture, throwing a shoe at a person was a sign of extreme disrespect.[87] But we needn't look any further than the Hebrew Bible to see how the use of shoes was a sign of disrespect. The law provided that if a man would not fulfill the levirate law to raise offspring for his dead brother, his brother's widow was allowed to remove his shoe from his foot and spit in his face (Deut. 25:7–10). And if a man would not redeem his brother's (or relative's) property, the person who did redeem it could publicly humiliate him by removing the offender's shoe (Ruth 4:7–10).

In some parts of West Africa, putting branches in the path of an oncoming chief or high official is a serious insult. Therefore, if the action of the crowd placing branches in the path of Jesus as he rode into Jerusalem (Matt. 21:8) is not explained either in the text or in the margin, it would be seriously misunderstood.[88]

The custom of levirate marriage may be odious to some cultures and may need some footnote explanation of its function in the Hebrew culture.[89] Those Americans who say that marriage is *only* between one man and one woman seem not to notice that Jacob had two main wives and two secondary (concubine) wives, David had several wives, and Solomon had seven hundred wives and three hundred concubines (1 Kings 11:3). So if marriage is only between one man and one woman, what does that make Jacob's second "wife," Rachel?

---

85   Nida and Reyburn, *op. cit.*, 48–54.

86   *Ibid.*, 64.

87   Williams, Timothy. "Iraqi Journalist Who threw Shoes at Bush Was Tortured in Jail, His Brother Says," nytines.com, Dec. 21, 2008. http://www.nytimes.com/2008/12/22/world/middleeast/22iraq.html.

88   Nida and Reyburn, *op. cit.*, 73; Nida and Taber, *op. cit.*, 111.

89   Nida, Eugene A. *God's Word in Man's Language.* New York: Harper & Brothers, 1952, 167–168.

The Problem of Ignorance

Another problem with translation is ignorance. To be ignorant does not mean to be dumb, but to not know something. How does one translate lions, camels, mustard, ship, and phylactery in a culture where they have no knowledge of these things without them being explained? Before the proliferation of books, what would the expression "sins as white as snow" mean to someone who was born in and lived his entire life in the jungle? Strange things have happened as a result of not understanding the actions of another culture. In the movie *Hawaii*,[90] Rev. Abner Hale (Max von Sydow), with his Yale theological education, arrogantly charges in and alienates the natives with his ethnocentrism, undermining his ability to proclaim the gospel, while his wife, Jerusha (Julie Andrews), accepts much of the Hawaiian culture, endearing her to them. In the movie *The Outlaw Josey Wales* (1976),[91] Josey Wales (Clint Eastwood) ends up with a Navajo wife because he does not understand their customs. Lone Watie (Chief Dan George) gleefully needles Wales, referring to the Navajo woman as Mrs. Wales.

Differences in Classification

All people classify things. They establish categories. For example, we classify people into categories like infant, toddler, child, adolescent, and adult. These divisions are arbitrarily decided. They are constructs. In the miniseries *Roots*,[92] there is no concept of adolescence. Kunta Kinte was considered a child one day, and his mother could treat him like a child. On the very next day, after his initiation, he became a man and a warrior, and his mother dared not treat him with the slightest hint of disrespect. In fact, in the Western world, the concept of adolescence was only coined by G. Stanley Hall in the late nineteenth century.[93] Even in some John Wayne movies, one can see that he often portrays himself as a man at twelve or thirteen when he leaves home to be on his own.

---

[90]   Hill, George Roy, dir. Metro-Goldwyn-Mayer Studios Inc., 1966. Film.

[91]   Eastwood, Clint, dir. Warner Brothers, 1976. Film.

[92]   Chomsky, Marvin, John Erman, David Greene, and Gilbert Moses, eds. 7-part series. David L. Wolper Productions, Warner Bros., 1977. Television.

[93]   "G. Stanley Hall," emergingadulthood.umwblogs.org; psyking.net.

BIBLICAL INTERPRETATION FOR LAYPEOPLE AND OTHER MARTYRS   81

The concept of race is also an arbitrary classification or construct. Can anyone really define race other than the human race? How does one decide that one belongs to a particular race? And what are the races? People influenced by the Bible in the past have assumed there were three races descended from Noah's sons Shem, Ham, and Japheth (Gen. 10–11). But in parts of the South, a person who had "one drop of black blood" was considered a Negro. So classifications, like art, are in the eye of the beholder and can be influenced by bias and vested interests.

The Israelites classified things. Physically speaking, "living beings were also classified as clean and unclean, those which could be eaten and those which could not."[94] Within a culture, definitions are based on perceptions, such as shape, size, and qualities; and they are grouped in the minds of people in that culture. When cultures come together, they share their perceptions. Before Carolus Linnaeus's binomial nomenclature, animals were perceived differently. My guess is that those who study biology in the Bantu languages have adopted words like "mammals," "amphibians," "reptiles," and "protozoa," just the way English-speaking Americans have adopted the words "veranda," "tacos," "patio,' and "déjà vu" (or as Yogi Berra said, "déjà vu all over again").

In the book of the prophet Jonah, Jonah was swallowed by a *dag* or *dagh* (Jon. 1:17; 2:1). Most English translations render the word "great fish" or "large fish." The same word is used in the first creation story and is translated just "fish" (Gen. 1:26). Yet everyone refers to Jonah being swallowed by a "whale." Aside from the fact that it was a figurative fish tale (not "fishtail"), to ask which it was is to ask an unanswerable question because the ancient Hebrews made no distinction between whales and large fish, although they did make a distinction between *dagh*s that have scales and those that do not (Lev. 11:9–12, Deut. 14:9–10). Since they swim, look alike, and do not have scales, whales and catfish were probably considered in the same category but were in a different category from fish with scales. I wonder how they categorized seahorses or whether there were seahorses in the Mediterranean Sea for them to wonder about. In New Guinea, a cassowary is not considered a bird because, although it has feathers, it does not fly. But a bat is considered a bird rather than a mammal because it does fly.[95]

---

[94]   Nida and Reyburn, *op. cit.*, 14–15.

[95]   Nida and Taber, *op. cit.*, 21.

82 DAVID W. MELBER

But since classifications are based on perceptions, they can also change over time. For Jews, pork has traditionally been considered unclean. But I once had a girlfriend who was a reformed Jew. One Saturday, I served her breakfast, which included bacon. As I put bacon on her plate, it hit me that she was a Jew. Startled at my own insensitivity, I immediately apologized and prepared to take it away. However, Joann was reformed and did not make distinctions between clean and unclean as the Orthodox still do. She ate the bacon heartily.

The Problem of Connotations

Aside from the dictionary definitions, connotations have to do with "our emotional reactions to words."[96] There are a number of words that can refer to the same thing, some of which are taboo because they have a more negative *connotation* than other words. However, there are both positive and negative connotations. For example, the Hebrew word "Yahweh," translated "LORD" (all capital letters) in most English translations, had such a positive connotation that it was taboo to speak it. "Toilet" (a perfectly good word from the French, dating from 1540) has such a connotation for some people that they use terms like "washroom," "comfort station," and "powder room." At singles' bars, the term "little girls' room" or "ladies' room" are sometimes used. Different military services have their own words for the phenomenon.

We sometimes use euphemisms with children that we do not use with adults because we believe the connotation would be offensive to them. And I have found it humorous when nurses in the hospital substitute the technical term "urinate" with "teetee," "weewee," or "peepee." And of course, there is the old standard "number one." Even to adults! I AM NOT KIDDING!

It is also true that the same word has different connotations in different environments. Nida and Taber point out that "*damn* used in church bears a quite different connotation from the same word used in a beer hall, even though uttered by the same person."[97]

African Americans are offended by whites calling them "nigger," but there are a sizable number of them who refer to their friends with this

---

[96] *Ibid.*, 91.

[97] *Ibid.*, 93.

BIBLICAL INTERPRETATION FOR LAYPEOPLE AND OTHER MARTYRS   83

otherwise offensive term. I had an African American roommate at the seminary (who was also in my wedding) whom I called "nigger" and who referred to me "po' white trash." However, if we got angry at each other, we would never use those epithets. We were rabid competitors on the basketball court, and neither of us was reluctant to foul hard enough to make sure the other did not score a basket. And although Sam and I participated in considerable good-natured trash talk, those terms would never be used in that context.

The Problem of Communicating Concepts

When one translates the Bible into another language, he may have concepts in the source language that do not exist in the receptor language. In order to communicate the concept from the source language, he may have to use terminology in the receptor language that in some way reflects ideas in the source language. To express the concept of "redemption" in the Bambara language of Mali, Burkina Faso, and Senegal, the expression "God took our heads out" is used because when a local chief paid an Arab slaver to redeem him, the iron collar around his neck was removed. So since they had no term for "redeem," to redeem a person, one would literally "take his head out of the iron collar." For them "taking our heads out" was a clear expression of our word "redemption."[98] The expression "take our head (or "your head") out" means something different altogether in English. I will not illustrate.

In Romans 12:20, when Paul referred to heaping "coals of fire" (*anthrax* in Greek) on his head, he was quoting Proverbs 25:21–22: "If your enemy is hungry, give him food to eat; if he is thirsty, give him water to drink. In doing this, you will heap burning coals on his head, and the Lord will reward you." This is the way Paul says we should treat enemies: "Do not overcome evil by evil, but overcome evil with good" (Rom. 12:22). Whether this meant it would shame him or give him an example in order to change his behavior or to "warm his heart" is a matter of debate.[99] But in some African countries, heaping coals on a person's head was a method of torture and killing.[100] If one quotes the

---

[98]   Nida, 1952, *op. cit.*

[99]   N. T. Wright, *The New Interpreter's Bible: The Letter to the Romans.* Vol. X, Leader E. Keck, ed. Nashville: Abingdon Press, 2002, 715.

[100]   Nida, *op. cit.*, 1952, 17.

statement attributed to Jesus in Revelation, "Behold I stand at the door and knock" (Rev. 3:20), the Zanaki people of Tanzania would assume Jesus was a thief because in their culture, an honest person would stand away from the house and call out to the people inside the house. Thieves would knock, and if they heard someone stirring in the house, they would run away. So for them, a translation that captures the idea might be "I stand in your yard and call out."[101] So if we used the original expression in Revelation, we would communicate just the opposite of what John of Patmos had in mind.

The Kare people of the Ubangi-Shari district of French Equatorial Africa[102] have no word for "faith," so they use the phrase "to hear and take into the soul."[103]

Reconciliation for the Uduks of Sudan is called "meet, snapping fingers together again" because rather than shaking hands when they meet a friend, they practice the snapping of fingers together. They only do this with close friends. The San Blas people speak of forgiveness as "erasing the evil heart."[104]

In Greek, the word for "sin" is *harmartia*, which means "missing the mark." For the Navajos, it is "that which is off to the side" compared with the straight truth. For the Shipibo language, sin is called "breaking someone else's pottery jar," which is an offense against someone. Hypocrisy for the Mixtecos is "having two heads." For the Tzeltals, it is "two hearts"; and for the Pames, it is to have "two mouths."[105]

To summarize Nida and Reyburn's attitude toward translation, a bad way is "formal correspondence: the form (syntax and classes of words) is preserved; the meaning is lost or distorted." A second bad way is to "paraphrase by addition, deletion, or skewing of the message." The good way is to establish a "dynamic equivalence: the form is restructured (different syntax and lexicon) to preserve the same meaning."[106]

---

[101] Nida, 1952, *op. cit.*, 45–46.

[102] French colony that comprised the countries of Chad, Central African Republic, Cameroon, the Republic of the Congo, and Gabon.

[103] Nida, 1952, *op. cit.*, 13.

[104] *Ibid.*, 141–146.

[105] *Ibid.*, 148–150.

[106] Nida and Reyburn, *op. cit.*, 173.

Chapter 5

METHODS OF INTERPRETATION

Schools of Hermeneutics

There are many ways of interpreting the Bible. Only a few general methods will be briefly described in order to illustrate the point.

Early Jewish Schools of Interpretation

Before the exile of Judah in 586 BCE, there were no schools of interpretation. There was little need. The focal point of their worship was the temple in Jerusalem. However, with the loss of the temple and their land and their having been scattered across the Babylonian Empire, they had to either make an adjustment or die as an ethnic people along with their religion, as the northern kingdom of Israel had done a century before. Until the eighth century BCE, there had been no writing prophets. But in the seventh century, men like Amos, Hosea, and Isaiah began to write down their prophecies. By the sixth century, there were a number of prophetic writings by Jeremiah, Ezekiel, Jonah (perhaps), Micah, etc. And although there is no indication of when, a new institution, the synagogue, emerged

85

during the exile. In order to maintain their religion, they began to focus on the prophetic writings; the Torah (writings attributed to Moses); historical documents like Joshua, Judges, Ruth, Kings, and Chronicles; wisdom literature like Proverbs; and the growing body of writings expressing personal and public worship (Psalms).

The first biblical interpreter we know of is Ezra. When a second wave of second- and third-generation Jewish exiles returned to Israel during the Persian rule, a body of literature was produced that came to be considered the basis of their religion. It probably involved many of the writings mentioned in the previous paragraph—mere speculation on my part. Many of the returning exiles could speak Aramaic but were losing their Hebrew language. Ezra gathered both men and women and "others who could understand" and read the book of the law to them (Neh. 9:1–18). But there were other scholars with him who interpreted (or translated) the words of Ezra for them, the first Targums (to explain). Because of his immense influence, it is reasonable to infer that Ezra was the leader of a school of interpretation.

In Israel before the Christian era, four types of interpretation or exegesis (midrash) emerged. Rabbis distinguished between the clear passages (*peshat*) and the hidden sense of the Mosaic law (*remaz*), the allegorical sense (*derush*) (expressed in legends), and the mystical or Cabalistic (*sod*) sense.[107] To what extent midrash can be applied to Ezra is not known because we know so little about how he or those who followed interpreted the law of Moses.

However, sometime later, the Qumran sect—known from the Dead Sea Scrolls, usually identified as Essenes—accumulated and perhaps wrote some commentaries on Old Testament books.[108] Regarding biblical texts, they often said, "The *peshar* is . . . (Aramaic for "to interpretation"). Theirs were a more literal and very legalistic interpretation. But they believed that everything written in the past had contemporary value and meaning."[109]

---

[107] Jacob Neusner. *What Is Midrash?* Philadelphia, PA: Fortress Press Books, 1987, 108–109. Quoted in Arnold G. Fruchtenbaum. *Midrash/Pesher and Hermeneutics.* Ariel Ministries. file:///C:/Users/David-PC/Documents/Writings/Biblical%20 Interp%20for%20Laypeople/2009-ChaferConf-Fruchtenbaum-Paper.pdf.

[108] Laypeople who want to acquaint themselves with the Dead Sea Scrolls don't have to know Hebrew, Aramaic, or Greek. Vermes Geza's *The Complete Dead Sea Scrolls in English* (New York, New York: Pelican Books, 1997) is available.

[109] Walter C. Kaiser Jr. and Moises Silva. *Introduction to Biblical Hermeneutics: The Search for Meaning* (Grand Rapids: Zondervan, 2007), 260–261.

Allegorizing Hermeneutics

The Greek philosopher Plato could not take the mythological writings of Homer and Hesiod seriously by interpreting them literally. So he established a method of interpreting them in order to make them acceptable. The method was allegorizing. Plato found hidden meaning behind the Greek myths, enabling him to accept them by not having to understand them literally. The historical sense is not necessarily denied, just ignored as unimportant.[110]

In the Alexandrian diaspora (the Jewish exiles) in Egypt influenced by Hellenism and the Greek language, Philo (20 BCE), a Jew from Alexandria, used the Septuagint version of the Old Testament, applying allegorizing to the Old Testament, and had an influence not only on Jewish hermeneutics but also on the early church. When he confronted passages that made no sense to him, he went below the literal interpretation to a "deeper truth," *hyponoia*, which he got by allegorical interpretation.

New Testament Interpretation

In the time of Jesus, two major schools developed in Jerusalem: the school of Hillel and the school of Shammai. Hillel emphasized the spirit of the scriptures, whereas Shammai emphasized the letter of the law. You could say Shammai was a law-and-order rabbi, and Hillel was a justice rabbi. Jesus's interpretation was much like Hillel's. In my novel, *The Making of A Messiah: Influences on Jesus' Childhood and Youth*, I have Jesus sitting at the feet of Hillel when he was twelve years old (Luke 2:41–51) because Hillel taught in Jerusalem at that time and died when Jesus was about fifteen years of age (pure speculation on my part). Time and again, Jesus showed his emphasis on loving God with one's whole heart and loving one's neighbor as oneself—even one's enemies. And if a dictum of the Old Testament contradicted that central teaching of Jesus, he had no compunction about putting it aside, with statements like "But I say unto you . . ." In addition, he taught in parables, a good rabbinical method.

Paul's fundamental interpretation was based on his understanding of the purpose of Jesus's life and who he was. For Paul, Jesus was the fulfillment of Jewish aspiration for a Messiah—not the strain that saw the Messiah reestablishing the political throne of David, but as the suffering servant of Isaiah, the sacrifice for sin. But rather than a Messiah just for

---

[110] *The Republic* (Tr. Benjamin Jowett). The Gutenberg Project (www.gutenberg.com).

the Jews, Paul saw Jesus as the second Adam, the Messiah who represented all mankind. And he had no problem allegorizing to make his point (Gal. 4:24–31). And his teachings on morality were also closer to Hillel's. Small wonder since Paul had been taught by Hillel's grandson, Gamaliel (Acts 22:3). Paul's morality was not based on legalism but was a response of gratitude to God for the work of Jesus. The author of Hebrews had a similar emphasis, stressing numerous Old Testament phenomena, or "types," that prefigured Jesus, including the priesthood, sacrifices, and the Tabernacle.

James had a similar interpretation but reacted to the abuse of Paul's emphasis on salvation by faith and ignoring Jesus's call to discipleship as expressed in Matthew 25. John showed a marked influence of Jesus's emphasis on love, stressing that we should love as he loved us (1 John 4:10). Peter's interpretation is not as clear-cut. His emphasis was on Jesus as his readers' hope (1 Pet. 1:3), their savior (1 Pet. 1:18–19), and their example (1 Pet. 2:21–24) in the midst of their suffering for the faith.

The Early Church Fathers

The Alexandrian school was led by Clement, who adopted the allegorizing method of Philo. His disciple Origen taught that there were three levels of interpretation: the corporeal (literal) for the simple, the soul (dealing with personal relationships), and the spirit (dealing with our relationship with God) for the more spiritually elite.[111] His disciple Eusebius of Caesarea even taught that Moses and the prophets did not even speak for their day, but for later Christians.

However, the Antiochian school, led by Theodore of Mopsuestia and John Chrysostom, argued that the natural or literal sense of the passage carried in it spiritual truth. A third school of patristic interpretation was the Western school, represented by Hilary, Ambrose, Jerome, and Augustine of Hippo, which stressed the literal sense as a basis for allegorical interpretation and also the role of tradition in interpretation called the *regula fidei* (rule of faith). St. Augustine of Hippo argued that there were four levels of meaning in the text: historical (obvious sense), allegorical (hidden meaning), tropological or analogy (moral sense), and anagogical or etiology (mystical or eschatological meaning).[112] Various versions of this approach

---

[111] A. Berkeley Mickelsen. *Interpreting the Bible* (Grand Rapids: Wm. B. Eerdmans Publishing Company, 1963), 32; Childs, 34.

[112] Brevard S. Childs. *Biblical Theology of the Old and New Testaments, A: Theological*

to interpretation were reflected in the hermeneutics of the Middle Ages. Thomas Aquinas said the literal sense was the basis of interpretation but said that putting heavenly concepts in earthly terms must use symbolism. This was, with some variations, the basic method of interpretation that held sway in the Western Church until Martin Luther.

Historical-Grammatical Hermeneutics

Martin Luther rejected allegorizing, arguing that by using that method, one could make the text say anything he wanted it to say. He said that one must take the literal meaning seriously. Luther emphasized the intended meaning of the original authors based on the grammatical and historical study of the text. His hermeneutic is probably best expressed at the Diet of Worms:[113] "Unless I can be instructed and convinced with evidence from the Holy Scripture or with open, clear, and distinct ground of reason [reasonable conclusions]—my conscience is captive to the Word of God—then I cannot and will not recant, because it is neither safe nor wise to act against conscience."[114] He emphasized the literal meaning, with reason serving scripture. The emphasis is that the Word addresses our understanding. But scripture had to be understood as serving the gospel. If it contradicted the gospel, it was suspect. That is why he had reservations about the epistle of James, believing it contradicted the gospel proclaimed in Galatians.

Fundamentalist-Literalistic Hermeneutics

Generally, fundamentalists believe the Bible to be absolutely errorless—accurate in all matters of science, history, and geography. The very words are considered to be inspired. Every word in it was exactly the ones God wanted.[115] It takes the words as they are without regard for figures of speech. For example, few believe that at the ends of time, all the armies of

---

Reflections on the Christian Bible (Minneapolis: Fortress Press, 1993), 38. Print.

[113] In another context, my daughter, Debbie Drury, pointed out to me that I may need to explain that the Diet of Worms is not a disgusting meal, but that a diet was a political meeting of the Holy Roman Empire in the city of Worms, Germany.

[114] James M. Kittelson. *Luther the Reformer: The Story of the Man and His Career* (Minneapolis: Augsburg Publishing House, 1986), 161.

[115] Donald K. McKim. *The Bible in Theology and Preaching: How Preachers Use Scripture* (Nashville: Abingdon Press, 1994), 57–59.

90 DAVID W. MELBER

a world of seven billion people in our age of modern weapons will actually be crammed into Armageddon (the valley of Megiddo) and fight with spears and swords. The expression you hear among fundamentalists is "the Bible says," and that ends the matter. And if the Bible says that Eve carried on a conversation with a snake (Gen. 3), that a donkey questions his rider because he sees more than the rider (Num. 22), that the sun stood still (Josh. 10), that time backs up (Isa. 38:7–8), then it is to be accepted without question. Of course, this approach ranges from soup to nuts, and literally nobody consistently exercises it.

Existentialist Hermeneutics

Existentialist interpretation emphasizes that we do not interpret the Bible; it interprets us. It calls us into question. It emphasizes that the words of the Bible are not the Word of God but *become* the Word of God in an encounter with God. Scripture is not revelation unless one receives it as revelation. The words only mean something in terms of the "revelatory events in history to which they witness . . . the Bible does not convey new content but a new dimension of ultimate meaning."[116] It requires a decision.

Historical-Critical Hermeneutics

The historical-critical method attempts to get behind the text to sources of the text. It emphasizes the cultural conditioning of the writers of the Bible. When you are reading scripture and do a double take, it is time to ask whether something is not as it is thought to be. For example, one cannot miss the fact that there are not only similarities in the two sets of beatitudes but also some glaring differences. Luke 6:20 says, "Blessed are you who are poor. For yours is the kingdom of God." But Matthew 5:2 says, "Blessed are the poor *in spirit,* for theirs is the kingdom of *heaven.*" Luke 6:21 says, "Blessed are you who hunger now, for you will be satisfied." But Matthew 5:6 says, "Blessed are those who hunger *and thirst for righteousness,* for they will be filled." From my perspective, Matthew seems to have watered down the radical impact of Luke's expression of Jesus's concern for the poor. Genesis had two stories of Ishmael being sent into the desert—one when he was a baby (Gen. 16:5–16) and one when he was a young man (Gen. 21:8–20).

---

[116] *Ibid.,* 108.

BIBLICAL INTERPRETATION FOR LAYPEOPLE AND OTHER MARTYRS   91

The historical-critical Method is used to get behind the text to sources. This method of studying the Pentateuch (first five books of the Bible) is usually called the documentary hypothesis. One source is called J, the Yahwist, which was from tenth century BCE in Judah, who used the name Yahweh for God. A second source was called E, the Elohist, an eighth-century northern Israelite source that used the name Elohim for God. A third source called D, the Deuteronomist, is responsible for most of Deuteronomy. Finally, a source called P, the Priestly Code, came later, maybe during the sixth century BCE. The basic scenario is that many of the stories in the Pentateuch grew as oral tradition, were written down and collected as literary sources, and were eventually brought together by an editor or redactor.[117]

There are two creation accounts: The first account is Genesis 1:1–2:4a. The second account is Genesis 2:4b–3:24. In the first account, God simply says, "Let there be . . .," and it happens. In the second account, God takes much more time and is much more personally involved. The two accounts used different words for "create." In Genesis 1:1–2:3, God is called Elohim. In the second account, God is called Yahweh Elohim. In the first account, Adam is both man and woman, created in God's image. In the second account, Adam is a male. The order of creation is different in the two accounts. The first story is a majestic creation, a positive view of creation, but very impersonal. The second account is not majestic. God is very personal with his creation, but it is pessimistic about human nature. Neither is a scientific account, but a story to make a point. Adam Hamilton points out that the stories are archetypal stories, Adam (meaning "human" and originally "of the ground") and Eve (meaning "bearer of life") are symbolic names that tell about the nature of God and ours.[118]

The story of Noah's flood is a story about God's feeling about the violence. God was so disappointed with humans that he was sorry he created the human race.[119] In Genesis 7:19, the text says that the flood covered all the highest mountains; many Christians argued that it must be believed, and yet in Acts 2:5, the text says that there were Jews from "every nation under heaven." I doubt that they think you must believe that

---

[117]   Exod. 1:1–5, 6:14–27; Gen. 37:2, 36:31–39; Num. 33.

[118]   Adam Hamilton. *Making Sense of the Bible: Rediscovering the Power of Scripture Today.* (New York: HarperCollins, Publishers, 2014), 193–194.

[119]   *Ibid.*, 196; http://en.wikipedia.org/w/index.php?title=Flood myth&oldid=607582294. Last modified on 8 May 2014 at 04:39.

there were Jews from Japan, Polynesia, Australia, and North and South America.

Process Hermeneutics

The process method of interpretation is based on the principle that our experiences in the present are related to all previous experiences and what we believe about the world stems from these experiences. The approach of process interpretation can be illustrated by the expression "We never step into the same ocean twice." That is, each time we read a text, we are a different person than we were the previous time we read the text. So because of our experiences in the meantime, for us, the text is not the same text. Based on our intervening experience, it says something different to us from what it did the previous time we read it. I suppose there is no one who has not read a text and said, "I have read that text hundreds of times, but I never saw *that* in it before." We didn't see it before because our experiences had been different before. Now that certain experiences have been lived, we see something different in a text.

For example, when people become parents, they read the Bible differently than they did before they became parents. They see things in texts that they had not seen before. After a death, divorce, or any traumatic experience, we see things in a text that we never saw before. For the process theologian, the Bible shows the nature of God and what humanity is called to be. Process hermeneutics portrays the unfolding action of God, providing people with new insights. For the process exegete, the Bible is not inspired so much as the reader is inspired by the text, which creates new meaning for the Bible.[120]

Narrative Hermeneutics

Part of our being human is our ability to communicate. Language enables us to connect to other people. It gives form to human consciousness and literally structures our thinking, enabling us to define ourselves as people.[121] And the words of others do a great deal to help define us. Images expressed by words enable us to interpret and give meaning to our

---

[120]   McKim, *op. cit.*, 121.

[121]   *Ibid.*, 130.

BIBLICAL INTERPRETATION FOR LAYPEOPLE AND OTHER MARTYRS   93

experiences. Without that ability, we would be like animals, which only respond to stimuli in terms of pleasure seeking or pain avoidance.

Words tell stories. All societies have "sacred stories about gods and heroes, tales of the cosmos, wisdom about human behavior, nature, and the miraculous. Personal and social identities were shaped by the stories . . . accepted behavior patterns were transmitted through these stories."[122] But if stories also have the power to generate a response and to imagine and influence behavior, people must be able to relate to the stories. In the South, if a white girl claims to be raped by a black man, her story—whether true or not—has the power to bring about a lynching. Stories about Abe Lincoln returning the penny and George Washington admitting that he chopped down the cherry tree, though not literally accurate stories, are used to influence people to be honest and truthful.

The authority of scripture means that in it, people find stories that teach them how to be faithful. Our own story is found in scripture. Biblical narratives were meant not to describe the world, but to change the world. The Bible tells the story of Jesus, whose story defines the nature of God's rule and how such a rule creates a world and society that God intended.[123]

Liberation Hermeneutics

Liberation theology addresses oppression. No oppressor ever admits to oppression. Oppressors always claim that they are maintaining law and order. But they exploit and dehumanize people. In Christ, God liberates people from the sin of oppression. People can only interpret the Bible out of the context of their own life situation. Since it is to their apparent benefit, the interpretation of the Bible by the privileged classes is apt to be ideologically "captive to the status quo." A "hermeneutic of suspicion" is one that suspects privileged classes of interpreting the Bible in light of vested interests. The Exodus is the paradigm for liberation hermeneutics, reflecting a God who takes the side of the poor and oppressed. Liberation proclaims freedom from "the sin of slavery as well as the slavery of sin."[124] At the cross, Jesus identified with the poor and oppressed and those who suffer injustice. The Resurrection is God's victory over oppression.

---

[122] *Ibid.*, 126.

[123] *Ibid.*, 127–133.

[124] *Ibid.*, 144–152.

94   DAVID W. MELBER

What the Bible *means now* is more important than what the Bible *meant*, the story is more important than the text, and the Bible has been used both to oppress *and* to liberate. Theology begins with "'praxis' or the combination of action and reflection that seeks to alter social oppression."[125]

Feminists have applied liberation to their condition. They emphasize that "the Bible is a book composed in cultures that had patriarchal biases. . . . [The] Bible has been interpreted predominantly by males and that in many ways sexist interpretations have been dominant ones."[126] Feminist hermeneutics generally fall into one of three categories: reclaiming texts, theological perspective, or historical reconstruction. Reclaiming texts focuses on texts that have been overlooked and/or misinterpreted. The theological perspective sees the Bible as a source of liberating paradigms, particularly the prophets' call for liberation of the oppressed. Liberationists argue that the early church was egalitarian and over the years became identified with the oppressors. Their call is a return to the egalitarianism of the early church.

Womanist Hermeneutics

Womanist hermeneutics reads the Bible through the lens of African American women to empower and liberate them. It sort of integrates the insights of feminist theology and black theology but is critical of their neglect of the realities of *black* women and all women of color. The term "womanist" was developed by the black theologian Alice Walker, author of the novel *The Color Purple*. It grew out of the theology of James Cone, Jacquelyn Grant, and Delores Williams. Cone developed black theology, which studied theology from black experience in America. He argued that "God is black" in order to show that God identifies with the oppressed.[127]

People like Walker[128] argued that Cone did not pay attention to the experience of black women because the oppression of black women is different from that of black men, emphasizing that black women also

---

[125]   *Ibid.*, 161.

[126]   *Ibid.*, 173.

[127]   James Cone. *Black Theology and Black Power.* New York: Seabury Press, 1969.

[128]   Alice Walker. *In Search of Our Mother's Gardens: Womanist Prose* (San Diego: Harcourt, 1983), xi.

BIBLICAL INTERPRETATION FOR LAYPEOPLE AND OTHER MARTYRS   95

suffer oppression from black men.[129] Some even criticize biblical texts that degrade women (as in Judg. 11:29–40, 19:1–30, 21:1–25) and people of color (Gen. 16:1–16, 21:1–7) and show how Hagar and Esther can be seen as models of resistance for women of color. It focuses on Jesus's love and women freed from white male supremacy. They are inclined to see the Bible as presenting "prototypes," as the possibility of transformation, rather than as "archetypes," as ideal forms of "unchanging, timeless pattern."[130]

Postmodern Hermeneutics

For the postmodernist, all experience and thought arise from the interaction with the physical and social environment. A worldview develops in us before we are even aware of it, including our knowledge, beliefs, value judgments, as well as the ends, ideals, and principles of conduct. We can understand the thinking of people only by comprehending the cultural environment and the thinking of individuals in that culture in a particular historical era. Nida and Reyburn point out that because no two individuals ever completely share the same linguistic and cultural background, "absolute communication is never possible."[131]

According to postmodern hermeneutics, there is no timeless truth existing "out there." Since no two people have the same experiences, we all have different perspectives and therefore different interpretations of the world. That means that since the author's experience is not exactly like ours, we can never completely grasp the mind and intention of the author. So the meaning of the text is derived from a dialogue between the text and the interpreter. This also implies that there is never one completely correct interpretation. We never state truth in the ultimate sense, but only truth in the context in which it is spoken or written. And since language is a social creation, each linguistic system expresses social convention and is therefore arbitrary.[132] Truth is ethnocentric, based on the way a particular society understands things,[133] or idiocentric, depending on the perspective of the

---

[129]   *Ibid.*, 317; 326–331.

[130]   McKim, *op. cit.*,185. http://en.wikipedia.org/wiki/Womanist theology. Modified on 25 July 2011 at 03:11.

[131]   Nida and Reyburn, *op. cit.*, 7.

[132]   Grenz, Stanley J. *A Primer on Postmodernism.* Grand Rapids: Eerdmans, 1996, 109–121.

[133]   *Ibid.*, 156–157.

individual. For example, the book of Samuel includes David's foibles and portrays him as a fallen leader, whereas Chronicles hides these issues and portrays him as the ideal king.[134]

General Hermeneutical Principles

Language

A Conventional Way of Communicating

The postmodernists are surely right about one thing: Words have no inherent meaning. They are conventional symbols to which a group of people have attached meaning. So those sound vibrations or configurations of ink on paper have no inherent meaning in themselves. They are social conventions and may mean different things to different groups. We all know what "plumbers" are. But in the Nixon White House, it took on a new meaning—people who plug up leaks of information escaping from the White House. In English, the word "bat" can mean different things. It can be an instrument with which a baseball is hit, a flying mammal, or one's mother-in-law (usually preceded by the word "old").

Usage

We pointed out in the previous section that there are often several meanings for the same word. An important issue is how the word is used. And translation needs to take that issue into consideration. For example, in English, we have one word for "time." Greek has two words. *Chronos* refers to "time" in the sense of measurement, dealing with issues of specific date and time of day. The other word is *kairos*. It does not mean a measurable time such as 5:00 a.m. on March 3. It means "the appropriate time," like the time for harvest or the time for a baby to be born. One does not say that harvest will occur or that a baby will be born on October 3 at 2:30 p.m. You can estimate when the appropriate time for these events will occur, but that is all. Harvest occurs when it is ready. Babies come when they feel like it, not when the doctor sets a date. We talk about babies coming "early" or "late," but they don't see it that way.

A good example of our use of words without knowing their meaning is the word "hallelujah." Have you ever wondered why sometimes we use

---

[134] Hamilton, *op. cit.*, 2014, 42.

the word "hallelujah" and other times it is "alleluia"? And what do they mean anyway? Does it really have any more meaning for us than the word "widget"? Like "selah," which shows up in numerous psalms, "hallelujah" is used only in the psalms. The "Hallel" was praise by making a high-pitched sound while flapping the tongue, making sort of an *L* sound. You may have seen it done in *Lawrence of Arabia* when they were leaving Wadi Rum to attack Aqaba or in *The Wind and the Lion* or any other movie about Africa or the Middle East. "Hallelujah" was the "Hallel" to ("lu") "Yah" (the first part of the name Yahweh). "Alleluia" is simply the Greek rendition of the Hebrew "hallelujah" because when the Gentiles read the Greek translation of the Old Testament, they did not know it started with an *h* sound. So when we say "hallelujah," rather than making the high-pitched flapping sound with our tongue, it is much like at an old Brooklyn Dodger game; instead of making the spitting "pffft" sound of the Bronx cheer, we would instead shout, "Bronx cheer! Bronx cheer!"

"World" in English can mean the geographical area, the planet as a whole, or the people that occupy the planet. In Greek, the *kosmos* can mean the people everywhere, the known Mediterranean world, the earth, or the people on earth. But in the New Testament, the term *kosmos* was given a *new* meaning, something like "all the other people besides Christians" or "everything that opposes God" (1 Cor. 2:12). This brings us to the next point—meaning changes.

Meaning Changes

Usage of a word can and does change over time. When I was a boy, we might say that a girl was "hot stuff." Nowadays, to communicate the same idea, young boys might say she is "cool." Or if he says a girl is "bad," he doesn't mean "bad" in the traditional dictionary sense, but "very good." You can tell what he means by the way he looks and the way he inflects his voice.

An example of how word usage changes over time is found by comparing 1 Timothy 2:4 in the KJV with modern versions. The KJV says, "[God] . . . Who *will have* all men to be saved, and to come unto the knowledge of the truth." In 1611, when the KJV was translated, the word "will" as a verb meant "volition" or "desire." So the text meant that God desires all people to be saved. But nowadays, "will" is a future auxiliary verb, taking it to mean salvation will be a future occurrence. If we read the KJV and are not aware of that change, we can misunderstand and miss the point.

In the KJV, Psalm 88:13 says, "But unto thee have I cried, O LORD; and in the morning shall my prayer *prevent thee*." Now what does "my prayer shall *prevent* thee" mean? Is the psalmist so arrogant that he thinks he can stop God from doing something? Well, we have to look at what "prevent" meant in 1611, when the KJV was translated. The prefix "pre" means "before" or "in front of," and "vent" means a "tube" or a "conduit." So it meant that the psalmist's prayer will "come out before" or "in front of" God.

Connotation Affects Interpretation

Another point is the connotation of words. Connotation is not the idea in a word, but the feeling it elicits. For example, the name Judas is a perfectly good name, but who names their son Judas? Who names their daughter Jezebel? The connotation and the emotional response that these names provoke prevent people from giving their children these names. Adolf was once a common German name. But except for neo-Nazis, nobody names their sons Adolf anymore because of the negative connotation of that name after World War II. And when one considers the fact that in the ghetto, it is often the mother who takes care of the family, works to support the family, and keeps it together, and "father" is someone who just impregnated the mother and is nowhere to be found, what connotation would God the *Father* communicate to children? How would one communicate to those children the attributes of the one whom we call "Father"? The word "mother" might communicate the concept better than the word "father." After all, God is a spirit and not literally of the male gender. The term is simply a metaphor to communicate a concept.

And the connotation of a word for one group may be different from that for another group. For example, the connotation of the word "nigger" for a white racist person has typically been negative. Blacks will not put up with hearing it from a white person, but many of them regularly use the term with a positive connotation among themselves.

Importance of Context

Context may be the most important concept in interpretation. The term "context" can be used in different ways. When one uses the term

BIBLICAL INTERPRETATION FOR LAYPEOPLE AND OTHER MARTYRS   99

"context," it could mean the historical context (what was happening and why), the cultural context (the ideas, values, and worldview of the time and place), the context of the entire Bible (the thread that runs through the whole collection of books, letters, songs, etc.), the context of the book (the train of thought in the book), or the immediate literary context (what precipitated the specific text, and what effect did it have?). When a text is used, one must use context in order to determine what the writer means.

Not understanding cultural context can cause problems. General Motors made a major financial mistake when it marketed the Chevy Nova south of the border because "No va" means "doesn't go" in Spanish.[135] The reluctance to buy the Nova may have cost General Motors millions of dollars. When President Reagan made a major faux pas in 1984 when he told a shopkeeper in China to "keep the change," it was considered an insult because tips are reserved for "lowly servants."[136]

Literary Context

I mentioned the fact that the word "bat" has different meanings. One does not know what the word "bat" means unless it is seen or heard in its context. Someone has said that "text without context is pretext." An example of that occurred when I was a sophomore at the University of Texas. I knew a senior student who was an unbeliever and was proud of it, and he liked to pull my chain. Periodically, he felt it necessary to attempt to burst my Christian bubble. And of course, I could not help picking up the gauntlet. At one point, he said, "Well, you know the Bible says, 'There is no God.'" Now I was quite sure that a book that spent so much time talking about the reality of God would not say that. So I asked for proof. He was unable to direct me to the text, but I found it. The text says, "The fool has said in his heart, 'There is no God'" (Pss. 14:1, 53:1). Now by ignoring the immediate literary context, he *made* the words seem to say the exact opposite of what the psalmist meant.

Historical Context

Over the course of history, the meaning of words and expressions change or are completely dropped. In the culture of the Old Testament,

---

135   Craig Storti. *The Art of Crossing Cultures* (Yarmouth, ME, 1990), xv.

136   US Department of Health and Human Services, *Crossing Cultures*. Quoted in Storti.

there was not nearly the passion for change as in our society, so words did not change as fast. It is possible that two hundred years from now, it will be more difficult to understand the English of today than it is the Hebrew of three millennia ago. Pretend you are an archeologist only five hundred years from now. Other games have replaced baseball. Nobody drives automobiles anymore. In your digging, you come across a fragment of a newspaper with these expressions:

The headline on the front page reads "MADD Meeting Rejects Legislation." You know that the word "mad" meant "angry" in 2018, but you are stumped. Did they misspell the word? And why did nobody notice that the word is in all capital letters? The editors must have overlooked it. But if the fragment includes the article, you will probably be able to figure it out.

In an article on baseball, you read, "So-and-so *'flew* out to left field.'" Does this mean that they had individual flying machines in 2018? Or were there human mutations that enabled some people to fly? Archeologists have not believed that individual flying machines were in use until the year 2026. To add to the confusion, you have read in an editorial section of the newspaper that a city councilman was "really out in left field" when he proposed that piece of legislation. So you wonder, "Why would he be proposing legislation while playing baseball?"

In the same baseball article, you read that a batter "tagged one to deep center field." You wonder, "Was this a price tag? No, it must have something to do with the game tag. But where were the holes in center field and how deep were they?" Further, you wonder if the game was called or delayed by having to replace a base when you read that so-and-so "stole second base." How did they know who stole the base? Did they catch him? Was he arrested? Was base theft considered a serious crime in those days? Was stealing a base a felony or misdemeanor?

You may also read a headline that says the Texas legislature raised the "sintax." Now you may know there is the word "syntax" (pronounced the same way) and wonder if the legislature was voting on adopting a specific type of sentence structure. But what does it mean that they "raised" it? You don't find the word "sintax" or the expression "sin tax" in any dictionary you are acquainted with. But if the fragment has the article with that headline, you might understand. That is, you would need context.

However, there are also some words in the Bible (especially Hebrew words) of which no one knows the meaning any longer. Sometimes translators

BIBLICAL INTERPRETATION FOR LAYPEOPLE AND OTHER MARTYRS   101

will just guess at the meaning based on the context, and some will guess at the meaning and put a footnote indicating they are not sure of the meaning. And sometimes they will simply put the word itself in, untranslated. In Genesis 6:4, we read that "the Nephilim" were in the land at that time. What were the Nephilim? Are they anything like Snuffalupagus? Well, nobody knows. The KJV and Today's English Version (TEV) translate the word as "giants." The Revised Standard Version (RSV), New International Version (NIV), New Revised Standard Version, (NRSV), Jerusalem Bible (JB), New American Standard Bible (NAS), and the New World Translation (NWT) just leave the word untranslated. Those that have a center-column reference refer you to Numbers 13:33, where the word is used again. The CEV translates it as "The children of the supernatural beings" and then adds, "They were called Nephilim." Exodus 14:20 in the TEV says, "The cloud made it dark for the Egyptians, but gave light to the people of Israel." But the footnote says that its translation is the probable meaning, but that the Hebrew is unclear.

Cultural Context

Different cultures understand the same things differently. Generally, in Asian culture, wearing shoes in a house of worship is considered a sign of disrespect. That is why when God appears to Moses, he tells him to take off his sandals. He is "on holy ground" (Exod. 3:5). But if one came into your church barefooted, it is likely that you would assume he is being disrespectful. And when Jesus referred to Herod Antipas as a "fox" (Luke 13:32), we assume that Jesus means Herod is "sly." But is that what he meant? That is our cultural connotation of the characteristics of a fox. But the first-century Jews' connotation of the characteristics of a fox was "voraciously destructive," or cruel.[137]

In the culture of both the Old and New Testament, there was a belief in supernatural beings (e.g., angels, demons, the devil) and in people who had the power to call down an efficacious curse or blessing on people.[138] And the Old Testament particularly emphasized corporate guilt rather than individual guilt (Josh. 7:1–26), the dominance of husbands, and the

---

[137]   R. Alan Culpepper. *The New Interpreter's Bible—Luke, John.* (Vol. X). Leander E. Keck (Ed.), (Nashville: Abingdon Press, 1995), 281. Fred B. Craddock. *Interpretation: A Bible Commentary for Teaching and Preaching—Luke.* James Luther Mays, ed., (Louisville: John Knox Press, 1990), 173.

[138]   Nida and Reyburn, *op. cit.*, 15.

retractability of parental blessings (Gen. 27).[139] To "know" did not mean to "have information about," but to "experience." The casting of lots could determine guilt or innocence. Virginity of the bride must be proved (but not the husband's), and a wife's maid could provide children for her (Gen. 16:1–4, 30:1–13).[140] They practiced herem, consecrating everything by extermination in honor of God (Josh. 6:17–19; 7:1–2; 8:2, 25), meaning they murdered enemy women and children and at times also all the livestock. They did not talk to women in private (John 4:27).[141]

Context of the Bible

The name of God is used often in the English Bible, as is the word "LORD." Since the Bible is about God, it would seem that the issue of God's name is pretty simple. Not necessarily! In the Old Testament, the Hebrew word "El," translated "god," occurs 238 times and is a common Semitic name for "god" in the ancient Near East. Although often used as a generic name for "God" or "gods," it was also a personal name of the head of the gods in Ras Shamra. El was a god in Canaanite and Israelite ancestral (polytheistic) religions.[142] The local Canaanite gods, including El, the head of the pantheon, were worshipped in sanctuaries eventually taken over by Israel.[143]

"Eloah," translated "god," is used fifty-seven times (mostly in Job). "El Shaddai," meaning "god of the mountain," occurs forty-eight times (mostly in Job). Sometimes the plural form, "Elohim" (or "gods"), is used. "Elohim" occurs about 2,600 times, beginning in Genesis 1:1.

In Exodus 3:1–17, "Elohim" is identified as "Yahweh." In the Hebrew Old Testament, "Yahweh" (YHWH), usually translated "LORD," occurs 6,828 times, although the exact pronunciation is not known for certain. When the KJV was translated, they believed the pronunciation was "Jehovah." Another name, Yahweh Tzabaoth (1 Sam. 1:3; 1 Kings 18:15; 1 Chron. 17:24; Ps. 24:10), usually translated "LORD of Hosts," occurs 279 times. For fear of accidentally using the name Yahweh in vain, the title

---

[139] *Ibid.*, 16.

[140] Nida and Reyburn, *op. cit.*, 17.

[141] *Ibid.*, 18.

[142] Leo G. Perdue. "names of God in the Old Testament," *HarperCollins Bible Dictionary*, 737.

[143] J. Andrew Dearman. *Religion & Culture in Ancient Israel* (Peabody, Mass.: Hendrickson Publishers, 1992), 16–18. 31.

"Adonai," meaning "my great Lord," was spoken in place of "Yahweh." The name does not occur in Ecclesiastes, Esther, or Song of Solomon.

Israel came out of a polytheistic culture where everyone had their own gods and nobody really questioned anyone else's god. Later, there was a stage of henotheism (a belief in many gods, but "our God can whip your god"). At this point, Yahweh, the name primarily associated with the covenant relationship, came to be used by the Israelites. We see this in Exodus 7:8–13, when the Egyptian magicians could turn rods into snakes, but Aaron's rod turned snake ate the Egyptians' snakes. Their gods were powerful, but Yahweh was more powerful. And when the Philistines captured the Ark of the Covenant and took it to Ashdod, according to the story, the chief Philistine god, Dagon, had the good sense to bow down to the ark (1 Sam. 5:2–7). Finally, Israel adopted monotheism. At Mount Carmel, Elijah's contest with the prophets of Baal and Asherah (1 Kings 18:19) prove that the Canaanites' gods were not really gods at all.

In the New Testament, the Greek word *theos*, translated "god," occurs 1,318 times, "often used by the LXX,[144] the Greek translation of the Old Testament, primarily as a translation of the usual Hebrew word for God, Elohim."[145] The term also is used for pagan gods. *Kurios*, translated "Lord," was used for Yahweh in the Septuagint. A majority of the 719 occurrences refer to Jesus.

Parallels

One example of context is the parallels. When we talk about parallels, we need to make sure that we are talking about the same thing. Parallels can be understood as an author or authors using the same terminology. If that is true, one needs to be careful that they are truly parallel. One must know whether it is a *verbal* or *real* parallel. Verbal or seeming parallels exist between two or more passages having approximately the same expressions that have different meanings. For example, both Paul (Rom. 9:8, Eph. 2:3, 2 Cor. 12:7) and John (John 1:14, 6:51) use the word "flesh," but they mean different things when they use the word. *Real* parallels exist in two or more passages that treat the same matter and have basically the same meaning.

---

[144] *The Septuagint of the Old Testament and Apocrypha with an English Translation of with Various Readings and Critical Notes* (London: Samuel Bagster and Sons, Limited).

[145] Boring, M. Eugene. "Names of God in the OT," *The HarperCollins Bible Dictionary*, Paul J. Achtemeier, gen. ed. (San Francisco: HarperSanFrancisco, 1996), 735.

It is important to be sure about parallels before drawing conclusions. Otherwise, we can be led into misinterpretation or misapplication. Often, when people use proof texts, they pay no attention to this fact.

Ephesians 1:7 says, "In him redemption through his blood, the forgiveness of sins, according to the richness of his grace." Colossians 1:14 says, "In whom we have redemption, the forgiveness of sins." This obvious parallel is one reason that some think that these two letters were written by the same person.[146] However, the use of the same wording is not necessarily proof that the same person said or wrote it. I have used the phrasing of Paul and Luther in my sermons and writings. One needs to be careful that premature conclusions are not drawn. People do repeat themselves, using exact wording. They also repeat themselves using similar wording. But others also use their wording at times.

In Luke 21:33, Jesus says, "Heaven and earth will pass away, but my word will not pass away." According to 1 Peter 1:25, "The word of the Lord stands forever." This seems to be a real parallel in that the same idea is conveyed by somewhat different terminology.

In Luke 15:1–2, we read that Jesus spoke to "tax collectors and sinners" gathered around to see him as he told the parable of the lost sheep. In Matthew 9:10, we read that as Jesus was at the home of Matthew (a tax collector), "tax collectors and sinners" came and ate with him and the disciples. Two different authors use the same terminology in different contexts to communicate basically the same idea—that Jesus cared about outcasts.

The Lord's Prayer is located in two places in the New Testament. In Matthew 6:9–13, it is included in a whole section of teaching on prayer. But in Luke 11:2–4, the disciples ask Jesus to teach them to pray. The wording in the two places is somewhat different, but the outline is basically the same.

Parallels are sometimes also used to develop a theme. This is done in the gospel of John regarding the concept of Jesus's "time" coming. It begins in chapter 2 of John. When Jesus's mother tells him they have run out of wine at the wedding in Cana, Jesus responds, "Woman, why do you involve me? My *time* has not yet come" (verse 4). In chapter 7, Jesus refuses to leave Galilee and go to Judea, saying, "The *right time* for me has not yet come"

---

[146] Some later manuscripts even add the words "through his blood" to make the parallel even stronger.

BIBLICAL INTERPRETATION FOR LAYPEOPLE AND OTHER MARTYRS   105

(verse 6).[147] But then, when he teaches in the temple that he is the Christ, John explains, "At this they tried to seize him, but no one laid a hand on him, because his time had not yet come" (verse 30).

When another conflict develops in the temple, John comments, "He spoke these words while teaching in the temple area near the place where the offerings were put. Yet no one seized him, because his *time* had not yet come" (John 8:20). Yet after his entry into Jerusalem on Palm Sunday, predicting his death, Jesus says, "The hour has come for the Son of Man to be glorified" (John 12:23). Then he tells his disciples, "The hour has come for the Son of Man to be glorified," (John 12:27), explaining that he is talking about his death. And just before Jesus washes the disciples' feet, John tells us, "It was just before the Passover Feast, Jesus knew that the time had come for him to leave this world and go to the Father" (John 13:1).

He even uses that same expression when he tells his disciples that they will be persecuted. "I have told you this," he adds, "so that when the time comes you will remember that I warned you" (John 16:4). Finally, as Jesus prays for himself, he implores the Father, "Father, the time has come. Glorify your Son, that your Son may glorify you" (John 17:1). These parallels develop the theme that, at the appropriate time, Jesus will glorify the Father through his death and that his disciples will face the same things that their Lord did.

When interpreting a text using context, one should use the immediate context both before and after the text to find out what prompted the story or what led up to the text. Find out what the response to the text is or how the author continues to develop his point. Look for parallels, particularly in the same book. Faithfulness to context will limit the potential for misuse of the text.

To determine what is real parallel and what is not, line up side by side certain questions about Matthew 26:6–7, Mark 14:3–4, Luke 7:36–37, and John 12:1–8. Ask questions such as the following: When did this happen? Who washed Jesus's feet (or head)? Who criticized? What was the point of the criticism? How did Jesus answer? You might think of others. What does this suggest about the story?

---

147   A different term is used, but it refers to the same concept.

Event	Matthew	Mark	Luke	John
Where happen?	26:6–13 Bethany, home of Simon the leper	14:3–9 Bethany house of Simon the leper	7:36–70 Pharisee's home Mary's home	12:1–8 Bethany Lazarus', Martha's
When happen?	2 days before Passover	2 days before Passover	Early in Jesus's ministry	Six days before Passover
What happened?	Woman with alabaster jar of perfume	Woman with alabaster jar of spikenard	Perfumed oil in alabaster jar	She took a pound of costly perfume
Where was she?	At his feet		Standing behind at his feet, weeping	
Who washed?	A woman	A woman	A woman of the city, a sinner	Mary
What washed?	Head as he reclined	Poured on head	Washed feet with tears, wiped feet with hair, kissed feet, poured perfume on feet	Poured on feet, wiped with hair
Who criticized?	Disciples	Some	Pharisee, who invited him	Judas Iscariot
Point of criticism	Waste, sold given to poor	Waste, sold for year's wages, given to poor	If he were a prophet, would know what kind of person touched him, a sinner	Could be sold and given to poor
Jesus's answer	Don't bother, she prepare him for burial, will be told as memorial	Let her alone poor you always have, poured on body for burial	If two debtors forgiven, who love the most? Host not give amenities, she lavished	Leave alone, she save perfume for burial, poor you always have

Meaning of Literal

When we talk about the term "literal," we need to know what we are talking about. It means different things to different people. There are at least three ways it is understood by people. For some, it means no allowance is made for the figurative at all. This is usually called "literalistic." Few people are consistently literalistic. A second meaning for "literal" is the usual or customary meaning of a word or phrase. The third meaning of "literal" is "the intended sense." It cannot always be assumed that words are used in the usual sense. Groups such as families and gangs use some of the same words that others use, but they use them in a special sense among themselves.

All messages have a first level of meaning, the literal meaning, on which virtually everyone in a given culture can agree. There are passages that are ambiguous or obscure and in some instances purposefully ambiguous. This is often a second level of meaning, such as a parable, which must be discovered. The story of the lost sheep is not about shepherding, but about God's concern for lost sinners (Luke 15:1–7). Nida and Reyburn point out that in the story of the prodigal son, there are many secondary levels—the results of a dissipated life, God's readiness to accept the penitent, a warning against self-righteousness, and a call for the "righteous" to also be forgiving. Sometimes repetition is even a significant hint. The repetition eight times of the fact that Ruth is a Moabite suggests that the author was emphasizing the fact. It may even be that Ruth was written to counteract the suffering of non-Jewish wives during the cruel rule of Ezra and Nehemiah.[148] It occurs to me that if Ezra had been around at the time of Ruth, he would have forced Boaz to abandon Ruth—and since Jesus was descended from Ruth, he would never have been born.

Traditional Hermeneutical Presuppositions

The presuppositions below are basically ones that Martin Luther used when he rebelled against allegorizing. Other Protestants have made modifications, but the presuppositions are basically used by traditional Protestant churches:

---

[148] Nida and Reyburn, *op. cit.*, 7–8.

Eyes of Faith

The first supposition is that Christians look at scripture through the eyes of faith. When they read the Bible, they see God at work. They read the same words as other people, but they read it with colored lenses from those who are not people of faith. An example would be the difference in the way Egyptians and Israelites viewed the Exodus. The Egyptians might have seen the plagues as a piece of really bad luck. The children of Israel saw *God at work*. When Christians open their Bible, because of their faith, they expect to hear God speaking. Berger puts it this way: "What appears as a human projection in one may appear as a reflection of divine realities in another."[149]

Christocentric

In scripture, Christians see God's grace leading them to reconciliation with God. They see the scriptures themselves as being the record of the redeeming acts of God and thereby an instrument of the redeeming act of God. Luther referred to the scriptures as the "cradle wherein Christ is laid." And although they couldn't phrase it the way Christians do, long before Jesus was born, Jews saw God's grace at work in the Hebrew Bible.

Scripture Interprets Scripture

With all its differences in styles, perspectives, and theologies, scripture is nevertheless seen as being a basic unity. Although written by human beings with different attitudes out of different cultural contexts, for different reasons and under different situations, it is seen basically as God's book. As such, it is seen as basically a unity. Therefore, the obscure passages are interpreted in light of the clear passages.

The New Testament Interprets the Old Testament

Scripture is considered to be a progressive revelation from the understandings in the Old Testament to those in the New Testament. When it was spoken and written, the contents of the Hebrew Bible must stand on their own as addressing the needs of God's people in their own time. But

---

[149] Berger, *op. cit.*, 1970, 46.

many Christians see the Old Testament as progressively preparing the world for the incarnation of the Son of God, fulfilled in Jesus of Nazareth. Yet the revelation was not completed. As indicated by the coming of the Holy Spirit on Pentecost, it continues to unfold. It may be seen as a building at different stages: the foundation, then the basic framework, the house in process, but never the completed structure.

The Interpreter Is Subject to Scripture

As the Word of God, the Bible is seen as an expression of God's authority. Therefore, the interpreter is subject to the Word and submits to its authority. When one "interprets" the Bible, she does not decide what it *should* say and then make it say what she wants to hear. She goes to scripture with the attitude of listening to God speak to her and responds in faith. This is not the attitude of people with an axe to grind.

Gospel Principle

The gospel is the foundation for interpreting scripture. It is the Holy Spirit that makes the understanding of the gospel possible. It is God's law informing human beings that they are not what God created them to be; but it is also God's love, calling alienated men and women back to harmony with God himself, with themselves, with their neighbors, and with the creation. It calls them to love God with all their hearts and their neighbors as themselves. And it gives examples of the way God's people have both succeeded and failed at their calling in their own cultures and in their own time. For Christians, it is the foundation for our lives from which we *understand the intent* of everything. I will have much more to say about this in chapter 11.

Which Is the Right Method of Interpretation?

So which method of interpretation is the right one? That's probably not the question to ask. Therefore, we should never become arrogant about our own interpretation.

So rather than asking which approach to interpretation is the right one, it is more helpful to ask in what way each approach can help us be what God calls us to be.

Chapter 6

SHORT FIGURES OF SPEECH

What Are Figures of Speech?

If you stopped to analyze how often we use figures of speech, I believe you would be amazed. Some 250 figures of speech have been catalogued. In this chapter, we will just address a few figures of speech. We use figures of speech every few minutes without even realizing it. So let's look at how we use figures of speech and how they were used in the Bible.

Definition

A figure of speech is an illustration of a relationship in one realm by means of a comparable relationship in another realm. Jesus often began comparisons by saying, "With what shall I compare this generation?" or "With what shall I compare the kingdom?" Jesus, the rural boy, compared the kingdom to agrarian life, fishing, and shepherding. Paul, the city slicker, compared sanctification to an athletic event. He compared the church to a human body, a building, a political entity, a bride of Christ.

A figure of speech can be compared to an arithmetic proportion. For example, Good Friday / New Testament = Passover / Old Testament. Or put in words, Good Friday is to the New Testament as the Passover is to the Old Testament.

Points of Comparison

In interpreting a figure of speech, one must be careful to draw only points of comparison *intended* by the author. When John the Baptist (Matt. 3:7) and Jesus (Matt. 12:34, 23:33) describe the Pharisees and Sadducees as a "brood of vipers," they are not saying that they have fangs, crawl on their stomachs, or are reptiles. The point is that they are deadly. It is fun to "find" comparisons, but we should find only what the author intended. The point of comparison can be illustrated by overlapping circles. There are many characteristics that Sadducees and Pharisees had—males, married, fathers, Jews, theologians, laity. There are many characteristics of serpents—reptiles, crawl on belly, hatched from eggs, tails. But the issue in the figure of speech is the characteristics seen as comparable in the two groups.

Interpretation Is Subconscious

Figures of speech are rarely conscious except when we purposely make a pun. The use of figures of speech is such a natural process that we usually don't even realize we are doing it. We pick up these principles long before we are even able to think about it. I recall when my twin daughters, Debbie and Angie, who were about five years old, first became aware of what figures of speech are. I had told them that I would do something with them after I finished working at my desk. They kept "bugging" (figure of speech) me, resulting in it actually taking me longer to finish what I was doing. So finally, when they again came in, I told them to "hit the road." Their eyes opened wide, and they said, "Okay." They ran out of the room, then out of the door to the street; they looked back to make sure I was watching them, clenched their fists, and hit the street pavement. By taking what I said literalistically, they were showing me that they understood the concept of figures of speech.

Types of Figures of Speech[150]

Direct Comparisons

Metaphor

A metaphor is a comparison by direct assertion, describing one thing in terms of something else. In the 1960s, a lot of opponents of the establishment referred to the police as "pigs." To say "You're a pig" is not a reference to anatomy. Because pigs are generally considered disgusting animals, it was the most derisive epithet of which they could think. Or to say "If he tries to steal second base, he'll be a dead duck" does not mean that a funeral is imminent.

The Bible is filled with metaphors. A delegation came to Jesus to inform him that Herod Antipas wanted an audience with him. Jesus insolently responded, "Go and tell that *fox*, 'Behold, I cast out demons and perform cures today and tomorrow, and the third day I finish my course'" (Luke 13:32). Jesus did not mean that Herod was a four-legged animal with pointed ears and a bushy tail. He was referring to the cultural understanding of the attributes of a fox, known for its cruelty.

Simile

A simile is an explicitly stated comparison using words such as "like" and "as." I can remember, as a boy, saying someone is "as crazy as a pet coon." I presume this is because raccoons, in captivity, exhibit bizarre behavior. But you don't have to understand the origin of a word in order to understand the meaning. "He runs like a deer" is a way of saying someone is very fast or maybe that he is graceful. Some can be very colorful. In *Naked Gun 33 1/3: The Final Insult*,[151] Lt. Frank Drebin says, "I knew that like a midget at a urinal, I'd have to stay on my toes." Tennessee Ernie Ford used to say, "I'm as nervous as a long-tailed cat in a room full of rocking chairs." Now that is really nervous!

Song of Solomon 6 says,

> Your teeth are *like* a flock of ewes,
> that have come up from the washing
> all of them bear twins,

---

[150] The outline for this section is largely based on the outline by Michelson.

[151] Peter Segal, dir. Paramount Pictures, 1994. Film.

not one among them is bereaved.
Your cheeks are *like* halves of a pomegranate
behind your veil. (verses 6–7)

The author's wife is a beautiful woman in his eyes. Her teeth are beautifully white and straight, with none missing, like freshly cleaned sheep, walking out of the water in matched pairs. Her cheeks are (we would say) "rosy"—even behind her veil.

Comparisons by Association

Metonymy

A metonymy is a figure of speech using the name of one thing for another because the two are frequently associated together or suggest the other. Often in newscasts, a reporter will say, "Today, the White House said . . ." We don't believe that a house can really talk. Usually, we think we know what it means. We generally think that it means something the president of the United States said. But at times, we find out that it was said by some representative of the White House staff, who is thought to be representative of the president's ideas. Yet at times, someone else from the White House rushes to explain that it does not represent the president's ideas or that she didn't mean it the way it sounded. At times, in the 1960s and 1970s, boys with long hair were called "hippies" not because their beliefs or lifestyles were anything like that of hippies, but simply because of the length of their hair.

There are several metonymies in this text from Micah 4:

He shall judge between many peoples,
and shall decide for strong nations afar off;
and they shall *beat their swords into plowshares,*
and their *spears into pruning hooks*;
nation shall *not lift up sword* against nation,
neither shall they learn war any more;
but they shall *sit every man under his vine and under his fig tree
and none shall make them afraid*;
for the mouth of the LORD of hosts has spoken. (verse 3)

In the text, "swords" and "spears" represent all the implements of warfare, and "plowshares" and "pruning hooks" represent implements of peace and agricultural production. And "sit every man under his vine and under his fig tree and none shall make them afraid" represents all the characteristics of peace, prosperity, and security.

Synecdoche

A synecdoche is a comparison in which a part is used for a whole or a whole for a part. When someone says, "Soon, we will hear the pitter-patter of little feet around the house," he means that he is about to have not feet, but a baby. Often, when the legislature adopts legislation, they say "the people have spoken" when in reality, only their representatives have "spoken."

In the parable of the rich man and Lazarus, the rich man begged father Abraham to send Lazarus back to tell his brothers about the place of torment in which he suffered. Abraham answered, "They have *Moses and the prophets*; let them hear them" (Luke 16:29). The expression "Moses and the prophets" (part of the Old Testament) refers to the entire Old Testament. And in the Lord's Prayer, Jesus offered the petition, "Give us this day our *daily bread*" (Matt. 6:11). "Daily bread" means, as Luther said in the explanation to this petition, "all that I need to preserve this body and life." Bread is so important for them in sustaining life; it is identified with the provisions one needs for life.

Figures of Speech Involving Personal Dimensions

Personification

A personification is a figure of speech in which a thing, a quality, or an idea is represented as a person. If a person is having difficulty with a new computer program, he might say, "This lousy computer has it in for me today," as if it had a mind.

The psalmist said, "The heavens *declare* the glory of God" (Ps. 114:4–6). That is, these inanimate objects, without vocal cords to speak, are portrayed *as if* they speak because they make known the glory of God. In Psalm 65, we read the following:

> The meadows *clothe* themselves with flocks,
> the valleys *deck* themselves with grain,
> they *shout* and *sing*
> together for joy. (verse 13)

Human beings clothe themselves and sing. Meadows and valleys do not. The psalmist seems enraptured by the beautiful image of white sheep on a backdrop of green grass and fields of grain. To him, they seem to shout for joy. What an ecstatic expression of emotion.

Apostrophe

The apostrophe is a figure of speech in which words are addressed directly to an inanimate object, a dead person, or an animal as if it were a live person. A frustrated person may say to his car that won't start, "Start, you lousy Ford." I can remember, in frustration, typing an obscene comment on the computer when it gave me the message that I had given it an illegitimate command. And people sometimes talk to their animals, saying things they know the animal doesn't understand, but which the person feels the need to express.

My mother used to love to tell people a story of when I was about ten years old. I had been scolded for something and was sitting on the back steps crying. Our dog, Scrappy, was sitting next to me. Through my tears, I sniffled, "Scrappy, nobody likes me!" as if he could understand what I was saying. Actually, my mother, looking through the window, said Scrappy was looking up at me as if he understood and sympathized.

In scripture, the psalmist utters the challenging question to inanimate objects:

> What ails you, O sea, that you flee?
> O Jordan, that you turn back?
> O mountains, that you skip like rams,
> O hills, like lambs. (Ps. 144:5–6)

And in anguish, David cries out to his dead son, Absalom, "And the king was deeply moved, and went up to the chamber over the gate, and wept; and as he went, he said, '*O my son Absalom, my son, my son Absalom! Would I had died instead of you, O Absalom, my son, my son!*'" (2 Sam. 18:33).

Exaggeration for Effect

Euphemism

A euphemism is a figure of speech in which a less-direct word or expression is used because the writer or speaker believes that the direct form would be offensive, unnecessarily harsh, or embarrassing to oneself or others—or just for jolting effect. A euphemism is often called an "understatement." Rather than saying a woman is pregnant, one might say, "She is in a delicate condition."

As he was stoned to death, Stephen knelt down and asked for the forgiveness of his killers; and "When he had said this, he *fell asleep*" (Acts 7:60). The expression "fell asleep" is a euphemism for dying because the expression "he died" seemed overly harsh. And Peter, understating his opinion of Judas's fate, said, "And they prayed and said, 'Lord, who knows the hearts of all men, show which one of these two thou have chosen to take the place in this ministry and apostleship from which Judas turned aside, *to go to his own place.*'" There is little disagreement that Peter believed Judas went to Hades but feels it is too harsh to say that directly in a prayer.

Hyperbole

A hyperbole is a figure of speech in which a conscious exaggeration is made by the speaker or writer in order to gain effect. Hyperbole is often called an "overstatement." I remember a young woman telling me that she had thought a former boyfriend was "the greatest thing since hair spray." Sometimes when a person wants to emphasize their original poverty, he may say, "When I got to town, I didn't have two cents to rub together."

In Psalm 6, the anguished singer utters his pangs of suffering:

> I am weary with my moaning;
> every night I *flood my bed* with tears;
> I *drench* my couch with my weeping. (verse 6)

The hyperboles "flood my bed" and "drench my couch" are gross overstatements to make the point of how anguished he is.

And the writer of John's gospel closes with this delightful hyperbole that communicates the truth well: "But there are also many other things which Jesus did; were every one of them to be written, I suppose that the world itself could not contain the books that would be written" (John 21:25). And Jesus uses this hyperbole to illustrate how the scribes and Pharisees were majoring in minors, missing the whole point of Judaism: "You blind guides, straining out a gnat and swallowing a camel!" (Matt. 23:24).

As Gideon came to face Israel's enemies, the author of Judges says, "And the Midianites and the Amalekites and all the people of the East lay

BIBLICAL INTERPRETATION FOR LAYPEOPLE AND OTHER MARTYRS   117

along the valley *like locusts for multitude; and their camels were without number, as the sand which is upon the seashore* for multitude" (Judg. 7:12). Comparing their numbers to a swarm of locusts and their camels to the number of sands on the seashore is a megaexaggeration. Of course, by using the word "like," a simile is also involved.

And to make his point to the Corinthians, from whom he had taken no financial support, Paul said, "I *robbed* other churches by accepting support from them in order to serve you" (2 Cor. 11:8). Although the money was given willingly, Paul talks as if he "robbed" them, exaggerating the meaning of his getting money from them.

And the psalmist says,

> I am poured out like water;
> and all my bones are out of joint;
> my heart is like wax,
> it is melted within my breast;
> my strength is dried up like a potsherd,
> and my tongue cleaves to my jaws;
> thou do lay me in the dust of death. (Ps. 22:14–15)

The exaggeration is obvious—he is "poured out like water," his "bones are out of joint," his heart is like[152] "melted wax," etc. The one thing that is obvious from this overstatement is that he is about as miserable as a person could be. And again, the exaggeration is used with similes.

Reversal of Meaning

Irony

Irony is a figure of speech in which words are used to express the exact opposite of what the words say. As a young man, I can remember being asked how I liked the blind date I had. Rolling back my eyes, I said, "Oh, she was a real doll." They knew I meant the opposite. The problem with irony is that it can be taken wrong, and if one is not careful, it can offend. It is much easier to express irony with the voice than it is in writing because the inflection of the voice can help one communicate the opposite meaning.

---

[152]   You might also notice there is a simile here. There are often more than one type of figure of speech in a text.

Paul castigates the Corinthian Christians for their spiritual pride and says in 1 Corinthians 4:8–13, "Already you are filled; already you have become rich; without us, you have become kings." He means the opposite of what he is saying. They have deluded themselves. They are none of these things. He shows he does not mean what he says by his next statement: "Would that you did reign" (verse 8).

And Paul is not above sticking it to the high priest with really biting sarcasm. During his interrogation before the Sanhedrin, the high priest has one of his attendants slap Paul. He shouts at the high priest, "God shall strike you, you whitewashed wall! Are you sitting to judge me according to the law, and yet contrary to the law you order me to be struck?" (Acts 23:3). When he is chided for his disrespect for the high priest, Paul (tongue in cheek) says, "*I did not know,_brethren, that he was the high priest*; for it is written, 'You shall not speak evil of a ruler of your people'" (Acts 23:5). Well, of course, Paul knew who the high priest was; but because of the high priest's behavior, he makes this ironic (and sarcastic) comment. And of course, calling the high priest Ananias a "whitewashed wall" was a major vilification of the high priest because it was an idiomatic expression to denote something that looks sound on the outside but is ugly on the inside.[153] It is even thought by some exegetes that Paul refers to Ananias as a "tomb,"[154] which would be an even more biting insult.

Rhetorical Question

A rhetorical question is a question that by implication draws a particular answer. The answer is couched in the question itself. The question is not asked to gain information, but to make a statement. One rhetorical question that almost all American parents ask in exasperation at least once in their lives is "What? Do you think money grows on trees?"

While Jesus is questioned by Pilate, Pilate queries, "*Am I a Jew?* Your own nation and the chief priests have handed you over to me; what have you done?" (John 18:35). Was Pilate asking for information? Didn't he know whether he was a Jew or not? Of course, he did. It was his way of saying, "I don't understand the issues involved here. Your own people are accusing you."

---

[153] *Bible Education Center Blog.* Reading.hopeinchampaign.com.

[154] Hermeneutics.kulikorskyonline.net.

BIBLICAL INTERPRETATION FOR LAYPEOPLE AND OTHER MARTYRS 119

Again, Paul, in anger, rails at the Corinthians about the divisiveness in the congregation, demanding, "Is Christ divided? Was Paul crucified for you? Or were you baptized in the name of Paul?" (1 Cor. 1:10–13). He is not trying to get information. He is making a statement with his question.

Descriptions of God

Anthropomorphism

An anthropomorphism is a figure of speech in which human physical features are ascribed to God. For example, Exodus says that the tables of the law were written "with the finger of God" (Exod. 31:18). And when the Egyptian magicians see the plagues, they opine, "This is the finger of God" (Exod. 8:19). And Exodus says, "Thus the LORD used to speak to Moses face to face, as a man speaks to his friend" (Exod. 33:11). The text speaks as if God had physical features that Moses could see and as if God had the limitations of human form.

Genesis uses this description of God: "And they heard the sound of the LORD *God walking in the garden in the cool of the day*, and the man and his wife hid themselves from the presence of the LORD God among the trees of the garden" (Gen. 3:8). It sounds like God is their next-door neighbor out for a pleasant evening stroll, who stops by to visit with his neighbors in their backyard.

Anthropopathism

An anthropopathism is a figure of speech in which human emotions are ascribed to God. Genesis says, "God was sorry he created man" (Gen. 6:7). And in Genesis 18:22–33, God is ready to destroy Sodom and Gomorrah. This characterization portrays God like a drunken Bubba who has lost his ability to reason. But Abraham, a cooler head and a good negotiator, continues to talk God into backing off from his irrational overreaction.

Figures Based on Sound

Pun

A pun is a figure of speech in which a word can have different meanings or a play on words when two different words that have a similar sound are used. When discussing the implications of the American Revolution,

Benjamin Franklin is reported to have said, "We had better all hang together, or we will hang separately," meaning they had better stick together or their fate would be their being hanged on the gallows. The pun is the figure of speech of which we are most aware. We consciously make puns. Much of our humor is based on puns.

In the country and western song "If I Said You Had a Beautiful Body Would You Hold It against Me," the play on the words "hold it against me" is obvious. It could mean "Would you be angry with me?" or "Would you press your body up against mine?" Many country songs use puns to make their point.

In the Bible, it is hard to detect a pun because the Bible we have is a translation. Puns are almost always lost in translations. Paul uses a pun in Philemon when he tells Philemon that he is sending back the slave Onesimus to him not as a slave, but as a brother in Christ—and he will be truly *onesimus* (useful). Paul is playing on the meaning of word *onesimus*, which means "useful." But we don't hear the pun in English because, unless we know Greek, we don't know the meaning of *onesimus*.

For us, the problem with biblical puns is that we are using a translation and therefore cannot "hear" the pun. For example, Isaiah 5:7 in English says,

> And [God] looked for justice,
> but behold, bloodshed,
> for righteousness,
> but behold, a cry!

One can almost hear the poetry without seeing it set off the way it is here, but we cannot hear the pun. In Hebrew, it says,

> And he looked for *mishpat*
> but behold *mispah*
> for *tzedhaqh*
> but behold, a *tzaqah.*

It is almost impossible to detect puns in the Bible unless we either know the language or accidentally run across one in a commentary.

Chapter 7

LONG FIGURES OF SPEECH

Long figures of speech are, obviously, longer—more than just a short sentence. They may have shorter figures of speech in them. They are often in the form of a story.

Similitude

A similitude is fairly simple to describe. It is an extended simile or series of similes. A man may say, "I had a date Friday night with a woman who ate like a horse, drank like a fish, cussed like a sailor, and fought like a demon."

In Song of Solomon 7, the bridegroom says of his new wife,

> How graceful are your feet in sandals,
> O queenly maiden?
> Your rounded thighs are *like* jewels,
> the work of a master hand.
> Your navel is a rounded bowl

121

that never lacks mixed wine.
Your belly is a heap of wheat
encircled with lilies.
Your two breasts are *like* two fawns,
twins of a gazelle.
Your neck is *like* an ivory tower
Your eyes are pools in Heshbon,
by the gate of Bath-rabbin
Your nose is *like* a tower of Lebanon,
overlooking Damascus (verses 1–4).

Now there is a man in love. You cannot miss the rapture as he gazes at his loved one's naked body.

Allegory

An allegory is an extended metaphor or a series of metaphors. Earlier, we talked about the method of interpretation called "allegorizing." It is important to explain the difference in allegory and allegorizing. An allegory is a figure of speech used *by the author.* Allegorizing is a method of interpretation used *by the interpreter.* In Genesis, the story of Ishmael and Isaac was not intended by its author to be an allegory. But in Galatians 4:21–26, Paul does a bit of allegorizing in picturing Ishmael as representing the law and Isaac as representing the gospel.

In interpreting an allegory, one must understand to whom the author is speaking, when he is speaking, under what circumstances, and the analogy on which it is based. In Galatians 4:21–26, it is important to understand that the writer was a Jew writing to Jews who wanted to require Gentile converts to practice circumcision in order to become a Christian, thus turning the freedom of the gospel into the fulfilling of legal requirements. Unless the readers know something about the story of Ishmael and Isaac, the allegory may not mean much.

In correctly interpreting allegories, one should do the following: First, understand the historical situation. It is at this point that one uses the context to determine to whom the author was speaking, when it was written, and under what circumstances. Second, one must determine the points of comparison. In an allegory, unlike a parable, there is often

BIBLICAL INTERPRETATION FOR LAYPEOPLE AND OTHER MARTYRS   123

more than one point of comparison. Third, use the post context to note any response or comment of the audience. How did they take the story? Were they amused? Were they offended? Did they react verbally or by action? Fourth, determine the meaning of the comparison for the points of comparison that were in the mind of the original author. Finally, determine how it relates to you and your present situation.

In Isaiah 5:1–7, God builds a vineyard. He is the vinedresser, the owner of the vineyard. He works hard on his vineyard. Israel is the vineyard. God expects the vineyard that he has cared for so lovingly to yield good fruit. The fruit is righteousness, living as God wanted them to live, caring for *all* Israelites. But they yielded sour grapes. Sour fruit is evil works, injustice. So God says he will destroy his vineyard. The protective walls will be broken down, they will be trampled, briars and thorns will come up, and there will be no rain. That is a threat of destruction.

And when one reads John 15:1–7, she cannot miss the point that the allegory is an application of the Isaiah allegory. It is applied to Jesus. In this case, the interpretation is given, beginning in verse 8. God is the vinedresser. Jesus is the vine. His people are the branches who are to bring forth good fruit. God gives Jesus to provide life-giving nutrition to Christians, enabling them to produce the kind of behavior that God expects.

And Ezekiel 16:1–19 is, to my mind, one of the Bible's most beautiful, poignant, and sad love stories of God toward his people. God pictures himself as a rich sheikh, walking along one day and finding a dying newborn baby girl (Israel) lying out in the desert on the verge of death. He takes her home and lavishes every blessing upon the girl. And at the time she comes of age, he gives her the ultimate honor of making her his wife. It is only logical that the sheikh would expect loyalty from her. But instead, she becomes a prostitute, serving other gods—a treasonous act toward the God who had been so gracious to her.

Matthew 13:3–17 (Mark 2ff.), usually called the parable of the sower, is actually an allegory (in the technical sense). Basically, the seed is the Word, and the ground is the heart to which the Word is addressed. Jesus gives his explanation, beginning in verse 18.

Parable

A parable is a story that may or may not be true, told in the past tense, may or may not be timelessly true, and usually has one point of comparison.

When interpreting a parable, try to determine how the "earthly details" were understood by the original hearers. Use context to determine what prompted the parable. Check the response of the listeners to determine how they understood the parable. Determine the point of comparison to understand the point of the parable. Then apply it to your own situation.

Let's look at Luke 10:30–37. The parable of the good Samaritan is known around the world by people who are not Christians. It may be the best-known parable in the Bible. However, many people do not get the full impact of the text. For many, it is an example story, showing that we should help stranded drivers on the highways or hitchhikers. If that is the way you see the parable, if you have become guilty of legalism, or if you conclude that one "gains eternal life" by picking up hitchhikers, you are in trouble. "Go straight to jail. Do not pass 'Go.' Do not collect $200."

First, we look at context. In verse 25, we see that a lawyer "put [Jesus] to the test," asking him how one inherits eternal life. Being the good pedagogue, Jesus asks him what he knows of the answer from the Torah of the Old Testament. The man answers with the summaries of the law: "You shall love the LORD your God with all your heart, and with all your soul, and with all your strength, and with all your mind" (Deut. 6:5) and "You shall love your neighbors yourself" (Lev. 19:18). "Bingo," says Jesus. "You got it. Do this and you will live" (verse 28). Luke now interprets the lawyer's intent, saying that "wishing to justify himself," he asks Jesus, "But who is my neighbor?" It is this question that prompts the parable.

You know the story. A man traveling from Jerusalem to Jericho was accosted by robbers, beat up, robbed, and left in such a condition that he could die. Along comes a priest and passes him by. Along comes a Levite and passes him by. Now comes the punch line, the point. The third time is always the charm. They were ready. Their ears perked up. Who is going to be the hero? But surprise of surprises, the hero is *a Samaritan*, a member of the group most hated by the Jews. Now Jesus asks the lawyer not "Who is my neighbor?" But he asks, "Who proved to *be* a neighbor?" Not wanting to say a Samaritan would be the hero, the lawyer answers, "The one who showed mercy." Jesus agrees that the lawyer has had sense enough to know which one was the neighbor and says, "Yep! Go and do the same."

You can imagine their shock. They do a double take. "Who did he say was the hero? A Samaritan? Surely not!" You see, the Samaritans were the

BIBLICAL INTERPRETATION FOR LAYPEOPLE AND OTHER MARTYRS 125

ultimate hated enemy. To go from Judah to Galilee, the most direct route was through Samaria. Because of their intense hatred of Samaritans, Jews would often detour across the Jordan River, travel east of the Sea of Galilee, and recross the Jordan River into Galilee. The trip might be two or three times as long; but to avoid Samaritans, many were willing to suffer the inconvenience, time, and expense. And now the hero in Jesus's story was a Samaritan? How could this be? This requires deeper thinking.

Well, not every exegete interprets the point of the parable the same, but there is one point on which all agree—it is not the emasculated story that many have made it. Some would argue that Jesus's answer suggests the impossibility of that kind of love, of being able to fulfill the requirements of God that well, thus calling for dependence on God. Others argue on the issue of with whom you identify in the story. They would not identify with the priest or Levite; they would definitely not identify with the Samaritan. That leaves only the person who was beat up and robbed. That might be the poor, simple layperson whom the lawyers have injured with their legalism.

A third interpretation, which is certainly in there somewhere, is the radical love God expects from his children—so radical that it would show love to a person that is so despised that the act of love is almost incomprehensible.

Another major parable is the parable of the prodigal son, which is the last in a trilogy of parables, with the lost sheep and the lost coin (Luke 15:4–32). Neither did these parables come out of thin air. What prompted the parable? Check the context. In verses 1–3, we learn that tax collectors and sinners were coming to hear Jesus. This got the goat of the Pharisees and scribes because he not only received them but also ate with them. In ancient times, meals were "ceremonies," which implied commonality, including status.[155] In this case, it is not "you are what you eat," but "you are *with whom* you eat." Jesus ate not only with the scribes and Pharisees, but also with social undesirables. One of these groups were the tax collectors. Unlike the chief tax collectors, these people were often unable to find a job elsewhere.[156] They might say to you, "Man, I needed a job. I had to feed my wife and kids." But for the Jew of that day, their Jewish counterparts

---

[155]   Bruce J. Malina and Richard L. Rohrbaugh. *Social-Science Commentary on the Synoptic Gospels* (Minneapolis: Fortress Press, 1992), 367.

[156]   *Ibid.*, 387–388.

who were collecting taxes for an occupying power, the Roman government, were traitors to the nation, considered to be the scum of the earth.

The word translated "sinners" (*hamartōlos*) literally means "one who misses the mark." Now some of these people may have erred with regard to the moral law,[157] but others were just ceremonially unclean. To the Pharisees, if Jesus came into contact with such "unclean" people, he would become unclean also. So we have three parables that respond to that attitude, the last of which is the parable of the "prodigal" son.

It is a story of a foolish young man who takes early retirement, leaves his family, blows his inheritance, resorts to the most repulsive job a Jew could imagine (feeding pigs and wishing that he could eat as well as they do), comes to his senses, and returns home in repentance. His father is berserk with happiness because his son has returned home where he belongs. But the older brother, who had been the compliant, responsible son, is resentful that the father made so much of the unfaithful, uncompliant son. The punch line is the father's pronouncement: "But we had to be merry and rejoice for this brother of yours was dead and has begun to live, and was lost and has been found" (verse 32). With this parable, the self-righteous scribes and Pharisees are called not just to be much more inclusive, but to rejoice over the response of the members of those despised groups of people to Jesus's ministry.

Fable

A fable is a story often using animals or inanimate objects as actors in order to convey a moral. They are usually intended to be timelessly true. Examples of fables are Uncle Remus's stories about Br'er Rabbit and Br'er Fox and Aesop's fable of the tortoise and the hare. In the story of the tortoise and the hare, the point is that although the hare got a fast start, he was too confident. The tortoise was slow, but persistent. The point is that those who pace themselves and keep at their job until they are finished are the best to emulate.

Fables are scarce in the Bible, but in Judges, we have a sample. Abimelech, the son of Gideon and a favorite judge of Israel, decided he wanted to be the first king of Israel. He had seventy of his brothers murdered to eliminate the competition. Then he met with the village of

---

[157] Spiros Zodhiates. *The Complete Word Study Dictionary--New Testament* (Iowa Falls, Iowa: World Bible Publishers, Inc., 1992), 131.

BIBLICAL INTERPRETATION FOR LAYPEOPLE AND OTHER MARTYRS 127

Shechem and offered himself as king. But Joash, the son of Gideon who had escaped the slaughter, stood on a high hill overlooking Shechem where he would be safe and told a fable about trees who decided to choose a king. All of the worthy trees declined to serve as king of the trees because they had important things to do. But the worthless bramble was happy to accept the job (Judg. 9:8–15). The point is obvious. Not that trees can talk or hold office, but that Abimelech, who coveted the office, was not worthy of it.

Legend

A legend is a nonhistorical or unverifiable story handed down by tradition from earlier times and is commonly accepted as being historical. Legends such as King Arthur, George Washington and the cherry tree, Abraham Lincoln walking miles to return a penny, and some of the stories about Davy Crockett and Daniel Boone are examples of our legendary lore. Legends are stories that are built around people that the storytellers believe are worthy of emulation. Neither the story about George Washington and the cherry tree nor the one about Abraham Lincoln returning the penny has any factual accuracy, but the people who constructed the stories admired the men and believed that the stories reflected the type of persons they were. And who can deny the importance of truthfulness and honesty?

There are numerous legends in the Bible. Many of the stories of the patriarchs are legendary. Abraham may not have actually taken Isaac to sacrifice the child of promise through whom the blessing would be fulfilled, but who can deny the importance of that kind of total devotion to God? While the facts may not be accurate, the truth of the story is real. Jesus was the kind of person that elicited legends. Stories of his walking on water (Mark 6:45–51, Matt. 14:22–33, John 6:16–21) and of feeding of four thousand with a few small fish and seven loaves of bread (Mark 8:1–13, Matt. 15:29–39) or of five thousand with five loaves and two fish (Mark 6:32–44, Matt. 14:13–21, Luke 9:10–17, John 6:1–14) may not be the kind of thing that one could have recorded with videotape, but these stories say something about Jesus, as well as point us toward ideals of sharing what we have with those in need.

Myth

A myth is a story about superhuman beings or imaginary persons that explains natural phenomena. It usually points to something real that people believe needs explaining. For example, the reason narcissus flowers grow along the side of rivers is because Narcissus, a handsome Greek god, once saw his own reflection in a river, fell in love with himself, and could not tear himself away from the edge of the river. So he just grew there. In America, we have stories about Pecos Bill and Paul Bunyan and Babe the Blue Ox, which, if not myths, certainly have mythological elements.

Genesis 1–3 have some mythological dimensions, but not nearly as fantastic as the myths of other cultures. The story contains a snake talking to a woman; a tree whose fruit *is not an apple*, but the knowledge of good and evil; and a tree whose fruit is life.

The following are some other stories that have mythological dimensions:

> God will not turn back His anger;
> Beneath Him crouch the helpers of Rahab. (Job 9:13)

Rahab, meaning "arrogant, raging, turbulent, afflicter,"[158] was the primeval sea monster that represented the chaos that God had to overcome.[159] The mythological dragon was overcome by God's victory over the forces of chaos in the Creation conflict. The chaos monster is portrayed in other earlier Middle Eastern mythology.[160]

> You split the sea with your power,
> You shattered the heads of the sea monsters on the water.
> You crushed Leviathan's heads.
> You gave it to the desert dwellers for food. (Ps. 74:13–14)

Leviathan, meaning "coiled one," was also a sea monster in serpentine form, which also represented the forces of chaos that God conquered, also

---

[158] For an excellent discussion of myth, see Northrop Frye. *The Great Code: The Bible and Literature* (San Diego: Harcourt Brace Jovanovich, Publishers, 1983), esp. 183–198.

[159] J Randall O'Brien. "Rahab," *Holman Bible Dictionary*. Trent C. Butler, gen. ed. (Nashville: Holman Bible Publishers, 1991), 1163–1164.

[160] Steve Wyrick. "Leviathan." *Holman Bible Dictionary*. Trent C. Butler, gen. ed. (Nashville: Holman Bible Publishers, 1991), 875.

BIBLICAL INTERPRETATION FOR LAYPEOPLE AND OTHER MARTYRS   129

known in ancient pagan myths.[161] Leviathan was a beast in ancient Near Eastern religions of Mesopotamia and Syria-Palestine, a dragon of the sea figured in creation stories.[162]

The Psalter has mythological imagery of a "primeval sea monster representing the forces of chaos God overcame in creation (Ps. 89:9ff.),"[163] as does Isaiah (40:28, 44:24, 45:7, 51:9ff., 65:17ff., 66:22–23). Also, in Psalm 104:26, God created Leviathan, the sea creature, "for sport."[164]

The mythological Adam tradition plays a minor role in the rest of the Old Testament, suggesting it is a relatively late story.[165] The Jewish philosopher Philo, influenced by Plato, saw Adam as the historical sinful father of humans and a perfect man in the mind of God.[166] The focus on Adam finds continuation in Paul (Rom. 5:14; 1 Cor. 15:10–22, 42–49).

Rahab, the dragon, is a mythological creature to designate chaos. God's primeval victory over the forces of chaos is portrayed. It portrays a creation conflict. The chaos monster is portrayed in other earlier Middle Eastern mythology.[167]

The author uses ancient Near Eastern chaos-dragon mythology for his imagery. In the Akkadian account of the *Enuma Elish*, Marduk slays the great dragon Tiamat, heaven and earth forming from the halves of her severed body. In the Canaanite version, the combat is between Baal and Yam (sea). In the Hebrew version, Rahab the dragon (*tannin*), the sea (*Yam*), and great deep (*tehom rebbah*) are used as the enemy slain by Yahweh.[168]

---

[161]   *Ibid.*

[162]   Gene M. Tucker. *New Interpreters' Bible, Isaiah 1-39.* Leander E. Keck, ed. (Nashville: Abingdon Press, 1994), 225.

[163]   *Ibid.*, 226.

[164]   *Ibid.*

[165]   Brevard S. Childs. *Biblical Theology of the Old and New Testaments: Theological Reflection on the Christian Bible* (Minneapolis: Fortress Press, 1992), 116.

[166]   Philo. *Allegory of the Jewish Law*, I, 31–32. http://www.earlyjewishwritings.com/text/philo/book2.html.

[167]   Tucker, *op. cit.*

[168]   Cuthbert A. Simpson, "The Book of Genesis," *The Interpreter's Bible, Vol. I*, George Buttrick (Gen. Ed.). (Nashville: Abingdon Press, 1956).

Does Knowing the Figure of Speech Matter?

We have spent considerable time discussing figures of speech in our language and the writings of today and of the Bible. And I believe it is important to be aware of figures of speech in the Bible as well as in our own communication. There are times when it is important to determine what type of literature with which we are working or whether an expression is factually accurate or not, but more often than not, it is not important.

Read the book of Jonah. It is very short and interesting. People have argued for centuries what type of literature it is. There have even been those who have said that unless it is taken as a factually accurate historical document, then it cannot be believed. I find this bizarre reasoning. The point of the book is very clear. It is an evangelism document. It assures us that God is forgiving to those who repent, even of those who have been considered enemies. Does the fact that it is not a historical event mean that the point of the book is not valid? If a pastor would illustrate a point by telling a story about Charlie Brown, who would be so silly as to say that unless one could prove that Charlie Brown and Snoopy were historical beings, the *point of the story* could not be believed? Rhetorical question!

Chapter 8

PROPHECY AND TYPOLOGY

Prophecy

Meaning of "Prophet"

When you ask someone what a prophet is, the answer will often be "one who predicts the future." However, that is a very minor dimension of what it means to be a prophet. In the Old Testament, there are two basic Hebrew words for "prophet." A *nabi* was "one who speaks a message for a superior."[169] The Hebrew word *chozeh* means a "seer." Generally, the *chozeh* tended to display ecstatic manifestations, whereas the *nabi* tended to focus on justice and political issues. In the New Testament, the Greek word *prophetēs* can mean "one who speaks for God," "a public expounder," or "one who foretells." As neat as these definitions seem, they were not. The meanings seemed to have overlapped and shifted over time. In fact, by the time 1 Samuel was finished, a transition had been made, for the author had to explain the following: "Before in Israel, if a man went to inquire of God,

---

[169]   Benjamin Davidson. *The Analytical Hebrew and Chaldee Lexicon.* (Peabody, MA: Hendrickson Publishers) (Second edition, 1850; Seventh Printing 1993), 530.

131

he would say, 'Come, let us go to the seer (*chozeh*), because the prophet *nabi* of today used to be called a seer (*chozeh*)'" (1 Sam. 9:9).

Development of the Prophets

Prophets developed out of the murky prehistory of Israel. Abimelech, king of Gerar, is told by God in a dream that Abraham is a *nabi* (Gen. 20:7). Aaron (Exod. 7:1) and Moses (Deut. 18:15–22) were called *nabiim* (*im* is plural). Of course, since the stories were passed on orally, sometimes for generations, there is no way to know what actually transpired or exactly what words were originally used. The priest Samuel is referred to as a *roeh* (1 Chron. 26:28, 29:29). After his anointing as king, Saul went into a "prophetic frenzy" and "became a "different person" (1 Sam. 10:5–13). He even was known to have stripped himself naked in a frenzy and is referred to as a *nabi* (1 Sam. 19:20–24).

Generally, prophets served from the end of the period of the judges to first half of the fifth century BCE.[170] In the mid-ninth century BCE arose a conscience-driven man named Elijah who felt Yahweh's call to condemn the practices of Ahab and Jezebel. In the eighth century BCE, the oral prophets like Elijah and Elisha (1 Kings 17–21, 2 Kings 1–9) focused on condemnation of the worship of Baal and for Jezebel's execution of Yahweh's prophets. Elijah escaped and appointed Jehu to overthrow Ahab and Jezebel. Elijah was a wild man wearing hairy clothing. Elisha, his protégé, was more settled and associated with a band of people who experienced ecstasy. Neither man left any written prophecy, but hero legends were told about them, attributing miracles to them that were claimed for no other prophet.[171]

Their words and deeds were passed on orally. Later, their words and deeds were written down by their disciples as best they could remember. By the mid-eighth century, prophets began writing their prophecies down. Books were written by Nathan the "prophet" (*nabi*), Samuel the "seer" (*chozeh*), and Gad the "seer" (1 Chron. 29:29); but they have been lost.

Over time, the role of the prophet changed. The prophets were the conscience of Israel and Judah. A *nabi* was distinguished from diviners, witches, interpreters of omens, sorcerers, ones who cast spells, mediums,

---

[170] Childs, *op. cit.*, 169.

[171] Boadt, *op. cit.*, 298–300.

BIBLICAL INTERPRETATION FOR LAYPEOPLE AND OTHER MARTYRS   133

spiritualists, and necromancers, who seem to do approximately the same things as a *nabi* (Deut. 18:15–22) but who are identified with those who make their sons and daughters pass through the fire (verses 10–14). There were also women prophets: Miriam, Moses and Aaron's sister (Exod. 15:20); Deborah, who gave Barak courage (Judg. 4:4); Huldah, wife of Shallum who approved the first canon of scripture (2 Chron. 34:22, 2 Kings 22:14);[172] Noadiah, who tried to intimidate Nehemiah (Neh. 6:14); and Isaiah's wife (whose name we do not know) (Isa. 8:3).

There were prophets on the courts of some kings. The prophet Gad was David's "seer" (2 Sam. 24:11; 1 Chron. 21:9, 25:5), and Nathan was a "prophet" for David (2 Chron. 29:25), suggesting that these two roles may have evolved into separate offices. When Amos came to Israel to expose the sin of Jeroboam II, he was told by Amaziah the priest, "Get out, you *seer*! Go back to the land of Judah. Earn your bread there and do your prophesying there. Don't prophesy anymore at Bethel, because this is the king's sanctuary and the temple of the kingdom" (Amos 7:12–14).

Isaiah, referred to as a prophet, was of major importance on the court of Ahaz and Hezekiah, serving as something like a secretary of state or at least a chief foreign policy advisor (2 Kings 19:20–20:19; Isa. 7:1–25, 36:1–39:8).

By the time of Zechariah (535/530 BCE), prophets were seen as a thing of the past (Zech. 1:4, 7:7, 11-12). But there was a hope that prophecy would be revived (Deut. 3:38, LXX; 1 Macc. 9:27, 4:46). Over time, prophecy seemed to have evolved into typology and apocalyptic literature. As the office of prophecy disappeared, the writing of prophetic texts arose in later generations. There were also groups of people known as sons of prophets (1 Kings 20:35, 2 Kings 2:3–15) and wives of prophets (2 Kings 4:1), but how they functioned is not clear.

False Prophets

According to the author of 2 Kings, Israel's destruction occurred because she ignored the warning of "every seer and prophet" (2 Kings 17:13), suggesting that they may have been distinguished from each other by that time. Isaiah accused the people of Judah of requiring the prophets and seers to tell them what they wanted to hear. "These are rebellious people, deceitful children, children unwilling to listen to the LORD's instruction.

---

[172]   In Kings, it doesn't even give her name.

They say to the seers, 'See no more visions!' and to the prophets, 'Give us no more visions of what is right! Tell us pleasant things; prophesy illusions. Leave this way, get off this path, and stop confronting us with the Holy One of Israel!'" (Isa. 30:9–11).

And there were some who caved in to that temptation. In dealing with "false prophets," God tells Ezekiel, "Son of man, prophesy against the prophets of Israel who are now prophesying. Say to those who prophesy out of their own imagination. . . . This is what the Sovereign LORD says: Woe to the foolish prophets who follow their own spirit and have seen nothing. Your prophets, O Israel, are like jackals among ruins" (Ezek. 13:2–4). Some of the women were also guilty of prophesying "out of their own imagination" for money (Ezek. 13:17). Although it was the people who wanted the prophets to tell them what they wanted to hear, when they did so, the prophets, the seers, *and the diviners* were not respected (Mic. 3:6–7). And part of the calamity that will come upon the people is that they will no longer be able to get a vision from the seer (Ezek. 7:26). Preachers in our day are also reluctant to confront their listeners with words they do not want to hear.

The Characteristics of a Prophet

What are the criteria for distinguishing the true from the false prophet (Deut. 13:1–5)? How does one know when a person is a prophet? Some did not even see themselves as prophets (Amos 7:14, Jer. 1:4–10). After all, false prophets were a thorn in the flesh of the community of faith. But no one has ever said to the community to which he is speaking, "I am a false prophet. Do not listen to me." Based on how prophets are described in various places, we can cull out the basic marks of a true prophet:

He Comes in the Name of Yahweh
He comes in the name of Yahweh and proclaims Yahweh's Word, not his own. Therefore, you hear the prophets saying, "Thus says Yahweh." But false prophets also make that claim. Some do it for money, others for prestige, others to preserve privilege, and others are simply deluded. On the other hand, prophets like Isaiah served at court and received financial remuneration for their services. Isaiah also had prestige and privilege. So how can one know if a prophet was deluded?

BIBLICAL INTERPRETATION FOR LAYPEOPLE AND OTHER MARTYRS 135

He Has the Ruach Yahweh

"The Spirit of the LORD" (*ruach Yahweh*) is the main characteristic of the prophet. At times, the truth of his prophecy is manifested by ecstasy. One can see this emphasis in 1 Samuel. When Saul joined a group of prophets and manifested certain atypical behavior, the people began to ask, "Is Saul also among the prophets?" (1 Sam. 10:11).

The Word Comes True

His word comes true, verifying him as a prophet. However, sometimes only hindsight tells who is the true prophet. In the meantime, people are bewildered and have to depend on faith.

Distinguishing the True Prophet from the False Prophet

Nevertheless, there were false prophets (Jer. 5:31) who "lie in my name" (Jer. 14:14–16, 23:21–31, 27:15–16, 29:9–21). "I have not spoken to them, but they prophesy any way" (Jer. 23:21). They divine for money (Mic. 3:11). But when one prophet is saying one thing and another is saying the opposite, how is one to tell which is true and which is false? Even true prophets could succumb to the temptation of confusing the voice of the people with the voice of God. In many instances, the prophets were compelled to indict the people and the so-called false prophets with the very same words (Isa. 30:8–14; Mic. 2:6, 3:5, 3:11; Jer. 26:8; Ezek. 13–14). That is no fun. Their message was often not popular in their time. Ahab had lots of prophets who would tell him what he wanted to hear. He disliked the prophet Micaiah because "he never prophesies good for me" (1 King 22:8–18; 2 Chron. 18:7–17).

Hananiah was the typical fanatic patriot who supported his nation right or wrong and accused Jeremiah of treason. Jeremiah counseled them to submit to Nebuchadnezzar because he wanted to preserve their lives. While Hananiah was blinded by his devotion to the king and perhaps his desire to ingratiate himself to the king, Jeremiah made a realistic assessment of the situation. But at one point, Jeremiah even says "Amen" to Hananiah's prediction (Jer. 28:6–9). Only later did he change his mind (Jer. 28:12–16).

No single secondary criterion can determine the difference between true and false prophecy (Deut. 13:2–3). The criterion must be the gospel. One must adapt the text, taking into consideration the dynamics of that situation. That is, it *ain't* always easy to clearly see who is the prophet of Yahweh and who is a false prophet. Deciding to whom one should listen requires a leap of faith.

Perspective of the Prophet

Although it will not always be found in this format, the general outline of prophetic proclamation has some common characteristics. They usually issue the following:

1. ***A reminder of God's past acts of grace.*** Often, the Exodus is used as an example of how God had blessed them and how God had a claim on their lives.
2. ***The response expected for a child of God is called for in the present.*** He often points to their apostasy or ingratitude for God's loving grace. From that point, the prophet often launches into a recitation of specific deeds of misconduct and of the suffering that they would soon be subjected to if they do not repent of their sin against God and the oppressed. So he calls them to a decision to change and follow God's justice in the present.
3. ***The future God has planned to create through his people depends on their response.*** The punishment will not come, or the present punishment will be abated by their *turning from their spiritual adultery* and again living faithfully as God's children.

Messianic Prophecy

When we talk about messianic prophecy, we are talking about proclamations of the coming of the messianic hope and examples of how the Old Testament had previously spoken of it. However, although we sometimes quote messianic prophesy glibly, we often completely ignore the original context and therefore do not know exactly what we mean.

Alfred von Rohr Sauer[173] has spoken of three different kinds of messianic prophecy.[174] He points out that most exegetes agree on these points: that it is important to establish the correct text by using textual

---

[173] Who was referred to affectionately by his students as Von Bull Rohr.

[174] Alfred von Rohr Sauer. "Problems of Messianic Interpretation," *Concordia Theological Monthly*, about 1962, 566–574.

BIBLICAL INTERPRETATION FOR LAYPEOPLE AND OTHER MARTYRS   137

criticism, that the literary form of a passage must be determined, that the historical context that produced the text must be understood, that the literal sense of the text must be determined in order to interpret the original writer's intended message to the people of his day, and that the interrelation of the two Testaments must be considered.[175] He further says that there are three kinds of messianic prophecy: direct prophecy, typical prophecy, and application.

Direct Prophecy

Direct prophecy is simple to understand. In this prophecy, the author looked directly to the messianic age, and the original hearers understood it that way.[176] For example, Micah 5:2 says, "But you, Bethlehem Ephrathah, though you are small among the clans of Judah, out of you will come for me one who will be ruler in Israel, whose origins are from of old, from ancient times." Matthew applied the text to Jesus's birth in Bethlehem, changing the text to say, "But you, Bethlehem, in the land of Judah, are *by no means least* among the rulers of Judah; for out of you will come a ruler who will be the shepherd of my people Israel" (Matt. 2:6). Nevertheless, both writer and reader understand it as a direct messianic prophecy.

Malachi 3:1 refers to the coming of the LORD's messenger who will prepare his way when he comes. It definitely referred to the coming of the LORD in the messianic age. In Malachi 4:5, he calls the messenger Elijah. Even though the gospel according to John records John the Baptist as denying that he was Elijah (John 1:21), Jesus identified him as the messenger to whom Malachi referred (Matt. 11:14).

The prophecy of Zechariah 9:9 regarding the king coming in humility mounted on an ass is portrayed by Matthew as being fulfilled by Jesus's entry into Jerusalem on Palm Sunday (Matt. 21:5).

Typical Prophecy

Sauer says that this type of prophecy has a "depth of profundity" because it has "an *immediate* meaning for their own day and an *ultimate* meaning that points toward the Messianic age."[177] The people understood

---

[175] *Ibid.*, 566.

[176] *Ibid.*, 567–568.

[177] *Ibid.*, 569.

it in terms of their time primarily but may have been able to see another meaning for the future.

Isaiah 40:3 says, "A voice of one calling: 'In the desert prepare the way for the LORD; make straight in the wilderness a highway for our God. Every valley shall be raised up, every mountain and hill made low; the rough ground shall become level, the rugged places a plain.'" But the Septuagint translates it as "a voice crying in the wilderness." The voice was Isaiah calling on the people of God to prepare the way for the LORD, who is coming to Babylon to lead his people home. When a monarch crossed through a country, it was considered important to make the highway smooth and level.[178] It was obviously meant for the people of that time to call the people to repentance. But Matthew uses the Septuagint version and sees it as a reference to John the Baptist, who was preparing the way for the messianic king (Matt. 3:1–3).

King Ahaz of Judah was concerned that Rezin of Syria and Pekah of Israel were going to attack him. As an assurance to Ahaz, Isaiah says (Isa. 7:14) that during the time of Ahaz, a "young woman" who is *already* pregnant will have a son, whom she will call Immanuel (a good Hebrew name for a boy). This is a sign that would guarantee that his enemies Rezin and Pekah would be defeated. The message was certainly meant for the age in which it was written.

But the Greek translation of the Old Testament, the Septuagint (LXX), translated the Hebrew word *alma* (young woman) with the Greek word *parthenos* (virgin). The prophecy of a virginal conception is based on the Greek translation.[179] Matthew uses the Greek word and sees the prophecy as applying to Jesus's birth to Mary (Matt. 1:22–23). So based on this text, the virgin birth of Jesus became an article of faith. Sauer considers this to be a typical prophecy. To me, it looks more like an obvious example of application.

Applications

Applications are texts of "perplexing obscurity" in that Old Testament passages are quoted as being fulfilled in the New Testament. But in the original Old Testament context, the text referred to something completely different, requiring a total recasting of the original. No contemporary of

---

[178]   *Ibid.*, 570.

[179]   Tucker, *op. cit.*, 112.

BIBLICAL INTERPRETATION FOR LAYPEOPLE AND OTHER MARTYRS   139

the original text would have understood the New Testament application. The author did not have anything long-range in mind, nor did the people understand it that way.

Referring to the destruction of the northern kingdom in 722 BCE, Jeremiah says that Rachel, considered the mother of the northern kingdom, was in mourning over her children and would not be comforted (Jer. 31:15–17). Herod the Great's killing of the male babies in Bethlehem is considered the fulfillment of the prophecy by Matthew, who recasts the original meaning in light of the New Testament massacre. The Old Testament hearers of Jeremiah's message understood it only as referring to the elimination of the Ten Lost Tribes of Israel and were completely unaware of the meaning Matthew 2:18 would later attribute to it.[180]

In Psalm 8, a creation hymn, the psalmist expresses amazement that God made the entire human race a little less than God, probably referring to their being created in the image of God. But Hebrews quotes the psalm from the Septuagint, which says man was created a little lower than the "angels" rather than "God." Also, the author of Hebrews interprets it to refer to Christ rather than human beings. Finally, he applies it to Christ's state of humiliation rather than humanity's rule over the creation.[181] Clearly application.

Hosea, referring to the Exodus of Israel from slavery in Egypt, says, "Out of Egypt I have called my son" (Hosea 11:1). From the context, it is clear that he is talking about God's delivering his people out of Egyptian slavery. But Matthew applies it to Joseph, Mary, and Jesus's return from Egypt to which they had fled to save Jesus's life from Herod's slaughter of the baby boys in Bethlehem (Matt. 2:13–15).

I find these distinctions helpful in understanding the New Testament messianic interpretations of Old Testament texts.

Typology

Typology may be considered a method of interpretation in which the interpreter finds a correspondence between an Old Testament phenomenon and a New Testament phenomenon. Although typology seems to be related

---

[180]   Sauer, *op. cit.,* 571.

[181]   *Ibid.,* 572.

to prophecy in some way, there is great difference of opinion regarding what typology is and in what way it is related to prophecy. Some believe it is somehow related to allegory. Others consider it related to prophecy. Sauer's analysis may give a hint to the transition. Childs says the bottom line is the issue of its soteriological (salvation) unity of the two Testaments (John 1:1–5, Col. 1:15–20, Heb. 1:2–3)[182] and that Jesus's message "transcended the particularity of Judaism and which summarized the essence to true religion."[183] In other words, it was for everyone.

New Testament as Interpretation of the Old Testament

For Christians, the New Testament writer is an interpreter of the Old Testament. The Christian interpreter's perspective colors the meaning of earlier revelation, recasting the words for the needs of his own time, thereby making it related to Sauer's application. For example, in Exodus 19:5–6, Israel is called a holy nation. In 1 Peter 2:9, the term "holy nation" is used to describe the Christian Church.

Typology and Prophecy

Typology seems to be, in some way, akin to prophecy[184] and may have developed out of it based on the assumption that there is a direct correspondence between the present and the past. Typology is definitely an interpretation. The Greek word *typos* has two basic meanings: It can mean "a pattern" or "that which is produced by the pattern" (product). So it can mean either the "original" or the "copy." In the New Testament, the Greek word *typos* is used in various ways. The term "type" is used in John 20:25 to refer to the "mark" or "print" of nails in Jesus's hand. In Acts 7:43, it refers to that which is formed, an image or statue of a god made by a man. In Romans 6:17, it is used for a "pattern" of teaching. In Acts 7:44 and Hebrews 8:6, it means "model" or "pattern." It is used as an "example" in several places (Phil. 3:17, 1 Thess. 1:7, 2 Thess. 3:9, 1 Tim. 4:12, Titus 2:7, 1 Pet. 5:3). In Acts 23:25, it is used as "content" of a letter.

---

[182] Childs, *op. cit.*, 14.

[183] *Ibid.*, 15.

[184] *Ibid.*, 13.

BIBLICAL INTERPRETATION FOR LAYPEOPLE AND OTHER MARTYRS   141

Typology in Interpretation

Typology, like beauty, is in the eye of the beholder. Use of typology assumes a "qualitative homogeneity" in God's revelation. But the contemporaries of the original *did not* recognize the event or person as typical. For them, it stood as God's revelation on its own. It was for *them* at that time. And when we interpret the Old Testament, we need to see it as directed first and foremost for the original hearers or readers. But according to Michelson, later generations "can see that God's earlier action became significant in his later action."[185] Yet unlike allegorizing, it is not something mysterious that was hidden in the text. It is considered by later generations as being clear.

Kinds of Types[186]

In the Bible, one finds several types—persons, events, deeds, actions, and things.

Types of Persons

Adam and Jesus. Paul finds a correspondence between Adam and Jesus. His argument is that just as Adam brought sin, judgment, and death to the world, righteousness and justice came through Jesus (Rom. 5:12–19). Adam was the natural human, whereas Jesus was the spiritual human (1 Cor. 15:45–49). Adam is representative of fallen humanity. Jesus is representative of a new redeemed humanity. Paul does not use the term "type" in 1 Corinthians, but he does in Romans 5:14.

Moses and Jesus. According to Deuteronomy, Yahweh will raise up a prophet like Moses and put his words in the prophet's mouth, and the prophet will speak all that God commands (Deut. 18:15–18). Without becoming very explicit, Matthew implies a correspondence between Moses and Jesus. Like Moses (Exod. 2:1–14), Jesus escaped the slaughter of Jewish children (Matt. 2:13–16). Just as Moses sojourned in the desert and was tempted for forty years (Deut. 29:5) and was on the mountain receiving the commandments for forty days (Exod. 24:18), Jesus was tempted in the desert for forty days (Matt. 4:1–11). As God gave the law through Moses

---

[185]   Much of this section comes from Michelson, 246–247.

[186]   I am heavily dependent on Michelson in this section.

(Exod. 20, Deut. 5), God gave Jesus to keep the law (Matt. 5:17). Jesus supersedes Moses in the "but I say to you" passages (Matt. 5:22; 28, 32, 34, 39, 44). People saw Jesus as a prophet. Jesus asked, "Who do men say I am?" One of the answers was "One of the prophets" (Matt. 16:14, Luke 9:19).

Elijah and John the Baptist. Malachi says that God will send his messenger before him, and the LORD will appear in his temple (Mal. 3:1, 4:5–6). Matthew sees a correspondence between the messenger and John the Baptist (Mal. 17:10–13).

Melchizedek and Jesus. God chose Aaron and his sons to be priests in Israel (Deut. 18:15). The author of Hebrews sees a correspondence between Jesus and the high priest. He sees Jesus as a high priest to make reconciliation for the sin of people (Heb. 2:17). But Jesus, who "passed through the heavens," was a greater high priest (Heb. 4:14). This high priest is "not a high priest who is unable to sympathize with our weaknesses, but one who in every respect has been tempted as we are, yet without sinning" (Heb. 4:15). Whereas Israel's priests made sacrifices continually and the high priest entered the Holy of Holies once every year on the Day of Atonement to make sacrifice for the people, Jesus entered "only once for all into the Holy Place, taking not the blood of goats and calves but his own blood, thus securing an eternal redemption" (Heb. 9:12; further developed in verses 13–29).

In Genesis, we find Abram meeting the mysterious person Melchizedek (Gen. 14:17–20, Ps. 110:4), priest-king of Salem (Jerusalem) and called priest of the Most High God, who brought bread and wine to Abram, blessed Abram (Gen. 14:18–20), and received a tenth of Abram's spoils from his defeat of the five kings. Hebrews quotes Psalm 110:4, contrasting the Levitical priesthood with Melchizedek (Heb. 7:1–10). He was more than a mere human. Melchizedek was "a Canaanite priest-king." Though as a believer in the true God, he was like the son of God.[187] And the author of Hebrews saw Jesus as a priest after the order of Melchizedek (Heb. 7:17–21).

Israel's Kings and Jesus. God promised to establish David's throne forever (2 Sam. 7:13, 2 Chron. 17:12, and many other places). Of course, that did not happen. The reign of David's descendants ended in 586 BCE, when Zedekiah was removed from the throne. The prophets carried on the hope of the return of the kingdom of Israel (Isa. 9:7, 11:1–5; Jer. 30:9, 33:17; Ezek. 34:23–24, 37:24–26; Amos 9:11). During the intertestamental period,

---

[187] Michelson, *op. cit.*, 250.

the hope of the return of the Davidic dynasty continued among some Jews. Although he was not of the Davidic bloodline, hope was stimulated when Aristobulus I (104–103 BCE) took the title of king. But others, such as the writer of the pseudepigraphical Psalms of Solomon, written in about the mid-first century BCE, complained that the Hasmonean family had usurped the monarchy and the Romans deposed them and prayed that a Davidic descendant would overthrow the foreign dominators (Ps. of Sol. 11:5–51).

When Jesus came, one of the expectations was that he would throw off Roman rule (Matt. 27:42, Mark 15:32, Luke 24:21). When Jesus entered Jerusalem on Palm Sunday, the people shouted, "Blessed is the king who comes in the name of the Lord!" (Luke 19:38). Mark also records them saying, "Blessed is the coming kingdom of our father David!" (Mark 11:10). Matthew recalls them saying, "Hosanna to the Son of David!" (Matt. 21:9), an obvious reference to the kingship. And John records them crying "Blessed is the King of Israel!" (John 12:13) and quotes this as a fulfillment of the prophecy: "Do not be afraid, O Daughter of Zion; see, your king is coming, seated on a donkey's colt" (Zech. 9:9). Pilate didn't ask Jesus if he was king of the Jews for nothing (Mark 15:2, Matt. 27:11). He had reason to be concerned.

Hagar and Sarah. Paul compares Hagar and Sarah (Gen. 16:1–16, 21:9–17, 25:12). For Paul, Hagar—the handmaiden of Abraham' wife, Sarah—represents the law, slavery, and the earthly Jerusalem. Sarah represents the gospel, freedom, and the Jerusalem above (Gal. 4:21–31).

Types of Events
The Passover and the Crucifixion. In the story of the Passover, blood of the paschal lamb (without blemish) was sprinkled on the doorposts of Israelite homes, which were passed over by the angel of death; and they were saved (Exod. 12:21–23). At the beginning of Jesus's ministry, John the Baptist proclaimed of Jesus, "Behold the lamb of God that takes away the sins of the world" (John 1:29). Paul referred to Jesus as the paschal lamb (1 Cor. 5:7). And Peter avers that "you were redeemed not with silver or gold, but with the precious blood [of Christ] as a lamb without spot or blemish" (1 Pet. 1:18–19). The author of Hebrews asserts the superiority of Christ's sacrifice (Heb. 9:1–10:18), for "by that [new covenant] we will have been sanctified through the offering of the body of Jesus Christ once for all" (Heb. 10:10).

The Exodus and Jesus's Escape to Egypt. In Israel's apostasy, God reminds them that he had called his son, Israel, out of Egypt, referring to the Exodus (Hosea 11:1). Matthew records Mary and Joseph escaping *to* Egypt to save Jesus's life, applying that text to their return with Jesus from Egypt (Matt. 2:15). Sometimes typology makes a long stretch to make a point.

Types of Actions

Lifting the Serpent and the Crucifixion. John sees a correspondence between the bronze serpent in Numbers and the Crucifixion. The book of Numbers has a story about God sending "fiery" serpents into Israel's camp because of their grumbling. God had Moses construct a bronze serpent and put it on a pole so that when they were bitten, they could look at it, trusting in God's promise, and live (Num. 21:4–9). In John's gospel, Jesus says, "As Moses lifted up the serpent in the wilderness, so must the Son of Man be lifted up, that whoever believes in him will have eternal life" (John 3:14–15). Just like in Numbers, as Jesus was lifted up on the cross, there was life for those who looked on, trusting God's promise.

Jonah's Entrapment and Jesus's Entrapment. Jonah was called to proclaim the Word of the LORD to Nineveh. Instead, he tried to avoid his mission by taking a Mediterranean cruise in the other direction (probably heading for the French Riviera). Therefore, God sent a storm. To quell the storm, Jonah was thrown overboard and swallowed by large fish. He was in the belly of the fish for three days and three nights (Jon. 1:17). So when obstinate scribes and Pharisees asked for a sign from Jesus to prove who he was, he said, "An evil and adulterous generation seeks for a sign; but no sign shall be given to it except the sign of the prophet Jonah. For as Jonah was three days and three nights in the belly of the whale, so will the Son of man be three days and three nights in the heart of the earth. The men of Nineveh will arise at the judgment with this generation and condemn it; for they repented at the preaching of Jonah, and behold, something greater than Jonah is here" (Matt. 12:39–41).

BIBLICAL INTERPRETATION FOR LAYPEOPLE AND OTHER MARTYRS 145

Types of Things

The People of Israel Compared to the Church. In the New Testament, a correspondence is found between Israel and the church. As Israel was God's people in the Old Testament, so the church is God's people in the New Testament (Acts 15:14; Rom. 9:25–26; 1 Pet. 2:9–10; Heb. 4:9, 13:12; Rev. 18:4, 21:3). As Israel was the true ethnic people of God, so the church is the true nonethnic people of God (Gal. 6:16, 1 Cor. 10:18, Rom. 9:6), the true "seed of Abraham (Gal. 3:29, Rom. 9:7–8), the true circumcision (i.e., Jews) (Phil. 3:3).

The Grief of the Northern Tribes Is Compared to the Grief of the Mothers in Bethlehem. God will turn the sorrow of Rachel, pictured as the mother of the northern tribes, from weeping over the slaughter of her children to joy (Jer. 31:15). Matthew takes this statement and turns it to Rachel *refusing* to be comforted, applying it to the women of Bethlehem who lost their children in Herod's slaughter of the baby boys in Bethlehem (Matt. 2:17–28). Whereas Sauer sees this as "typical prophecy," Michelson sees it as "typology." I'm inclined to agree with Michelson. Perhaps there is no difference between the two.

Michelson says that typology works because God is "a God who builds upon what he has said and done before."[188] While I would not argue with his point, I would add that typology is a way of thinking, is in the eye of the beholder, and is used for illustration purposes.

---

[188] *Ibid.*, 240.

Chapter 9

SYMBOLISM AND APOCALYPTIC LITERATURE

Symbolism

A symbol is a sign that *suggests* meaning rather than stating it directly. Symbols are everywhere. When we see a swastika, we immediately think of Nazis. When we see a *V* superimposed on the middle of a *W*, we think of a Volkswagen. When we see a swoosh, we think of Nike. But the symbol brings to mind not only the *thing* represented by the symbol, but also the *emotion* that the thing or idea elicits. For example, the symbol that we call a swastika elicits great emotional reactions, especially among Jews. The Confederate flag elicits emotions to black people because it is a symbol of their slavery and the thousands of deaths to preserve it.

However, just because the swastika meant Nazism in Europe, Nazism is not its inherent meaning. Some Native Americans of the Southwest had the same symbol hundreds of years before Nazism. "KKK" can mean "Ku Klux Klan" for many people. For others, it is the name of the Kappa Kappa Kappa fraternity.

Symbols can also change meaning. In Jesus's day, the cross was a symbol of capital punishment and degradation. But the meaning, or

146

connotation, has changed for that symbol. In our day, for Christians, the cross has become a symbol of pride. So symbols have no inherent meaning. The Greek uppercase letter omega (Ω) means an ohm (unit of resistance) in electricity for the electrician. During the late 1960s and early 1970s, it was used as a symbol of resistance to the establishment. The theta (θ) in trigonometry has a meaning that is different from the meaning of the Greek letter during the 1960s and 1970s, when it was used to symbolize death (*thanatos*, which is Greek for "death").

In general, a symbol is something that, by conventional agreement, represents something else. A symbol is a sign that *suggests* meaning rather than stating it clearly and *may* hide the meaning from those for whom the message is not meant. Fraternities, secret organizations, and gangs have secret handshakes, languages, and signs that they use to communicate to one another. Because of this, one must be careful in interpreting symbols. In fact, not all symbols are conventional. In Ezekiel, the prophet is instructed to lie on his left side for a certain period of time and on his right side for a certain period of time to express Judah's captivity, which would be limited to that particular situation (Ezek. 4:4–8).

Principles for Interpreting Symbols

In the interpreting of symbols, one needs to understand the qualities of the literal object. If the symbol is a lion, an eagle, a lamb, or a lamp, what is the quality of a lion or lamp that makes it a good symbol?

Kinds of Symbols

Symbols are arbitrarily chosen either by an individual or within a culture. A symbol is a literal entity that is used to convey some lesson or truth. The idea to be conveyed by a person who uses the object is determined by the connection between the literal object and the meaning of the symbol.

Word as Symbol
The basic symbols used by human beings are words. Words make us human. They bridge the chasm between our individual loneliness and

enable us to be part of one another's lives.[189] But there is no inherent meaning in the configuration of sound vibrations or ink on a page. Their meaning is culturally defined. The word "gut" has no inherent meaning. The same lettering occurs in English and German. In German, it is pronounced "goot" and means "good," whereas in English, it is pronounced "guht" and means "the intestines" or the abdominal area. (Boy, can you have fun with that!) Dan Houston, my friend in high school German class, would invariably say "guht." Our teacher would also invariably respond, "Mein Himmel, Herr Houston! Das ist nicht 'guht,' aber 'gut.'" Boy, could Dan blush? (rhetorical question).

Picture or Design Symbols

When certain pictures or designs are seen, they communicate something specific to people; and with it, certain emotional responses are attached. When one sees a multicolored apple with a bite in its upper right hand side, only Forrest Gump thinks of it as fruit. The rest of us think of computers.

In the early post–New Testament church, the cross became a symbol of Christianity. But perhaps an even earlier symbol was the "fish." The first letters of the Greek words Ιησους Χριστους Θεου ʽΥιους Σωτηρ (Iēsous Christous Theou Huious Sōter), which in English means "Jesus Christ God's Son Savior," spells ΙΧΘΥΣ, the word "fish" in Greek. In the early church, a fish, with or without the letters, became both a symbol and confession of the early church. By drawing that simple symbol, during times of persecution, one Christian could communicate with another without others realizing they were both Christians.

Symbolic Numbers

Numbers also have special meanings for certain groups of people. The Fab Four, "the terrible twos," the Forty-Niners, "unlucky 13," "7 come 11," "lucky 7," "a 110 percent" (a sports commentator's hyperbole)—all these numbers mean something to most people in our culture. But for sports fans, 11, 9, and 5 have sports teams meaning.

---

[189] Marty, Martin. *The Hidden Discipline* (St. Louis: Concordia Publishing House, 1962), 6.

The Jewish people loved to use numbers with symbolic meaning. The number 4 referred to the four winds (Jer. 49:36; Ezek. 37:9; Dan. 7:2, 8:8; Zech. 2:6; Rev. 7:1) and the four corners of the earth (Isa. 11:12, Ezek. 7:2, Rev. 7:1). Now even though we know that there are an infinite number of directions from which the winds come, we still use the terminology to mean "winds from every direction." And although we know the earth is round, we still use the expression "four corners of the earth" to mean "everywhere."

In Revelation 1:4, the seven spirits may refer to Isaiah 11:1–2: "A shoot will come up from the stump of Jesse; from his roots a Branch will bear fruit. The Spirit of the LORD will rest on him—the spirit of wisdom and of understanding, the spirit of council and power, the spirit of knowledge and of the fear of the LORD—and he will delight in the fear of the LORD."

Revelation 7:4 says, "Then I heard the number of those who were sealed: 144,000 from all the tribes of Israel." The number 12 is the number of the people of God. It began with the twelve tribes of Israel. Squaring a number or multiplying the number by ten intensified the number. Jesus chose twelve disciples as his nucleus followers. And when Judas abdicated, the followers of Jesus chose Matthias to take his place because Peter said it was necessary to do so (Acts 1:1–26). We will see it multiple times in Revelation.

Symbolic Actions

In Austin, Texas, where I grew up, the index and pinky fingers held in the air with the middle and ring fingers held down with the thumb is virtually a sacred symbol. It is the symbol of the Texas Longhorns. If you cut in front of another driver on the road, he may honor you with a symbolic action involving the extension of only one finger. We clap when we want to express congratulations. We smile to show approval. We wave to say goodbye or hello. A thumb up means affirmation or "Way to go!" The hand held in front with the palm perpendicular means "stop." To show disapproval, Americans boo, and Mexicans whistle. An entire language for the deaf (American Sign Language) is based on actions that communicate.

In the Bible, sitting in sackcloth and ashes was a symbol of sorrow (Isa. 58:5, Esther 4:1, Dan. 9:3). Tearing the clothes was another way of expressing grief or distress (Mark 14:63).

Symbolic Colors

In our culture, yellow is a symbol for cowardice, blue is the color of faithfulness, white is the color of purity, and green for envy or ecological issues. White was the symbol of purity in the Bible also (Rev. 7:9). In scriptural times, purple was a color symbolizing royalty. Red was a symbol for blood or fire.

Symbolic Things

Apocalyptic Literature

Apocalypsis is the Greek word for "uncovering" or "revealing." It is a type of literature that usually grows out of the unique situation of persecution, drawing heavily on symbolism, hiding its meaning from those from whom it is to be hidden, and revealing to those to whom it is to be revealed. Parts of Ezekiel and most of Revelation are apocalyptic. But it is not a genre of literature that was limited to the Bible. It was used by other Near Eastern cultures and by the Hebrews in the intertestamental period as well.

Apocalypsis has come to be identified with a specific type of literature that claimed a special revelation by God.[190] It may have developed out of prophecy in the Old Testament but became widely used in the Hellenistic period. In the Old Testament, it is used in Daniel as well as in parts of Isaiah, Ezekiel, and Zechariah. It is also used in the apocryphal books of IV Ezra, II Baruch, and I Enoch. A considerable amount is also recorded in the Nag Hammadi library in Egypt. Most of it was written from the second century BCE into the fourth century CE.[191]

Characteristics of Apocalyptic Literature

The basic characteristics of apocalyptic literature, according to Michelson,[192] are as follows:

---

[190]   cf. Childs, *op. cit.*, ch. 3, XII.

[191]   *Ibid.*, 318.

[192]   *Op. cit.*

BIBLICAL INTERPRETATION FOR LAYPEOPLE AND OTHER MARTYRS   151

Professedly Revelatory

The prophets often made the claim that "the LORD appeared to me" (Deut. 8:1). In whatever way it is portrayed, the prophet made the claim that his words came directly from God.

Visions

Hundreds of examples of visions are recorded in scripture: Abraham concerning his descendants (Gen. 15:1–7), Jacob's ladder (Gen. 28), Moses's burning bush (Exod. 3:2), Elisha seeing Elijah translated to heaven (2 Kings 2:11), Ezekiel's valley of the dry bones (Ezek. 37:1–14), Daniel's visions of the four beasts (Dan. 7) and of the Ancient of Days (Dan. 7:9–27), the angel's promise to Zechariah of the birth of John the Baptist (Luke 1:13–22), Paul on the road to Damascus (Acts 9:3–6) and the call of the man from Macedonia (Acts 16:9), Peter and the sheet of unclean animals (Acts 10:9–18), and dozens of visions by John on the isle of Patmos (Revelation).

Dreams

There are also many examples of revelations coming through dreams. The LORD appeared to Solomon and promised him glory (1 Kings 3:5–15). Joseph's dream was interpreted to mean that his brothers and parents would bow down to him (Gen. 37:5–11). But even nonprophets had dreams. Abimelech had a dream warning him to stay away from Sarah because she was Abraham's wife (Gen. 20:3). The charlatan Laban had one telling him that he not verbally attack Jacob (Gen. 31:24). Joseph had a dream concerning Mary's innocence (Matt. 1:20–21) and another one warning him to flee to Egypt (Matt. 2:13) and to return into Palestine (Matt. 2:19–22).

There were also dreams by non-Israelites, Jews, or Christians that are interpreted by God's people. The Babylonian king Nebuchadnezzar had a dream, interpreted by Daniel, that was fulfilled (Dan. 4:4–37). The dreams of Pharaoh and those of his cupbearer and baker that Joseph interpreted (Gen. 40:1–23) as portending prosperity were followed by a devastating famine (Gen. 41:1–32). A man's dream about a cake of barley bread rolling down the hill into the Midianite camp was regarded as a sign of Gideon's victory (Judg. 7:13).[193]

---

[193]   See also Dan. 2:16–23. 28–30.

152   DAVID W. MELBER

On the other hand, Jeremiah had disdain for prophets who said they had a dream and proclaimed it to the people. He contrasted their dreams from true prophecy as the difference between wheat and straw (Jer. 23:25–32).[194] But he didn't opine whether they were charlatans or just self-deluded. And the similitude in Isaiah 29:7–8 definitely referred to those who attacked Israel thinking they would defeat the city; they were deluded like a hungry person dreaming of eating only to wake up disappointed.

According to Deuteronomy, if a prophet or interpreter of dreams tries to lead Israel away from Yahweh to another god, even if he performs a "sign" or "wonder," he is to be executed (Deut. 13:1–5). There is no suggestion of concern for the person's intent either, whether he is devious or deluded.

Some of these passages remind us of the mean-spirited, vitriolic pronouncements of public "Christian" leaders who make pronouncements regarding who are being punished when an earthquake or hurricane hits an area, killing innocent children, as well as adults the pronouncement is against.

Often Imitative of Earlier Writing

Visionary experience was often "plagiarism" in Western understanding. In the book of Revelation, apocalyptic imagery of Ezekiel, Daniel, and Zechariah is used most. The rebellious nations of Psalm 2 (Rev. 2:27), the cosmic chaos of Joel 2 (Rev. 6:12), and the new heavens and earth of Isaiah 66 (Rev. 21:1) are examples.[195]

Often Pseudonymous

Apocalyptic literature is often attributed to an important person who may have lived hundreds of years before. The writers were not necessarily being deceitful. They may have believed they were portraying the teaching of the famous person.[196]

Predictive or Pseudopredictive

Although it claims to predict events, apocalyptic literature is often written ex post facto and claims to be predictive. The more precisely accurate it is, the less likely it is to have actually been predictive of future events. For example, if it predicts the exact name of someone who is going

---

[194]   Also, Jer. 27:9, 29:8; Zech. 10:2.

[195]   Childs, *op. cit.*, 321.

[196]   *The Nag Hammadi Library in English (op. cit.)* has many examples, like the Gospel of Thomas.

BIBLICAL INTERPRETATION FOR LAYPEOPLE AND OTHER MARTYRS   153

to do something a century or two in the future, you can be certain it was
written ex post facto.

Evil Is Often Personified

Figures such as Beliar, Korah, the Antichrist, Satan, the devil, and
the "man of perdition"[197] are personifications of evil and considered the
perpetrators of evil.

Outlook of Apocalyptic Literature

Apocalyptic literature has a fairly specific outlook toward life. It is the
following:

> ***Dualistic.*** Apocalyptic literature portrays the present world
> order versus the world to come. The strife is between the forces
> of good and the forces of evil, making conflict inevitable. There
> is no reconciling, no compromising, no gray areas, no middle
> ground, and no conversion expected with the evil.

> ***Deterministic.*** The future is in God's hands in such a way
> that nothing can change it. Apocalyptic literature is usually
> written to people who are suffering under persecution. It gives
> assurance that despite how things look, God has everything
> under control.

> ***Pessimistic.*** Most of it came out of a time of chaos and
> persecution. The righteous are *bound* to suffer at the hands of
> an evil world. Before the culmination of history, evil will be
> unchecked, and God's faithful people will endure persecution.

> ***Ethically Passive.*** There is no need for God's people to fight
> it because the evil world will not change. But signs of the times
> are encouragements to the suffering community of believers.
> Despite the fact that "desecration reaches its fanatical climax,"

---

[197]   Childs, *op. cit.*, 318–21.

154   DAVID W. MELBER

God will intervene with final judgment, vindicating his saints
and punishing their persecutors.[198]

Apocalyptic Literature in the Bible

There are small apocalypses in Mark 13, Matthew 24 and 25, and
Luke 21. Mark uses Daniel 13 as its basis. Jesus predicts that many will
come in his name, saying "I am *He*," and will lead many astray. He
predicts tribulations such as wars, rumors of war, famines, and cosmic
catastrophes such as earthquakes. The disciples will be persecuted and
dragged into courts and synagogues. Of course, all these things have
already occurred. The gospel will be proclaimed to all nations. This has
probably also already happened. There will be familial chaos. But they
needn't be frightened, for these are signs of the end of time. The great
suffering ushers in the "abomination of desolation" (Dan. 9:27). The sun
and moon will be darkened, and the heavens will be shaken when the
Son of Man descends from the clouds to gather the elect and to judge the
wicked (Dan. 7:9–14).

Because of the way it is written, Daniel can be interpreted by later
generations in response to discouragement during their suffering (Mark
13:30). Apocalyptic literature is meant to encourage Christians who are
being persecuted and can be used to encourage them to be faithful until
their death. But it is also easily used to manipulate the gullible. It has been
abused by many, including Hal Lindsey in his popular book in the early
1970s, *The Late Great Planet Earth*. I can't tell you how many confused,
stressed-out students came to me after having read that book, which
incidentally has long since been proven false.

In 2 Thessalonians, the coming "day of the Lord" will be followed by
rebellion and the coming of the "man of lawlessness" (2 Thess. 2:3) who
tries to deceive God's people with false signs and miracles. In the letters of
2 Peter and Jude, the major concern "is to identify the threat of heresy and
to guard the community against these ungodly persons."[199]

---

[198]   *Ibid.*, 318.

[199]   *Ibid.*, 320.

Apocalyptic literature does not lie in the future but is reinterpreted as completed action. God rules now as well as in the kingdom to come (Rev. 7:10, 11:15, 19:6). Satan is already defeated by the Lamb and has already been cast out of heaven. Apocalyptic literature focuses on the church's continuous struggle with evil, false prophets, and oppression, calling for faithfulness and endurance to death (Rev. 2:10).[200]

---

[200] *Ibid.*, 321.

Chapter 10

THE CANON OF SCRIPTURE

Introduction

But what is the Bible, and how did the Bible come about? In 2 Timothy
3:15–17, Paul says, "All Scripture is given by inspiration of God." What is
he talking about? Quite often, this is used as a proof text that the entire
Protestant Bible as we have it is inspired by God. However, that is not
what Paul was referring to. He certainly was not talking about the New
Testament. He was referring to the writings that Jews of his time considered
authoritative, which may have also included the Apocrypha—perhaps
even certain writings called the pseudepigrapha.[201]

---

[201] The Biblical Apocrypha (from the Greek word ἀπόκρυφος, *apókruphos*, meaning
"hidden") refers to the collection of ancient books found in some Bibles. Jerome,
in the early fifth century, distinguished between the Hebrew and Greek Old
Testaments, stating that books not found in the Hebrew were not canonical.
They were called deuterocanonical (secondary biblical) by Roman Catholics
and *anagignoskomena* (ἀναγιγνωσκόμενα, or "worthy to be read") by the Eastern
Orthodox. Jerome's Latin Vulgate translation in 405 CE, which did include the
Apocrypha, became the authoritative Bible in the Western church. His prologues
to the books identified some as apocryphal or noncanonical. Martin Luther (ca.

156

BIBLICAL INTERPRETATION FOR LAYPEOPLE AND OTHER MARTYRS   157

Well, let's take a look at how the biblical canon developed, how it was accepted, and why it was accepted. Christians believe it came from God. But it came to us in a cause-effect world. It came through a process we understand, including political conflict.

The Development of Writing

Before the writings of the Old Testament scripture came to us, they had to be written down. In order to be written down, there must be writing. So far, so good. But how and why was writing invented? Did Fred Flintstone one day sit down and say, "I think today I'll invent writing"? No! Plato said that necessity is the mother of invention.[202] Well, necessity is the mother of the invention of writing.

Before Writing

Writing develops under specific social circumstances. The earliest and simplest social structure is the hunting and gathering society. They are generally quite egalitarian. Economic activity involves finding food. Their social structure is built around that activity. The next level is usually either horticultural and/or nomadic herding. Horticultural societies involve seminomadic farming, often involving slash-and-burn procedures. Natural vegetation is cut down and burned, providing nutrients for the soil. Holes are dug with a sharp stick, and seeds are put in individual holes. When the crop is harvested, the tribe moves to another location to repeat the same procedure. Their social structure is primarily based on that economic activity.

1534) accepted only the books in the Hebrew Bible as canonical, but he accepted the Apocrypha as being worthy of study, including them in between the two Testaments in the German translation. The Council of Trent (April 8, 1546) accepted them as canonical. The English King James Version (KJV) of 1611 followed Luther's distinctions. Generally speaking, a pseudepigraphon is a book claiming to be written by an authority figure who did not write it. They will be discussed later.

[202]   *The Republic*, Book II, 369c, p. 63in www.gutenberg.net, Release Date: May 22, 2008 [EBook #150], Benjamin Jowett (Tr.).

Herding societies do approximately the same thing with animals. They have domesticated animals and move them from one grazing ground to another as grass runs out. Their social structure is built around that economic activity. There is more stability in these last two types of societies with regard to providing food for the tribe. As long as there is grass and water available, the food supply is usually plentiful and stable. Economic life is still simple with little specialization, and there is no need for writing.

During the Neolithic Revolution, about 6000–8000 BCE, people began to migrate out of the mountains into Mesopotamia (the Tigris and Euphrates river valley), where agriculture began about 5000 BCE. Agriculture is a more settled economic activity.

Although Abram grew up in an agricultural society, his family were nomadic herders. His father, Terah, moved his family from Ur of the Chaldees (in what is now Iraq) (Gen. 11:31) on or near the coast of the Persian Gulf, probably around 1900 or 1800 BC. They moved their flocks and herds north to Haran (in what is now Syria). It is from there, after his father died, that Abram (by then called Abraham) migrated to Canaan (in what is now Israel and Palestine) (Gen. 12:1–6).

The Development of Writing

Prior to writing, information and traditions passed orally from generation to generation, including "sacred stories about gods and heroes, tales of the cosmos, wisdom about human behavior, nature, and the miraculous. . . . Leadership roles, systems of kin, social structures, and accepted behavior patterns were transmitted through these stories."[203]

However, things began to change radically with the development of agriculture. Agriculture had begun along the Tigris and Euphrates Rivers about 5000 BCE. Agricultural societies, unlike horticultural societies, involve the farming of larger tracts of land and remaining in one place. Planting is done by "broadcasting." A natural outcome of permanently living in one place is the building of permanent dwellings and the idea of ownership of land. Since surpluses of food are produced, not everyone is needed in food production. Nor is work to produce food required all year. It can be stored. Specialization develops because the farmers can provide food for others who provide special services to them, such as the making

---

[203] McKim, *op. cit.*, 126.

BIBLICAL INTERPRETATION FOR LAYPEOPLE AND OTHER MARTYRS   159

of weapons, tools, pottery, shoes, and clothing, as well as keeping them connected with the gods.

It is also at that point, when large surpluses exist, that the need for recordkeeping ensues. A number system develops to keep accurate records of surpluses and transfers of items in trade. At first, when surpluses are small, records are simple. Recording of numbers begins with simple lines to record numbers. As numbers get larger, someone makes it easier to see amounts by grouping. Others built on that laziness. Farmers and merchants agreed, so an individual (or committee) [204] is appointed to work on a truly efficient system. Therefore, symbols are designated for larger numbers. For example, the Romans developed groupings, designated by V (5), X (10), C (100), D (500), and M (1,000).

A system of designating symbols to represent grain and/or animals is developed to designate what is being counted. These symbols become written picture language. At the beginning, there are usually symbols that represent specific things, such as sheep and cattle. But being the lazy individuals they are, human beings figure out ways to shorten their workload so they can spend more quality time with the wives and kids or blowing their recently purchased goats at the camel races. So they develop shorthand.

Later, some of these symbols are developed to represent sounds, and the language becomes phonetic (based on syllables for sound) rather than glyphic (pictures of things and concepts). In Hebrew, aleph (א), which means "ox," comes to symbolize the sound "ah"; and beth (ב), meaning "house," comes to symbolize the sound "b."

And it is much handier to have a central place for craftsmen and merchants to bring their goods to trade. Permanent structures are the next natural step. As disputes erupt between traders, people are chosen to settle disputes. And if the toughest, meanest guy around refuses to honor the decision of the judge, people are needed to enforce the decision. But if farmer Nahor wants to buy shoes for the family, pottery for storing water so his wife doesn't have to make so many trips to the well, or a newfangled wheeled cart because he doesn't want to walk all over creation—MM cubits to one merchant, ML cubits to another, and MMLC cubits to

---

[204] Committees must have existed at that time. The reason we know that is clear. Someone has observed that a camel is a horse designed by a committee. And camels existed in Mesopotamia and Egypt at that time.

another. He wants the convenience of having them close together. Markets develop so that shopping can be convenient.

Entrepreneurs learn this quickly and find they can have higher-volume sales and have more contented customers by agreeing to have all the merchants gathering in a centralized place—the Oasis of the Ten Date Palms. A village begins to develop. As disputes need to be settled, defense from raiders is needed, and services are demanded, a city government begins to evolve. A military comes into being. In previous types of societies, fighting occurred, but it was done by members of the family or tribe. However, agricultural societies developed special groups of people who died to protect the belongings of the rich farmers and the evolving merchant class. But there has to be incentive to risk one's life to protect someone else's wealth. Therefore, looting is allowed—as well as the taking advantage of all the conquered people's young women. The religion makes it a saintly thing to die for the country and justify the bad behavior of soldiers. Writing is also required to keep records in the military and pass messages between the military personnel.

Writing in the Near East

Writing was very expensive and was used by the rich or the priests, who were supported by the government. Writing was known throughout the area by 3100 BCE[205] in southern Mesopotamia long before Abram left Ur. The early writing was pictographic. It evolved into the cuneiform script of the Sumerians.

Development of Hebrew Writing

Since writing was expensive, families that didn't have flocks or herds numbering in the hundreds probably had no need to learn to write or hire anyone who could. Their stories and traditions were handed down orally from generation to generation and repeated so often that they were memorized. It is unlikely, therefore, that the patriarchs did any writing. Much of the Old Testament was originally progressively developed over hundreds or thousands of years, passed on orally from parents to children.

---

[205]   D. J. Wiseman. "writing," *The New Bible Dictionary*. J. D. Douglas, Organizing Ed. (Grand Rapids: Wm. B. Eerdmans Publishing Co.), 1341.

BIBLICAL INTERPRETATION FOR LAYPEOPLE AND OTHER MARTYRS   161

As writing came to be used in the Hebrew culture, written traditions were progressively assembled.

Early Hints

During the time before the Exodus, it is likely that along with their herding, the Israelites practiced some agriculture in the land of Goshen, located in the northeastern Nile Delta. Assuming that an exodus occurred under an educated man named Moses, he may have learned to write Egyptian hieroglyphics, proto-Canaanite, and the cuneiform of the Mesopotamian world. Therefore, Moses would have been able to record case law as major decisions were made. When Israel settled in Canaan and established agriculture, records may have been kept, although oral tradition was still the main way of transmitting cultural information. According to Exodus, Moses wrote the law code (Exod. 24:3–8), which the priests carried in the Ark of the Covenant (Deut. 31:9ff.). If so, he obviously did not write it all. Joshua wrote down the words of the covenant on stone (Josh. 8:31–32, 24:25–26). By the time of the Judges, traditions began to be written down (Josh. 8:32–34, 24:25–26). Samuel wrote down the rights and duties of a king (1 Sam. 10:25)—a constitution.

Kingdoms Need Records

Kingdoms usually emerge as agricultural societies develop. Those who have land want to keep others from taking it from them, so they hire people to protect it for them. Armies are formed. Warriors are fed from the surplus food produced. Other economic specialization occurs as well. Local feuding over lands becomes destructive. Rich land owners realize that the petty wars destroy crops, preventing them from producing food and accumulating wealth. A "social contract" is made with someone to keep the peace, thus protecting their interests. A king is chosen for this purpose. With kings come taxes, armies, bureaucracies, and recordkeeping. Writing becomes an ongoing need.

The beginning of bureaucracy is recorded during David's administration. Joab was head of the joint chiefs of staff, Jehoshaphat was recorder, Seraiah was secretary, and David's sons were chief ministers (2 Sam. 8:16–18). One needs to keep records of who is available to tax in order to pay that growing bureaucracy and the military and maintaining the

162   DAVID W. MELBER

king in a lifestyle he believes is appropriate for a king. Besides, if he wants to go to war, he needs to know what human cannon fodder is available. So he takes a census. David's census (2 Sam. 24:1–9) required extensive records.

But it was during Solomon's reign that constant, extensive recordkeeping was required. He established a marriage alliance with the Egyptian Pharaoh (1 Kings 3:1) and had seven hundred other wives, virtually all probably representing treaty relationships (1 Kings 11:3). All of this required a greatly expanded bureaucracy (1 Kings 4:1–19), treaties, and recordkeeping. Solomon had no computer, so the accumulation of funds was so lavish that they gave up on keeping records (1 Kings 7:1–47), a formula for corruption.

Nation building requires records of holdings, decisions, and treaties. Such writings did occur as witnessed by references in Exodus through Deuteronomy. In Numbers, we learn that there was a record called the "book of the wars of the LORD" (Num. 21:14). Joshua refers to the book of Jasher (Josh. 10:13). Samuel wrote ordinances of the kingdom in the book (1 Sam. 10:25). The acts of David were written in "the Chronicles of Samuel the seer, of Nathan the prophet, and of Gad the seer" (1 Chr. 29:29). The acts of Solomon and the records of Nathan were recorded in the prophecy of Ahijah the Shilonite and in visions of Iddo the seer concerning Jeroboam, the son of Nebat (2 Chron. 9:29). Solomon's activities were "written in the book of the acts of Solomon" (1 Kings 11:41). Acts of Rehoboam were written in the records of Shamaiah the prophet and of Iddo the seer (2 Chron. 12:15). In 1 Kings the "book of the Chronicles of the Kings of Israel" (1 Kings 14:19) and the "books of the Chronicles of the Kings of Judah" (1 Kings 15:7) are referred to.

Writing of the Prophets

The knowledge revolution exploded under the influence of writing. It began with government and religion, but later, others made use of writing. A number of the prophets put their thoughts to "paper." The first prophets we know about were not writing prophets. They spoke the word, perhaps not thinking that what they had to say would be relevant to future generations. But later, their words were recorded (1 King 17–22). Finally, prophets began to write down their own words. Some of the prophets not only wrote but dated their writing (Isa. 1:1; 6:1; Jer. 1:2–3, 24:1; Hosea 1:1; Amos 1:1). Isaiah even says the LORD gave directions regarding *what* to write: "Then the LORD said to me, 'Take for yourself a large tablet and

BIBLICAL INTERPRETATION FOR LAYPEOPLE AND OTHER MARTYRS   163

write on it in ordinary letters" (Isa. 8:1). Now one might wonder *how* "God said." Was it in a dream, a trance, or insight? Some indicate that the word came in a dream, trance, or vision (Isa. 1:1, Dan. 1:17, Obad. 1, Nah. 1:1, Hab. 2:2). But for others, it was probably insight.

Jeremiah had a secretary named Baruch (Jer. 32:12–16, 36, 43:1–6, 45:1–2). Jeremiah sent a letter to exiles in Babylon as prophecy (Jer. 29:1). Jeremiah's scroll was read in the temple (Jer. 36:1ff.). King Jehoiakim didn't like the contents, so he had it burned (Jer. 36:20ff.). Jeremiah "spoke" (Jer. 50:1), but it was recorded in the book bearing his name.

Biblical Languages

Hebrew

Most of the Old Testament was written in Hebrew. Hebrew is a language related to Ugarit, Phoenician, and Moabite. Although it had been the language of Israel long before, the designation for the language first occurred in Ben Sira (ca. 130 BCE). The script descends from Phoenician script. It is written from right to left and was originally a consonantal language. That is, there were no vowels. Let's illustrate the difficulty in English. If you were to read the sentence, "Thr r tn cts n th hs," if you added vowels, it could have several meanings. It could be the following: There are ten cats in the house. There are ten cots in the house. There are ten cuts in the hose. Or the first word would be "three." The second word could be "or." The fifth word could be "on" or "no." The last word could be "hour," "his," "has," "hose," and perhaps others. One must use the immediate context of the words definitely known in order to determine the meaning of the words that are not certain. But a couple of symbols were added to make vowel sounds. In the 800s CE, systems of vocalization were attempted.

Aramaic

Although very little of the Bible is written in Aramaic, it is quite important because it was the international language of economics and diplomacy during much of the Old Testament times and was the language of the Jews during Jesus's time. Aramaeans were a seminomadic

164   DAVID W. MELBER

Semitic-speaking people who immigrated into Syria and Mesopotamia
from the area of Arabia in the third millennium BCE.[206] Abraham is
referred to as a "wandering Aramaean" (Deut. 26:5).

After the ninth century BCE, Aramaic became the international
language. In the time of Sennacherib (705–681 BCE), Aramaic was a
diplomatic language. In 701 BCE, when Sennacherib's Assyrian army
surrounded Jerusalem, Hezekiah's officers requested that the Assyrians
address them in Aramaic rather than Hebrew so the citizens couldn't
understand the threats the Assyrians were making (2 Kings 18:26).
Aramaic is a close cognate of Hebrew (Dan. 2:4–7, 28; Ezra 4:8–4, 18;
7:12–26; Jer. 10:11).[207]

Greek

The New Testament was written in *koine*, or "common" Greek. Because
of the conquests of Alexander the Great, it became the international
language of the Mediterranean world in the time that the New Testament
was written. The New Testament writings, although all written in Koine
Greek, betray a wide variety of abilities to write in Greek.[208] Because Greek
was such an international language, wherever Paul traveled throughout the
Roman Empire, people may not have known Latin, the native language of
the Romans; but he could understand the message of the gospel in Greek.

Old Testament Jewish Interpretation

Preservation of the Canon

Some of the stories in Genesis are about things that occurred before the
development of writing and were transmitted orally, perhaps a response to
a question asked by a child. Over the years, as the story became popular,
it was passed on to future generations as later storytellers added to or
dropped out parts. At some point, someone wrote the story down. The
stories were finally gathered together and passed on to future generations.

---

[206] K. A. Kitchen. "Aramaic," *The New Bible Dictionary*, 56.

[207] W. J. Martin. "Writing," *The New Bible Dictionary*, 712.

[208] *Ibid.*, 715–716.

BIBLICAL INTERPRETATION FOR LAYPEOPLE AND OTHER MARTYRS   165

Moses

The early chapters of Genesis are attempts to explain phenomena such as how the world came into being (Gen. 1–2). Genesis 1 focuses on the creation of the world. Although attempting to explain the creation, another story in Genesis 2–3 focuses on explaining why people are mean to one another, why people have to work so hard, why men are in charge, and why women must suffer in childbirth. It may have also addressed the question of the alienation between people and snakes. It may have even addressed the question of why people wear clothes. Chapter 4 explains just how far sin can go—to the murder of a brother. Chapters 4 and 5 also attempt to explain the development of such things as music, technology, and cities. It ends by asserting that "at that time men began to call on the name of the LORD (Yahweh)" (Gen. 4:26). It provides genealogy down to Noah (chapter 5). It also reflects traditions that had been heard about a major flood (chapters 6–9), which was earlier recorded in the Babylonian flood story, *The Epic of Gilgamesh*. It attempts to explain the existence of nations and different languages (chapters 10–11). One could see a child asking, "Daddy, why do some people speak in ways we cannot understand?" and hearing the father saying, "Well, son, originally, everyone spoke Hebrew. But here's what happened . . ."

Beginning with chapter 12, stories about Israelite tribal leaders are gathered together. Oral stories are written down by different people out of different Israelite traditions. Finally, someone gathered them together and wrote them down. Genesis ends with an explanation of why Israel was in Egypt.

Exodus through Numbers is the accumulation of stories about Israel's escape from Egyptian slavery, its years of wandering in the desert of Sinai, its sense of being Yahweh's covenant people, its establishment of the Aaronic priesthood, the building of the Tabernacle, its accumulation of the Torah, and its preparation to enter Canaan.

Rediscovery of the Law Code

The story of the rediscovery of the law code (2 Kings 23:3ff.) caused Josiah to initiate a reform, including a renovation of the temple. During the cleaning process, Hilkiah, the priest, said he found the book of the law. However, in Chronicles, the story is reversed. During the reform, which included the cleansing of the temple, the law was discovered (2 Chron.

34:3–32). Writings of prophets and psalms demonstrate acquaintance with the law, but apparently, they had been working with secondary sources. Once it was found, the book of the law was taken to every city and taught to the residents (2 Chron. 17:9).

Ezra Preserved the Law

The Persian king Cyrus I issued his edict allowing Jews to return to their homeland and appointing Ezra to govern the province "Beyond the River," according to the "wisdom of God which is in your hand" (Ezra 7:25).

By the time of Ezra (about 458 or 398 BCE),[209] Aramaic was the official language of Jewish men and women on the street. Ezra read the book of the law publicly to the people (Ezra 8:1–6), and scribes had to "explain" Hebrew scripture (Neh. 8:7–8) in Aramaic.

Ezra acted as an instructor of the entire people (Ezra 7:14, 25). Many "professionals" like him developed in the synagogues, an institution that sprang up during the exile. Scribes were learned men who were in charge of teaching the law of Moses.

Antiochus Epiphanes tried to destroy copies of the Torah and punish those who retained them (1 Macc. 1:56–57). After the rebellion and victory of the Maccabees, Judas Maccabeus is said to have "collected all the books that had been lost on account of the war that had come upon us, and they are in our possession" (2 Macc. 2:14)."[210]

The Septuagint

Its Origin

As often happens when immigrants are in a foreign nation, the kids begin to lose the language of "the old country." At the very time Jews were becoming the people of the book, their children in Egypt began to lose their Hebrew language. They were learning Greek and Aramaic. As mentioned earlier, part of the Hebrew Bible was translated into Greek. The

---

[209] Depending on which king he served under. Richard Coggins. "The Book of Ezra," *The HarperCollins Bible Dictionary*. Paul J. Achtemeier, Gen. ed. (San Francisco: HarperSanFrancisco, 1996), 324.

[210] *Ibid.*, 10.

BIBLICAL INTERPRETATION FOR LAYPEOPLE AND OTHER MARTYRS   167

tradition says Ptolemy Philadelphus (285–248 BCE), king of Egypt, had the entire Old Testament translated into Greek all at one time. Because the tradition also says that seventy-two rabbis were involved in the translation, it is called the Septuagint (seventy) and is often designated LXX. Actually, possibly only the Pentateuch (the Five Books of Moses) was translated at that time.

Others were added a bit at a time. This Hellenistic Greek Bible includes Ecclesiasticus. (Ben Sira), Judith, 1 Maccabees, Tobit, 1 Esdras, Wisdom of Solomon, Baruch, 2 Maccabees, Additions to Esther, Susanna, Song of the Three Children, Bel and the Dragon, and Prayer of Manassas (Additions to Daniel). In about 117 BCE, the grandson of Ben Sira (the author of Ecclesiasticus) referred to all the books in the Hebrew Bible. But the fact that other books were included in some copies suggests that the concept of "canon" was by no means a settled issue.

The Roman Catholic Bible is based on the Septuagint. The books in the LXX that are not found in the Hebrew Bible are called Apocrypha ("hidden" in Greek) by Protestants and "deuterocanonical" by the Roman Catholic Church, which are included in the Roman Catholic Bible. Other works (3–4 Maccabees, Prayer of Manasseh, 1–2 Esdras) are sometimes printed in Bibles but are not considered canonical by either Protestants or Catholics. The Greek Orthodox Church includes these books as well as 3 Maccabees and 2 Esdras. The Ethiopian Orthodox canon also contains 1 Enoch, Jubilees, Pseudo-Josephus, and others.[211] So one of the contemporary issues that will need to be dealt with in the ecumenical movement will be the canon of the Bible.

Septuagint's Contents

Esdras is a parallel account of parts of Chronicles, Ezra, and Nehemiah, plus a debate with pagans that Zerubbabel wins, allowing him to remind the Persian king that he has obligated himself to rebuild the temple. Esdras is an apocalyptic writing involving seven visions that question the reasons Jews suffer, concluding that the reason is incomprehensible. It promises that the age to come will be preceded by signs of the end of time, Rome being displaced by the Messiah.

Tobit is about a Jew who suffers persecution under Shalmaneser, being blinded by accident. Meanwhile, a Jewish woman named Sarah has had

---

[211]   *Ibid.*, 8.

seven husbands die on their wedding night, afflicted by a demon named Asmodeus. Tobias, Tobit's son, marries Sarah, surviving because of a smelly potion prescribed by the angel Raphael, which drives off the demon. He also uses a concoction to restore sight to his father.

Judith is about a Jewish woman who murders a Babylonian general, Holofernes, who besieges her city of Bethulia by enticing him, getting him drunk, and beheading him, saving her town. It is a thoroughly feminist writing. Additions to Daniel is a record of the prayer of Azariah in the fiery furnace and the record of the song of the three children in the furnace. Susanna, a beautiful Jewish woman, is accused by Jewish elders of adultery because she refuses to sleep with them. She is convicted of adultery. Daniel protests, she is retried, and the accusers are caught in their lie. It is also feminist in that Susanna is far superior ethically to the men in the story.

In Bel and the Dragon, Daniel proves that the priests of Bel eat the offering to the idol rather than the idol itself. He destroys a dragon worshipped by Babylon, is put in the lion's den, is saved by Habakkuk, then is released. It was one of the later books, written about 100 BCE. Additions to Esther is more about the book of Esther, involving Mordecai's dream that saved the king from a conspiracy. The edict for the destruction of the Jews, prayers of Esther and Mordecai, Esther's audience with the king, the edict allowing Jewish self-defense, and an interpretation of Mordecai's dream are included. The Prayer of Manassas is a prayer from 2 Chronicles 33:11–19. The epistle of Jeremiah purports to be a letter from Jeremiah to exiles in Babylon, ridiculing idols.

Baruch purports to be by Jeremiah's secretary, supposedly written in Babylonia in 597 BCE. He addresses the exiles, offering a confession of sins, a prayer for forgiveness, and a prayer for their salvation. Another part praises Wisdom as found in the law of Moses. There is an assurance that they will return to their homeland. Ecclesiasticus, the Wisdom of Joshua ben Sira, gives advice for a successful life. Another part is the praise of famous men of Israel.[212] The Wisdom of Solomon personifies Wisdom as a celestial female, the greatest creature of God. It reviews the history of the Jews as a record of Wisdom's care of them and the punishment of her adversaries. It speaks of the immortality of the soul and shows Greek thinking.

The book 1 Maccabees covers 175 to 134 BCE, including the struggle of the Jews with Antiochus Epiphanes, and was probably written just

---

[212]   *Ibid.*, 10.

BIBLICAL INTERPRETATION FOR LAYPEOPLE AND OTHER MARTYRS   169

after the death of John Hyrcanus in 103 BCE. It glorifies the Maccabean rebellion and features the purification of the temple. The same period but with fewer years is covered in 2 Maccabees.

By the time of Jesus Ben Sira (second century BCE), the LXX was complete.[213] The LXX is extremely significant. It has preserved the meaning of Hebrew words, which had been lost, by the Greek words we know. In addition, it enables us to make a historical, linguistic, and theological connection between the Hebrew of the Old Testament and the Greek of the New Testament. It was the Bible to generations of Greek-speaking Jews in many countries, and it is often quoted in the New Testament. As the Vulgate became the official version of the Roman Catholic Church, the LXX became the official version of the Greek Orthodox Church.

Development of Synagogue and Readings

With the loss of the temple, their central place of worship, in 586–587 BCE and their scattering all over the Near Eastern world, the Jews developed ingenious adaptations. One was the gathering of a set of documents that they used for their spiritual needs during the exile, as well as adding others they found to be helpful to them. The second adaptation was the establishment of a new institution, the synagogue. It functioned as a place of worship, a place for the spiritual education of their children, and as a place for social gatherings. These functions, facilitated by the synagogue, enabled them, against all odds, to adjust and maintain their identity as the people of God, even through the horrendous persecution under Antiochus IV.

Completion of the Jewish Canon

There was widespread consensus that the Pentateuch received canonical status by about 400 BCE. Canonization of the prophets was close to 200 BCE. Although used much earlier, the Writings were adopted at the end of the first century CE when at the Synod of Jamnia (CE 90), the rabbis established the Jewish canon. But it was somewhat in

---

[213] David Ewert and Bruce M. Metzger. "Texts, Versions, Manuscripts, Editions." *HarperCollins Bible Dictionary*, Paul J. Achtemeier, ed., 1116.

flux for a long period. Ben Sira,[214] author of Ecclesiasticus (ca. 180 BCE), considered the Torah to be authoritative but also knew the prophetic books (Ecclus. 49:10). Ben Sira (ca. 180 BCE) in writing Ecclesiasticus 24:32–34 believed he was writing a continuation of prophets. In about 130 BCE, his grandson was vague about what was included. Debates between Jesus and the Pharisees assume there is a body of writings to which they appeal. But it was not always clear which ones. Josephus, in about 93–95 CE, speaks of twenty-two books.[215]

In the first century, the Jewish scholar Josephus[216] says that the writings had come to an end and must be believed. He saw the twenty-two writings of the Hebrew Bible as being of a different quality from other writings. The traditional number of twenty-four was first recorded in 4 Ezra 14:45–46.

The basic Hebrew canon may have been relatively fixed sometime before the Council of Jamnia (ca. 90 CE), perhaps even by the second century BCE,[217] but may have officially been closed for most Jews at Jamnia (the Greek name for Yavneh-Yam), a small village near Jerusalem. At Jamnia, because of the threat to their entire culture, a group of rabbis under Rabbi Yohanan ben Zakkai attempted to establish a body of documents to be considered authoritative. The devastation of Palestine, which occurred in 70 CE, when Jerusalem was destroyed, was one of the greatest crises is Jewish history. A second reason for their establishing a canon may have been the threat of books produced by a new Jewish heresy called Christianity. Though not accepted by all Jews, the canon established at Jamnia was accepted by most.

Hillel and Shammai

Two main schools of Jewish interpretation developed between 168 BCE and 100 CE. During Jesus's childhood, one school followed Hillel, who could have been a teacher of Jesus. He was generally not legalistic but emphasized the circumstances that were qualifying factors in how the law

---

[214]   Sometimes also spelled "Sirach."

[215]   Childs, *op. cit.*, 56–58.

[216]   "Antiquity of the Jews: Flavius Josephus Against Apion" (Book I, 8), *Josephus: Complete Works* (William Whitson, Grand Rapids: Kregel Publication, 1960), 609.

[217]   Harrington, *op. cit.*, 9–11.

BIBLICAL INTERPRETATION FOR LAYPEOPLE AND OTHER MARTYRS   171

should be interpreted and applied in a specific situation. The other school followed Shammai, who interpreted the law rigidly.

New Testament's Use of the Old Testament

The Christian canon arose as various writings were experienced and acknowledged as authoritative through the actual use of Christian communities.[218]

The New Testament refers to the "Holy Writings" (2 Tim. 3:15, Rom. 1:2), "God-breathed" or "inspired" (2 Tim. 3:16), and speakers spoke "by the Holy Spirit" (Matt. 22:43, Acts 4:25). The problem is that we are not told specifically to what they are referring. Nowhere in the New Testament is Obadiah, Nahum, Zephaniah, Esther, Ecclesiastes, or Song of Solomon quoted. However, it does quote 1 Maccabees (Matt. 24:15–16), Enoch (Jude 4:6, 13–15), Wisdom of Solomon (Matt. 12:42), Sirach (Matt. 6:19–20; 7:16–20; 4:5, 16–17), Martyrdom of Isaiah (Heb. 11:37), Judith (Matt. 9:36, Mark 9:48), Assumption of Moses (Jude 9), and the Apocalypse of Elias (Tobit 3:8, 4:15, 7:11, 7:18). They are *not* treated fundamentally different from the Old Testament canon. Philo, a Jewish contemporary of Jesus (40 CE), used every book of Hebrew canon, using terms like "sacred oracles" and "holy scriptures."

Conclusion regarding Development

Most of the Old Testament writers and speakers addressed their audience as proclaiming God's Word for that occasion. Generally, they did not have in mind the use of their writings by later generations. They were written to address a specific issue at a specific time and were not intended to be for all time. However, later on, they "were viewed as also having lasting value and significance for other churches."[219] But not all the books were accepted unanimously. The books that were not welcomed with open arms were Ecclesiastes (because of its negativism), Song of Songs (because of its eroticism), Ezekiel and Proverbs (because

---

[218]   Childs, *op. cit.*, 65.

[219]   Harrington, *op. cit.*, 13.

they contradicted the Torah), and Esther (because it never mentions God).[220]

Isagogics of the Old Testament

Isagogics is a fifty-cent word that just refers to the study of texts, addressing issues of who wrote the text, when it was written, to whom it was written, and the purpose of the writing.

Before I go any further, I need to address another issue that is described with another fifty-cent word. Ethnocentrism is the process of evaluating things in light of one's own culture—whose culture is assumed to be the correct one. Frankly, it is difficult (if not partially impossible) not to be ethnocentric because our culture is there at our birth and affects how we think of everything "from how to raise children to the nature of God and ultimate reality."[221] Dennis Bratcher argues that this is a tendency toward cultural imperialism that "hinders understanding and relationship across very real if unknown cultural divides."[222] For example, whereas Westerners tend to believe the individual is most important, in much of the world, in tribal cultures, the primary concern is the family or the community. In Western cultures, an individual is defined by what they achieve personally. But in other cultures, people's reputation is based on what they contribute to the group—the family, the clan, or the tribe to which they belong. According to Bratcher, in cultures like that of Korea, Russia, and Kazakhstan, cooperation and collaboration are emphasized over competition. In many communal and tribal cultures, they have no concept of private real estate property. The Bible was produced in an Eastern culture.

Now regarding scripture, biblical writers did not think of "author" the way we do and were not concerned about issues such as plagiarism and were less inclined to believe that ideas could be owned by individuals. Nor did they write for profit or "sell ideas as property."[223] Therefore, they had

---

[220] *Ibid.*, 9.

[221] Bratcher, Dennis. *Cultural Influence in Biblical Studies*, "Community and Testimony." http://www.crivoice.org/historyculture.html.

[222] *Ibid.*

[223] *Ibid.*

BIBLICAL INTERPRETATION FOR LAYPEOPLE AND OTHER MARTYRS   173

no copyright laws or laws about "intellectual property." Ideas were seen as part of the "accumulated wisdom of the community . . . to be used in the instruction of the young and the guidance of the community as a whole."[224] So documents written by an author, such as Isaiah, could be added to in the name of the originator and was considered an honor to him. It is obvious that Deuteronomy was written by more than just Moses, whose sermon it was supposed to be because it spoke of Moses in the past (Deut. 1:1, 5:1) and discussed his burial (Deut. 34:1–12), as well as having laws regarding real estate property (Deut. 19:14, 20:5–6), which were obviously included in the law long after the time of Moses. Numerous letters that we refer to as Paul's letters are from Paul and others—1 Corinthians 1:1 (Paul and Sosthenes), 2 Corinthians 1:1 (Paul and Timothy), Philippians 1:1 (Paul and Timothy), Colossians 1:1 (Paul and Timothy, if not written later), 1 Thessalonians 1:1 (Paul, Silvanus, and Timothy), 2 Thessalonians 1:1 (Paul, Silvanus, and Timothy), and Philemon 1 (Paul and Timothy). It is even suggested by 2 Thessalonians that the letter was not actually penned by Paul, when he says in 3:17, "I, Paul, write the greeting in my own hand, and this is a distinguishing mark in every letter, this is the way I write" (New American Standard Version).

Early Collections

How the collections came about is not known, but there were collections. The songs in 2 Samuel 22 and Psalm 18 are almost identical. Psalm 14 and Psalm 53 are almost identical. One is probably a copy of the other. It is much like English fairy tales that were passed on by word of mouth. As they were passed on, they changed a bit. Later, the stories were written down independently, resulting in different versions.

Rabbinical Tradition

We also learn from the Talmud about how the Old Testament was understood by the Jews. The Talmud is a collection of Targums (Aramaic paraphrase); Gemara, a commentary on the Mishnah; and midrash, a commentary on scripture in Hebrew and Aramaic.

---

[224]   *Ibid.*

174   DAVID W. MELBER

Manuscripts

Scrolls

The earliest Old Testament manuscripts were written on papyri or parchments and were rolled into scrolls.[225] Some of the more important parchments are the Dead Sea Scrolls, the most famous text discovery of all time. It includes fragments and complete documents of about two hundred scrolls, including all of the Old Testament except Esther.[226]

Codices (singular "Codex")

A codex is a text in book form developed around 100 CE. Some of the more important Hebrew codices are Cairo Codex (896 CE), which includes the prophets. The Leningrad Codex (L), dated 1009–1010 CE, is the earliest complete Hebrew Bible with vowel points, which was devised in Tiberias by rabbis called Masoretes.[227] Codex Neofiti I is a Targum ("translation" in Aramaic), which is a paraphrase and commentary. It includes the Pentateuch. Targum Onkelos dates from the second or third century.

With one exception, codices are generally designated with either a Latin letter or an arabic numeral, like *A* or "12." Codex Vaticanus (B), dating from 325 to 350 CE, contained all the books of the Bible but part of Hebrews, Paul's letters to individuals, and Revelation. But it included Maccabees. Another important codex is Codex Sinaiticus, a fourth-century manuscript containing most of the Old Testament and all twenty-seven books of the New Testament, plus the *Epistle of Barnabas* and part of the *Shepherd of Hermas.* The fifth-century Codex Alexandrinus (A) includes the New Testament, the Greek Old Testament, 1 Clement, part of 2 Clement, and the Psalms of Solomon.[228] These differences in books included in different early manuscripts indicate that the New Testament canon was not nailed down.

---

[225]   Ewert and Metzger, *op. cit.,*1113.

[226]   *Ibid.,* 1114.

[227]   Sanders, James A. and Astrid Beck. "The Leningrad Codex: Rediscovering the Oldest Complete Hebrew Bible." *Bible Review,* Vol. XIII, Number 4, Aug 1997, 32-34.

[228]   Harrington, *op. cit.,* 15.

Transmission

Because of controversy within the church, a standard text of the Old Testament emerged about 100 CE, and LXX lost its popularity in Jerusalem.[229] As early as the first century CE, Christian scholars began writing their works in codex form rather than scrolls. The Jews, however, did not use the codex until about the seventh century.[230]

New Testament Canon

The Reasons for Preserving

As the early church began to talk about Jesus, his teachings were circulated orally. Since many believed the Second Coming would be relatively soon, there may have been little effort to write them down at the beginning. The first documents that began to be collected were the letters of Paul to the churches that he had visited (except for Rome) and to individuals. They were written for specific occasions, especially problems within the churches. The gospels seem to have been written because, contrary to expectations, Jesus's second coming did not occur during the lives of his contemporaries. In addition, Jerusalem had been destroyed in 70 CE, and followers of Jesus feared that the stories about Jesus's life might be lost. So attempts were made to reconstruct Jesus's teaching and works, which were called gospels. And each gospel writer had a specific message about Jesus that he wanted to express. Most scholars believe that some sayings were written down and were viewed as "having lasting value and significance for other churches."[231]

---

[229] Ewert and Metzger, *op. cit.*, 1117.

[230] "Scroll and Codex" http://penelope.uchicago.edu/~grout/encyclopaedia romana/scroll/scrollcodex.html#anchor171306.
"The Scroll versus the Codex," http://www.biblewheel.com/Canon/Scroll vs Codex.php.
"From Scroll to Codex," http://courses.educ.ubc.ca/etec540/July03/batchelorj/researchtopic/.

[231] Harrington, *op. cit.*, 1994, 13.

Biblical Claims of Authority

References to Authority of Jesus's Instruction

There are not many references to the sayings of Jesus in the earliest New Testament writings, the letters of Paul. However, Paul did say, "I received from the Lord what I also passed on to you: The Lord Jesus, on the night he was betrayed, took bread, and when he had given thanks, he broke it and said, 'This is my body, which is for you do this in remembrance to me.' In the same way, after supper he took the cup, saying, 'This cup is the new covenant in my blood; do this, whenever you drink it, in remembrance of me'" (1 Cor. 11:23–25). And again, "For what I received I passed on to you as of first importance: that Christ died for our sins according to the scriptures, that he was buried, that he was raised on the third day according to the scriptures, and that he appeared to Peter, and then to the Twelve" (1 Cor. 15:3–5).

Apostolic Claims of Authority

Of his own writing, Paul said, "I give this commandment (not I, but the Lord)" (1 Cor. 7:10). And two verses later, "I say this (I, not the Lord)" (1 Cor. 7:12). And later in the same chapter, "I have no command from the Lord, but I give my judgment as one who by the Lord's mercy is trustworthy" (1 Cor. 7:25); and "In my judgment . . . and I think that I too have the Spirit of God" (1 Cor. 7:40). Paul fluctuates between claiming theological authority and claiming only opinion—sanctified opinion, but opinion nonetheless.

Letters Read in Church

Paul instructs the leader of the church in Thessalonica to "read it to the brethren" (1 Thess. 5:26–27). The early churches were urban. Paul went to synagogues in cities or the agora (market) in Athens. A Christian merchant from Thessalonica might go to Corinth and gather with the brethren and worship while he was there. They might share a letter they received from Paul. It was so good he had it photocopied (well, maybe not photocopied) and informed them his congregation received a letter from him also. They wanted a copy, so he agreed to fax (well, maybe not fax) them a copy when he got back home. That is how I conceive of the collection forming. According to Justin Martyr, by 150 CE, they were read in the churches

BIBLICAL INTERPRETATION FOR LAYPEOPLE AND OTHER MARTYRS   177

along with the Old Testament—"the memoirs of the apostles or the writings of the prophets and read, as long as time permits."[232]

Post-apostolic Claims

There were documents contemporary with and written soon after the New Testament texts that were considered by some to be part of the canon. Much can be learned about what the early Christians considered to be canon and how it was understood. Some of the earliest writings were 1 Clement (after 95 CE), 2 Clement (120–140 CE), Ignatius (early second century), Polycarp (early second century), the *Didache*[233] (early second century), the *Epistle of Barnabas* (early or mid-second century), the *Shepherd of Hermas* (before 180 CE), the *Epistle to Diognetus* (150 CE or later), and Papias (130–140 CE).[234] Some were written less than a century after the first New Testament canonical book was written, and most were less than fifty years after the last one was written.

Early church fathers make reference to New Testament writings. First Clement (ca. 95 CE) quoted Matthew, Romans, 1 Corinthians, and Hebrews. The epistle of Polycarp, bishop of Smyrna (150 CE), knew Matthew, Romans through 2 Thessalonians, 1 Peter, and 1 John. The *Didache*, about 150 CE, knew Matthew and Luke. Justin Martyr (ca. 140) knew Matthew through Romans, 2 Corinthians through Ephesians, Colossians, 2 Thessalonians, 1 Peter, and Revelation. Irenaeus, bishop of Lyons (ca. 170), knew Matthew through Titus, Hebrews, 1 Peter, 1 and 2 John, and Revelation. Marcion (ca. 140) referred specifically to Luke, Romans through 2 Thessalonians, and Philemon. The value of Jesus's words is expressed by Clement[235] and Ignatius.[236] Justin Martyr spoke of

---

[232] "The First Apology of Justin," LXVII, 3, *The Ante-Nicene Fathers* (Alex Roberts and James Donaldson, Eds.) (Grand Rapids: Eerdmans, 1981), 186.

[233] "The Teaching of the Apostles," *The Apostolic Fathers* J. B. Lightfoot (trans. and ed.). (Grand Rapids: Baker Book House, 1962).

[234] Although Papias was apparently quite influential, we have no copy of his writing, only quotes from other apostolic fathers.

[235] *The Ante-Nicene Fathers*, "First Epistle of Clement to the Corinthians" XIII, p. 8; XL, 17.

[236] *The Ante-Nicene Fathers*, "The Epistle of Ignatius to the Smyrnaeans," VII, p. 89; "The Epistle of Ignatius to the Philadelphians," VIII, 84.

memoirs of apostles *read with the prophets*[237] in about 150 CE. The concept of a collection of "canon" was forming.[238]

The Muratorian Canon (ca. 170), which was a listing of the canon, refers specifically to Matthew through Philemon and 1 John through Revelation.[239] Finally, Athanasius, bishop of Alexandria (367 CE), listed the twenty-seven books that now make up the New Testament canon, saying that no one is to add or take away from it.[240]

Jerome

Because many different Latin versions were in circulation at the time, in 382 CE, Pope Damascus asked Eusebius Sophronius Hieronymus, later known as St. Jerome, to translate an authoritative version of the Bible into Latin. It was known as the Vulgate (common) translation. Jerome used Athanasius's listing, insisting on using the Hebrew canon. However, he included the Apocrypha, putting it between the Old and New Testament, referring to it as "deuterocanonical" (secondary canon). He believed it was good for the church, but not to be used as a basis for doctrine. However, as it came into use, the Apocrypha gained status by its inclusion. By the late fourth century, the church generally accepted the twenty-seven-book New Testament canon.[241]

Decisions of the Councils

The issue was addressed by church councils in North Africa. The Council of Hippo (393 CE) and the Third Council of Carthage (397 CE), neither of which reflected the feelings of the whole church, resolved that only canonical writings should be read in church in North Africa. By that time, they were referring to all the books included in Jerome's Latin Vulgate, including the Apocrypha, or deuterocanonical, books.

---

[237] Justin Martyr, "The First Apology of Justin," LXVII, *The Ante-Nicene Fathers.* Grand Rapids: Eerdmans, 186.

[238] Most found in the *Ante-Nicene Fathers*, Vol. I.

[239] Merrill C. Tenny. *The New Testament: An Historical and Analytic Survey* (Grand Rapids: Eerdmans, 1953), 147.

[240] Harrington, "Introduction to the New Interpreters' Bible," 1994, 15.

[241] *Ibid.*

The Issue during the Reformation

The question of canon arose again at the time of the sixteenth-century Reformation. While the reformers adopted the principle of *sola scriptura* (theology should be based solely on the Bible), they raised the question of what constitutes scripture. As well as his rejection of the Apocrypha as authoritative, Luther had problems with Hebrews, James, Jude, and Revelation. The Roman Catholic Church responded at the Council of Trent (1546), for the first time making the content of the Bible an article of faith. They did not accept Jerome's concept of canon but adopted the wider one.[242]

Manuscripts

When the English King James Version of the Bible was translated in 1611, the earliest manuscript available was the *Textus Receptus*, a combination of several texts from about six hundred to eight hundred years after the last book of the canon was written. The nice thing is that over the last two hundred years, a plethora of much earlier manuscripts of the Bible have been found, some fragments even dating to the second and third centuries. Because they are copies much closer to the original texts (autographs), they provide much more potential for determining the original wording of the Bible.

Closing of the Canon

Deciding What Is Biblical

But how does one decide what is "biblical" and what is not? The early church tried to deal with the issue, but had no unanimous agreement. One of the early church fathers, the historian, Eusebius, bishop of Caesarea (303 CE), said that the criteria was "orthodoxy of content, apostolic origin, and general acceptance by the churches."[243] Actually, the early church

---

[242]   *Ibid.*, 12–16.

[243]   Eusebius. *The Ecclesiastical History of Eusebius Pamphilus* (Grand Rapids: Baker Book House, 1962), 3, 24; Harrington, *op. cit.*, 14.

did *not* generally agree on either orthodoxy or apostolic origin. Indeed, some members of the early church killed one another over these issues. But by 200 CE, there was general acceptance in the churches of the four gospels, Acts, Paul's epistles, 1 Peter, and 1 John. But there was controversy over James, 2 Peter, 2 and 3 John, Jude, and Revelation. And there were supporters of the inclusion of the *Shepherd of Hermas*, 1 Clement, and the *Epistle of Barnabas*.[244]

The Question of a Closed Canon

Adding to the Canon

In 1 Corinthians, Paul talks about a "previous letter" (1 Cor. 5:9); and in Colossians 4:16, he refers to his letter to the Laodiceans. If archeologists were to dig one of them up, would it be considered canonical? Some believe that the Gospel of Thomas, found at Nag Hammadi library in Egypt, contains Jesus's sayings that are older and more original than in the canonical gospels.[245] And our received text has 150 psalms. However, in the Dead Scrolls Library, a Psalm 151 was discovered in the psalms.

Could spiritual classics like Augustine's *Confessions*, Luther's *Small Catechism*, Milton's *Paradise Lost*, C. S. Lewis's *Screwtape Letters*, Martin Luther King Jr.'s "Letter from a Birmingham Jail,"[246] and Dietrich Bonhoeffer's *Cost of Discipleship* be added to the canon? And of course, there is the Book of Mormon. All of these are more edifying than *some* parts of scripture, such as the dimensions of the Tabernacle and the medical procedures of the priests and certainly the evil Psalm 137.

Removing from the Canon

And what about those books we idealize as being in the canon, but which we treat as noncanonical by completely ignoring them, such as Habakkuk and parts of Leviticus that give details about the curtains in the

---

[244] "The Pastor of Hermas," The Ante-Nicene Fathers (Vo. II), Alexander Roberts and James Donaldson, Eds. (Grand Rapids: Eerdmns1979), 1 ff; St. Clement, "Epistle to the Corinthians," The Ante-Nicene Fathers (Vol. I), Alexander Roberts and James Donaldson, Eds. (Grand Rapids: Eerdmans, 1981), 151ff.; Barnabas, "Epistle," The Ante-Nicene Fathers (Vol. I), Alexander Roberts and James Donaldson, Eds. (Grand Rapids: Eerdmans, 1981), 133ff.

[245] Harrington, *op. cit.*, 18–19.

[246] *Ibid.*, 18.

BIBLICAL INTERPRETATION FOR LAYPEOPLE AND OTHER MARTYRS   181

Tabernacle? Should we maintain the illusion that we honor them as God's Word or just consider them valuable historical documents? Or should the Bible itself be seen that way?

Development of the Text

A theory about Jesus's teaching is that although it wasn't done at the beginning, someone decided to compile a collection of his sayings, to which both Matthew and Luke had access when they wrote their gospels. This hypothetical document is referred to as Q, standing for *Quelle*, meaning "source" in German. The gospel of John concluded, "Jesus did many other things as well. If every one of them were written down, I suppose that even the whole world would not have room for the books that would be written" (John 21:25). If Q indeed existed as a body of oral and/or written tradition, would it, if found, be canonical? Or was Paul's letter to the Romans canonical until the secretary Tertius stuck in his little note: "I Tertius, who wrote this letter, greet you in the Lord" (Rom. 16:22).

Changes in the Text

The earliest available copies of the same documents do not all agree on the wording in later copies. Mark is particularly problematic since the earliest available texts do not include Mark 16:9–20. Because they are not found in the earliest manuscripts, John 7:53–8:11 and Mark 16:9–20 were apparently added many years later. Even the gospels regarding the same events do not agree on details. Although considered canonical, these sections were almost certainly not written by John or Mark.[247]

Canon and Tradition

Roman Catholics argue that the gradual development and acceptance of the biblical canon is proof that the Bible is the church's book, that acceptance of individual books grew out of the church's experience and were only declared canonical by the church later on,[248] and the Bible is part of the tradition. The truth is the writings grew out of the experience and life of the church and were, though not unanimously, declared to be canonical by the church. The Roman Catholics emphasized the importance of

---

[247]   *Ibid.*, 17–18.

[248]   *Ibid.*, 20.

tradition in choosing of the Christian Bible.[249] Protestants need to take that fact more seriously.

Which Canon Is Authoritative?

Christian

We have already discussed the different canons of the Roman Catholic and Protestant churches. The Eastern Orthodox churches also recognize 1 Esdras, Psalm 151, the Prayer of Manasseh, and 3 Maccabees (with 4 Maccabees in an appendix). The Russian Orthodox Church adds 2 Esdras.[250] The Coptic (Ethiopian) Church includes those and certain pseudepigraphical books, such as 1 Enoch.

Quran

Muhammad (570–632 CE) produced the Quran, as God's (Allah's) final guidance for humankind in all aspects of human life, personal and social. Muhammad repeated his revelations verbatim to his close followers. A group under the leadership of Zayd ibn Thabit (died 666 CE), Muhammad's secretary, collected the writings into a book. The Quran says that in Allah's grace, he sent messengers (Adam, Noah, Abraham, Moses, and Jesus) to communicate his will and that Muhammad is the last of the prophets. The Quran is considered by most Muslims to be verbally inspired and therefore infallible. God expects a response of gratitude and obedience and that one's deeds will be weighed in the balance.[251]

Book of Mormon

Mormons believe that divine revelation was given to Joseph Smith Jr. in 1820. They teach that a tribe of Israel sailed to America about 600 BCE and were visited by Jesus after his resurrection. In the time of the

---

[249] Childs, *op. cit.*, 66–67.

[250] Murphy, Roland F. "Bible, The," *The HarperCollins Bible Dictionary*. Paul J. Achtemeier, ed. (San Francisco: HarperSanFrancisco, 1996), 121.

[251] Richard C. Martin. "Jesus Christ," *The HarperCollins Dictionary of Religion*. Jonathan Z. Smith, ed. (San Francisco: HarperSanFrancisco, 1995), 514–517.

prophet Mormon and his son Moroni (about 500 CE), the Lamanites (Native Americans) defeated the righteous Nephites. Moroni buried the history recorded by his father and appeared to Smith to reveal records written or gold plates in "Reformed Egyptian," which ironically were lost. The Book of Mormon is the official scripture of the Church of Jesus Christ of Latter-Day Saints, along with the Protestant Bible. Additionally, the proclamations of the president of the church have binding authority.[252]

Preaching and Teaching

God's Word has a vitality that goes beyond the book. Most Christians believe that preaching also is a proclamation of the Word of God. However, it is generally believed that the Word is based on the teachings of the Bible or an application of the Bible. There have been some, however, who believe that because the Bible was written in a culture that is not as "sophisticated" as ours, Christian teaching must go beyond the Bible. After all, because there were no nukes, birth control, corporations, computers, automobiles, or Facebook, the Bible does not address issues related to their abuse.

---

[252] Lawrence S. Cunningham. "Latter-day Saints, Church of Jesus Christ of," *The HarperCollins Dictionary of Religion*. Smith, Jonathan Z., ed. (San Francisco: HarperSanFrancisco, 1995), 652–653.

Chapter 11

THE INSPIRATION AND AUTHORITY

Foundation

Little Thought Given to Question

As I suggested earlier, when one quotes "All Scripture is inspired by God" (2 Tim. 3:15–16), it is rare that Christians think about the issue of how the Bible was developed, *who* decided it was the Word of God, or *how* it was decided which books were canonical and which were not. If it is thought of at all, it is often thought of as some immaculate production that God dropped out of heaven, fully dictated and spell-checked. Most people completely ignore the issue, thus avoiding a problem for themselves. Others may live a life of schizophrenia, living in two different worlds, one of reality and one of fancy. Brevard Childs, in referring to *hē graphē* (Greek for "the Scriptures") says, "When one asks what was the scope and precise form of the scripture[s] . . . a host of complex historical questions arise."[253]

When we use the term "scripture," we make some assumptions also. The text is quoted as if it refers to the entire Bible, but it definitely did not

---

[253] Childs, *op. cit.*, 55.

BIBLICAL INTERPRETATION FOR LAYPEOPLE AND OTHER MARTYRS 185

refer to the New Testament, for not all of it had been written and collected yet. It may have referred to the Septuagint. It may even have referred to the Apocrypha or certain pseudepigrapha. We do not know.

The second passage often quoted is "Holy men of God spoke as they were moved by the Holy Spirit" (2 Pet. 1:21). But here, it refers to men "speaking," which certainly does not refer to the Bible, which is "written." My guess is that it referred to the oral communication of the prophets. However, it could also have been referring to the oral proclamations of Peter and Paul, whose messages had been proclaimed perhaps as many as fifty years earlier.

Both of these passages assert that God has communicated through human beings. And since the Christian Church confesses that the Bible is "God's Word," we should think about exactly what that means. The Bible was written by people during different cultural periods who wrote according to the limitations that their cultures put on them.

Problem of *Verbal* Inspiration

I began this book by saying that the clergy often are not honest with the laity about what they really know and believe about the Bible. Rather than helping the laity grow, the clergy often are satisfied to leave the laity with a children's understanding of the Bible. We do them a disservice because they are not prepared to face the world with an adult level of understanding of the faith. I believe that we help people fall away when they get to be adults by leaving them at that level when the rest of their understanding has grown.

There are those who argue that every word in the Bible is absolutely correct in every way, including historical and scientific information. But the Bible itself does not agree with that point of view.

Jesus acted out an historical drama. Obviously, he did specific things that are not all recorded. It is impossible to record everything that anyone does. So specific episodes are chosen and portrayed in a way to communicate the message that the gospel writer wanted to get across. That is why there are four gospels that are very different from one another, sometimes even disagreeing with one another over details. Some of the things recorded may not have happened in the sense that they could be recorded on film and tape. But history (as written or told) is not the important thing. It is only the framework for the message.

The story within the history is the important thing. Martin Luther said that the Bible is the crib in which Christ lay. The crib is not the important thing. The Christ within the crib is what is important. It is the message that is important, not the trappings. However, the message is communicated *through* the trappings. One can argue endlessly, for example, about what type of literature the book of Jonah is. And in wasting all that time, one can evade the message of Jonah, a message that, regardless of what kind of literature it is, is quite clear. But there are those who argue that unless Jonah is understood as history, it cannot be believed. It seems incredible that anyone would argue that.

The person who makes such stipulation for accepting the Bible as "true" or the Word of God has not put trust in the Bible or the God he claims to accept, but in himself and his own decision as to how he will allow God to communicate. He is idolatrous in deciding in what way he will allow God to communicate. It is very important to distinguish between the *message* of the Bible itself and what we have been told that we *should* believe about it.

Some of Scripture Is Not What God Wanted

Jesus did not believe in verbal inspiration. To justify their easy divorce laws toward women, which was supported by Rabbi Hillel, the Pharisees say to Jesus, "Moses allowed us to divorce our wives by writing her a 'writ of divorcement'" (Deut. 24:1–4). Their reasoning was since it is in the law of Moses, it must be okay. Divorce was very easy for Jewish males to get. The school of Hillel, Gamaliel's grandfather, taught that a man could divorce his wife for burning food. These views won out over the view of the school of Shammai that adultery was the only cause for divorce.[254] But Jesus answered, "It is because of the hardness of your heart that Moses allowed you to divorce your wives. But that was not God's original intent. From the beginning, God made them male and female. A man leaves mother and father and they become one flesh" (Matt. 19:8–9, my wording). So we learn that because of human obstinacy and for political expediency, things got into the law of Moses that God did *not* intend. So the content of scripture is influenced by the sinful desires of people as well as righteous ones. Therefore, Jesus had no compunctions about attacking such laws.

---

[254] Mollenkott, 1977, *op. cit.*, 9.

BIBLICAL INTERPRETATION FOR LAYPEOPLE AND OTHER MARTYRS   187

There were other instances in which Jesus either intensified what the Old Testament said or contradicted it. He said that the Bible had said "do not murder," but Jesus said that anyone who is angry with his brother is subject to judgment (Matt. 5:21–22). He pointed out that the Bible said "you shall not commit adultery," but Jesus said that anyone who looks at a woman with lust is guilty of adultery in his heart (Matt. 5:27–30). He pointed out that the Bible says that an oath in God's name should be kept, but Jesus said to not take oaths, but to let your "yes" be "yes" and your "no" be "no" (Matt. 5:33–37). Again, he pointed out that the Bible said "an eye for an eye and a tooth for a tooth" (Exod. 21:23–24, Lev. 24:19–20, Deut. 19:21), but Jesus said, "I say to you, do not resist an evil person. If someone strikes you on the right cheek, turn to him the other" (Matt. 5:38–42). Finally, he said, "You have heard that it was said, 'Love your neighbor and hate your enemy.' But I tell you: Love your enemies and pray for those who persecute you, that you may be sons of your Father in heaven. He causes his sun to rise on the evil and the good, and sends rain on the righteous and the unrighteous" (Matt. 5:43–45). Although the Old Testament never actually says that, some texts (especially numerous psalms) definitely spew hatred toward enemies, even asserting that God hates them (Ps. 5:5, Hosea 9:15, Mal. 1:13). Jesus had no problem with rejecting a part of scripture that did not measure up to God's standards as he understood them.

Contradictory Ideas

Unless one avoids reading the Bible or completely closes his eyes while doing so, one cannot miss the fact that not all writings in scripture agree with one another. For example, Ecclesiastes and Daniel do not agree on life after death. Ecclesiastes says, "Man's fate is like that of the animals: the same fate awaits them both: As one dies, so dies the other. . . . All go to the same place, all come from dust, and to dust all return. Who knows if the spirit of man rises upward and if the spirit of the animal goes down into the earth?" (Eccles. 3:19–21). But Daniel says, "Multitudes who sleep in the dust of the earth will awake: some to everlasting life, others to shame and everlasting contempt" (Dan. 12:2). In 1 Samuel 8 and 12, God says Israel's desire for a king is a rejection of God's rule but was tolerated by God (1 Sam. 8:22, 12:17). The initiative to have a king reflected the disobedience

188   DAVID W. MELBER

of the people. On the other hand, 1 Samuel 9:1–10, 16 and 11:1–15 place
the initiative for establishment of monarchy with Yahweh himself.[255]

Sanctified Opinion

In 1 Corinthians 7:25, Paul makes a distinction between his opinions
and God's commands when he says he has "no command from the Lord"
but gives his sanctified opinion on how to deal with the present critical
situation. So not everything in scripture is God's antecedent will.

Unworthy Texts

The ban (herem) referred to the total destruction of towns or persons
and their possessions.[256] Moses claimed that the LORD was giving the cities
Israel attacked to them and "not leave anything alive that breathes" (Deut.
20:16). As Joshua prepared to enter Israel, the mysterious "commander of
the LORD's army" ordered him to totally destroy Jericho and every living
thing—men and women, young and old, cattle, sheep, and donkeys—and
to burn everything in it, except for Rahab and her family. But they were
to take all the silver, gold, and articles of bronze and iron for the priests
(Josh. 6:1–21). Regarding Ai, there was no intermediary. It was the LORD
himself who told Joshua that he would deliver Ai into Israel's hands, except
that they were to carry off their plunder and livestock for themselves—
which they did to Ai (Josh. 8:1–27) and numerous other towns and villages
(Josh. 9–11). The claim was even made that "it was the LORD himself
who hardened their hearts to wage war against Israel, so that he might
destroy them totally, exterminating them without mercy, as the LORD had
commanded Moses" (Josh. 11:20). Samuel claimed that he was speaking for
the LORD when he told Saul to "attack the Amalekites and totally destroy
everything that belong to them. Do not spare them; put to death men and
women, children and infants, cattle and sheep, camels and donkeys." (1
Sam. 15:2–3). These texts reflect the history of Israel and the opinion of
the writers of the Old Testament but are unworthy of the God we worship.

And regarding texts like Psalm 137:89, Virginia Mollenkott points out
that texts which blesses bashing out the brains of the enemy's baby (see also

---

[255]   Childs, *op. cit.,* 150–153.

[256]   Robert G. Boling. "ban," *The HarperCollins Bible Dictionary (Paul* J. Achtemeier,
        gen. ed.) (San Francisco: HarperSanFrancisco, 1996), 101.

BIBLICAL INTERPRETATION FOR LAYPEOPLE AND OTHER MARTYRS   189

Ps. 109:10, 12–13) violates the spirit of the Old Testament as represented by Proverbs 24:17: "Do not gloat when your enemy falls; when he stumbles, do not let your heart rejoice."[257] And it certainly contradicts Jesus's teaching to "love your enemy" (Matt. 5:43–48, Luke 6:27–28). So such texts may be part of the traditions of Israel but certainly can't be considered "inspired" in the same sense of John 3:16 or Philippians 2:1–11. And Luther had no problem with rejecting parts of scripture that he believed were contrary to the gospel. He had theological problems with Hebrews, James, Jude, and Revelation.[258]

Texts Ignoring Reprehensible Behavior

Virginia Mollenkott claims that not every text reflects the will of God and must be evaluated in light of God's intent for his people. Therefore, she says that we must "suspect any meaning which contradicts the thrust of the whole Bible toward human justice and oneness in Christ."[259] Phyllis Trible illustrates Mollenkott's point by referring to pericopes that fail to defend women.

Hagar

Since Abram's (later named Abraham) wife, Sarai (later named Sarah), had borne him no children, she suggested he have intercourse with her Egyptian handmaiden, Hagar. There are two stories about this event. In one story, Hagar conceives and is impudent toward her mistress, who retaliates by treating her badly, causing her to run away. Hagar is confronted by an angel, who tells her to return, which she does with her son, Ishmael (Gen. 16:1–16).

In the other story, Ishmael is weaned. Hagar mocks Sarah, who complains to Abraham, who resists sending Ishmael away. But God intervenes and tells Abraham to send her and Ishmael away. They run out of water, and the boy almost dies. But God speaks to Hagar from heaven and shows her a well. They survive, and he marries an Egyptian woman (Gen. 21:8–21). In both stories, the promise is made that Ishmael will be the father of a great nation.

---

257   Mollenkott, 1977, *op. cit.*, 104.

258   Harrington, *op. cit.*, 16.

259   Mollenkott, 1977, *op. cit.*, 118–119.

As males have read scriptures, certain passages have caused them to do a double take, but their discomfort with the texts are often rationalized, insisting that the Bible just "tells it like it is" about human nature and the reality of sin. However, feminists like Phyllis Trible take exception to these texts, not only at what befell these women, but also by the silence of scriptural writers in defense of the ravaged women. Scripture does *not* just "tell it as it is." There are a plethora of texts that condemn bad behavior in no uncertain terms. Trible also points out that there are two stories in which Abraham is willing to betray Sarah and allow others to have sexual relations with her (Gen. 12:10–20, 20:1–19).[260]

Trible refers to the injustice to Hagar: "As a symbol of the oppressed. . . . She is the faithful maid exploited, the black woman used by the male and abused by the female of the ruling class, the surrogate mother, the resident alien without legal recourse, the other woman, the runaway youth, the religious fleeing from affliction, the pregnant young woman alone, the expelled wife, the divorced mother with child, the shopping bag lady carrying bread and water, the homeless woman, the indigent relying upon handouts from the power structures, the welfare mother, and the self-effacing female whose own identity shrinks in service of others."[261]

Tamar's Rape

A second story that Trible highlights is the rape of Tamar (Gen. 38). A son of David, Amnon, rapes Tamar, his half sister. David hears about it but ignores the brutality of the incident. Although he is her father, he does nothing about it. Trible comments that the father turns his back on his daughter and identifies with his rapist son to deny justice to the female. And if there is no outrage, Amnon's behavior comes off as if not reprehensible, at least intolerable. Trible points out that Proverbs warns boys to avoid the loose women (Prov. 7:4–5) but says nothing to protect innocent girls from loose men.[262]

A Levite's Unknown Concubine (Judges 19–21)

Trible's third story is the story of a Levite and his concubine who spend the night in Gibeah. That evening, men of the village want to have sex with him. In order to protect his Levite guest, the host offers his virgin daughter

---

[260] Trible, Phyllis. *Texts of Terror*. Minneapolis: Fortress Press, 1984, 9.

[261] *Ibid.*, 24.

[262] *Ibid.*, 46–57.

BIBLICAL INTERPRETATION FOR LAYPEOPLE AND OTHER MARTYRS   191

and the concubine instead. The Levite puts his concubine out the door, and the men gang-rape her all night. In the morning, he steps out on the porch and tells her to get up. She can't because she is dead. He shows no remorse, but anger. He cuts her up into twelve pieces and sends them to the tribes of Israel, seeking revenge.

Trible points out that neither he nor the narrator shows any concern for the girl. When the avenging army attacks Gibeah, no woman, child, or beast survives. Six hundred men escape. But in strange compassion for the men of Gibeah, they save four hundred young women of Jabesh-Gilead and abduct two hundred more young women for the men of Gibeah. So the rape and murder of one woman has become the rape of six hundred. What these men claim to abhor, they reenact themselves.[263] There is no comment suggesting that anything was wrong in this story.

Jephthah's Daughter (Judges 11)

Trible's fourth story has to do with Jephthah's daughter. Jephthah makes a vow that if he is successful in battle, he will sacrifice the first thing he sees when he gets back. He is successful. As irony would have it, the first thing he sees is his daughter. She is sacrificed for Jephthah's ridiculous vow (verse 29). The narrator of the biblical text makes no judgment of Jephthah. Unlike other books that make strong criticism of evil actions, these stories are told with no commentary, no criticism. In the sacrifice of Jephthah's unnamed daughter, Trible argues that the expression "the spirit of Yahweh came upon Jephthah" (Judg. 11:29) puts God's stamp of approval on the story. Trible concludes that these writers of the biblical text were so influenced by their patriarchal culture and had so little regard for women that they never even noticed the heinous dimension of the behavior.[264]

The Influence of Culture

The Culture of Scripture

The effect of the patriarchal culture in which the Bible was written had significant repercussions. Four thousand years of masculine biblical

---

[263]   *Ibid.*, 21–23, 66–83.

[264]   *Ibid.*, 96–107.

images of God have left the impression that male is the norm for humanity and that women are inferior.[265]

God is pictured often in male images. But there are also many female images of God in the Bible. We have simply ignored them. Yahweh is pictured as having labor pains (Isa. 42:14). Jesus refers to a childbirth image, including playing on the concept of the breaking of water in the womb (John 3:5–7). And images such as being "born of God" (1 John 4:7), "new-birth" (1 Pet. 2:2–3), being "born again" uses mother images for God. Jesus compares his act of redemption to a woman who forgets her pain after childbirth (John 16:21).

God refers to creation as bearing the sea out of her womb (Job 38:8) and wrapping the clouds in swaddling bands (Job 38:9), as well of bearing ice from her womb and giving birth to the frost from the heavens (Job 38:29). A similar image is used toward Israel. God conceives Israel and carries him since birth (Isa. 46:3–4), comparing her relation to Israel to a mother nursing a child (Isa. 49:15) and having labor pains (Isa. 42:14). Moses asks, "Was it I who conceived all this people, was it I who gave them birth. . . ." This was a rhetorical question, meaning "No it was God" (Num. 11:12–13).

In numerous places, God is also described as doing women's work, work that no self-respecting male would do—cleansing a woman after her defilement (Ezek. 36:25), sewing clothing (Gen. 3:21, Job 10:10–12), wiping away tears (Isa. 25:8, Rev. 21:4), washing a child (Ps. 51:2, 7), a mother comforting her child (Isa. 66:13–14), teaching Ephraim to walk and taking him in her arms (Hosea 11:3), and lifting an infant close to her cheek (Hosea 11:4). Virginia Mollenkott goes into great detail regarding feminine images of God in the Bible.[266]

In addition, the Hebrew word for "Spirit" (*ruach*) is feminine in gender, and the Greek word for "Spirit" (*pneuma*) is neuter. So there is no reason for referring to the Spirit of God as masculine. Mollenkott points out that God is described with animal similes and metaphors: mother bear (Hosea 13:8) and mother eagle (Deut. 32:11–12), and Jesus as mother hen (Matt. 23:37, Luke 13:34). Even though God and Jesus are described as animals or having animal characteristics, no one envisions

---

[265] Mollenkott, Virginia Ramey. *The Divine Feminine: The Biblical Imagery of God as Female* (New York: Crossroad Publishing Company, 1988), 3.

[266] *Ibid.*, 15–27.

God as an animal. So why think of God as male just because male images are used for God?[267]

Cultural Influence

The culture of the time was one that understood the world in terms of natural orders. God was at the top of the hierarchy, then angels, man, woman, child, and animals. Old Testament and rabbinic teaching reflect a culture of patriarchy. And there are vestiges of rabbinic conditioning in Paul's writing. He says in 1 Corinthians 14 that in the church, "women are not allowed to speak, but must be in submission" (verses 34–35). Yet in 1 Corinthians 11, Paul has no problem with women prophesying as long as they have their heads covered (verses 7–9), appealing to "nature" and "practice" (verses 13–16), an expression of cultural thinking.[268] He was torn between his culture and the gospel, expressing some confusion over women's role in the worship service.

Another issue is factual accuracy. In order to support their view that all of the Bible is factually accurate in all its details, some have quoted the following statement of Jesus: "Your word is truth" (John 17:17). In order to make that point and use this as a proof text, they have to lift the text completely out of its literary context and ignore everything they know about John's use of the word "truth" (*alētheia*). Every exegete agrees that John uses the term somewhat consistently. So how much sense does it make to use the definition of "factual accuracy" for "truth" in the expression that he had come to testify to the truth (John 18:37), that the Spirit "will guide you in all truth" (John 16:13), "I am the way, the truth, and the life" (John 14:6), and "the truth will make you free" (John 8:32)? When Jesus says he is the "truth," does that mean he is factual accuracy? When he says "the truth will make you free," is he saying factual accuracy will make people free? Not hardly. It means something much deeper than factual accuracy.

Over the last thirty or forty years, one group of exegetes has pointed out that ignoring the cultural content of scripture has adversely affected our understanding of women. As women studied the Bible through their set of lenses, a different view of the Bible and our whole way of interpreting it have been scrutinized. Mollenkott argues that our concept of the Bible

---

[267] Mollenkott, 1977, *op. cit.*, 93–95; 1983, *op. cit.*, 15–35.

[268] *Ibid.*, 1977, 91–100.

is often the problem. The Bible should not become "an icon (something to be admired but never touched)."[269] The treatment of women is a good illustration of the relation between inspiration and culture.

Mollenkott argues that we must conquer our fear of undercutting the doctrine of inspiration.[270] The problem is not if the Bible is inspired, but our understanding of inspiration. She also points out that not everything recorded in scripture is God's "antecedent" (my term) will (permitting men to divorce their wives) (Matt. 19:3–9, Deut. 24:1–3). Therefore, "we must immediately suspect any meaning which contradicts the thrust of the whole Bible toward human justice and oneness in Christ."[271] Women have begun to "destabilize" traditional teaching about women by interpreting the Bible through a different set of lenses. They have seen things that male-dominated exegesis has overlooked.

Finally, even within the highly patriarchal culture of the Bible, there are numerous instances in which women are portrayed as the heroine. Moses's sister, Miriam, was a "prophetess" (Exod. 14:20) and honored as a leader of Israel (Mic. 6:4). Deborah, the prophetess, played a major role in Israel. "She held court under the Palm of Deborah between Ramah and Bethel in the hill country of Ephraim, and the Israelites came to her to have their disputes decided" (Judg. 4:5). It was she whose influence persuaded the reluctant Gideon to foment rebellion against the Canaanites, who would not take military leadership unless Deborah went with him (Judg. 4:4–9). And the Canaanite general, Sisera, died at the hands of a woman, Jael (Judg. 4:17–22). Huldah, the prophetess, authenticated the "book of the Law" discovered during Josiah's reformation, making her the first person to establish the canon of scripture (2 Kings 22). Persian queen Esther took her life in her hands to courageously stand before the Persian king to plead on behalf of her persecuted people (Esther 5). Judith saved her people by killing Babylonian general Holofernes (Jdth. 13:1–10). In the book named for her, Susanna was morally superior to the elders of Israel. Lydia was an independent Jewish businesswoman who had considerable authority and provided hospitality for Paul (Acts 16:11–15). Nympha was a leader in the Colossian congregation, holding church in her house (Col. 4:16).

---

[269] Harrington, *op. cit.*, 20.

[270] Mollenkott, 1977, *op. cit.*, 104–105.

[271] *Ibid.*, 119.

BIBLICAL INTERPRETATION FOR LAYPEOPLE AND OTHER MARTYRS   195

Therefore, feminists point to a different approach toward inspiration, one that focuses on the intent of God in the gospel, which is harmony between God and humans and among humans, which includes suspicion of any text that undermines justice in the treatment of any people, including women.

Biblical Culture and Violence

Religion has often been the justification for violence, including genocide. Despite the teachings of Jesus, people like Ferdinand and Isabella, Philip II, King Leopold of Belgium, Cecil Rhodes, Hernando Cortés, Francisco Pizarro, and a plethora of others ignored all they had heard about Jesus and Christianity. Thousands of white Americans killed Native Americans who had the audacity to defend their homes and families against the invaders who wanted to take their land. And the Ku Klux Klan and White Citizens' Councils abused scripture to justify their unbridled abuse of African Americans.

Adam Hamilton reviewed the violence in the Old Testament. The death penalty was applied to Israelites for sacrificing to other gods (Exod. 22:20); to a child who violently hits a parent (Exod. 21:15); to a child who curses his parent (Exod. 21:17); to a stubborn and rebellious child who is a drunkard (Deut. 21:18–21); to people working on the Sabbath, including starting a fire (Exod. 35:2–3); to adulterers (Lev. 20:10); to a woman not being able to prove she is a virgin (Deut. 22:20–21); and to male homosexuals (Lev. 20:13). A priest was to burn his daughter alive if she was a prostitute (Lev. 21:9) or for encouraging family or friends to worship another god (Deut. 13:6–10). Sounds like the Taliban in Afghanistan because their culture was very similar to the Taliban's culture.

At Moses's orders, the Levites killed family members who presumably had participated in worshipping the golden calf. However, Aaron, who had constructed the golden calf, was not punished (Exod. 32:27–29). *Strange*. Well, maybe not so strange since he was part of the privileged class. In 2 Samuel 24, the claim is that God killed seventy thousand people because he was angry at David for taking a census (verses 1–15). God is portrayed as commanding that Israel exterminate all the inhabitants of cities in Canaan that they conquered, including children (Deut. 20:16–18), oxen, sheep, and donkeys (Josh. 6:20–23).[272]

---

[272]   Hamilton, *op. cit.*, 107–111.

However, this ban contradicted Deuteronomy, which says that when they were about to attack a city, they should offer peace terms, meaning they should give them the option to surrender (Deut. 20:10). If they submit, they should be forced to become "forced labor" (Deut. 20:11). If they refused and fought Israel and Israel won, the men should be put to death; but the women, children, and animals should become booty (Deut. 20:13–14). And if the woman was beautiful and the Israelite man wanted her for his wife, he could take her but first give her a month to mourn the loss of her parents before he had intercourse with her (Deut. 21:10–14).

Israel justified their cruelty toward other cultures, including murdering women and children, very much like Americans justified the virtual extermination of the American Indians, much like Cecil Rhodes and King Leopold of Belgium did to Africans and much like Hitler did to the Jews. However, Hamilton points out that the Old Testament "was written by human beings whose understanding and experiences of God were shaped by their culture, their theological assumptions, and the time"[273] in which they lived, expressing what they believed about God rather than what God actually wanted. We have already pointed out that Jesus argued that not everything in the Bible is what God wanted.

But it is important to notice that Israel was part of an entire Middle Eastern culture. On the Moabite Stone, King Mesha planned to do the very same thing to Israel—to invade and wipe out all the Israelites. That was part of the culture of the time. So the Old Testament "[tells] us more about the people who wrote them and the times that they were living in than about the God in whose name they claimed [the] authority to do these things."[274] That part of culture is almost international. Even today, "my nation right or wrong," a totally unchristian attitude, still prevails so that "when America marches to war, patriotism and faith are quickly melded so that to be a good Christians is to support the war effort,"[275] regardless of its justifiability. And if they seemed cruel, remember the thousands of children who were killed in Hiroshima, Nagasaki, and Dresden. And look at how many evangelicals have sold their immortal souls out to a man who has no moral compass whatsoever.

---

[273] *Ibid.*, 249.

[274] *Ibid.*, 214.

[275] *Ibid.*, 216.

View of Inspiration

Absolutizing Culture

Hamilton argues that "some still regard the New Testament (or even the entire Bible) as a sort of magic book whose 'meaning' has little to do with what the first century authors intended, and a lot to do with how some particular contemporary group has been accustomed to hear in it a call to a particular sort of spirituality or lifestyle."[276] Some even "treat it as if it fell from the sky in the King James Authorized Version."[277] I personally experienced this attitude in the summer of 1956, when I sold Bibles door-to-door out of Kingwood and Philippi, West Virginia. Nelson had recently put out the Revised Standard Version of the Bible. The "new-fangled" version was a threat to numerous people who wanted me to assure them that I was not selling that new heretical version, but that I was selling the authentic "King Virgin Bible." This is a true story. I swear it.

Mollenkott argues that in order for God to be able to communicate with us, just as we should refrain from absolutizing the political culture (kingdoms and slavery), so we should do the same for gender. Christians should concern themselves with "the power of the gospel instead of clinging to the sinful social order."[278]

Prototype Rather Than Archetype

Therefore, we are not to "absolutize" texts as if they were the important thing to hold on to once for all time. There is a more foundational principle. Texts are to be used as "paradigms" or prototypes of what might be appropriate for the kingdom at a specific time. James Sanders put it this way: "Since the Bible comes to us cloaked in the idioms, mores, and cultural 'givens' of the five culture eras . . . [we should] not generalize on or absolutize any of them but try to discern . . . [the way that] our ancestors

---

[276] Wright, N. T. *The New Testament and the Peoples of God* (Minneapolis: Fortress Press, 1992), 4.

[277] *Ibid.*, 5.

[278] Mollenkott, 1977, *op. cit.*, 92–95.

in the faith affirmed God's oneness, or integrity, in their day—then take that as inspiration and energy for going and doing likewise in our day."[279]

With these points in mind, it strains our reasoning to maintain the view that the Bible is a perfect archetypal writing, *un*influenced by the culture in which the Bible itself was written.[280]

Harrington says that those who use the Bible as a prototype are "directed by the tradition of faith, they come to the canon of Scripture expecting to find in it guidance for their lives . . . Then reflecting on how the Scriptures have been used within the faith-community (Jewish and Christian), they try to discern what the text might be saying to their own social and/or personal situation."[281]

This brings us to the issue of the purpose of the Bible.

---

[279] Sanders, *op. cit.*, 5.

[280] Harrington, *op. cit.*, 20.

[281] *Ibid.*, 21.

Chapter 12

PURPOSE OF SCRIPTURE

Have you ever sat in church during a sermon and looked around, figuring out who should pay attention to that part of the sermon or who should be in church to hear the sermon? Isn't it fun knowing who should be uncomfortably squirming in their pew? Well, I suppose there are times when we may identify with those proclaiming the message. But if God is to speak to us, we should generally be identifying with the ones *to whom the message is directed*. The same is true of the Bible. Sanders says, "Whenever our reading of a biblical passage makes us feel self-righteous, we can be confident we have misread it."[282]

Application of the Bible to New Situations

When we hear the same person (Jesus) say, on the one hand, "Judge not that you be not judged" (Luke 6:37) and then tell us to make judgments, "By their fruits you shall know them" (Matt. 7:16), we have a dilemma. That is, not all texts take the same side in an argument. In the eighth or

---

[282] Sanders, *op. cit.*, 71.

ninth century BCE, Joel said, "Beat your plowshares into swords and your pruning hooks into spears" (Joel 3:10), just the opposite of Isaiah 2:4 (750–686 BCE) and Micah 4:3 (after 701 BCE) that all peoples "will beat their swords into plowshares and their spears into pruning hooks." Apparently, the need was different when Joel wrote than it was when Isaiah and Micah wrote. John says Jesus gave his disciples his peace (John 14:27). In Luke, Jesus says he has come not to bring peace, but a sword (Luke 12:51). Apparently, the need was different when John's gospel was written than when Luke wrote his gospel. Sanders sees the Bible as producing *paradigms based on our need*. He argues that this reflects the "integrity (oneness) of God, ontologically [who he is] and ethically [what we do]," even working through man's sin.[283]

Interpreting in Context

To those overburdened with their sense of guilt, Jesus said, "My yoke is easy" (Matt. 11:30). The sin of the woman caught in adultery was public. To those who wanted to exercise the prescription of the law and stone her, Jesus challenges the crowd, daring them, "Let him without sin cast the first stone." When the accusers walk away, Jesus asked rhetorically if they did not stone her. When she says they did not condemn her, Jesus says, "Neither do I condemn you," calling her to change her life (John 8:3–11). With this, he challenged not only them, but also, by implication, the law of Moses that made stoning the punishment for adultery (Lev. 20:10, Deut. 22:22).

On the other hand, there are times when the self-satisfied who are passive conspirators in an unjust situation simply need an explanation of the unjust nature of the situation. As Martin Luther King Jr. said, "The ultimate tragedy is not the oppression and cruelty of the bad people but the silence of that by the good people."[284] My mother was like that. Raised in the South with segregation a part of the cultural fabric from the time she was born, she thought that segregation was okay and the way things were meant to be. When confronted with the conspiratorial nature of segregation and the injustice of it, she completely reversed her attitude. There are people who go along with injustice because they do not see it

---

[283] *Ibid.*, 8.

[284] Martin Luther King Jr., (n.d.). BrainyQuote.com. Retrieved July 7, 2016, from Brainy Quotecom Web site: http://www.brainyquote. Com/quote/quotes/m/martinluth390143.html.

BIBLICAL INTERPRETATION FOR LAYPEOPLE AND OTHER MARTYRS   201

and, because of their integrity, will change their minds when confronted with the truth. And yes, there are also those who will twist scripture in the worst, evil ways in order to support their own selfishness.

And so there are times when the hearers/readers may need the strong dose of indigestion-producing word of the law. For the obstinate, the unjust, the hypocritical, the self-righteous, and the duplicitous, what Luther called the second use of the law is necessary medicine, exposing our self-delusion about ourselves before God. One has difficulty conceiving of pastors in our day spewing forth the kind of severe law that Jesus vented on the highly regarded Pharisees (Matt. 23:1–36). He would lose parishioners and perhaps his pension.

Jesus told a rich man who claimed he wanted to follow Jesus to sell all he had, give it to the poor, and follow Jesus (Matt. 19:22–23). So what's the point? He didn't tell everyone to do that. Nicodemus, Mary, Martha, and Lazarus were well-to-do; but he never told them to sell all they had, give it to the poor, and follow him. In one text, he strokes his listeners. In the other, he rattles him. His message was based on his perception of the needs of the hearers. That is properly dividing the word of truth (2 Tim. 2:15), law and gospel, condemning and forgiving, killing and making alive— depending on the need.

Sanders says that discerning whether the historical hour stands under God's wrath or forgiveness "requires both intimate knowledge of the traditions or 'texts' of the ways of God in Israel's past (its *mythos* or Torah story) and a dynamic ability to perceive the salient facts of one's own moment in time"[285] Finally, both condemnation and forgiveness should always be motivated by love, which will be discussed later.

Transmission of the Message

If one reads this book as a Jew or Christian, there may be some benefit. I hope some insight is gained into understanding the process of communication better and thereby to better be able to transmit and receive communication not only in the Bible, but also in any piece of verbal communication. It would make me ecstatic to think that among all this analysis, there was enough of the proclamation of the gospel (good news) of the love of God in the history and traditions of Israel and in the person of Jesus Christ to bring the reader to faith. For those of the

---

[285]   *Op. cit.*, 93.

household of faith—whether a weathered and seasoned Christian who has fought the battles of faith for decades, one who has been a complacent quasi-Christian on whom God's Spirit has only recently broken down concupiscent defenses, or one who has recently been confronted with the gift of God's grace—God has a message in the form of inky configurations on the pages of the Bible.

In the Bible, individuals attempt to communicate a message of a nongender, non-image, noncorporeal, and nonvocal transcendent God to "finite," gendered, corporeal, vocal human beings, who, when they think of God, cannot help but think of God in gender, image, corporeal, and vocal terms. Those human beings have different experiences, different levels of education, different levels of communion, have prejudices, insights, limitations, good experiences, bad experiences, habits of thinking, vested interests, a penchant for status quo, or a penchant for change. They are all different. They think in different categories of thought. Some have been very conscious of God's call to proclaim the word (such as Ezekiel). Some were not at all aware of it (such as fathers and mothers whose stories told to their children were passed through those children to future generations, were finally written down, and eventually made it into scripture). Then there were those like Paul, who believed when he wrote to the churches that he was just writing for a specific situation and never conceived of his letters being put on the same level as the prophets of the Old Testament. Some were deluded by vested interests in staying in power but spoke the truth anyway, such as Caiaphas: "It is necessary that one man die for the people" (John 11:49–51).

Applying Love to Specific Situations

In Matthew 28, Jesus summarizes discipleship: "All authority in heaven and on earth has been given to me. Therefore, go and make disciples of all nations, baptizing them in the name of the Father and of the Son and of the Holy Spirit, and teaching them to obey everything I have commanded you. And surely I am with you always, to the very end of the age" (Matt. 28:18b–20). This was Jesus's call to his disciples (students) to be his apostles (those who are sent). His teachings had to do with the treatment of other people. But what are the guidelines for exercising discipleship to social situations?

A good guide is Jesus's injunction to his disciples to be "wise as serpents and innocent as doves" (Matt. 10:16). In other words, the Christian is to use both his heart and his head. Peter Berger, a Christian sociologist, illustrates the application of this text. He first argues that "'innocence' refers to a quality of the heart, not the head."[286] But how does one go about being "wise as serpents"?

Berger argues that the emphasis of the gospel is not enough. We also need to know what the real situation is to which we apply the gospel. If we misread the situation, even though our motive is a good one, our ignorance could be detrimental. As we study the Old and New Testament, we need to understand how the laws and statements functioned in that cultural context and apply them to our situation within our own cultural context.

So Berger says we need to study issues closely regarding the personal, social, economic, and political decisions that we have to make. In addition to the motivation of the gospel, he also needs to correctly diagnose the situation. With God's love moving us and the wisdom of discerning reality guiding us, we will be more apt to be instruments of God's creative purpose. Berger says that although we may work through the church, the decision to be a Christian is not for the religious institution itself, but for Jesus. But that also involves actions to do something as a Christian. Berger argues, "The diagnosis without the doctrine may lead to resignation, which is bad, but the doctrine without the diagnosis almost certainly leads to illusion, which is much worse."[287] Therefore, he says, "Christian commitment demands a relentless intellectual honesty, because it concerns God, who is truth and who is offended if He is worshipped as anything less than truth."[288]

There are two mistakes one can make regarding truth: One is to be committed to ideology, "a set of ideas serving the vested interests of a particular social group . . . parallel to the psychological concept of rationalization. And . . . [it] involves a distorted view of reality."[289] Ideology is dishonest in that the practitioner is not interested in the truth, but in defending his own vested interest or point of view. Berger argues—correctly, I believe—that "the people who would make of God an ideological weapon in our political conflicts are engaged in blasphemy."[290] It is not that we

---

[286] Berger, Peter L. *The Noise of Solemn Assemblies* (Garden City, NY: Doubleday, 1961), 13.

[287] *Ibid.*, 131.

[288] *Ibid.*, 10.

[289] *Ibid.*, 53.

[290] *Ibid.*, 131.

should avoid using our faith in viewing political situations, but that we should avoid using God to defend injustice.

Yet since nobody knows everything, it is important to be cautious about absolutes. "An individual possessed of absolute certainty with regard to his own perceptions and values . . . would then proceed to seek explanations as to why these other people are so blind to what to him are obvious truth. . . ."[291] Certainty tends to close one's eyes to further information, particularly if it is contradictory to what one already believes. That is the response of ideology. "An ideology is a set of definitions of reality delegitimizing specific vested interests in society."[292]

For example, the Christian faith has been used by the Ku Klux Klan to justify the murder of African Americans and by whites who supported them during Reconstruction and again during in the civil rights movement. Christians used a skewed interpretation of the Curse of Ham, whom they consider to be the father of the black race, to justify their racism. But the curse was not even pronounced on Ham, but on Canaan, who was considered to be the ancestor of the Canaanites (Gen. 9:24–27). Second, the man who pronounced the curse was in a drunken state. But all these facts are ignored so that the text could be used to justify the slavery of African Americans and later segregation and every kind of injustice toward black Americans. The same was true of those who took the Native Americans' land and killed them if they defended their families from such usurpation.

The second mistake is to have an incorrect understanding of the situation. "What everybody knows" is not always correct. For example, everybody knew that the world was flat, justifying the execution of Galileo for teaching that the earth was round. Unfortunately, too often, we respond on the basis of our perception of reality rather than reality itself. Berger argues, "Relevance presupposes a perception of the real situation."[293]

Berger points out that "religion always exists within a certain historical and social situation."[294] Before the Christian can understand how to apply his faith's response to a given situation, he must clearly understand

---

[291] Peter L. Berger and Hansfried Kellner. *Sociology Reinterpreted: An Essay on Method and Vocation* (Garden City, New York: Anchor Press, 1981), 57.

[292] *Ibid.*, 68.

[293] *Ibid.*, 37.

[294] *Ibid.*, 30.

BIBLICAL INTERPRETATION FOR LAYPEOPLE AND OTHER MARTYRS   205

his present situation. The goal of the sociologist is to provide correct information regarding social situations.

Berger and Kellner point out that "sociology is . . . an *attempt to understand*[295] . . . by clearing away collective illusions."[296] Sociology's insight is that things are not necessarily what they seem to be.[297] So "the sociologist will seek to penetrate the smoke screen of official versions of reality"[298] and "disturb the comfortable assumptions on which he rests his own social existence . . . unmaking 'the pretensions and propaganda.'"[299]

Our problem is that sociological and historical information, based on studies of the real situation, will often contradict our strongly held perceptions. Berger further says, "The concern of a sociologist, as a sociologist, is not to decide the issue but to provide an objective analysis"[300] and to provide correct information. In other words, the sociologist asks what *is* without asking what *ought* to be. Therefore, with the motivation of the gospel *and* the correct information regarding a social situation, a Christian has a much better chance of being a blessing rather than a curse.

The message needed in one social situation may be the opposite of what is needed in another. One only needs to look at Galatians and James to see that. It seems as if James read Galatians and contradicted it. But Galatians was apparently addressed to those who wanted to make the Christian faith a matter of observing certain "legal" requirements. Paul directs them to faith in the grace of God.

But James comes along with the opposite emphasis. He says faith without works (doing the right thing for people) is dead. His is not necessarily a contradictory message, but the need for the opposite emphasis. Apparently, there were people identifying with the Christian Church who wanted to become Christian for selfish reasons—that is to say, "King's X" to perdition—and not caring about others who were suffering. James addressed those who wanted to *use* justification by faith as an excuse for loveless unconcern for their fellow men and women. It was addressed for those who wanted to say, "If I believe in Jesus, I'll be saved, and that's

---

[295]   *Ibid.*, 4.

[296]   *Ibid.*, 6.

[297]   *Ibid.*, 23.

[298]   *Ibid.*, 35.

[299]   *Ibid.*, 38.

[300]   *Ibid.*, 39–40.

all that counts." James blasts that selfishness in no uncertain terms. One can see that abuse in politicians who parade their faith by focusing on Paul's interpretation of Jesus's work of redemption (for them, of course) while ignoring the actual teachings of Jesus about caring for the poor and outcasts and his warning about the potential for selfishness of the rich.

Example of How Changed Context Changes the Message

The record in Jeremiah says that when the Babylonians had Jerusalem surrounded, Hananiah assured the Jews that everything would be okay. God would take care of them. Sanders points out that when Hananiah spoke those comforting words to Judah (Jer. 28:1–4), Jeremiah was most ready to pray that it be God's will to break the yoke of their Babylonian oppressor (verses 5–9). But as time went on and the situation became more dire because Jeremiah saw no change, his message changed from that of hope to condemnation of Hananiah for leading the people to trust in a lie (verses 12–17).[301] Deuteronomy says to shun the prophet who tries to lead you astray (Deut. 13:1–5). A prophet was a prophet because he could perceive the situation correctly for the good of the people and spoke out on it. One way you will know if the prophet is a true prophet is whether his word comes true or not (Deut. 18:15–22). But at that point, you do not have the privilege of hindsight. Being a Monday morning quarterback is not the world's oldest profession, but it is the easiest. The problem is that decisions must be made in the present—on game day. It is not often that we can tell whether the prophet has evil intention.

Sanders does not believe that the false prophet is necessarily a false prophet because he intends to deceive (although it could be), but because his message *caused* deceit and falsehood. Jeremiah came to perceive that the earlier message was no longer relevant. In fact, it led the people astray. So if the same text can be appealed to with opposing conclusions, "the difference lies not in theological tradition . . . but in the hermeneutics applied to that tradition."[302]

Even though "the torah story was eternal, holy, and good,"[303] laws that worked well during the Bronze Age and Iron Age might be discarded

---

[301] Sanders, E. P. *The Historical Figure of Jesus* (New York: New York: Penguin Press, 1993), 90.

[302] *Ibid.*, 100.

[303] *Ibid.*, 108.

because they no longer worked during a later era. Laws that reflect justice during the nomadic period might be irrelevant or even unjust during the agricultural period. If laws or statements conflict, God's people must decide which is appropriate in the present situation.[304] For example, in a rural society in which children are needed to work the farm, they are an economic asset. So it might be important to encourage large families. But in an urban society in which many children might be a burden, it might be important (for the good of families and the society) to encourage limiting the number of children a family has. And as an escalating world population puts a strain on the ability to feed everyone and contributes to pollution, it might also be important to limit family size.

The Foundation

So what do we hang on to? Jesus agreed with the teacher of the law who perceived that the two foundation laws of the Old Testament were as follows: "You shall love the LORD your God with all your heart, and with all your soul, and with all your mind" (Deut. 6:5) and "You shall love your neighbor as yourself" (Lev. 19:18). Sanders argues that when Jesus said, "On these two hang the law and the prophets" (Matt. 22:37–44), he was teaching "that all Scripture depends on theologizing first, loving God with all the self, and moralizing thereafter, loving neighbor as self . . ."[305] And that moralizing is not first and foremost sticking to a set of laws. When Jesus was criticized for allowing his disciples to pick up heads of grain to eat on the Sabbath, which was against the law of Moses (Deut. 23:25), Jesus responded by pointing out that for the good of his men, David had broken the Sabbath (Mark 25–26) and added his interpretation that "the Sabbath was made for humankind, not humankind for the Sabbath" (Mark 2:27), emphasizing the spirit of the law rather than the letter of the law. When Jesus said "fulfill the law" (Matt. 5:17), he didn't mean the letter, but the spirit of the law since Jesus often "violated many of the ritual interpretations of the law."[306]

---

[304]   *Ibid.*

[305]   *Ibid.*, 7.

[306]   Nida and Taber, *op. cit.*, 24.

The Three Functions of the Law

So how does the law work? Martin Luther[307] and the Reformation theologians[308] said the law operates in three distinct ways.

The Law as Curb

How does law (in the sense of proscription) function for our good? Since not everyone responds out of God's love, the law is sometimes required to curb human selfishness or civil use of the law (Deut. 13:6–11, 19:16–21; Rom. 13:3–4), the "judicial" and punitive sense. If you break the law, you will be punished—jailed, have your life taken, fined, spanked, have your privileges taken away, or sent to time-out. Conformity to the law is not motivated by the love of God or man, but by the desire to avoid punishment and live a pleasant life. All human beings, to some extent, operate with this function of the law.

Another way of understanding the "law" is in terms of "a principle." A friend of mine, Hilmer Krause, likes to say it is like the laws of nature. If we obey the laws of nature, it will be to our benefit. For example, if we obey the law of gravity, we will be okay. But if we defy the law of gravity, we are liable to end up with broken bones and abrasions or worse. Keeping the law of gravity, we will live in harmony with God and creation.

The Law as Mirror

A second way the law functions is as a mirror. When we look at ourselves in the clear mirror of God's law, our efforts to justify ourselves are frustrated. All our illusions about ourselves that have been propped up by defense mechanisms like rationalization are completely undermined (Rom. 3:20, 4:15, 5:13, 7:7–11). This causes us to look to Jesus (Gal. 3:19–24),

---

[307] Edward A. Engelbrecht. "Luther's Threefold Use of the Law," *Concordia Theological Quarterly*, Vol.75:1–2 (January/April 2011), referring to Martin Luther, *Luthers Werke: Kritische Gesamtausgabe [Scriften]*, 65 vols. (Weimar: H. Böhlau, 1883–1993) 10:I:456–457; 26:17.

[308] James Andreae, Nicholas Selnecker, Andrew Musculus, Christopher Koerner, Chytraeus, Martin Chemnitz. "Formula of Concord," *The Book of Concord: The Confessions of the Evangelical Lutheran Church*. G. Tappert, Tr. and ed. (St. Louis: Concordia Publishing House, 1959), 563–568.

the author and finisher of our faith (Heb. 12:2). Take the example of the parable of the good Samaritan (Luke 10:15–37). The power of this parable is missed if one does not know the cultural context. It does not refer to helping stranded travelers with flat tires or about helping old ladies across the street. As commendable as these actions might be, they are tepid and watered down compared with the dynamite of Jesus's message.

The Samaritans were hated by the Jews. They were considered the scum of the earth. Samaria was between Galilee and Judea. In going from Judea to Galilee, they had to make the choice of whether to take the short route through Samaria or go a long way out of the way to avoid going through Samaria. Because of their fanatical hatred of the Samaritans and the Samaritans' fanatical hatred of Jews, which actually could make it dangerous for a Jew to go through Samaria, it was common for them to take the long way. To go the long way, they had to travel east, cross over the Jordan River, travel north, and turn west to cross back over the Jordan River just south of the Sea of Galilee, making their trip twice the distance and taking twice as much time.

So the last person in the world that the Jews would expect to be the hero in the story was a Samaritan. The story would be extremely offensive to almost all Jews. So why did Jesus choose a Samaritan as the hero of his story? Because it is an example of the radical love that God expects. It shows what "neighbor" is really like in God's eyes, to show the utter and complete love required to keep this commandment. I believe the parable may be to show the impossibility of being able to *earn* God's favor, which was the issue in the original question that elicited the parable. It may be a way of directing the man who asked "Who is my neighbor?" to God's grace. It causes them to ask, "Then who can be saved?" The answer is the same answer given to the bewildered disciples after Jesus told the rich man that if he wanted to inherit eternal life, he should sell all that he had and give it to the poor—namely, "With man it is impossible, but with God nothing is impossible" (Matt. 19:16–26).

In the Old Testament, the second use of the law was a way of turning Israel to Yahweh's grace in what God had been doing for Israel and to what their sins of injustice were leading them. For Christians, the second use of the law is a way of turning us to God's grace in Christ. It is what we saw God do for and through Israel that calls one to be God's child. It is in Christ's cross and resurrection that we find the power of redemption and harmony with God and our neighbor. It is God that frees us from guilt, from shame, fear, selfishness, and the crass use of others as mere utensils for our own unworthy ends. It is he who frees us from slavery to sin, as well as the sin of slavery. It is God whose fulfillment of the law turns the law from being our accuser to being our friend.

The Law as Guide

The third use of the law is as a guide. Having been freed from the oppression of the law, in thankfulness to God and as free agents, we look to God and ask, "How can I serve you?" He answers, "Look into my law. It was meant for your good in the first place. If you want to serve me, then keep your eyes focused on me the only answer to life's needs, and put away all those false trinkets on which people are pathetically inclined to depend for meaning in their lives. Don't throw my name around in a destructive way or as an expression of your language poverty, for when you want to use it seriously, nobody will take you seriously. Do not neglect worship and use of my word in your life, for they are for your benefit, rejuvenating your spirit by imbibing My Spirit.

"Do not kill or embitter the lives of my children of any age, class, or ethnic group, but help them maintain, enhance, and enjoy their lives. Do not be a party to destruction of your marriage or your neighbor's marriage, but support and honor marriage. For I gave husband and wife to each other, not for treason and bitterness, but for happiness, pleasure, and mutual delight and support. In fact, do not use sex as a means of expressing selfish lust, but use it as a way of expressing my love and commitment to me by demonstrating love and commitment to my children. I give you my relation to the church as an example of what your relationship should be to your spouse or other loved ones. He loved the church so much that my son gave his own life for it. That is how you should love your partner" (Eph. 5:25).

"If you love me and want to serve me, do not steal from your brothers and sisters, either by legal or illegal means, but help them maintain what they need in this life. Do not be quick to gossip about your brothers and sisters or tear down their reputation. Do not delight in hearing about the failures of my children to be all that I created them to be. Make sure that what you say about them, even if it must be something negative, is not to tear them down, but is to their benefit and the protection of the reputation of others who are innocent. Insofar as you can, assume the best possible interpretation on what they do, not gleefully jumping at the chance to interpret what they do in a negative way.

"In fact, if you love me and love my creation, do not even harbor in your heart the desire to have what is your neighbor's, because it is out of the heart that proceed either good or evil actions toward your brothers and sisters."

In case you didn't notice, I went through an interpretation of the third use of the law for the entire Ten Commandments. It was not anything original. I stole those ideas from Martin Luther's explanation of the commandments in *Small Catechism*.[309] That is what God says regarding the third use of the law (Rom. 6:14, 7:4, 6; 1 Cor. 9:20; Gal. 2:15–19, 3:25).

Basis of the Commandments

According to Luther, the basis of our keeping of the commandments is to "fear and love God, *so that . . .*" There is no sentimental moralism here. Luther places our relation to our neighbor as expressed in the Ten Commandments squarely on our prior relationship to God.

Positive Emphasis

The second thing is that Luther does not see the commandments as a bunch of "don't do this and don't do that" to prevent us from enjoying life. In each of his explanations to the commandments, he emphasizes. "We *do not* do this . . . but we *do* do that." It is not negative, but positive. Nor is it a "minimum daily requirement" type religion. It is not an emphasis on what we can get by with without God zapping us. This is no "staying out of hell" emphasis and no use of faith as merely fire insurance. That emphasis would be completely self-centered and not focused on love for God or care for our brothers and sisters. The emphasis begins with not hurting our neighbor, but it does not stop there. The positive side is what God would have us do because of our love of God to enhance our neighbor's life and because God has made us brothers and sisters.

---

[309] "Enchiridion: The Small Catechism of Dr. Martin Luther for Ordinary Pastors and Preachers," *The Book of Concord: The Confessions of the Evangelical Lutheran Church.* Theodore G. Tappert, tr. and ed. (St. Louis, MO: Concordia, 1959), 342–344.

Specific Example

The first three commandments (in the Lutheran and Roman Catholic numbering) are summed up in the words "You shall love the LORD your God with all your heart, with all your strength, and with all your mind" (Deut. 6:5). Commandments 4–10 are summarized in the words "You shall love your neighbor as yourself" (Lev. 19:19). Now let's face it. In dealing with people, if the church collectively and Christians individually asked ourselves how we would want to be treated, our entire society would be different and would be stood on its head. We would have a different attitude about welfare. We wouldn't use the term "welfare reform" as self-delusional, hypocritical justification for doing as little as possible for the poor. If we asked ourselves how we would want to be treated in similar circumstances, we would have a completely different attitude and therefore completely different behavior toward the unemployed, the homeless, children of welfare mothers, contraception, gays and lesbians, members of other religions, national health care, nuclear weapons, gun control, massive corporate welfare, and bloodthirsty dictators whose countries happen to have resources and products that we want to buy and a totally different tax structure—one that requires the filthy rich to share with the poor who work themselves full-time to the bone and still don't have enough to be able to support their children. Although our conclusions may not change on specific issues, our approach to the problem would be completely different on many of them.

Limiting the Gospel

Christians often have a very narrow definition of the gospel and thereby limit God's activity in the world through his children. Marcus Borg points out that our image of Jesus affects our perception of the Christian life, giving shape to our lives as Christians, making Christianity either credible or not credible to the world.[310]

The gospel is expressed in many more ways than what Christians call the "vicarious atonement"—that is, Jesus's sacrifice on the cross to forgive sins. Borg shares three of what he calls "macro-stories" in scripture. The first is the story of exodus—basically a story of bondage, liberation, a journey, and destination, inviting us to ask, "To what am I in bondage?"

---

[310] Borg, 1994, *op. cit.*, 2.

BIBLICAL INTERPRETATION FOR LAYPEOPLE AND OTHER MARTYRS   213

Bondage could be to anything—drugs, alcohol, sex, work, texting, computer games, nation, political party. The possibilities are endless. Borg says that like Israel, the way out of bondage is through the wilderness—a place of fear and anxiety. In other words, "It ain't easy." Other texts that deal with being enslaved but given freedom are Galatians 5:1, Romans 8:2 and 6:6-9, 14-20, 22, and John 8:32–36. It is a struggle to become free.

A second macro story is the story of exile and return, which, like Israel's Babylonian exile, is the experience of separation from the familiar and dear. The experience of exile is one of estrangement and alienation and is felt as a loss of connection with meaning in life. Estrangement can be from husband, wife, mom, dad, friends, nation, boss, reality, or oneself. Besides the exile, I believe Genesis 2–3 express that same alienation. The story of Adam and Eve reflect the alienation from each other (they blame each other), from themselves (they experience shame), from the environment (life will become a matter of sweating to struggle, and childbirth will be a struggle), and from God (they hid from him).

That alienation can be seen when "Christian" leaders with an immature or negative understanding of the faith make public vitriolic, hateful pronouncements. Non-Christians, making the false assumption that they are speaking for the essence of the Christian faith, are so turned off by the hatemongers that they are turned off to Christianity and never get a chance to hear the gospel.

Read the gospels and see whom Jesus embraces and whom he condemns. He does not condemn the outcasts. He ministers to them. He calls them to himself. The people that Jesus condemns are the self-righteous religious establishment and the duplicitous who speak piously one way but act differently when it comes to their treatment of people. That bears repeating. The two groups of people that Jesus condemns are the self-righteous and the duplicitous. They were often the religious leaders who looked down on people, the Sadducees and Pharisees. And those religious leaders were often the people who pontificated about people's objective keeping of the law but had no compassion for those in need of care.

The priestly story is the paradigm of which Christians usually think. It is a story of sin, guilt, sacrifice, and forgiveness, involving ideas of impurity, defilement, and uncleanness and therefore of images of cleansing, washing, and covering over. It has to do with being redeemed from the bad things that we do to others. Now it is true that there are times in our lives that we have done things of which we are guilty. We have hurt other people.

It may be relatively benign by just doing or saying something thoughtless or mean-spirited that hurt someone deeply by what we said or did. Or it may be something extremely serious, like injuring or killing someone by drunk driving or online bullying. In some instances, we have been guilty of embittering or destroying the life of someone that God loves.[311]

Borg argues that exclusive focus on the priestly story results in distortions. It may lead to political domestication, a passive understanding of the Christian life, a belief that God has done everything that needs to be done, and a focus on the afterlife to the exclusion of the call to discipleship. The problem is the idea that all we have to do is to believe the story. Second, some people do not feel much guilt but may feel in bondage or strong alienation and estrangement.[312] Those people will not be helped by total emphasis on the priestly story.

Borg points out that Jesus challenged the dominant thinking and that an interpretation of scripture that is faithful to Jesus is one that "sees the Bible through the lens of compassion, not purity."[313] And the way we see the world determines the way that we live. Conventional wisdom reflects the values of a culture, based on rewards and punishments, as the basis for identity and self-esteem. Jesus reversed the thinking of the time, focusing on the will of the Father.[314]

Jesus himself gave us the example. It has been said in many ways by others. Paul wrote, "Whether you eat or drink, or whatsoever you do, do all to the glory of God" (1 Cor. 10:31). Again, he wrote, "He died for all that those who live should no longer live for themselves, but for him who died for them and rose again" (2 Cor. 5:15). But Paul articulated it most beautifully in his letter to the Philippians in what may have been a hymn of his day. He wrote,

> Let the same mind be in you that was in Christ Jesus,
> who, though he was in the form of God
> did not regard equality with God as something to be exploited,
> but emptied himself, taking the form of a slave, being born in human likeness.

---

[311] *Ibid.*, 124–127.

[312] *Ibid.*, 130–132.

[313] *Ibid.*, 49–59.

[314] *Ibid.*, 74–80.

BIBLICAL INTERPRETATION FOR LAYPEOPLE AND OTHER MARTYRS 215

And being found in human form, he humbled himself
and became obedient to the point of death—even death on a
cross.
Therefore, God also highly exalted him and gave him the name
that is above every name,
so that at the name of Jesus every knee should bend,
in heaven and on earth and under the earth,
and every tongue should confess that Jesus Christ is Lord,
to the glory of God the Father. (Phil. 2:4–12).

That is the motivation—our response to God's incredible love for us. Paul calls on believers to have the same mind as Jesus had.

But in addition to the macro stories, there are many other stories and expressions that reflect human need and God's address of those needs with the gospel. They are expressed with many figures of speech. A few are lost but found by God, like the lost sheep (Luke 15:1–7), lost coin (Luke 15:8–10), and the prodigal son (Luke 15:24); being in the dark or blind, but being enlightened (John 1:5, 3:20); being dead and made alive again (Rom. 6:4, Luke 15:24); being enemies of God but made friends, at-one-ment (Col. 1:21–22, Rom. 5:10); being afraid or losing heart and being given courage (Ps. 34:7, Rom. 8:15); being estranged from the Father and the family and being accepted back (Luke 15:11–32); being wounded and being healed (Mal. 4:2, Jer. 17:44, Luke 9:11); being attacked and being defended (many psalms); being reviled and being vindicated (John 9:28 and many psalms); being outside the law and being justified (Rom. 3:24–28); being hungry and being fed (Neh. 9:15, Matt. 5:6); and numerous others. And if you look closely at all, you see that in many instances, these metaphors address our situations or feelings about life.

All of these images express the devastating experience of distance from God. (Even when I say "distance" from God, I am using a metaphor). Borg adds that they all involve a new identity, one that senses acceptance by God. The reason we need these different stories is because different people have different needs. Each story is a story of a transforming relationship to God into a compassionate people, "into the likeness of Christ."[315] And that is what the Christian faith is all about.

---

[315] *Ibid.*, 133–136.

Connecting Ancient Man and Modern Man

In the case of neither the ancient world nor in the modern world is our worldview (*Weltanschauung* in German) something we consciously obtain. It is given to us by our society from our very birth. It is the world as we find it when we are born. The father buys a truck for boy, a doll for the girl, roughhouses with the boy, is gentle with the girl. Long before we are able to reflect on the stimuli in our environment, we observe what others do, learn from them, and "know" what is appropriate. If we saw a woman walking in a mall with her breasts flopping in the wind, she might be arrested, and we would "realize" that there was something wrong about that. But if we had grown up in a tribe in New Guinea or among Australia's aborigines, where the women's breasts are exposed, we wouldn't even notice them. As many have repeated, we learn more by what is "caught" than what is "taught." And we reify the world. That is, from our very earliest days as children, we assume that the world as it is in our experience is the way it is *supposed to be.*[316]

We pointed out earlier that the *writers* of scripture were "afflicted" with cultural and personal limitations. So are those to whom the word comes. Our problem is learning God's intent for us and therefore the intended meaning of scripture *for us*. Modern man is spoken to by ancient man. The difficulty is that the worldviews (*Weltanschauungen*) of the two is totally different. However, the social dynamics that construct our understanding of the world are the same. "The world view of the New Testament writers was constructed and maintained by the same kind of social processes that construct and maintain the world view of contemporary 'radical' theologians."[317] However, for most of us, "world views remain firmly anchored in *subjective* certainty"[318]

---

[316] Peter L. Berger and Thomas Luckmann. *The Social Construction of Reality* (Garden City, New York: Anchor Books/Doubleday, 1966), 89–92, 196–187.

[317] Peter L. Berger. *A Rumor of Angels: Modern Society and the Rediscovery of the Supernatural* (Garden City, New York: Anchor Books/Doubleday & Company, Inc., 1970), 41.

[318] *Ibid.*, 42; italics mine.

Ancient Man's World

Ancient man lived in an open system. For him, "history . . . is set in motion and controlled by . . . supernatural powers."[319] He lived in a flat world, with God living locally "up there," us living "here" on earth, and devils living "down there." God was localized. He lived in mountains. He lived in tabernacles. He lived in temples. Ancient man lived in a world where people could cast spells, where a person's name could change his very being, and where magic was taken very seriously. He lived in an honor-shame culture of one-upsmanship by marshaling honor for oneself and shaming others. And even today, you get a glimpse of that in taunting in sports and the need to have a better house than the Joneses. Of ultimate importance in life (aside from God) was to maintain the family's good name. People looked for cause and effect but looked outside what most of us would call "rational" causes to what we would call superstitious causes. When the disciples saw a man born blind, because of their way of thinking, it was natural for them to ask Jesus, "Rabbi, who sinned so that he was born blind, this man or his parents?" (John. 9:1). That was the way they thought.

Modern Man's World

Modern man lives in a closed system in which he also looks for cause-effect relationships. If he cannot find it, he still is sure that it is there. He lives in a world that is not at all the center of an infinite universe in which God is not localized, but ubiquitous, and who works through natural processes. If a hurricane hits a city, only the vitriolic who want to pronounce judgment on someone or some group for a sin (including the infants) will pontificate about God's judgment raining down. Look at the irrational pronouncements of so-called Christian leaders regarding the earthquake that hit Haiti in 2010 and Hurricane Katrina's devastation of New Orleans. The rest of us look for earthquakes in the shifting of tectonic plates and for hurricanes in the wind currents in the Atlantic that were a natural result of the warming and cooling of ocean currents. Otherwise, we would pay no attention to the predictions of geologists regarding the potential for earthquakes or meteorologists for weather predictions based on such phenomena. The God in which modern man believes does not

---

[319] Rudolf Bultmann,. "New Testament and Mythology," *Kerygma and Myth: A Theological Debate*, ed. (London: SPCK, 1953), 1.

supernaturally break in and put aside the "laws of nature." Modern man expects there to be a scientific explanation for everything, even if no one now knows what that explanation is.

Talking Past Each Other

In applying scripture to present-day situations, we need to avoid having modern man and ancient man talk past each other. As indicated in the second chapter, the purpose of interpretation is to take a piece of literature written thousands of years ago by people with a completely different way of understanding the world and transmitting the meaning of that message to people in our modern culture in such a way that we apply the intent of the original message to our own modern situation in light of the two great commandments.

Nomadic Law

Now let's apply the broad commandments in specific situations. The Old Testament has many examples of how the commandments are to be kept in specific situations. The fifth commandment says, "You shall not kill." Now the main point of this commandment is *God's concern for human life*. So how does one keep the commandment? During Israel's nomadic period, there was a law that said that if a man has an ox that has a tendency to gore people, the ox is to be kept tethered. If the owner is so unconcerned with the lives of his neighbors that he does not tether this ox and it gores someone, the ox is to be killed, and the owner is to make heavy remuneration. If the ox kills someone, the lives of both the owner and the ox are to be taken (Exod. 21:28–32). It does not say whether the ox was given to the deceased's family as an expression of compensation for their loss. My guess is that the priests got it. Since nomads could not maintain prisons, they needed a reasonable way to make sure people were responsible toward the neighbors. Death seemed reasonable—the life of the offender for the life of the victim.

Application

The commandments don't give neat little answers (for that matter, neither does the whole Bible). God's law is not a convenient index by which one can look up chapter and verse and know exactly what to do in every situation. That is legalism. Indeed, that is the problem with bureaucracy. Bureaucracy is an extremely efficient way to deal with thousands or millions of typical situations. However, not all situations are typical. Bureaucracies are notoriously inept in dealing with atypical situations. Life is just not always typical.

Ancient man did not have to deal with weapons of mass destruction, overpopulation, environmental destruction, computer hacking, identity theft, or the competition between CD sales and Internet streaming. The law as we have it recorded was given to a small nomadic tribe of Bedouin herders of cattle and sheep, later a loose confederation of relatively small tribes of small farmers and herders, then a small but fairly powerful kingdom, followed by two beleaguered squabbling small kingdoms engaged in fratricide, and finally an ethnic people without a country or temple. It occurred during the Bronze Age and early Iron Age. The laws deal with God's people in those kinds of social structures, structures that are considerably different from ours.

To find the point of the law, let me suggest that we look at people in need *as if we were those people* and then ask what we would like others to do for us if we were in that situation. That is the point the Old Testament makes. But then we would also have to really understand their true situation rather than the way uncaring demagogues like to present the situation. We need to actually understand the person's situation as best we can rather than stereotyping based on commonly held self-justifying misperceptions. And in the New Testament, Jesus affirms that approach toward the treatment of our brothers and sisters (Luke 10:27).

So how might we apply that ox-tethering law to our situation? If we know that drinking alcohol and driving a car or texting while driving are lethal combinations, then if someone has so little regard for his brothers' and sisters' lives that he participates in such a lethal combination, he will be heavily fined and lose his driver's license. If he has a wreck under that condition, *he* pays for the victim's car and the bills of the injured parties and remains in jail in a work-release program until the bill is paid. If a person is killed in the accident, he is imprisoned like anyone else who commits intentional manslaughter, also serving in a work-release program until an appropriate amount (always a guess) is fulfilled. But here I am talking about the legal system. We as individuals within the community of faith address the issue of how to treat others with the motivation of the gospel.

Chapter 13

APPLICATION OF BIBLE TO MODERN ISSUES

Scriptural Guidance for Jewish and Christians Ethics

So what does all this emphasis on biblical interpretation and applying it to the present time mean? Where do we start? We said earlier that the basis of interpreting the scriptures had to do with applying "love God with all your heart and love your neighbor as yourself." But what is the real essence of our beliefs about morality? Some would argue that it is not "smoking, drinking, or running around with wild women" (that expression shows how old I am). Others would argue that honesty, not lying, is the best policy. Others focus on the Bill of Rights as the foundation of morality. Others consider that the separation of church and state (which is, incidentally, not what the First Amendment to the Constitution says) is a foundation principle. One implication of that concept for some people is that the church and private charitable institutions should take care of the needs of the poor and that the government has no business getting involved in their need of social relief. You observe that kind of thinking in the case of politicians who tout their Christian faith but focus completely on Paul's

BIBLICAL INTERPRETATION FOR LAYPEOPLE AND OTHER MARTYRS   221

interpretation of who Jesus was and neglect what Jesus taught about taking care of people. Unfortunately, even people who claim Christ can be very selfish and uncaring.

Those opposed to the Supplemental Nutrition Assistance Program (SNAP, the descendant of the Food Stamp Program), health care of the poor and their children, Section 8 housing, and other programs to maintain the lives of the poor turn their backs on the people about whom Jesus was most concerned.

The main argument against the government providing care for the needy is an ideological interpretation of John 22:21. Wanting to trap Jesus in his words in order to have an excuse for having him put to death, the Pharisees come to him with sugary sweet hypocritical flattery, asking, "Teacher, we know you are a man of integrity and that you teach the way of God in accordance with the truth. You aren't swayed by men because you pay no attention to who they are. Tell us, then, what is your opinion? Is it right to pay taxes to Caesar or not?"

It is not hard to see their intent. If Jesus had said no, this would have been, for the Romans, a treasonable statement. If he had said yes, it would have been a treasonable statement to the Jews. So he didn't answer their question. Instead, he said, "You hypocrites, why are you trying to trap me? Show me the coin used for paying the tax." When they produced a denarius, he asked, "Whose portrait is this? And whose inscription?" They answer, "Caesar's." Jesus responded with an evasive statement, avoiding the trap: "Give to Caesar what is Caesar's, and to God what is God's" (Matt. 22:15–21). So in the sacred precincts of the temple, they produced a coin that was sacrilegious to Jews, for the inscription said, "Tiberius Caesar, august son of the divine Augustus, high priest." His evasive answer could be interpreted in pretty much any way they wanted to interpret it, but it avoids answering the question originally asked of him.[320] The Romans could have no problem with the statement, and the Jews knew that Jesus agreed that their ultimate loyalty was to God.

So what does it mean to love your neighbor as yourself? It means if you were in the same situation, how would you want to be treated by those

---

[320]   This is not the only time Jesus avoided answering dangerous questions (Matt. 21:23–28, Mark 11:27, Luke 20:1–8). Bruce J. Malina and Richard L. Rohrbaugh's *Social Science Commentary on the Synoptic Gospels* gives numerous examples of such thrust and parry in the "honor-shame" culture in which Jesus lived.

who have the power to do something about it? The purpose of humans is not to squirrel away enough to maintain them for a hundred lifetimes, but to care for the needs of people whom God loves.

What did Jesus teach? His background began with what he knew about the teachings of the Old Testament. Another way of saying "love your neighbor as yourself" is "exercise justice." The way many people think of justice is "make the punishment fit the crime." But in the Bible, the term is most often used to demand that those in power treat those without power with equity or fairness. It was emphasized time and time again by the prophets. Nothing seems to have been more important to them. Isaiah says that a king rules to promote justice (Isa. 32:1). And who will be able to live under God's scrutiny? Isaiah says,

> The one who walks righteously and speaks truthfully,
> who rejects profit from extortion,
> who waves away a bribe instead of grabbing it,
> who won't listen to bloody plots,
> and who won't contemplate doing something evil. (Isa. 33:15,
> Common English Bible [CEB])[321]

Jeremiah joins Isaiah's call for justice, saying, "The LORD proclaims: 'Do what is just and right; rescue the oppressed from the power of the oppressor. Don't exploit or mistreat the refugee, the orphan, and the widow. Don't spill the blood of the innocent in this place'" (Jer. 22:3, CEB).

And regarding his servant, God says in Isaiah,

> But here is my servant, the one I uphold;
> my chosen, who brings me delight.
> I've put my spirit upon him;
> he will bring justice to the nations.
> but he will surely bring justice. (Isa. 42:1–4, CEB)

And regarding his ministry, Isaiah uses words that Jesus would quote five hundred years later at the foundation of his ministry:

---

[321] Joel B. Green, gen. ed. *The CEB Study Bible with Apocrypha*. Nashville: Common English Bible, 2013.

940514

Statement

DATE 02/27/19

TERMS

TO Erik S.

IN ACCOUNT WITH

Rev. David W. Melber
Alpha Omega Publishing
7600 Glenhill Cove - Austin, TX 78752
(512) 922-8888   dwmelber@aol.com

1		Bib Interp				19	99
					Tot / 65		
		PA					

| CURRENT | OVER 30 DAYS | OVER 60 DAYS | TOTAL AMOUNT | 2 64 |

adams· DC5812

01-11

The LORD God's spirit is upon me,
because the LORD has anointed me.
He has sent me
to bring good news to the poor,
to bind up the brokenhearted,
to proclaim release for captives,
and liberation for prisoners,
to proclaim the year of the LORD's favor
and a day of vindication for our God,
to comfort all who mourn,
to provide for Zion's mourners,
to give them a crown in place of ashes,
oil of joy in place of mourning,
a mantle of praise in place of discouragement.
I, the LORD, love justice;
I hate robbery and dishonesty.
I will faithfully give them their wage,
and make with them an enduring covenant. (Isa. 61:1–3,
8, CEB)

And Jeremiah comments on what makes a person a good king, namely,

He defended the rights of the poor and needy;
then it went well.
"Isn't that what it means to know me?"
declares the LORD.
(Jer. 22:15)

And in Jeremiah, God shows how serious he is about treating the disenfranchised with justice, threatening the rich and powerful because they

have grown fat and sleek!
To be sure, their evil deeds exceed all limits,
and yet they prosper.
They are indifferent to the plight of the orphan,
reluctant to defend the rights of the poor. (Jer. 5:28, CEB)

In Deuteronomy, the LORD tells "Moses" to appoint judges who will judge the people fairly (Deut. 16:18) and warns them, "Don't delay justice; don't show favoritism. Don't take a bribe because bribery blinds the vision of the wise and twists the words of the righteous" (Deut. 16:19).

The psalmist takes the positive approach, instructing his people to "defend the cause of the weak and fatherless; maintain the rights of the poor and oppressed. Rescue the weak and the needy; deliver them from the hand of the wicked" (Ps. 82:3–4).

Amos is one of the LORD's earliest prophetic representative critics, threatening punishment for the oppressive treatment of the poor:

> The LORD proclaims:
> For three crimes of Israel,
> and for four, I won't hold back the punishment,
> because they have sold the innocent for silver,
> and those in need for a pair of sandals.
> They crush the head of the poor into the dust of the earth,
> and push the afflicted out of the way. (Amos 2:6–7, CEB)

> He criticizes the degrading opulent lifestyle while ignoring
> the important issue of justice:
> Hear this word, you cows of Bashan,
> who are on Mount Samaria,
> who cheat the weak,
> who crush the needy,
> who say to their husbands, "Bring drinks, so we can get
> drunk!" (Amos 4:1, CEB)

He expresses disdain for the greedy perverters of justice:

> Hear this, you who trample on the needy and destroy
> the poor of the land, saying,
> "When will the new moon
> be over so that we may sell grain,
> and the Sabbath
> so that we may offer wheat for sale,
> make the ephah smaller, enlarge the shekel,
> and deceive with false balances,

in order to buy the needy for silver
and the helpless for sandals,
and sell garbage as grain?" (Amos 4:4–6, CEB)

This suggests the need for regulations and oversight of the merchant class, which, of course, they would vociferously oppose.

Micah adds his threats:

Doom to those who devise wickedness,
to those who plan evil when they are in bed.
By the light of morning they do it,
for they are very powerful.
They covet fields and seize them,
houses and take them away.
They oppress a householder
and those in his house,
a man and his estate. (Mic. 2:1–2, CEB)

Even after the exile, Zechariah had to emphasize the same theme: The LORD of heavenly forces proclaims:

"Don't oppress the widow, the orphan, the stranger, and the poor; don't plan evil against each other!" But they refused to pay attention.

They turned a cold shoulder and stopped listening. (Zech. 7:9a, 10–11, CEB)

And Malachi adds,
"I will be quick to testify against . . .
those who cheat the day laborers out of their wages
as well as oppress the widow and the orphan,
and against those who brush aside the foreigner and do not
revere me,"
says the LORD of heavenly forces. (Mal. 3:5–6, CEB)

As legalism began to overtake Israel and the well-to-do were keeping the letter of the law but ignoring the spirit of the law so that they were prospering and the poor were suffering, prophets called Israel up on the carpet, pointing out that God was more interested in the way his people treated others than he was about their scrupulously adhering to a set of requirements. And Micah assures Israel that simply being a Jew is not assurance from God:

> With what should I approach the LORD
> and bow down before God on high?
> Should I come before him with entirely burned offerings,
> with year-old calves?
> Will the LORD be pleased with thousands of rams,
> with many torrents of oil?
> Should I give my oldest child for my crime;
> the fruit of my body for the sin of my spirit?
> He has told you, human one, what is good and
> what the LORD requires from you:
> to do justice, embrace faithful love, and walk humbly with
> your God.
> Can I approve wicked scales and a bag of false weights
> in a city whose wealthy are full of violence
> and whose inhabitants speak falsehood
> with lying tongues in their mouths? (Mic. 6:6–8, 11–12, CEB)

In Amos, the LORD is even more vitriolic regarding the hypocrisy of worship and injustice:

> I hate, I reject your festivals;
> I don't enjoy your joyous assemblies.
> If you bring me your entirely burned offerings and gifts of food—
> I won't be pleased;
> I won't even look at your offerings of well-fed animals.
> Take away the noise of your songs;
> I won't listen to the melody of your harps.
> But let justice roll down like waters,
> and righteousness like an ever-flowing stream. (Amos 5:21–24, CEB)

BIBLICAL INTERPRETATION FOR LAYPEOPLE AND OTHER MARTYRS   227

So the Old Testament is where Jesus's orientation comes from. But Luke also records that when Jesus's mother, Mary, found out that she was pregnant, she sang,

> [God] has scattered those who are proud in their inmost
> thoughts.
> He has brought down rulers from their thrones
> but has lifted up the humble.
> He has filled the hungry with good things
> but has sent the rich away empty.
> He has helped his servant Israel
> remembering to be merciful
> to Abraham and his descendants forever,
> just as he promised our ancestors. (Luke 1:46–55)

Of course, as a young child, Jesus learned a great deal from his parents. Hillel, a leading rabbi in Jerusalem, died when Jesus was about fifteen. So it is also possible that when Jesus was twelve, he also learned from Hillel, who, for the most part, emphasized the two major commandments.

Jesus's teaching began with John the Baptist, his cousin and apparently his mentor. When the crowds came to John, he attacked them or the Pharisees and Sadducees, depending on which gospel you accept, calling them a brood of vipers, calling on them to produce fruits that reflected repentance, assuring them that they could not depend on their ethnic heritage, claiming, "We have Abraham as our father," and saying that "Every tree that does not produce good fruit will be cut down and thrown into the fire'" (Matt. 3:5–10, Luke 3:7–9).

Luke added questions from the crowd: "What should we do then?" John answered, "Anyone who has two shirts should share with the one who has none, and anyone who has food should do the same." Even tax collectors came to be baptized. "Teacher," they asked, "what should we do?" To them, he said, "Don't collect any more than you are required to," he told them. Then some soldiers (perhaps Jewish mercenaries in the Roman army) asked him, "And what should we do?" He replied, "Don't extort money and don't accuse people falsely—be content with your pay" (Luke 3:8–17). This reflected the values of the Old Testament prophets but had been conveniently overlooked by many Jews.

The Old Testament law had made punishment more humane than the traditional ethics of the time. Rather than retaliating against anyone in another tribe that had injured someone in one's own tribe, the law was made to punish the actual person who committed the injury. And if someone in one's tribe or family was injured, they were not allowed to kill the person, but only to exercise a "proportional" injury, like "an eye for an eye" (Exod. 21:24, Lev. 24:20, Deut. 19:21).

But Jesus takes the law even further, saying,

> You have heard that it was said, "An eye for eye, and tooth for tooth." But I tell you, do not resist an evil person. If anyone slaps you turn the other cheek. And if anyone wants to sue you and take your shirt, hand over your coat as well. If anyone forces you to go one mile, go with them two miles. Give to the one who asks you, and do not turn away from the one who wants to borrow from you. You have heard that it was said, "Love your neighbor[322] and hate your enemy." But I tell you, love your enemies and pray for those who persecute you, that you may be children of your Father in heaven. He causes his sun to rise on the evil and the good, and sends rain on the righteous and the unrighteous. If you love those who love you, what reward will you get? Are not even the tax collectors doing that? And if you greet only your own people, what are you doing more than others? Do not even pagans do that? Be perfect, therefore, as your heavenly Father is perfect. (Matt. 5:38–48)

In Nazareth at the beginning of his ministry, Jesus went into the synagogue on the Sabbath. He read the scroll of Isaiah that said,

> The Spirit of the LORD is on me,
> because he has anointed me
> to proclaim good news to the poor
> He has sent me to proclaim freedom for the prisoners
> and recovery of sight for the blind,

---

[322] Lev. 19:18.

BIBLICAL INTERPRETATION FOR LAYPEOPLE AND OTHER MARTYRS   229

> to set the oppressed free,
> to proclaim the year of the LORD's favor.[323]
>
> Then he claimed, "Today this scripture is fulfilled in your
> hearing" (Luke 4:16–21).

Jesus claimed that his ministry was to the poor, those who were imprisoned (probably for political reasons), the disabled, and the oppressed. "The year of the LORD's favor" referred to the fiftieth year at the end of seven sabbatical cycles in which all land was to be returned to its ancestral owner (who had lost it because of poverty), all indentured slaves were to be freed, and the land was to be left fallow for a year (Lev. 25:8–17, 23–55, 27:16–25).[324] The essence of Jesus's ministry was a relationship with God that influenced our relationship to other people as well as the earth.

Jesus asserted that the Spirit would move him to exercise justice and support those who were weak in faith. And when John the Baptist sent representatives to Jesus to determine exactly how he saw himself, Jesus authenticated his ministry, saying, "The blind receive sight, the lame walk, those who have leprosy[325] are cleansed, the deaf hear, the dead are raised, and the good news is proclaimed to the poor. Blessed is anyone who does not stumble on account of me" (Matt. 11:5–6). Here, Jesus applied Psalm 146:7–9 to his ministry. They would have recognized the connection.

Regarding moral soundness, Jesus proclaimed that we should "do to others what we would have them do to you, for that is the sum of the teachings in the Law and the Prophets" (Matt. 7:12). He quoted the prophet Hosea, who said, "'I desire mercy, not sacrifice.'[326] For I have not come to call the righteous, but sinners" (Matt. 9:13).

Jesus also distinguished between secondary rules and the essence of Jewish morality, replying the following to a Pharisee's question regarding handwashing:

---

[323]   Isa. 61:1–2 (see Septuagint); Isa. 58:6.

[324]   Lawrence H. Schiffman. "Jubilees, Book of," *The HarperCollins Bible Dictionary.* Gen. Ed. Paul J. Achtemeier. (San Francisco: HarperSanFrancisco, 1996), 549.

[325]   The Greek word traditionally translated "leprosy" was used for various diseases affecting the skin.

[326]   Hosea 6:6.

And why do you break the command of God for the sake of your tradition? For God said, "Honor your father and mother"[327] and "Anyone who curses their father or mother is to be put to death."[328] But you say that if anyone declares that what might have been used to help their father or mother is "devoted to God," they are not to "honor their father or mother" with it. Thus you nullify the word of God for the sake of your tradition. You hypocrites! Isaiah was right when he prophesied about you, "These people honor me with their lips, but their hearts are far from me. They worship me in vain; their teachings are but rules taught by men." (Matt. 15:3–7, Mark 7:8–13)

And again, "Woe to you, teachers of the law and Pharisees, you hypocrites! You give a tenth of your spices—mint, dill and cumin. But you have neglected the more important matters of the law—justice, mercy and faithfulness. You should have practiced the latter, without neglecting the former. You blind guides! You strain out a gnat but swallow a camel" (Matt. 23:23–24). It is not that Jesus says the teachers of the law cannot be saved, but is a warning to his followers and perhaps a call to the teachers to reevaluate where their hearts are.

With example after example, it may seem like I am killing a mosquito with a hand grenade. But I wanted to point out, contrary to often public opinion, that Jesus and the prophets were concerned only about personal morality rather than political, social, and economic issues. For example, slavery is both a moral and political issue. But the foundation of issues such as justice and mercy for the weak and powerless goes to the very heart of our being as not only Christians, but also as humans regardless of the issue.

And on one occasion, a man asked Jesus what good he must do to inherit eternal life. Jesus told him that in order to enter life, he should keep the commandments. So he asked Jesus which ones he should keep. Jesus replied, "You shall not murder, you shall not commit adultery, you shall not steal, you shall not give false testimony, honor your father and mother"[329] and "love your neighbor as yourself."[330] Taken aback, the man protests,

---

[327] Exod. 20:12, Deut. 5:16.

[328] Exod. 21:17, Lev. 20.

[329] Exod. 20:12–16, Deut. 5:16–20.

[330] Lev. 19:18.

BIBLICAL INTERPRETATION FOR LAYPEOPLE AND OTHER MARTYRS   231

"All these I have kept. What do I still lack?" Jesus answered, "If you want to be perfect, go, sell your possessions, and give to the poor. And you will have treasure in heaven. Then come follow me." When the young man heard this, he went away sad because he had great wealth. Jesus probably took a deep breath before saying, "How hard it is for the rich to enter the kingdom of God! Indeed, it is easier for a camel to go through the eye of a needle than for someone who is rich to enter the kingdom of God" (Matt. 19:24; also in Mark 10:25). Not that Jesus hated wealthy people, but he knew the pressure that wealth put on people to hoard or conspicuously spend rather than putting it to good use.

One day, an expert in the law asked Jesus, "What must I do to inherit eternal life?" Rather than answering, he asked the man, "What is written in the law?" He correctly answered, "Love the Lord your God with all your heart and with all your soul and with all your strength and with all your mind"[331] and "Love your neighbor as yourself."[332] Jesus agreed. But to justify himself, the lawyer asked, "And who is my neighbor?"

Jesus replied with a parable about a man traveling from Jerusalem to Jericho who was attacked and robbed by men who stripped him of his clothes, beat him, and left him half-dead. Then a priest came along but passed by on the other side. Next, a Levite came by and passed by on the other side. But a hated Samaritan came by; and when he saw the man, he took pity on him, bandaged his wounds, and poured on oil and wine. He put the man on his own donkey, brought him to an inn, and took care of him. The next day, he took out two denarii, which was equivalent to two days' wages for a laborer, and gave them to the innkeeper, promising to reimburse him for any additional expense.

After finishing the story, I would imagine Jesus allowed a pregnant pause, looking the man in the eye. He then asked, "Which of these three do you think was a neighbor to the man who fell into the hands of robbers?" Not being willing to say a Samaritan was the hero in the story, the expert in the law simply responded, "The one who had mercy on him." I imagine Jesus nodded pensively as he said, "Go and do likewise" (Luke 10:25–37).

---

[331]   Deut. 6:5.

[332]   Lev. 19:18.

The purpose of his ministry and that of his followers was expressed in the parable of the sheep and the goats. Jesus told the parable, saying to the group on his right, "Come, you who are blessed by my Father. Take your inheritance the kingdom prepared for you since the creation of the world." Because he was hungry, they fed him. Because he was thirsty, they gave him something to drink. Because he was a stranger, they invited him in. Because he needed clothes, they clothed him. Because he was sick, they looked after him. Because he was in prison, they visited him.

The righteous were amazed, asking when they had done these things. He replied, "Truly I tell you, whatever you did for one of the least of these brothers and sisters of mine, you did for me." On the other hand, to those on his left, he said, "Depart from me, you who are cursed, into the eternal fire prepared for the devil and his angels. For I was hungry, and you did not feed me; thirsty and you gave me nothing to drink; a stranger and you did not invite me in. I needed clothes, and you did not clothe me. I was sick and in prison, and you did not look after me."

They too were astounded and asked, "Lord, when did we see you hungry or thirsty or a stranger or needing clothes or sick or in prison and did not help you?" You could see his answer coming. He replied, "Truly I tell you, whatever you did not do for one of the least of these, you did not do for me. Then they will go away to eternal punishment, but the righteous to eternal life" (Matt. 25:31–46).

On various occasions, the issue of which commandments were the most important came up. One day, a teacher of the law came to Jesus while he was arguing with the Sadducees and asked him what the most important commandment was. Jesus answered, "'Hear, O Israel: The Lord our God, the Lord is one. Love the Lord your God with all your heart and with all your soul and with all your mind and with all your strength.'[333] The second is this: 'Love your neighbor as yourself.'[334] There is no commandment greater than these."

"Well said, teacher," the man replied. "You are right in saying that God is one, and there is no other but him. To love him with all your heart, with all your understanding, and with all your strength and to love your neighbor as yourself are more important than all burnt offerings and sacrifices." When Jesus saw that he had answered wisely, he said to him,

---

[333] Deut. 6:4–5.

[334] Lev. 19:18.

"You are not far from the kingdom of God." And from then on, no one dared ask him any more questions (Mark 12:29–34).[335]

The Torah and the prophets had commanded Israel to exercise justice not only to their own people, but also to the immigrant because "you too were aliens in Egypt (Exod. 22:21, 23:9; Lev. 19:33–34; Deut. 1:16, 10:19, 24:14, 17, 27:19; Jer. 7:6, 22:3; Ezek. 22:29; Mal. 3:5). But Jesus took it a lot further. Many psalms are vitriolic expressions of hatred (Pss. 3:7, 31:6, 111:113, 139:21–22) and even claim that God hates certain people (Ps. 5:5). But Jesus tells them to love their enemies.

He pointed out that it is no big deal to love those who love you because even the worst people love those who love them. And if you lend to those from whom you expect repayment, what credit is that to you? But you are to love your enemies, do good to them, and lend to them without expecting to get anything back. Then your reward will be great, and you will be children of the Most High, concluding, "Be merciful, just as your Father is merciful."

He warns his listeners not to be judgmental so that they will not be judged or condemn so that they will not be condemned, but to forgive and they will be forgiven. For with the measure they use, it will be measured to them (Luke 6:20–40).

Like the Old Testament prophets, Jesus had a special concern for the poor. In the beatitudes in Luke, Jesus shows his concern for the poor:

> Blessed are you who are poor,
> for yours is the kingdom of God.
> Blessed are you who hunger now,
> for you will be satisfied.
> Blessed are you who weep now,
> for you will laugh. . . .
> But woe to you who are rich,
> for you have already received your comfort.
> Woe to you who are well fed now,
> for you will go hungry.
> Woe to you who laugh now,
> for you will mourn and weep.
> Woe to you when everyone speaks well of you,

---

[335] Matt. 22:37–39.

for that is how their ancestors treated the false prophets.
(Luke 6:20–26)

Once, a Pharisee invited Jesus to eat with him. The Pharisee expressed surprise when Jesus did not first wash before the meal. Jesus responded, "You Pharisees clean the outside of the cup and dish, but inside, you are full of greed and wickedness. You foolish people! Did not the one who made the outside make the inside also? But now as for what is inside you—be generous to the poor, and everything will be clean for you."

Then he pronounced condemnation on the Pharisees because they give God a tenth of their mint, rue, and all other kinds of garden herbs (which was not commanded in the law) but neglected justice and the love of God. He condemned them for loving popularity more than justice (Matt. 23:23).

And when one expert in the law pointed out that Jesus insulted them with his condemnation, he replied that they loaded people down with irrelevant laws that even they themselves could not carry while they would not lift one finger to help the ordinary Jew.

He continued that they even built monuments for the prophets who were killed by their ancestors even though they approved of what their ancestors did. He predicted that they would do the same things their ancestors, who had killed the prophets from Abel to Zechariah, had done. He concluded that by their example, not only had they taken away the key to knowledge for people who looked up to them, but also were actually leading others away from God (Luke 11:37–53).

Perhaps Jesus's most direct message about the greed of the rich and turning their backs on the poor was a parable about an extremely rich man who was dressed in purple and fine linen and basked in his luxury. Just outside his gate, a beggar named Lazarus lay, covered with sores. Since he was so disabled, he could not work and had to eat whatever people would give him. He would have settled for what fell from the rich man's table. Although the rich man ignored him, his dogs licked the poor man's sores, soothing his pain.

Finally, the beggar died and went to heaven, where he met Abraham. The rich man also died and was in torment in Hades. He could see Abraham and Lazarus. So he pleaded with Abraham to send Lazarus to dip the tip of his finger in water and cool his parched tongue because he was in agony.

But Abraham replied, "Son, remember that in your lifetime, you received your good things while Lazarus received bad things. But now he

BIBLICAL INTERPRETATION FOR LAYPEOPLE AND OTHER MARTYRS   235

is comforted here, and you are in agony. And there is a chasm between us that cannot be crossed." In desperation, the rich man answered, "Then I beg you, send Lazarus to my family, for I have five brothers. Let him warn them so that they will not also come to this place of torment."

Abraham replied, "They have the writings of Moses and the prophets. Let them listen to them." But he protested, "No, Father Abraham. But if someone from the dead goes to them, they will repent." Abraham responded, "If they do not listen to Moses and the prophets, they will not be convinced even if someone rises from the dead" (Luke 16:9–31). That is, the Old Testament had given the rich man and his brothers guidance regarding their moral responsibility. Although he had ignored what the prophets and Moses had said, his brothers still had the same opportunity to pay attention to their words.

Again, regarding greed, someone had asked him to tell his brother to divide the inheritance with him. Jesus warned him, "Watch out! Be on your guard against all kinds of greed. Life does not consist in an abundance of possessions." To illustrate, he told a parable of a rich man who had so much that he had to tear down his barns to build bigger ones to store his grain. Then he thought he would retire, take life easy, to eat, drink, and be merry. But here's the problem. God was watching and said, "You fool! This very night, your life will be demanded from you. Then who will get what you have prepared for yourself?" Jesus then concluded with his punch line: "This is how it will be with whoever stores up things for themselves but is not rich toward God" (Luke 12:13–21). What a condemnation of the rich who continue to build up fortunes, passing them on to their children while ignoring or giving a pittance to care for the poor!

Americans especially need to pay particular attention and not set their hearts on what they can consume, for the pagan runs after such things. But they should be satisfied with what they have, for God knows what they need. And his punch line is extremely important, but also extremely difficult to remember: "For where your treasure is, there your heart will be also" (Luke 12:29–34).

So far, this book has addressed principles valid for all time. But how do the principles apply in early twenty-first-century America? Too often, when Christians discuss issues of social and political importance, they forget who they are and focus on arguments that either are personally beneficial to them or stroke their desire to feel macho or that just sound good. In dealing with issues, Christians should be focusing on the fact that they *are Christians* and should attempt to apply what they know about Jesus to the issue at hand. A second problem is generalizing from one or two specific experiences or observations. Fearnside and Holther, in their book on the rules of argumentation, say, "Far from weaving a tight lattice of systematic investigations, individuals make isolated observations. Since man must understand so that he may move and act, he leaps to some hasty generalization and 'induces' some broad principles from scraps of evidence."[336] Such conclusions, according to Fearnside and Holther, are "faulty generalizations."[337]

Knowledge and Intuition

We all hold dearly held beliefs that we are sure are true simply because we believe them. How many times have we heard the response "Oh, you know he did so-and-so" or "She had to have known . . ." The movies like *The Da Vinci Code* and *JFK* have a plethora of actual historical information but fill it in with suppositions that *could be true* and misinformation that never actually happened. This writer personally believes that there was indeed a conspiracy to kill President Kennedy because of the incredibly improper and clandestine nature of the autopsy, the statistical improbability of so many material witnesses dying under mysterious circumstances, and the slipshod job of the Warren Commission, which was criticized by the more thorough investigation of the House Select Committee on Assassinations fifteen years later. But the fact that I believe it doesn't necessarily make it true. I also believe that we will never learn the whole truth. We can only approach it.

Public opinion polls attempt to measure people's thinking. Polling is a multiple-billion-dollar industry, and yet they claim their analysis could suffer from a margin of error by 3 percent in either direction. And in their interviews, they are noted for hedging their bets. One wonders how they can make so much money. But they do. Politicians who are leading in the polls listen to them intently (and those who are behind in the polls say they don't).

---

[336] W. Ward Fearnside and William B. Holther. *Fallacy: The Counterfeit of Argument* (Englewood Cliffs, NJ, 1959), 8.

[337] *Ibid.*, 10.

BIBLICAL INTERPRETATION FOR LAYPEOPLE AND OTHER MARTYRS   237

Part of the reason for the slipperiness of the polls is that people change their minds, sometimes for having gotten additional information that helps them understand the situation better and sometimes just because a change in their own circumstances leads them to look at things differently.

And then, of course, people also hold contradictory beliefs at the same time. Not consciously, but they do. For example, Americans criticize companies who move to other countries because the labor costs are lower. On the other hand, they love to buy those products because they are cheaper to purchase than the ones produced in the United States. From the time of the Declaration of Independence, we have said we believe all "men are created equal" while at the same time practicing slavery of blacks, genocide of American Indians, and discrimination against Hispanics and Orientals. While we still practiced "segregation" in the United States, we had the audacity to criticize "apartheid" in South Africa. On the one hand, we claim to believe in democracy, or the rule of the majority, as well as in individualism, which is contradictory to the rule of the majority. More than once, I have heard a person say that the United States cannot be the world's policeman and, in the same conversation, defend intervention in other countries.

Very few major issues are simple and require nuancing. But people want simple answers to difficult issues. Have you ever noticed that people who know very little about an issue know exactly what needs to be done to rectify the problem while the person who had deeply researched the issue is much less inclined to make a blanket statement about the answer to the problem?

Therefore, politicians use propaganda because their listeners want to hear a simple one-liner statement of the problem and the answer to the problem. Second, propaganda appeals not to the understanding, but to the emotions. Appeals to patriotism, protection of the family, fear, and pride are simple ways to move people from reason to emotion. Third, successful propaganda depends on "incessant repetition of simple, emotional themes, slogans, and captions."[338] Political cartoonists are particularly good at it.

Fourth, propaganda does use selectively chosen facts in order to draw conclusions that may have nothing to do with the chosen facts. Fifth, propaganda shields the public from uncomfortable facts that may contradict their line of reasoning or conclusions. Sixth, the propagandist

---

[338]   Robert A. Liston. *Why We Think As We Do* (New York: Franklin Watts, 1977), 12.

must "lie *credibly*."[339] One might want to review such books as *Fallacy: The Counterfeit of Argument* to review how people can be distracted from the facts with faulty reasoning and non sequitur arguments.[340]

Americans like to believe that we have become such a rich nation because compared with other nations, we have been the most hardworking, industrious, and entrepreneurial nation in the world. We ignore the fact that an important part of our riches is the fact that our forefathers had lots of room for expansion, fertile ground, and incredible natural resources that we took our land away from the defenseless people who were here first. We also ignore the fact that because of our geographical isolation, we have not wasted our human and physical resources on incessant war (except against people who had no planes, tanks, and explosives).

And because we seem to have an endless supply of resources, we ignore the side effects and have become the most "profligate wasters the world has ever known."[341]

We live in what many call the information age. One can go on the Internet and find virtually anything. But we could also call our age the misinformation age. You can put anything on YouTube. I have a cousin who has passed on misinformation that he received over YouTube from other people who believe like him. I do not believe he passed on such stories because he intended to pass on lies, but because he uncritically trusted the sources of his information and because he *wanted* it to be true. People who think like this about issues but who do not have the integrity he does and makes up lies bear false witness against their neighbors. Berger and Kellner point out that "an individual possessed of absolute certainty with regard to his own perceptions and values . . . would then proceed to seek explanations as to why these other people are so blind to what to him are obvious truth. . . ."[342] Of course, ideologists do not want information because they already know what is right.

But even the truth can be used to promote misinformation by selection of the facts. Because the media depends on readership, listenership, or viewership, they tend to focus on the outrageous and exciting because that is what people want to read, hear, and see. For example, after the 9/11

---

[339]   *Ibid.*

[340]   Fearnside and Holther, *op. cit.*

[341]   Liston, *op. cit.*, 18.

[342]   Berger and Kellner, 1981, *op. cit.*, 57.

destruction of the Twin Towers and damage to the Pentagon, the media recorded a few thousand Palestinians out in the streets rejoicing over the catastrophe. However, there were 3,309,977 Palestinians.[343] So about 98 percent of Palestinians were not out in the street rejoicing. However, those people were not covered by the media, leaving the impression that the few thousand in the streets represented all Palestinians.

Another is that "what everybody knows" is often intuitive. Research is often counterintuitive. Until about World War I, it was assumed that women were not capable of being secretaries. However, with the male shortage during the war, it became necessary to use women as secretaries. Then it became obvious that businesses could hire female secretaries for a lower income than that of men. Before long, businesses found that women were *more* appropriate as secretaries than men.

Until about the twentieth century, it was assumed that in a divorce, men should get custody of the children. Over time, until about the 1970s, it became assumed that women should get custody of the children in a divorce. At that point, the assumption changed again so that, at least theoretically, all things being equal, the parents should have an equal opportunity to have custody of the children and that the most qualified should have custody or that it should be shared.

People may have an experience with someone of a particular ethnic, religious, or whatnot group and generalize it to assume that it is a trait of a group. Ronald Reagan used the example of Linda Taylor, who had abused the welfare system in Chicago in order to reduce welfare in California.[344] In the movie *The Defiant Ones* with Sidney Poitier and Tony Curtis, a young boy who is protected by the black man from the white man assumes that it is the white man who had protected him from the black man.[345]

It is also important to keep in mind Peter Berger's insight that in order to properly address an issue as a Christian, he needs both the motivation of the gospel *and* an understanding of the actual situation. He points out that it is important to address issues based on information from actual

---

[343] *Population Pyramids of the World from 1950 to 2100: State of Palestine.* http://www.populationpyramid.net/state-of-palestine/2001/.

[344] Kathryn J. Edin and H. Luke Shaefer. "Ronald Reagan's 'welfare queen' myth: How the Gipper kickstarted the war on the working poor," salon.com, Sunday, Sep 27, 2015 10:59 AM CDT; NewsOne Staff, "Linda Taylor: Ronald Reagan's 'Welfare Queen' Was Real . . . And White." Newsome.com.

[345] Stanley Kramer, dir. United Artists, Sept. 24, 1988. Film.

research rather than faulty perception, arguing that "the diagnosis without the doctrine may lead to resignation, which is bad, but the doctrine without the diagnosis almost certainly leads to illusion, which is much worse."[346]

Second, as we address the issues, the information we have will always be somewhat limited, and our application may also be somewhat flawed. Therefore, it is important to remain constantly ready to modify or change our ideas as Jeremiah did regarding the fate of Jerusalem. Having said that, I will attempt to address some issues on the basis of actual information rather than of flawed perception or the ideologies of vested interests

Third, I personally find that words like "conservative" and "liberal" are virtually useless because they don't mean anything specific. The way we use the terms doesn't really communicate their meaning. Generally speaking, "reactionary" refers to those people who want to go back to the way things were in the "good old days." They tend to fantasize about the past, as when sixty-year-olds refer to their childhood as a more innocent time, ignoring segregation and the prejudicial treatment of Hispanics, women, and homosexuals. "Conservative" refers to someone who wants to preserve the existing conditions, which may be good or not. "Liberal" refers to those who are favorable to incremental progress or reform, which may or may not be a positive development. The change they want is incremental. "Radical" describes those who desire extreme rather than incremental change of existing conditions. "Revolutionary" refers to those who favor overthrowing the whole present social order in favor of something totally different. Presently, some people distinguish between social conservatives and economic conservatives. But although there may be some validity to the general characteristics in these terms, they say little or nothing about the specific values or ideas held by any of the groups of people to which they refer. So rather than generalizing, let's address some specific issues.

Poverty and Social Welfare

So what does the Bible tell us about God's attitude toward this issue of poverty and welfare? The Mosaic law said that if you lend to the poor, don't charge interest (Exod. 22:25) and if you get collateral for a loan, "the lender is to give the pawned coat back by sunset so they can sleep in their own coat. They will bless you, and you will be considered righteous before

---

[346] Berger, 1961, *op. cit.*, 131.

the LORD your God" (Deut. 24:12–13). And Jesus says to lend to the poor without demanding repayment (Luke 6:34–35). I am sure this sounds completely unrealistic to those bankers who reaped millions by preying on the ignorance of the poor, hiding the fact that their loans had escalating interest rates, which caused so many foreclosures in the 2010s, leading to defaults, or payday loan officers, some of whom ended up charging over 500 percent interest. Jesus would have us take a whole different perspective toward dealing with the poor.

The book of Proverbs was not written by one person, but was a collection of folk wisdom. It seems that one proverbist had the same erroneous perception about poverty as many Americans who ignore the sociological research, who believe that if one is poor, it is his own fault, that the poor are lazy, loving sleep rather than work: "Don't love sleep or you will be poor; stay alert and you will have plenty to eat" (Prov. 20:13). One can always find a few who will fit that stereotype. Alcoholism is acknowledged as a cause of poverty by one proverbist (Prov. 23:21), which it certainly is in some cases. The experiences and observations of the proverbists are reflected in their proverbs. They may reflect reality, and they may not. Aldus Huxley said, "But proverbs are always platitudes until you have experienced the truth of them."[347]

But on the other hand, another proverb addresses the affluent: "Those who close their ears to the cries of the poor will themselves call out but receive no answer" (Prov. 21:13). And another focuses more on the lack of certainty that personal industry will always pay off economically: "A poor person's land might produce much food, but it is unjustly swept away" (Prov. 13:23). The fatalist who wrote Hannah's song seemed to believe that it made no difference how hard one worked because God made people rich or poor (1 Sam. 27:8) as did the author of the book of Job. The author of Ecclesiastes is more realistic: "When I next observed all the oppressions that take place under the sun, I saw the tears of the oppressed—and they have no one to comfort them. Their oppressors wield power—but they have no one to comfort them" (Eccles. 4:1). Amos castigates the rich for taking advantage of the poor (Amos 2:6–7; 8:4–6). Deuteronomy encourages compassion on the poor (Deut. 15:16–17). Proverbs says that the righteous care for the poor, but the wicked do not (Prov. 29:7).

---

[347] Aldus Huxley, *Jesting Pilate: A Diary of a Journey* (Doran, New York: Doran Co., 1926), 207.

Numerous texts encourage the care and defense of the poor (Ps. 82:3; Prov. 14:20–21). One who responds to the cries for the poor honors God (Prov. 14:31; 19:17; 22:2; Jer. 22:16), those who care for the poor will be blessed (Pss. 41:1–3; 112:4–9), but those who neglect the poor will be punished (Pss. 28:27, 109:16; Ezek. 16:49).[348]

Beginning in the eighth century BCE, a commercial and landed aristocracy in Israel began to exploit the poor (Isa. 3:14–15), and foreclosures concentrated land in the hands of a few rich families (Isa. 5:8). And like those rich Israelites in the eighth century, for those who think "I got mine" and don't worry about the poor, the biblical faith has explicit answers.

First, God hears the cries of the poor (Ps. 12:5). The Mosaic law, the governmental rules of Israel, had a great deal to say about special provisions for the poor. The land was to be left fallow one out of seven years for the poor (Exod. 23:11), and that year, the debts of the poor were *cancelled* (Deut. 15:2). Provisions were made so that the landless poor had enough to eat during the growing season (Deut. 23:24–25) and after harvest by not picking up the gleanings in the field (Lev. 19:9–10). The entire twenty-fifth chapter of Leviticus is given to making sure that all people of the nation had sufficient livelihood. And laws protected debtors in order to prevent destitution (Deut. 24:6; Exod. 22:26). In addition to Leviticus 25, all of Deuteronomy 15, 24, and 25 deal with laws generous toward the poor, including the foreigner (Deut. 24). That is the religious-cultural milieu into which Jesus was born and grew up.

But what did Jesus himself say? The callous who want to justify their heartlessness crassly quote Mark 14:7: "The poor you always have with you." But that ignores the context and portrays Jesus as making a point that he was not making. In fact, some argue that this text was a reminder of the permanence of the obligation to the poor handed down in Deuteronomy. 15:11.[349]

Jesus had compassion for the poor with utmost seriousness. He says to give alms (Luke 11:41), to give to them that ask (Matt. 5:42), to invite the poor rather than the rich to meals (Luke 14:12–14). As mentioned earlier,

---

[348] *The Poverty and Justice Bible* is a wonderful source for finding Bible passages regarding treatment of the poor and issues of justice, in that it has the passages highlighted. Contemporary English Version. (New York: American Bible Society, 2008).

[349] Stephen C. Mott. "poor," *HarperCollins Bible Dictionary*, ed. Paul J. Achtemeier (San Francisco: HarperSanFrancisco, 1966), 866.

BIBLICAL INTERPRETATION FOR LAYPEOPLE AND OTHER MARTYRS   243

in his parable of the rich man and Lazarus, the rich man is punished severely because of his ignoring of the poor man (Luke 16:19–25). And he told a story about a foolish rich man, who had so much that he had to build bigger barns to hold all that he had, but did not live to enjoy his selfishness (Luke 12:15–21).

To test one man who came to Jesus claiming he wanted to be in his innermost discipleship class, Jesus even told him to sell all that he had and give all to the poor (Matt. 19:21; Luke 18:22). In another place, he argues that if we have enough to be comfortable, we should share what we have with the poor (Luke 3:11). Tim Anderson agrees with the "American Social History Project," which said, "The test of our progress is not whether we add more to the abundance of those who have too much; it is whether we provide enough for those who have too little."[350] I think Jesus would say "Amen."

Probably remembering some of the Old Testament passages on the subject (Prov. 14:31, 19:17, 22:2; Jer. 22:16; Ps. 41:1–3, 112:4–9) in Jesus's parable of the sheep and the goats, he stresses that compassionate behavior toward those in need is actually done to God, promising a blessing to the compassionate and issuing a threat to the tight-fisted and uncaring (Matt. 25:42–45).

So what was the response of those who followed Jesus? The very earliest response was to completely commit all that they had to sharing with each other, so that "none of them would say, 'This is mine!' about any of their possessions, but had everything in common" (Acts 4:32) and gave sacrificially to see to it that their needy had what they needed (Acts 4:33–37). Paul says that Jesus taught that it is more blessed to give than to receive (Acts 20:35). In Romans, Paul entreated the congregation that "if your *enemy* hungers, feed him" (12:20). And he spent much of his ministry collecting money for the Christians in Judea who were suffering from the devastating effects of a drought (1 Cor. 16:1–2; 2 Cor. 8–9; Gal. 2:10; Rom. 15:26). James argues that it is *hypocrisy* to confess the faith and refuse to help the poor (James 2:14–20). And the author of 1 John says, "But if a person has material possessions and sees a brother or sister in need and that person doesn't care—how can the love of God remain in him? Little children, let's not love with words and speech but with action and truth"

---

[350]   T. Carlos Anderson, 2014, 64, quoting "American Social History Project website, http://historymatters.gmu.edu/d/5105/, retrieved January 7, 2014.

(3:17–18). This is only a smattering of the plethora of passages that address the issue of help for the poor.

Popular conscience-soothing folklore maintains that poor people, or at least the vast majority of the poor, are poor because they are lazy and shiftless. And there was always the red herring about the poor owning Cadillacs, which everyone knows about, but which nobody has actually seen (unless it was a $500 clunker).[351] But the facts discovered by research give lie to this myth. Never mind the fact that over 16 million of the poor are children. Over 22 percent of all children live in families that are below the official poverty level (even though families need about twice that much to cover basic expenses),[352] *most of whose parents work full-time in low-wage jobs.* Plenty of research has shown that poverty can adversely affect children's ability to learn and contributes to social, emotional, and behavioral problems, as well as poor physical and mental health.[353] People complain about crime, but often don't want to share with those who are forced into crime because they can't get by. So we end up suffering as a society because we refuse to provide fair minimum wage and fair tax structure, giving welfare to the rich and failing to provide adequately for the poor.

When I was a pastor in DeKalb, Illinois, I recall a newspaper article about the opening of a new hotel in Chicago with 500 jobs available. Some 20,000 people waited outside in line in subfreezing weather to fill out an application. That means 19,500 did not get a job. I doubt they waited in that long line because they were lazy.

One in five American children live in poverty, the highest rate of any industrialized nation. In any given year, about 1.35 million children will be *homeless.* About 22 percent of the homeless are homeless because of mental problems, a significant percentage of whom are veterans traumatized by

---

[351] Or it may be a situation of which I knew personally. A Mrs. O'Brien, the mother-in-law of multimillionaire (or perhaps billionaire) Stanley Marsh of the Amarillo Cadillac Ranch fame, was a social worker without a salary. She took the food stamps of disabled people to the store to make purchases for them in her brand-new Cadillac and dressed in the most incredibly beautiful, expensive dresses. I can imagine how the grocery store employees rolled their eyes when she came in to make the purchases. I still have a soft spot in my heart for this courageous woman.

[352] National Center for Children in Poverty. Columbia University, http://www.nccp.org/topics/child poverty.html.

[353] Lauer & Lauer, op. cit., 165–173.

war defending the citizens of this nation. As the richest nation in the world, we should be ashamed.

In the richest nation in the world, the gap between the top 1 percent and the rest of the nation has continued to grow since the 1970s, the widest gap of any industrialized nation. Over half of the welfare recipients are children, the elderly, the disabled, or mothers with small children.[354]

Only the most ideological liberal would deny that some of the poverty has to do with the irresponsible behavior of pregnancy of unmarried women and the guys who impregnated them. But is that justification for not helping their children? In Elvis Presley's song "In the Ghetto," the song makes the point that if the child isn't helped, he may be killed *and the cycle will continue.*[355] Only the most ideological conservative would deny that those who control wealth have the greatest influence in getting laws passed that benefit them. Laws that were supposed to benefit the poor often do not do so or are inadequate. Medicaid, which was supposed to benefit the poor, was rejected for a time by some states, and is still inadequate in most states, so that a majority of the poor is still not covered or has inadequate coverage. The Temporary Assistance of Needy Families (TANF) passed in 1996 to replace Aid to Families with Dependent Children (AFDC) does not, even with the addition of food stamps, temporarily pull people out of poverty.

But the real tragedy is that subsidies of the nonpoor are much greater than the subsidies for the poor. Lauer and Lauer point out that "the federal government loses four times as much in revenue by allowing people to deduct mortgage interest from income taxes as it spends on housing programs for low-income Americans" and "in 2001, 59 percent of mortgage interest deduction savings went to households with income of $100,000 a year or more."[356] This means that renters are paying taxes to support welfare of the mortgage holders. Subsidies for large oil companies and large farm corporations are gigantic. In 2012, the biggest oil companies were raking in record profits. And on top of these record profits, oil companies were also getting billions a year in taxpayer subsidies.[357] So investors were getting

---

[354]   *Ibid.*

[355]   Elvis Presley, RCA Victor, April 1969, record. Written by Mac Davis, it was originally called "The Vicious Cycle."

[356]   Ibid., 174.

[357]   Megan Slack, *Five Reasons to Repeal Subsidies for Oil Companies*, March 29, 2012, 11:57 AM EDT. http://www.whitehouse.gov/blog/2012/03/29/repeal-subsidies-oil-companies.

welfare on the backs of taxpayers. This corporate welfare is usually totally overlooked by those condemning welfare for the poor. In 2010 alone, the federal government doled out $3.7 billion in subsidies "to oil-related industries."[358] Deductions such as country club membership, entertainment of clients, automobiles for families of business owners, and lunches are deductions that can be made by the affluent, but not the poor. My wife and I were once taken to dinner by a corporate executive who bragged that the previous evening, he and three others had spent $500 for the dinner on their business trip, which, of course, was deductible.

The nonpoor receive much more welfare than the poor through subsidies, multi-billion-dollar corporate bailouts, and tax deductions such as the income deduction on mortgage interest. And yet the paltry amount that the poor get in comparison allows many of the nonpoor to refer to the poor as "freeloaders." This is the conclusion of sociological and journalistic research.

This makes one wonder how legislators who tout their "Christian" faith can sleep at night when they cut food stamps and other programs that help the poor while passing legislation that subsidizes and bails out rich investors and CEOs who receive golden parachutes, even when their companies lose money. A nation that calls itself a "Christian" nation should restructure its priorities and legislation to reflect the values of Jesus Christ, whom it claims to follow.

Knowing that riches had a hold on people, Jesus warned the poor that it was extremely difficult for the rich to enter the kingdom of God (Matt. 19:24). But there are rich people who have the integrity to which Jesus called us. Responding to a question about the Supreme Court's *Citizens United* decision to allow unlimited anonymous political contributions, former president Jimmy Carter, one of the most Christian presidents in American history, said on the nationally syndicated radio show the *Thom Hartmann Show* that the United States is now "an oligarchy with unlimited political bribery." He said that decision of the Supreme Court has created "a complete subversion of our political system as a payoff to major contributors."[359] The hypocrisy of the Supreme Court's decision in *Citizens United v. FEC*, which concluded that a corporation was a person

---

[358]   Russell Hooper, *Two Big Things You Didn't Know About Oil Subsidies*, Nov. 20, 2013. http://www. policymic.com/articles/73903/two-big-things-you-didn-t-know-about-oil-subsidies.

[359]   "Jimmy Carter: The U.S. Is an 'Oligarchy With Unlimited Political Bribery'." http://www.thomhartmann.com, July 30 2015, 6:09 PM, radio.

whose massive contributions to political campaigns is the free speech guaranteed in the Bill of Rights[360] is as great as the hypocrisy of the *Dred Scott* decision that said Dred Scott was *not* a person and therefore had no standing before the court.[361]

There are some American millionaires, calling themselves the Patriotic Millionaires, who have committed themselves to caring about the poor. They describe themselves this way: "The Patriotic Millionaires are a group of more than 200 Americans with annual incomes over $1 million and/or assets of more than $5 million who believe that the country's current level of economic inequality is both dangerous and immoral. They recognize that while there are many causes of inequality, the current level of economic disparity is largely the result of a multi-decade effort by wealthy elites to enact legislation designed to enhance their personal wealth and their political power with little or no regard for the negative consequences such policies predictably wreaked on the vast majority of Americans. The Patriotic Millionaires are dedicated to reversing these policies and to ensuring that the legislative capture that led to their adoption comes to an end."[362] So perhaps there is hope for the future, hope that Christians will live up to the teachings of Jesus and Americans will live up to the ideals of the Bill of Rights.

Anderson points out that "through the 1950s, the marginal tax rate on any personal income over $200,000 was stable at 91 percent. . . . Those who argued that the high taxes undermined initiative and investment were a small minority branded as ideological cranks. Profits were high, wages were climbing, the middle class was growing, and the American Dream was for many a tangible reality."[363] However, ideology of those who want to maintain their riches and let the rest of the nation pay for government programs argue in favor of "trickle-down economics."

Supply-side economics has been touted by several presidents. It has been referred to as "trickle-down economics," a term first used by Will Rogers, who said that "money was all appropriated for the top in hopes that it would trickle down to the needy."[364] In his Cross of Gold speech in

---

[360] Citizens United v. Federal Election Commission, 558 U.S. 310 (2010).

[361] Dred Scott v. Sandford, 60 U.S. 393 (1857).

[362] · http://patrioticmillionaires.org/.

[363] Anderson, op. cit., 57.

[364] D. M. Giangreco and Kathryn Moore (1999). *Dear Harry: Truman's Mailroom,*

1896, Democratic presidential candidate William Jennings Bryan said, "There are two ideas of government. There are those who believe that if you just legislate to make the well-to-do prosperous, that their prosperity will leak through on those below. The Democratic idea has been that if you legislate to make the masses prosperous their prosperity will find its way up and through every class that rests upon it."[365] Economist John Kenneth Galbraith blamed the Panic of 1896 on the "horse and sparrow theory," saying, "If you feed the horse enough oats, some will pass through to the road for the sparrows,"[366] a somewhat earthy way of describing trickle-down economics. One might be surprised that Ross Perot called trickle-down economics "political voodoo."[367] Pope Francis called trickle-down theories a "naïve trust in the goodness of those wielding economic power and in the sacralized workings of the prevailing economic system."[368]

However, a 2012 study by the Tax Justice Network concluded that "wealth of the super-rich does not trickle down to improve the economy, but tends to be amassed and sheltered in tax havens with a negative effect on the tax bases of the home economy."[369] And a 2015 report by the International Monetary Fund concluded that "there is no trickle-down effect as the rich get richer: [I]f the income share of the top 20 percent (the rich) increases, then GDP growth actually declines over the medium term, suggesting that the benefits do not trickle down. In contrast, an increase in the income share of the bottom 20 percent (the poor) is associated with higher GDP growth."[370]

1945-1953. ISBN 0-8117-0482-3, quoted in https://en.wikipedia.org/w/index.php!title=Trickledown_economics&oldid= 713856282. Last modified on 6 April 2016, at 05:42.

[365] Bryan's "Cross of Gold" Speech: Mesmerizing the Masses. historymatters.com.

[366] John Kenneth, Galbraith, "Recession Economics," *New York Review of Books* 29, no. 1 (February 4, 1982).

[367] "Trickle Down," Perot campaign ad. n.p.

[368] *La Santa Sede*, http://w2.vatican.va/content/francesco/en/apost-exhortations/documents/papa-francesco_esortazione-ap_20131124_evangelii-gaudium.htmo#No_to_an_economy_of_exclusion, quoted in https://en.wikipedia.org/w/index.php!title=Trickle-down_economics&oldid=713856282. Last modified on 6 April 2016, at 05:42.

[369] Heather Stewart, *"Wealth doesn't trickle down – it just floods offshore, research reveals." The Guardian (London)*, July 21, 2012. Retrieved August 6, 2012.

[370] Era Dabla-Norris, Kalpana Kochhar, Nujin Suphaphiphat, Frantisek Ricka, and

When I was a boy, people believed one should work for what they get. Now they justify passing on untold millions and billions to their children while others who are unable or can't find work (and their children) are of little or no concern. That is not what Jesus taught.

Since the stock market doesn't necessarily reflect the reality of profits made by a company, but rather what investors think the stock *might be worth*, investors can make money on nonexistent corporate worth—until the overheated rise in stock prices get to the point at which people realize that it is overheated and (to mix a metaphor) the "bubble bursts," and stocks plunge—sometimes destroying the company. In 1929, it caused the world's worst depression. The same thing happened (along with deregulation) in the savings and loan crisis in the 1980s, in the dot-com crisis in the late 1990s, and the banking industry in 2008. Trickle-down definitely does not occur under such circumstances. But we learned in Economics 101 that putting money into the hands of people who *need* to make purchases means that purchases will be made. When purchases are made, the products must be produced to satisfy the market, meaning that people must be hired in order to produce the products. If people are hired to produce these products, they have income to make purchases, stimulating the need to produce more products, which means . . . etc., etc., etc. Therefore, putting money in the hands of the poor is more likely to stimulate a truly healthy economy than one based simply on the hope of the escalating value of stocks with no foundation under them.

Environment: The World in Which We Live

The Problem

"God blessed [the man and woman] and said to them, 'Be fruitful and increase in number, fill the earth and subdue it. Rule over the fish of the sea and the birds of the air and over every living creature that moves on the ground" (Gen. 1:28). This text has been used to defend both unbridled population growth and abuse of the environment. First, God did *not* mean that humans ravage the earth, but take care of it. Fretheim says, "A study of the verb *have dominion* ['subdue' in King James Version] . . . . reveals it must be understood

---

Evridiki Tsounta, *Causes and Consequences of Income Inequality: A Global Perspective. International Monetary Fund* (June 15, 2015), 4. Retrieved June 25, 2015.

in terms of care-giving, even nurturing, not exploitation. As the image of God, human beings should relate to the nonhuman as God relates to them."[371]

Second, be fruitful and increase in number may have been fine when there were only two people on earth. It may have been fine when there were a hundred million. It may have even been fine when there were one billion. But the population is escalating at a geometric rate.

In 8000 BC, there were about 5 million people on earth, 100 million in about 500 BC.[372] At the time of Jesus's birth, two thousand years ago, the world population was approximately 170 million[373] and about 200 million between AD 500 and 600. By 1250, there were 400 to 416 million. Plagues and wars took their toll before the 1400s. But by about 1805, there were about 1 billion. It took over 100,000 years to reach that figure. The growth was slowed by the White Lotus Revolution in China, which killed about 16 million. Despite about 20 million deaths in World War I, it took only about a hundred years (1927) to reach 2 billion. China's Great Leap and Russia's famine and Stalin's policies took the lives of probably between 10 and 15 million in the 1930s. But despite these losses and about 60 million deaths in World War II, earth's population reached 3 billion in 1959 (baby boomers).

Only fifteen years later, in 1974, we reached 4 billion. On July 11, 1987, we reached 5 billion. On October 12, 1989, we reached 6 billion, and on Oct. 31, 2001, 7 billon earthlings. However, the population when I checked it at 8:47 a.m. (CST) on March 1, 2014, was 7,216,586,702. And it is increasing at a geometric rate. When I wrote this section in 2014, for the 22,612,283 births that have occurred, 9,330,190 deaths have occurred, meaning that in the first two months of 2014,[374] the world population had increased by 13,282,093 people. When I was finishing the book at 12:36 a.m. On July 6, 2017, the population was 7,401,893,021, an increase of 18,530,632.[375] There are now over 7.5 billion, and it is estimated that we will reach 8 billion in 2025, 9 billion before 2050, and 10 billion by 2100.[376]

---

[371] . Terence Fretheim, "The Book of Genesis," *The New Interpreter's Bible*, vol. 1, ed. Leander E. Keck (Nashville: Abingdon Press, 1994), 346; see Ezek. 34:1–4 and Ps. 72:8–14.

[372] Stephanie Pappas, "7 Population Milestones for 7 Billion People," *LiveScience.com*, October, 2011, 11:06 AM ET.

[373] *Worldometers*, http://www.worldometers.info/world-population/.

[374] *Worldometers*, http://www.worldometers.info/world-population/.

[375] https://www.census.gov/popclock/.

[376] Stephanie Pappas, "7 Population Milestones for 7 Billion People," *LiveScience.com*,

The graph below illustrates the escalation of population growth.

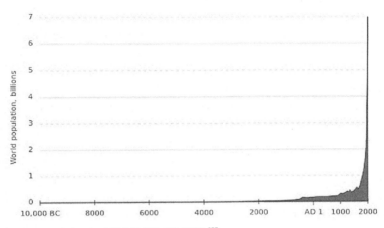

World human population (est.) 10,000 BC–AD 2000.[377]

It is obvious that if we want to live in the world as God intended, something has to be done to retard the growth of the population. For one thing, the earth cannot sustain the human demand for food. It is true that the dire predictions of people such as Malthus[378] have not come true. Malthus did not know how scientists would alter plants such as wheat, corn, and rice to produce more per acre. But food is not the biggest problem.

Disease

The main problem is the refuse left by of consumption of merchandise, especially the pollution produced by automobiles and industry. The ecosystem may be defined as "the interrelationship between living things and the environment."[379] And because of the interrelationship between everything in the environment, every change in one area has some effect on another. Children in elementary school learn that if it were not for photosynthesis, humans could not have oxygen to sustain life, and if

---

October 2011, 11:06 AM ET.

[377] http://en.wikipedia.org/wiki/File:Population_curve.svg.

[378] Thomas Robert Malthus, *An Essay on the Principles of Population*, 4th ed. (London: J. Johnson, 1807).

[379] Lauer and Lauer, *op. cit.*, 442.

humans and other animals did not give off carbon dioxide, plants could not carry on photosynthesis. We depend on each other.

With the development of the Industrial Revolution, we have benefitted in ways that don't require enumeration. However, many diseases are rampant that didn't exist before or were minor—cancer, emphysema, and asthma have a definite known correlation; others like autism and Alzheimer's disease *may* be correlated. The Industrial Revolution also produced acid rain, which is produced when sulfur dioxide emissions from coal-burning plants and factories combine with water vapor in the air to produce sulfuric acid. And nitrogen oxides from automobile exhausts mixes with water vapor, producing nitric acid, which falls to the earth killing birds and fish, reducing crop yields, damaging buildings, irritating eyes, and creating health problems. In the 1970s, one could not drive on the Tri-State Turnpike through East Chicago, Hammond, and Calumet City, Indiana, without either rolling up the windows of the car or holding one's breath as the pollutants belched out of the smokestacks. Lake Michigan was dying, and still 78 percent of the Great Lakes shorelines are polluted.[380] Thanks to government regulations, pollution has been significantly reduced, the air in these cities is significantly better, and Lake Michigan is recovering.

In 2005, Congress passed a cap and trade law for emissions of sulfur dioxide and nitrogen oxide, the two main causes of acid rain. And since then, emissions have dropped 40 percent. Europe has an even stricter cap and trade law, and they have managed to have these compounds drop by about 75 percent.[381]

Ozone

Ozone is a trioxidane form of the oxygen molecule (which, as middle school students know, is ordinarily diatomic), produced by lightning and high-voltage electrical equipment. It is toxic for humans. On ozone-action days, which we have several of every summer in Austin, Texas, especially young children whose lungs are still developing and elderly whose lungs are less robust, we are encouraged to stay inside. But as it rises in the atmosphere, ozone produces a layer between 6 and 31 miles above the

---

[380] *Ibid.*, 450.

[381] Andrew Isenberg. *Lectures in History*, "Origins of Environmental Commercialism," C-SPAN3.

surface of the earth that filters out ultraviolet rays of the sun, preventing skin cancer and the burning of crops. Depletion of the ozone layer is produced by nitrogen fertilizers, supersonic airplanes, chlorofluorocarbons in aerosol spray cans, and nuclear explosions. In 1998, the National Aeronautics and Space Administration (NASA) announced the existence of a hole (actually, depletion) in the ozone layer from Antarctica to Australia,[382] causing an escalation of skin cancer in Australia. The depleted ozone layer reduces crop yield and causes climate change, dry skin, skin cancer, and cataracts. With the banning of chlorofluorocarbons in aerosol cans at the Montreal Protocol of 1987 and the Clean Air Act of 1990, and almost total elimination of nuclear tests, the hole is closing.[383]

Atmospheric Pollution

Although one can see the particulate matter belching out of factory smokestacks, most atmospheric pollution is not immediately observable. One example is the vapors of a deadly pesticide that escaped from a faulty valve in Bhopal, India, in 1984, killing 2,500 people and making thousands of others critically ill.

Incineration in landfills, which reduces the buildup of waste, also adds pollution and potentially toxic chemicals to the air, which was mitigated by the Clean Air Act of 1970, resulting in a change to "sanitary landfills." The problem is where to put all that waste that is not being burned up. Since the burning of garbage was mostly prohibited, large holes became garbage dumps. The holes were available because they were created by the removal of dirt to build highway overpasses, on-ramps, and off-ramps as a result of the Interstate Highway Act (1956). Contractors bought the pits for next to nothing to market them for people to dump garbage for a small fee. However, they weren't lined to prevent toxins from leaking into the ground. In 1982, the Environmental Protection Agency (EPA) did a study of public water systems supplied by groundwater and found that 45

---

[382] *Imagine the Universe*, National Aeronautics and Space Administration: Goddard Space Flight Center, http://imagine.gsfc.nasa.gov/docs/ask astro/ answers/980403a.html. This site is no longer available. A discussion can be found on en.wikipedia.org/wiki/Ozone depletion, but the site warns that it may be technical for most readers. It was!

[383] Andrew Isenberg, *Lectures in History*, "Origins of Environmental Consumerism," C-SPAN3.

254   DAVID W. MELBER

percent of them were contaminated by chemicals that seeped out of solid
waste dumps.

In sanitary landfills, paper and other organic material eventually
decompose, but very slowly. However, plastics, the use of which has grown
enormously, does not decompose because it is packed so tight that it cannot
get the air it needs to decompose.[384] The landfills were composed of 40
percent paper, 18 percent plastic, 14 percent metal, 11 percent food waste,
2 percent disposable diapers, and other stuff 15 percent. The year 1980
was the height of garbage production in the United States with 150 million
tons of garbage per year in 1980s. Now, because of reuse and recycling, we
produce only about 100 million tons of garbage per year[385] despite the rise
in the population by 18–20 million.[386]

Erosion

Erosion is another problem. Abuse of the land by strip mining and
deforestation is also causing significant erosion. Between 2000 and 2005,
Africa lost 3.2 percent of their forests and South America lost 2.5 percent,
causing a buildup of carbon dioxide.[387] Without trees to hold the soil in
place, it is sent down rivers into the ocean or creates mudslides that destroy
residential areas. Another kind of land and water pollution is eutrophication,
overfertilization leading to nitrogen and sulfur in groundwater, leading to
algae growth and oxygen depletion.[388]

Water Pollution

Water pollution from organic sewage, overfertilization, waterborne
bacteria and viruses, pesticides and insecticides, inorganic chemicals, and
radioactive substances (e.g., Fukushima, Japan, and Chernobyl, Ukraine),
and oil spills (Exxon Valdez, 1989; Gulf oil spill, 2010) have contributed
to the pollution of lakes, rivers, and the oceans, killing wildlife, disrupting
the ecosystems, and costing billions of dollars to clean up and reclaim.

---

[384]   Lauer and Lauer, *op. cit.*, 451.

[385]   Andrew Isenberg, *Lectures in History*, "Origins of Environmental Consumerism,"
        C-SPAN.

[386]   *U.S. Population in Millions: 1940 to 2050.* Census.gov.

[387]   *Ibid.*, 452.

[388]   *Ibid.*, 444.

BIBLICAL INTERPRETATION FOR LAYPEOPLE AND OTHER MARTYRS   255

Threats to Coastal Cities

But global warming, produced by greenhouse gases trapping solar energy in the atmosphere, may be the biggest threat to the future of the world because it is adversely affecting crop production, causing the melting of polar icecaps and glaciers, resulting in the rise of ocean levels, and threatening coastal cities. According to NASA, although the consequences of the greenhouse effect are difficult to predict with precision, the earth will become warmer, leading to both more evaporation and precipitation, some regions becoming wetter and others dryer. It is warming the oceans, melting glaciers and other ice, thus increasing the sea level.[389]

In 2015 and 2016, a 225-square-mile chunk of the Pine Island ice shelf (the floating edge of the Pine Island Glacier), part of the West Antarctic ice sheet, broke off and drifted into the Amundsen Sea, on the Pacific coast of Antarctica.[390] The ice sheet is up to two and a half miles thick and covers an area twice the size of Texas, but most resting on the floor of the sea 5,000 feet below sea level. If the shelf breaks away, as researchers believe it might, "it would raise sea level by roughly 10 feet, drowning coasts around the world."[391] These "ice shelves are weakening and the glaciers behind them are flowing faster into the sea. The Pine Island Ice Shelf, about 1,300 feet thick . . . [has] thinned by an average of 150 feet from 1994 to 2012. But even more worrisome is the neighboring Thwaites Glacier, which could destabilize most of the West Antarctic Ice Sheet if it collapsed."[392]

Eric Rignot, a glaciologist at NASA's jet propulsion laboratory in Pasadena, believes that the collapse of the West Antarctic ice sheet is only a matter of time. It could take 500 years or fewer than a hundred years. A current of melted ice is streaming out from under the ice shelf. Warm saltwater from the South Pacific flows along the floor of submarine canyons. The warm "grounding line" where the glacier lifts off the seafloor erodes it. Because it is less dense, it is rising above the warmer water, flowing back out to the sea under the shelf, causing it to lose 13 cubic miles of ice per year.

---

[389]   "Global Climate Change: Vital Signs of the Planet," *NASA*, http://climate.nasa.gov/causes/, last updated October 29, 2015.

[390]   Douglas Fox, "The Crisis on the Ice," *National Geographic* 232, no. 1 (July 2017), 32.

[391]   *Ibid.*

[392]   *Ibid.*, 41.

Stan Jacobs, an oceanographer from the Lamont-Doherty Earth Observatory, and Adrian Jenkin, a glaciologist from the British Antarctic Survey in Cambridge, found that between 1996 and 2009, the rate of melting had increased by about 50 percent. Fox says that large swaths of West Antarctica were "hemorrhaging ice."[393]

The Antarctic Peninsula is hit by warm air and water from farther north, causing the average annual temperatures to rise nearly 5 degrees Fahrenheit since 1950, which is several times faster than the rest of the planet, with winters warming "an astonishing 9 degrees."[394] Thus, the Larsen A Ice Shelf collapsed in January 1995, losing about 1,500 square kilometers of ice.[395] Larsen B collapsed in 2002, an acceleration of about 300 percent and a mass loss of from 2–4 gigatonnes[396] per year in 1996 and 2000 to between 22 and 40 gigatonnes per year in 2006.[397] Swansea researchers argue that a large rapidly growing crack in Larsen C risks eventually following Larsen B[398] because "the glaciers they once stabilized have stampeded into the ocean, accelerating to two, five, even nine times the original speed."[399] The scientists were right. While I was reading the prediction in the July edition of *National Geographic*, on July 11, Swansea University's MIDAS project announced that a one-trillion-metric-tonne[400] iceberg of 5,800 square kilometers, one of the biggest ever recorded, calved away from Larsen C between July 10 and 12.[401]

Since most of it was already floating before it calved away, it has no immediate impact on sea level, but reduces Larsen C area by more than 12 percent. Ice may remain in the area for decades or may drift north into

---

[393] *Ibid.*, 41–43.

[394] *Ibid.*, 43.

[395] Rebecca Lindsey, "Collapse of the Larsen-B Ice Shelf," January 31, 2002, https://www. earthobservatory.nasa.gov/Features/WorldOfChange/larsenb.php.

[396] One metric gigatons or one billion gigatons = 1,102,311,311 US tons.

[397] Lindsey, *op. cit.*; a gigatonne is one billion metric tonnes.

[398] Swansea University, "The one trillion ton iceberg: Larsen C Ice Shelf rift finally breaks through," *ScienceDaily*, 12 July 2017, www.sciencedaily.com/releases/2017/07/170712110527.htm.

[399] Fox, *op. cit.*, 43.

[400] 1,102,311,311,000 US tons.

[401] 2,239.39252 sq. mi.

BIBLICAL INTERPRETATION FOR LAYPEOPLE AND OTHER MARTYRS   257

warmer waters. The thickness of 200 to 600 meters floats on the ocean at the edge of the Antarctic Peninsula.[402]

In November, Ian Howat, glaciologist from the Byrd Polar and Climate Research Center in Columbus, Ohio, "reported two ominous new rifts" spreading across the Pine Island Ice Shelf that threaten to break off. The water flowing underneath it is 4 to 6 degrees Fahrenheit *above freezing*. This may not sound like it causes a great loss, but Fox says, "Roughly 3,000 cubic miles of ['warm water'] arrives every year, which means the ice shelf is receiving an amount of heat that exceeds the output of a hundred nuclear power plants, operating 24/7."[403]

As meltwater undercuts the ice, the unsupported ice sags, causing the entire shelf to bend, creating crevasses along lines of stress. Research by Eric Rignot, glaciologist at the NASA Jet Propulsion Laboratory, "indicates that the collapse of several major glaciers flowing into the Amundsen Sea is now unstoppable." Helen Fricker of the Scripps Institution of Oceanography in San Diego says that the ice shelves "are the canary in the coal mine." She says that "they signal that a rise is imminent, as the glaciers behind them accelerate." She and her team "have found that from 1994 to 2012, the amount of ice disappearing from all Antarctic ice shelves . . . increased 12-fold, from six cubic miles to 74 cubic miles per year."[404]

Scientists are concerned about the Thwaites Glacier, which could raise global sea level four feet. Fox says, "Throw in Greenland and other rapidly melting glaciers around the world, and sea level could plausibly rise three to seven feet by 2100."[405]

In the East Antarctic with more than three-fourths of all the ice on earth,[406] glacially carved channels drop as far as 8,500 feet below sea level, where the Totten Glacier, the largest coastal outlet in this region, is located. If it collapsed, global sea level could rise 13 feet. In 2016, the team of Donald Blankenship, a University of Texas glaciologist, reported evidence that Totten has retreated 100 to 200 miles inland.[407] If it should slide into the sea, it would mean "abandoning many of the world's largest cities,

---

[402]   Swansea University, *op. cit.*

[403]   Fox, *op. cit.*, 46.

[404]   *Ibid.*, 46.

[405]   *Ibid.*, 47.

[406]   *Ibid.*

[407]   *Ibid.*, 48.

including New York, Los Angles, Copenhagen, Shanghai, and dozens of others—and it's looking less crazy all the time."[408]

Fox says, "Geologists studying ancient shorelines have concluded that 125,000 years ago, when the Earth was only slightly warmer than today, sea levels were 20 to 30 feet higher. Some three million years ago, the last time atmospheric carbon dioxide was as high as it is today, and the temperature was about what it's expected to be in 2050, sea levels were up to 70 feet higher than today."[409]

Another unanticipated problem developing from global warming is that many pests that harm crops would not be killed by winter freezes. Acidification of oceans are causing destruction of coral reefs and seashell-forming organisms because CO_2 in H_2O forms H_2CO_3, carbonic acid, which affects the pH level in oceans and dissolves the calcium carbonates needed for corals and seashell-forming organisms.[410]

Other results of climate change are wildfires, unusual rain patterns, and hurricanes. At the same time that the eastern and southern part of the United States is inundated with rain, wildfires burn the western United States. According to the Scripps Institution of Oceanography, since 1987, global warming has contributed to the increase of wildfires four times, the area burned has increased by a factor of four, and the fire season is five weeks longer.

Another issue is hurricanes. They draw their energy from the heat in the ocean, and as the heat in the ocean becomes warmer, the storms become more powerful. Between 1990 and 2006, the number of category 4 and 5 hurricanes has doubled each year.[411]

On October 8, 2018, the Intergovernmental Panel on Climate Change (IPCC), "the leading world body for assessing the science related to climate change, its impacts and potential future risks, and possible response options," issued its latest report and most dire prediction. The report involved ninety-one authors and review editors from 40 countries, more than 6,000 scientific studies, and the contribution of thousands of

---

[408] *Ibid.*, 49.

[409] *Ibid.*, 47.

[410] Friedman (2008), *op. cit.*, 110.

[411] Anthony Westerling, Hugo Hidalgo, Dan Cayan, and Tom Swetnam, "Warming Comate Plays Large Role in Western U.S. Wildfires, Scripps-led Study Shows," *Scripps Institution of Oceanography,* July 6, 2006, 12:00 AM PDT.

expert and government reviewers worldwide, with a 42,001 expert and government review comments.

It is made up of three major working groups. Working Group I assesses the physical science basis of climate change; Working Group II addresses impacts, adaptation, and vulnerability; and Working Group III deals with the mitigation of climate change.

The report concluded that limiting global warming to 1.5°C instead of the 2.0°C currently anticipated "would require rapid, far-reaching and unprecedented changes in all aspects of society," resulting in "clear benefits to people and natural ecosystems." Scientists have been predicting for about four decades the radical and catastrophic changes in weather and environmental patterns that we see today, such as the death of coral reefs, increased number and intensity of hurricanes, the loss of shorelines from rising sea levels, increased drying resulting in more forest fires in some areas, and increased torrential rain and flooding in other areas. "One of the key messages . . . from this report is that we are already seeing the consequences of 1°C of global warming through more extreme weather, rising sea levels and diminishing Arctic sea ice, among other changes," said Panmao Zhai, cochair of IPCC Working Group I.

The report says that the catastrophic impact could be avoided by limiting global warming to 1.5°C compared to 2°C by 2100. For instance, by 2100, global sea level rise would be 10 centimeters lower compared with 2°C. But it would require "rapid and far-reaching" transitions in land, energy, industry, buildings, transport, and cities. Global net human-caused emissions of carbon dioxide (CO_2) would need to fall by about 45 percent from 2010 levels by 2030, reaching "net zero" around 2050, including removing CO_2 already from the air. "Limiting warming to 1.5°C . . . would require unprecedented changes," said Jim Skea, cochair of IPCC Working Group III. "Limiting global warming to 1.5°C compared with 2°C would reduce challenging impacts on ecosystems, human health and well-being, making it easier to achieve the United Nations Sustainable Development Goals," said Priyardarshi Shukla, cochair of IPCC Working Group III. The decisions we make today "are critical in ensuring a safe and sustainable world for everyone, both now and in the future," said Debra Roberts, cochair of IPCC Working Group II.[412]

---

[412] "The Summary for Policymakers of the Special Report on Global Warming of 1.5°C," *The Intergovernmental Panel on Climate Change*, October 8, 2018. The Intergovernmental Panel on Climate Change (IPCC) is "the UN body

The Role of Human Activity

Although some cynical politicians refer to global warming as a "myth," or even worse, a "hoax,"[413] the overwhelming majority of climatologists, meteorologists, oceanographers, botanists, zoologists, and geologists who study the situation do agree that the situation is becoming critical.

There have been other periods of warming that had nothing to do with industrial pollution. The earth has gone through periods of warming and cooling all on its own. Opponents of environmental protection argue that this is what is happening with global warming. However, Andrew Isenberg argues, "But those are not mutually exclusive arguments. If in fact, the earth is getting warmer all on its own because of whatever pattern it's in, the last thing we want to be doing is contributing to that problem by adding carbon to the atmosphere."[414]

In its "Fourth Assessment Report," the Intergovernmental Panel on Climate Change (IPCC), a group of 1,300 independent scientists under the auspices of the United Nations, concluded that there is more than a 90 percent probability that human activities over the past 250 years have caused warming of the planet.[415]

---

for assessing the science related to climate change. It was established by the United Nations Environment Programme (UN Environment) and the World Meteorological Organization (WMO) in 1988 to provide policymakers with regular scientific assessments concerning climate change, its implications and potential future risks, as well as to put forward adaptation and mitigation strategies. It has 195 member states. IPCC assessments provide governments, at all levels, with scientific information that they can use to develop climate policies. IPCC assessments are a key input into the international negotiations to tackle climate change. IPCC reports are drafted and reviewed in several stages, thus guaranteeing objectivity and transparency. The IPCC assesses the thousands of scientific papers published each year to tell policymakers what we know and don't know about the risks related to climate change. To produce its reports, the IPCC mobilizes hundreds of scientists drawn from diverse backgrounds." The full report can be found at https://www.ipcc.ch/report/sr15.

[413] I say cynical because they are not ignorant. They, above all others except the scientists, have the information.

[414] *Lectures in History,* "Origins of Environmental Consumerism," C-SPAN3.

[415] *IPCC Fourth Assessment Report, 2007,* "Global Climate Change Impacts in the United States," United States Global Change Research Program, Cambridge University Press, 2009, http://climate.nasa.gov/ causes/. Naomi Oreskes, "The Scientific Consensus on Climate Change," *Science* 3 December 2004: Vol. 306

BIBLICAL INTERPRETATION FOR LAYPEOPLE AND OTHER MARTYRS   261

The Union of Concerned Scientists (UCS) is a science network that collaborates with nearly 17,000 scientists and technical experts across the country, including physicists, ecologists, engineers, public health professionals, economists, and energy analysts. The organization contends that it has been so difficult to achieve meaningful solutions to global warming because "media pundits, partisan think tanks, and special interest groups raise doubts about the truth of global warming. This barrage of misinformation misleads and confuses the public — and makes it more difficult to implement effective solutions."[416]

They say that we "are overloading our atmosphere with carbon dioxide, which traps heat and steadily drives up the planet's temperature. . . . The fossil fuels we burn for energy—coal, natural gas, and oil—plus the loss of forests due to deforestation, especially in the tropics. [and] . . . Global warming is already having . . . harmful effects on our communities, our health, and our climate."[417]

The UCS says, "Within the scientific community, *there is no debate*.[418] An overwhelming majority of climate scientists agree that global warming is happening and that human activity is the primary cause."[419] And according to six different studies that surveyed 11,944 peer-reviewed abstracts of research on global warming from 1991 to 2001, between 90 percent and 100 percent of the researchers concluded that global warming was anthropogenic global warming (AGW), that is, human-caused. Summarizing the studies, which used different methods, Cook et al. concluded that 97.2 percent agreed that AGW is the major or contributing cause of climate change and/or global warming.[420] Another finding is

---

no. 5702, 1686, doi: 10.1126/science.1103618.

[416] Union of Concerned Scientists: Science for a healthy planet and safer world, http://www.ucsusa.org/ global_warming#.VjZzrbSFNyQ. See also https://climate.nasa.gov/scientific-consensus/.

[417] *Ibid.*

[418] Italics mine.

[419] *Ibid.*

[420] John Cook, Naomi Oreskes, Peter T. Doran, William R. L. Anderegg, Bart Verheggen, Ed W. Maibach, J. Stuart, Carlton, Stephan Lewandowsky, Andrew G. Skuce, and Sarah A. Green, "Consensus on consensus: a synthesis of consensus estimates on human-caused global warming," *Environmental Research Letters*, published 13 April 2016, IOP Publishing Ltd., http://iopscience.iop.org/article/10.1088/1748-9326/11/4/048002/meta. Tol (2016), a contrarian on the

262   DAVID W. MELBER

that the higher the level of expertise, the higher the agreement in climate science that global warming is anthropogenic.[421] Additionally, the National Academies of Science from 80 countries have endorsed this position.[422]

A 2011 paper published in the *International Journal of Public Opinion Research*, researchers from George Mason University found that of 489 American scientists from academia, government, and industry, 97 percent agreed that global temperatures have risen over the past century and 84 percent agreed that "human-induced greenhouse warming" is now occurring. Only 5 percent disagreed that human activity is a significant cause.[423]

Every year for the past 37 years has been warmer than the twentieth-century average, the 12 warmest years on record occurring since 1998, the hottest year of all occurring in 2012. Globally, the average surface temperature has increased more than one degree Fahrenheit since the late 1800s, most of which has occurred over the past three decades.[424] This was the information I got when I first did the research. Since then, however, according to the World Meteorological Organization (WMO), "the ten hottest years since thermometer records became available in 1860 all occurred between 1995 and 2005."[425] That was true until the WMO published its findings on January 18, 2017, confirming that 2015 was the hottest until 2016, which surpassed the previous year.[426]

---

climate issue, obtained a lower consensus estimate. The flaws in Tol's article were giving nonexperts the same credibility as the view of experts who had actually done peer-reviewed research. The second flaw was assuming that a paper that simple did the research and did not comment one way or the other was taken to be a negative.

[421]   Oreskes 2004, Doran and Zimmerman 2009, Anderegg 2010, Verheggen et al. 2014.

[422]   *Joint science academies' statement: Global response to climate change*, http:// nationalacademies. org/onpi/06072005.pdf.

[423]   http://en.wikipedia.org/wiki/Global_Warming#Scientific_discussion.

[424]   *Ibid.*

[425]   Friedman (2008) *op. cit.*, 33.

[426]   "WMO confirms 2016 as hottest year on record, about 1.1°C above pre-industrial era," World Meteorological Organization, https://public.wmo.int/en/media/ press-release/wmo-confirms-2016-hottest-year-record-about-11°c-above-pre-industrial-era.

BIBLICAL INTERPRETATION FOR LAYPEOPLE AND OTHER MARTYRS   263

The IPCC concluded that "there's a better than 90 percent probability that human-produced greenhouse gases . . . have caused much of the observed increase in Earth's temperatures over the past 50 years."[427] They said that although it is reasonable to *assume* that changes in the sun's output have caused the climate to change (which some have claimed), the evidence shows that current global warming cannot be explained by changes in the sun's energy. Tests, such as ice cores, permafrost cores, and tree ring samples, show that since 1750, the energy from the sun has either remained constant or increased only slightly. Second, if the warming were caused by the sun, there would be warmer temperatures in all layers of the atmosphere. However, there is cooling in the upper atmosphere (stratosphere and above), but warming at the lower atmosphere (troposphere) and the earth's surface, trapping heat in the lower atmosphere.[428]

The *UCS* expresses the urgency of the problem: "We must take immediate action to address global warming or these consequences will continue to intensify, grow ever more costly, and increasingly affect the entire planet—including you, your community, and your family."[429]

Growing International Middle Class

But pollution is not the only problem. Another problem is depletion of resources. Until recently, America, with about 7 percent of the population of the earth used up about half the resources in the world. Without reducing America's usage, recently China and India have greatly increased their ability to use up resources.

The more people there are, the greater the impact on the ecosystem. But it is not just the number of people, but also the fact that a rapidly escalating number of humans are moving into the middle class with much more money to spend on merchandise. Along with the growth of the middle class in India, with the fall of communism in China, 200 million people came out of abject poverty in the 1980s and 1990s in China and India, enabling them to consume more, produce more, and discard more.[430] Beginning with the Great Leap Forward under Deng Xiaoping, China has become

---

[427] http://climate.nasa.gov/causes/; the panel's full Summary for Policymakers report is online at http://www.ipcc.ch/pdf/assessment-report/ar4/syr/ar4_syr_spm.pdf.

[428] *Ibid.*

[429] http://www.ucsusa.org/global_warming#.VjZzrbSFNyQ.

[430] Friedman (2008), *op. cit.*, 27.

264 DAVID W. MELBER

increasingly successful but has caused significant air pollution, much of it blowing on wind currents across the Pacific Ocean to the United States.[431]

In about 1974, when China opened to the outside world, an economics professor from West Texas State University was among the first group to visit China. He told some of us that he was amazed about the plethora of bicycles in China. Everyone rode bicycles. However, as China moved from communism to capitalism, the most bicycling nation in the world quickly became one of the most automobile-driving nations in the world. In 2008, China took over the United States' role as leading carbon emitter.[432] Therefore, their eleventh Five-Year Plan under Hu Jintao target 20 percent below 2005 levels of gas emissions by 2010, far more ambitious than the 1997 Kyoto Protocol, was based on the scientific consensus.[433]

Nissan has entered the world's biggest auto market, China, producing the Sylphy Zero Emission, partnering with Dongfeng Motor Group, claiming 210 miles on a charge. Government subsidies help Chinese drivers to purchase the electric cars. General Motors and Volkswagen are poised to launch electric sedans, minivans, SUVs designed "for Chinese tastes and budgets." And "Tesla, GM and others sell imports or electrified versions of models made by Chinese partners, but the market is dominated by low-cost local rivals including BYD Auto." [434]

In the nineteenth and twentieth centuries, America "treated things like pollution, waste, and CO^2 emissions as essentially irrelevant 'externalities' . . . any cost or benefit resulting from a commercial transaction that is borne by or received by parties not directly involved in the transaction."[435] Issues like asthma and downstream water pollution are examples. The most recent example was the contaminated water in Flint, Michigan.[436] Other famous ones in the United States are the near nuclear meltdown in Three-Mile

---

[431] *Ibid.*, 316.

[432] *Ibid.*, 246.

[433] *Ibid.*, 321.

[434] "Nissan launches electric sedan targeted at China," *Austin American-Statesman*, August 28, 2018, B5, Associated Press.

[435] "Nate Lewis Leads US Energy Innovation Hub at Caltech," *Planning Report: Insider's Guide to Planning & Infrastructure*, August 7, 2013, 235, <https://www.verdexchange.org/news/nate-lewis-leads-us-energy-innovation-hub-caltech>.

[436] Sara Ganim and Linh Tran, "How tap water became topic in Flint, Michigan," CNN, January 13, 2016, 10:53 AM ET, CNN.com.

BIBLICAL INTERPRETATION FOR LAYPEOPLE AND OTHER MARTYRS   265

Island,[437] the major disaster at Love's Canal,[438] and the one made famous in the movie *Erin Brockovich*,[439] starring Julia Roberts, in which numerous people's lives in Hinckley, California, were ruined by cancer and related illnesses by contaminated groundwater produced by Pacific Gas & Electric (PG&E), which was settled for $333 million.[440]

American Culture

The contribution to resource depletion and pollution is the change in attitude toward science and technology. The United States is afflicted with the "I gotta have the newest tech" bug.

After World War II, the environmental catastrophe in the USA really began, perhaps because after so much self-sacrifice during the war, with accumulated war savings in veterans' hands and incentives such as the VA loan program, America focused on short-term benefits. As families got smaller, houses got bigger. Capitalism, with its emphasis on constant growth, contributed to the problem. Existing market needs were filled, and innovations in advertising created new markets by convincing people they must have things they did not need. But unbridled capitalism was not the only culprit. Environmental abuse also occurred under the communist governments of the Soviet Union and the People's Republic of China, which paid no attention to protecting the environment at all. The attitudes were very similar—increase production regardless of what damage occurred to the environment.

For decades, we complained about planned obsolescence, which has exacerbated the problem by causing a large increase in the volume of discarded objects. Lobbying by corporations for legislation favorable to their interests has contributed to environmental degradation. For all these reasons, the environment is not a high priority for politicians. And when profits to the individual or company outweigh the costs to the environment, there is little chance that the offending individual or company will alter its behavior unless it is accountable for paying for the damage it causes to the

---

[437]   "Three Mile Island accident," en.wikipedia.org/wiki/Three_Mile_Island_acident, last edited on 7 June 2017 at 02:46.

[438]   https://en.wikipedia.org/wiki/Love_Canal, last edited on 18 June 2017, at 21:40.

[439]   Soderbergh, Steven, dir. Universal Pictures, 2000.

[440]   https://en.wikipedia.org/wiki/Erin_Brockovich, last edited on 23 May 2017, at 12:50.

environment, as with PG&E. Again, Neubeck says "that the activities of business and industry frequently run counter to environmental sanity."[441]

This is a cultural issue and attitudes can change if people are convinced that the cost outweighs the benefit. Economic issues are important. But since human life is more important, we should support specific behaviors and laws that will be beneficial to as many people as possible, especially in life and death issues.

Growing Change in Attitude

In 1949, the world changed. Two Volkswagen Beetles, originally derided as the "Hitler Car," were sold in the United States. In 1950, 157 were sold. But by the end of 1977, 21,529,464 Beetles were sold.[442] Despite its lack of debonairness, its price, dependability, and gas mileage made it "cool," particularly among young people. But that was not the end. The other World War II enemy, Japan, developed a car that was also more durable than American-made cars. In 1969, when the music died, as Ritchie Valens, Buddy Holly, and the Big Bopper died in an Iowa farm field, Honda invaded America.[443] It was more "sedanish" and high-end than the VW, more to the liking of middle-class moms and dads. The Big Three no longer had their cozy monopoly. With the success of Volkswagen and Honda, the floodgates opened with Toyota, Nissan, Saab, Subaru, Hyundai, Kia, BMW, Mercedes-Benz, Isuzu, and the Yugo, some of whom have been successful, some of whom failed.

In about 1970, rising public concern for the environment among Americans led to the first Earth Day. The campus-related congregation in which I served hosted the first Earth Day ecumenical worship service at Northern Illinois University. Concern has steadily grown since then. A large part of the problem initially was ignorance of the problem. Like Adam, we are called to care for the earth (Gen. 1:28). It is incumbent on Christians to become "wise as serpents" (Matt. 10:16) in dealing with the environmental issues so that our children and grandchildren will have an earth that is livable.

---

[441] Kenneth J. Neubeck, *Social Problems: A Critical Approach* (New York: McGraw-Hill, 1991).

[442] "The first Volkswagen Beetle in America looked like this," *Autoweek*, January 29, 2014, http://autoweek.com/article/car-news/first-volkswagen-beetle-america-looked.

[443] "Fifty Years of Honda in America," *Automobile*, July 7, 2009, http://www.automobilemag.com/ news/fifty-years-of-honda-history/.

BIBLICAL INTERPRETATION FOR LAYPEOPLE AND OTHER MARTYRS   267

In 1973–1974, the Arab oil embargo briefly precipitated a drive toward energy efficiency. In early 1973, the Organization of the Petroleum Exporting Countries (OPEC) met in Kuwait and decided to raise the price of oil from $3 a barrel to $5 a barrel to punish the United States for supporting Israel in the 1973 Arab-Israeli War. In December, they met in Tehran and raised it to $11 a barrel, raising their income from $4 billion in 1970 to $60 billion in 1974. In 1972, it cost Europe and the United States $20 billion to import oil they needed. In 1974, it cost $100 billion, causing 10 percent inflation in the United States. By the summer of 1974, 20 percent of US gas stations had no fuel to sell. Others had long lines and rationing. Industries that relied on fuels looked for ways to cut costs.[444]

In 1975, Congress passed the Energy Policy and Conservation Act that required passenger vehicle efficiency for new cars to reach 27.5 miles per gallon within ten years. Between 1975 and 1985, American miles per gallon went from around 13.5 per gallon to 27.5, weakening OPEC and helping to unravel the Soviet Union, the world's second-largest oil producer.[445] But when oil prices went down, we got readdicted to imported oil. In 1989, G. H. W. Bush introduced a "production tax credit on renewable energy."[446] But after liberating Kuwait, oil prices went down and gas-guzzling Hummers became faddish.

The Big Three automakers and the United Automobile Workers (UAW) opposed mileage standards to Congress. Interlocking directories undermine such progress. Oil men on the board of directors of automobile companies were definitely *not* inclined for their automobiles to have greater gasoline efficiency. So attitudes in the United States have changed, but very slowly.

Attitudes changed in China also. In 2003, China announced fuel economy standards for new cars. Only in 2007 did Congress act again, moving standards to 35 miles per gallon by 2020, where Europe was already.[447] But under George W. Bush, we became "more dependent on China to finance our deficit and on Saudi Arabia to fill up our gas tanks,"[448]

---

[444]   Andrew Isenberg, "Origins of Environmental Consumerism," *Lectures in History*, C-SPAN3.

[445]   Friedman (2008), op. cit., 13.

[446]   *Ibid.*, 14.

[447]   *Ibid.*

[448]   *Ibid.*, p. 19.

causing us to support some of the world's worst autocracies—Saudi Arabia, Iran, Iraq, Russia.

Resistance to Change

There is a minority of people who deny global warming and the role of human activity in it. However, just as in the denial of the ill effects of tobacco in decades past, for the most part, the deniers are people who benefit from ignoring the ill effects of global warming, such as the "think tank," the Heartland Institute.[449] Nevertheless, scientists have been documenting the effects of global warming for decades—the almost total loss of Glacier National Park; receding of the ice at both poles, Patagonia, Mt. Kilimanjaro; the devastation of the Brazilian rain forest; and the rising of the ocean level. However, 31,487 American scientists have signed a petition asking the US government to reject the global warming agreement adopted in Kyoto, Japan, in December 1997, even saying that it would "damage the health and welfare of mankind." However, only 9,029 of them had PhDs, and there is, so far, no evidence that any of them have done research on climate or global warming.[450]

The strange reasoning of Americans is reflected in a Yale University poll that found that more than half of Americans believe that climate change will "harm people in the U.S.," but fewer than 40 percent believed it would "harm me personally."[451]

Friedman says that the climate-change deniers are those paid by fossil fuel companies, those who have concluded that the rapid increase in greenhouse gases is not a major threat, and the conservatives who refuse to accept the reality because they hate government intervention, particularly regulations.[452]

There is almost unanimous agreement among climate scientists that the main cause of current global warming is human production of carbon dioxide (CO_2). Increased atmospheric CO_2 increases the "greenhouse effect," warming that results from the atmosphere trapping heat radiating

---

[449] http://www.sourcewatch.org/index.php/SourceWatch.

[450] *Global Warning Petition*, http://www.petitionproject.org/.

[451] Nadja Popovich, John Schwartz, and Tatiana Schlossberg, "How Americans Think about Climate Change, in Six Maps," *New York Times*, March 21, 2017, https://www.nytimes.com/interactive/2017/03/21/ climate/how-americans-think-about-climate-change-in-six-maps.html.

[452] Friedman (2008), *op. cit.*, p. 104.

from earth like the inside of a car on a hot day with the windows rolled up. The warming is caused by gases, like carbon dioxide, which is produced mainly by deforestation and burning fossil fuels, increasing "atmospheric CO_2 concentration by a third since the Industrial Revolution began."[453]

Another hydrocarbon gas is methane, produced by the decomposition of wastes in landfills, agricultural cultivation (especially rice), ruminant digestion, and livestock manure. And chlorofluorocarbons (CFCs), synthetic compounds used in air conditioning and aerosol cans, have been responsible for a hole in the ozone layer,[454] which allows more skin-cancer-causing ultraviolet rays.

According to Nate Lewis, a solar fuels/solar chemical researcher at Caltech, the composition of the earth's atmosphere has been relatively unchanged for twenty million years, but it has dramatically changed in the last hundred years. He says that ice core samples show that the level of carbon dioxide in the atmosphere stood at about 280 parts per million (ppm) by volume. But it started to change in the 1950s. In 1997, the level was 384 ppm, climbing at a rate of about 2 ppm per year.[455] My guess is, he got this figure from the National Oceanic and Atmospheric Administration (NOAA) research, which had documented it from Mauna Loa Observatory since 1955.[456] The earth has become 1 degree warmer over the last 100 years.[457]

Lewis says that the change in global average temperature from glacial to interglacial periods is too big to account for the sun's radiation or

---

[453] http://climate.nasa.gov/causes/, last updated Oct. 29, 2015. See also http://www.ucsusa.org/global warming#.VjZzrbSFNyQ.

[454] http://climate.nasa.gov/causes/, last updated October 29, 2015.

[455] sos.noaa.gov/_media/cms/sosx/climate_change_and_carbon_dioxide_lesson_teacher.pdf.

[456] *Global Climate Change and Carbon Dioxide Lesson – Earth & Environmental Science* – Teacher Version (with answers), sos.noaa.gov/_media/cms/sosx/climate_change_and_carbon_dioxide_lesson_ teacher.pdf. Nathan S. Lewis is head of the Lewis Research group and has written over 500 papers on the issue of solar issues (http://nsl.caltech.edu/home/). The National Aeronautics and Space Administration (NASA), along with NOAA, provide a great deal of research information on climate change. The Environmental Protection Agency (EPA) used to provide volumes of research data also, but much of it was taken down within a couple of weeks after President Trump was sworn in.

[457] Andrew Isenberg, "Origins of Environmental Consumerism," *Lectures in History*, C-SPAN3. Isenberg is editor of *The Oxford Handbook of Environmental History*.

variations in the earth's orbit. The concentrations of CO_2 between glacial and interglacial periods varied by about 120 parts of CO_2 per million, from 180 ppm to 300 ppm and back to cause 6° Celsius (10.8° F) temperature changes. For the last 10,000 years, it has been stable at about 280 ppm of CO_2, and our climate has been stable.

That changed, beginning in about 1750 with the Industrial Revolution, and particularly in the last fifty years, when the amount of CO_2 in the earth's atmosphere jumped from 280 ppm to 384 ppm, where it has probably never been for twenty million years. And we are now on track to add 100 or more ppm of CO_2 to the atmosphere in the next fifty years from burning fossil fuels and deforestation. Carbon dating measurements show that the carbon dioxide increase in the atmosphere in the last fifty years has come from fossil fuel consumption.[458] "And we know that this increase of CO_2 is going to give us a different climate than the one we now know, because in 670,000 straight years, whenever CO_2 has gone up, temperatures have gone up, and whenever CO_2 in the atmosphere has gone down, temperatures have gone down. So, to say that the addition of CO_2 added by humans is not a problem is to bet against 670,000 straight years of data, and to hope that we are going to get lucky this time."[459]

Reaction to Growing International Middle Class

A major question that must be answered in the future is "whether the poor nations can achieve the same standard of living as the rich nations" or not.[460] It will require richer nations to reduce their emphasis on the present opulence. It is unreasonable for affluent nations to try to force nations with emerging economies to limit themselves while richer nations refuse to do so. As Neubeck points out, "Just as rich nations consume and pollute at far higher rates than poorer ones, the affluent minority in this country makes a greater contribution to environmental deterioration than its numbers would indicate."[461]

---

[458] Freedman (2008), *op. cit.*, 108.

[459] "Nate Lewis Leads US Energy Innovation Hub at Caltech," *The Planning Report: Insider's Guide to Planning & Infrastructure*, August 7, 2013, https://www.verdexchange.org/news/nate-lewis-leads-us-energy-innovation-hub-caltech. Also quoted in Friedman (2008), *op. cit.*, 109. Obviously, the report was presented earlier somewhere else since Friedman quotes it in 2008.

[460] Lauer and Lauer, *op. cit.*, 460.

[461] Neubeck, *op. cit.*, 145.

BIBLICAL INTERPRETATION FOR LAYPEOPLE AND OTHER MARTYRS   271

Nevertheless, there is hopefulness: "The good news is that we have the practical solutions at hand to dramatically reduce our carbon emissions, slow the pace of global warming, and pass on a healthier, safer world to future generations."[462]

For the good of the planet, *perhaps* even to save life on the planet, numerous things need to be done by individuals, the business community, and government. Laws such as the Clean Air Act are a good start.[463] The Environmental Protection Agency regulations have set pollution standards.[464] Mass transit can carry seventy times the number of people as cars on the highway can while consuming only 1 percent of the hydrocarbon fuels and costing one-tenth as much as it does to build the same amount of highway.[465]

An economical way to capture and use methane gas would solve numerous problems. Using scrap metal to build new cars and the skeletons of new buildings, building cars that get better gas mileage, the development of alternate energy such as geothermal, fuel cells, solar, and wind would have a major benefit to our life on earth. Although atomic power is a great source of energy, it is extremely deadly, as we learned from Chernobyl's radioactive meltdown, which perhaps ultimately killed a 100,000 people,[466] and Fukushima. The Japanese accident had contaminated part of Japan; the reactors continue to bleed radiation into the groundwater and then into the Pacific Ocean, and Japan does not know what to do with nearly a million tons of radioactive water.[467] In 1956, the cast and crew of the movie *The*

---

[462]   http://www.ucsusa.org/global_warming#.VjZzrbSFNyQ.

[463]   Lauer and Lauer, *op. cit.*, 456

[464]   *Ibid.*, 448.

[465]   *Ibid.*, 466.

[466]   The actual number is difficult to determine. Russia, Belarus, and Ukraine suffered the most. However, estimates have varied widely, partly because wind currents carried contaminated material as far northwest as Sweden, which was first to be exposed to the fallout in their atmosphere. The New York Academy of Science published an analysis of scientific literature, concluding that medical records between 1986 and 2004 reflect 985,000 premature deaths as a result of the radioactivity released. "Chernobyl: Consequences of the Catastrophe for People and the Environment," *Annals of the New York Academy of Science*, no. 1181 (December 2009), nyas.org. Retrieved 15 March 2011.

[467]   Tyler Durden, "Fukushima Five Years Later: The Fuel Rods Melted through Containment and Nobody Knows Where They Are Now," zerohedge.com, 3/11/2016 23:27.

Conqueror were downwind from the nuclear test site in southeastern Nevada. Of the 220 members of the cast and crew, 91 developed cancer, including Patrick and Michael Wayne, and 46 died of cancer, including John Wayne, Susan Hayward, Agnes Moorhead, Pedro Armendariz, and Dick Powell.[468]

A second problem with the use of atomic energy is the storage of radioactive wastes because of the length of time it takes radioactive elements to break down and the possibility of contamination of the earth and underground water.[469]

Other ways to help preserve our environment are by the recycling of plastics, paper, metals, lumber; by stopping the use of disposables, such as diapers; by using rheostats that turn off lights thirty seconds after people leave the room;[470] by refilling plastic bottles rather than throwing them away. These are a sample of things that can be done to make the world a more livable place. Christians can influence their senators and congressmen, their businesses at work, and in their own lives. Also, individuals might learn that they can be just as happy with less. The church can help our cultural values evolve away from individualism toward an emphasis on community well-being.[471]

The most ambitious international agreement thus far was the Paris Agreement, adopted by representatives of 197 nations. On December 12, 2015, parties to the United Nations Framework Convention on Climate Change (UNFCCC) reached a landmark agreement to combat climate change. It brought virtually all nations into a common cause. The central aim was to keep a global temperature rise this century well below 2 degrees Celsius above preindustrial levels and under 1.5 degrees Celsius if possible. It makes provision for financial resources through a Green Climate Fund (GCF) and provides new technology supporting action by developing countries and the most vulnerable countries to strengthen

---

[468] Wikipedia, s.v. "John Wayne," en.wikipedia/org/wiki/John_Wayne, last modified Nov. 2, 2015 at 15:31 and https://en.wikipedia.org/wiki/The_Conqueror, last modified on 5 March 2016 at 17:06.

[469] Lauer and Lauer, *op. cit.*, 453.

[470] Japan has been using motion detectors to turn lights on and off for at least thirty years.

[471] Al Gore, *An Inconvenient Truth*, Davis Guggenheim, Paramount Classics, 2006. Supported by *Alliance for Climate Protection, Climate Reality Project, Natural Resources Defense Council, National Wildlife Federation,* and *Stop Global Warming.* Carefully documents the growth of the problem and suggested some remedies.

BIBLICAL INTERPRETATION FOR LAYPEOPLE AND OTHER MARTYRS   273

their ability to deal with the impacts of climate change. It requires all parties to put forward their best efforts through "nationally determined contributions" (NDCs) and report regularly on their emissions and on their implementation efforts. Participation is voluntary. It also makes provision for climate change education, training, public awareness, public participation, and public access to information. While representatives from 197 voted in favor of the provisions, the governments of 152 nations have actually adopted it.[472]

Unfortunately, in 2017, while almost 200 nations are, to one extent or another, pulling together to deal with the crisis, the United States began to reverse a several decades' direction when Donald Trump promised to withdraw from the Paris Agreement, appointed Scott Pruett head of Environmental Protection Agency, and began reversing the presidential directives of President Obama regarding regulations in the energy-producing industries.

Michael Oppenheimer, professor of geosciences at Princeton and a member of the panel for climate change, said on the *PBS News Hour*, that as a result of EPA regulations, global emissions of greenhouse gases have decreased slightly over the last three years, even though the population and the global economy is growing. Almost every country in the world has committed to the Paris Accords, including the biggest emitter, China. Because of its recent development of industry and a growing middle class that is increasing consumption, China has a great air pollution problem, so much so that in cities like Beijing, people wear face masks to filter out the particulate. China is reducing emissions and moving in the direction of making money on the new ecological technology. It is the leading producer of solar photocells and the leading producer of wind turbines. Oppenheimer argues that the United States will be left in the dust economically if we do not compete in the increasing production of clean energy products. He further claimed that in the United States, the renewable energy industry now has four times as much employment as in coal production.[473]

The leadership of Exxon, Chevron, Microsoft, Apple, Johnson & Johnson, Monsanto, Dell Chemical, and numerous other corporations

---

[472]   United Nations Framework Convention on Climate Change, http://unfccc.int/ paris_agreement/ items/9485.php.

[473]   Judy Woodruff, anchor, *PBS News Hour*, KUT, Wednesday, May 31, 1917, PBS.org.

have agreed that the United States should continue its commitment to the Paris Accords, even making economic arguments for it.

Norway, which considers itself the world's most pristine nation, has become the world's fastest-growing electric car market. Despite the fact that Norway's major income is from gas and oil production, they are opting to reduce their dependence on fossil fuels by embracing electric cars. The government has encouraged the use of electric cars by providing them with free parking, increasing number of charging stations, lowering yearly fees to use roads, and exempting electric cars from paying tolls. They have high taxes in Norway, but no sales tax on electric cars. Gas is about $7 gallon in Norway. All these incentives make electric cars almost irresistible. Norwegians drive over 100,000 electric cars. Although that does not sound like much, Norway has the highest per capita ownership level in the world. They expect the number of electric cars to pass gas-driven cars by 2025.[474]

The Opel Ampera-E,[475] in a collaboration between GM and South Korea's LG,[476] which will sell for $35,000, was expected to launch in May 2017. It gets 300 miles on a charge. There is a fifteen-month waiting list.[477] Any automotive company would lick its chops for that kind of waiting list. In July 2017, Tesla Model 3 electric car began rolling off the line, costing $35,000 less the $7,500 federal electric car tax credit. It can go 215 miles between charges. But others are competing. GM's Chevrolet Bolt recently came out, going 238 miles per charge. Audi plans an electric SUV with 300 miles range next year. In 2020, Ford plans to have one out. Volkswagen plans several models in 2025.[478] These innovations should have a significant benefit to the environment. But perhaps the biggest impetus for the whole automotive industry is the announcement of Volvo that is based in Sweden, but owned by the Chinese firm Geely, that it would be *completely* phasing out gasoline-only cars beginning in 2019. Audi and Mercedes-Benz are already producing hybrids in Europe. Volvo plans to roll out five completely electric models

---

[474] Judy Woodruff, anchor, *PBS News Hour*, KUT, May 29, 2017.

[475] "'Das Elektroauto': Opel Ampera- impresses with electrifying high-tech," *Automotive World*, Automotiveworld.com.

[476] "LG Chem sees GM selling over 30,000 Bolt electric vehicles next year," *Reuters*, 18 Oct. 2016, 4:22 AM, Businessinsider.com.

[477] Woodruff, op. cit., Wednesday, 29 May 1917.

[478] "Tesla Model 3 to roll off the line Friday," *Austin American-Statesman*, Tuesday, July 4, 2017, B5.

BIBLICAL INTERPRETATION FOR LAYPEOPLE AND OTHER MARTYRS 275

between 2019 and 2021, which will go 310 miles between charges. Although two years ago, they were not thinking of such a thing, they changed because technology has progressed faster than expected and customer demand is increasing.[479]

Food Production

More good news. With the population of the earth growing to 7.6 billion by August, 2018, and that growth displacing farmland, the issue of food production is also an issue. However, ingenious innovations are being developed in food production. The Dutch have been leading the way in a combination of food production and environmental protection, operated by the Plant Science Group at Wageningen University & Research (WUR), fifty miles southeast of Amsterdam.[480] In about 2000, the Dutch made a national commitment: "Twice as much food using half as many resources."[481] The Food Valley is an expanse of agricultural technology start-ups and experimental farms, a merger of "academia and entrepreneurship," using climate-controlled greenhouses, some over 150 acres, enabling them to be the worlds' top exporter of potatoes and onions and the second-largest exporter of vegetables overall."[482]

Its accomplishments are phenomenal, becoming the globe's number two exporter of food measured by value, second only to the United States, which is 270 times the size of Holland. In excess of half of Holland's land area is used for agriculture and horticulture.[483] Since 2000, Dutch farmers *have reduced dependence on water by as much as 90 percent* and have almost completely eliminated the use of chemical pesticides on plants in greenhouses. Since 2009, Dutch poultry and livestock producers have reduced the use of antibiotics by about 60 percent. Jacob van den Borne's

---

[479] "Volvo to go electric and ditch gas-only vehicles," *Austin American-Statesman*, Thursday, July 6, 2017.

[480] Frank Viviano, "A tiny country feeds the world: Agricultural giant Holland is changing the way we farm," *National Geographic*, September 2017, 93.

[481] *Ibid.*, 92.

[482] *Ibid.*, 93.

[483] *Ibid.*, 92–93. As distinguished from agriculture, horticulture is "the cultivation of a garden, orchard, or nursery; the cultivation of flowers, fruits, vegetables, or ornamental plants."

fields produce more than twenty tons of potatoes per acre, compared to the global average of nine tons.[484]

Ernst van den Ende, managing director of WUR's Plant Sciences Group, says that they must produce "more food in the next four decades than all farmers in history have harvested over the past 8,000 years" because by 2050, the earth could have 10 billion people, up from today's 7.5 billion.[485] Van der Ende says, "If massive increases in agricultural yield are not achieved, matched by massive decreases in the use of water and fossil fuels, a billion or more people may face starvation."[486] One of the innovations of van den Ende is that the absence of nutrients in the soil is offset by cultivating plants that act symbiotically with certain bacteria to produce their own fertilizer. He further argues that by use of grasshoppers, one hectare of land can yield fifty tons of livestock feed per year with insect protein compared to one metric ton of soy protein.[487]

The Duijvestijn brothers have constructed a self-contained food systems in their thirty-six-acre greenhouse that produces tomato vines rooted in fibers spun from basalt and chalk rather than soil. According to Frank Viviano, "The growing environment is kept at optimal temperatures year-round by heat generated from geothermal aquifers that simmer under at least half of the Netherlands."[488] Tomatoes from Duijvestijn's plants requires less than one-fourth the amount of water required for plants in open fields. The old vines are processed to make packaging crates. Rather than pesticides, they use mites that feed on the tomato-eating spider mites.[489]

Koppert Biological Systems, a global leader in biological pest and disease control, can provide cotton bags of ladybug larvae that mature into consumers of aphids, a bottle of 2,000 mites that feed on spider mites, or a box of 500 million nematodes that feed on fly larvae that prey on commercial mushrooms. Their beehives increase yields of fruit 20 to 30 percent by weight for less than half the cost of artificial pollination. Rijk

---

[484] *Ibid.*, 92.

[485] *Ibid.*

[486] *Ibid.*, 94.

[487] *Ibid.*

[488] *Ibid.*, 94, 100.

[489] *Ibid.*, 100.

BIBLICAL INTERPRETATION FOR LAYPEOPLE AND OTHER MARTYRS 277

Zwann, a high-tech breeder of greenhouse tomato seeds, produces 150 pounds of tomatoes at less than $0.50.[490]

A team from SoilCares, a Dutch agricultural technology firm, produces a handheld device that, using a cell phone app, analyzes the soil's pH, organic matter, and other properties of soil in the Rift Valley of Africa, uploading the results to a database in the Netherlands and returning a detailed report of optimal fertilizer use and nutrient needs in less than 10 minutes.[491] Graduates of WUR are returning to their homes in China, Indonesia, Uganda, Nepal, Kenya, Peru, Guatemala, Tanzania, Nicaragua, Mozambique, Bangladesh, and even the United States to put into use what they have learned.[492]

Although the term "global warming" is still used when specifically dealing with that issue, the term "climate change" is now more often used because global warming is triggering more than just the warming of the planet. It is causing weather events that seem contradictory. While hotter heat spells and droughts are occurring in some places, the heat causes more evaporation, resulting in heavier snows, violent storms, and torrential rains, forest fires, and species loss in other places.

Friedman says, "I would have thought that conservatives, of all people, would be most insistent on being *conservative*—being prudent, and siding in the debate with those who say that even if there is a 10 percent chance of a major disruption as a result of climate change, we should make sure to *conserve* the world we have."[493] If the climate skeptics are correct, no real problem. We are still better off. If they are wrong and we listen to them, disaster.

Human nature being what it is, there is always resistance to reduction of income in order to benefit the environment. However, human beings are capable of making rational decisions, especially if they have a social conscience—or fear of not addressing the issue. Christians have a better reason than those. God has given us the responsibility of caring for the world God has created.

---

[490] *Ibid.*, 100–101.

[491] *Ibid.*, 109.

[492] *Ibid.*, 102–103, 108.

[493] Friedman (2008), *op. cit.*, 125.

Immigration: The Populating of America

Biblical Foundation—Justice for the Alien

An issue about which many Americans have a strong opinion is immigration, especially undocumented workers. This was a very important issue for the people of ancient Israel. The Old Testament was most emphatic that the Israelites care for the alien. Because of their own experience as aliens in Egypt, they should be compassionate toward not just the poor in Israel, but also toward the aliens among them. "Do not deprive the alien or the fatherless of justice, or take the cloak of the widow as a pledge. Remember that you were slaves in Egypt and the LORD your God redeemed you from there. That is why I command you to do this. When you are harvesting in your field and you overlook a sheaf, do not go back and get it. Leave it for the alien, the fatherless and the widow, so that the LORD your God may bless you in all the work of your hands" (Deut. 24:17–19). And the psalmist says, "The LORD watches over the alien and sustains the fatherless and the widow, but he frustrates the ways of the wicked" (Ps. 146:9). Deuteronomy puts it even more seriously: "Cursed is the man who withholds justice for the alien, the fatherless or the widow" (27:19).

And Jeremiah makes a promise to those who are compassionate toward the alien: "Do not trust in deceptive words and say, 'This is the temple of the LORD, the temple of the LORD, the temple of the LORD! If you really change your ways and your actions and deal with each other justly, *if you do not oppress the alien*, the fatherless or the widow and do not shed innocent blood in this place, and if you do not follow other gods to your own harm, then I will let you live in this place, in the land I gave your forefathers for ever and ever" (Jer. 7:4–8).[494] Since they had been a mistreated alien minority in Egypt, they knew what it was like to be at the mercy of another nation (Deut. 17:12).[495] Therefore, they should have sympathy toward aliens in their land.

---

[494] See other texts that reflect this attitude (Deut. 14:29, 16:11, 26:12–13, 27:19; Ezek. 22:7; Zech. 7:10).

[495] The King James Version uses the terms "stranger" and "sojourner." There are over fifty references in Exodus, Leviticus, Numbers, and Deuteronomy alone demanding moral treatment of the ethnic and religious minorities among them.

BIBLICAL INTERPRETATION FOR LAYPEOPLE AND OTHER MARTYRS   279

Then shouldn't we be supporting the poor immigrants who are trying to take care of their families? And for those touting "family values," should they be sending back to Mexico the parents of citizens born here and force children to make a choice between their families and the opportunities they, as American citizens, have by living in the United States?

The most often quoted estimate of illegal immigrants in the United States is 12 million, one out of thirty US residents. If we could actually find all of them (putting the moral issue aside) and deport them, what would happen to the United States' economy? The states where illegals reside would be financially devastated because there would be a significant loss of sales tax revenue as well as the loss of low-paid employees. Second, it would devastate the merchants, forcing some out of business.[496] The loss of workers would be devastating to the economy.

---

[496]   "Bush calls for changes on illegal workers," *CNN*, January 08, 2004, http://articles.cnn.com/2004-01-07/politics/bush.immigration_1_immigration-laws-illegal-immigrants-immigration-proposals?_s=PM:ALLPOLITICS.

History of US Immigration

The United States is a nation of immigrants. The American Dream is the belief that with hard work and determination, an immigrant can achieve a better life, attracting them to the United States. But despite Emma Lazarus's poem, "Give me your tired, your poor, Your huddled masses yearning to breathe free, The wretched refuse of your teeming shore. Send these, the homeless, the tempest-tost to me," written at the base of the Statue of Liberty, the United States has not had a completely stellar record on immigration.

As new waves of immigrants have entered, there have always been some voices from previous immigration groups who oppose the coming of later immigrant groups. There was no immigration law until the Page Act of 1875 and the Chinese Exclusion Act of 1882, which defined Asians as "undesirables" and which behind their flowery language were racist laws. The Page Act could not be passed until after May 1869 because Chinese workers were needed to complete the Transcontinental Railroad. They were desirable until that date. The Emergency Quota Act of 1921 and the Immigration Act of 1924 also reflected prejudices in that they restricted immigration of Southern and Eastern Europeans, especially Jews, Italians, and Slavs.

Immigration from South of the Border

The Great Depression saw more emigration from the United States than to it, largely due to the Mexican repatriation program, which removed Mexicans without due process of law, who had been welcomed during the early 1900s to work on farms and ranches in the southwest. And despite the fact that Jews were fleeing for their lives from the Nazi regime, Jews were turned away from coming to the United States. In 1954, Operation Wetback deported over a million Mexicans. Finally, in 1965, some of the racist policies were reversed by the Immigration and Nationality Act, which abolished national origin quotas.

Since 1986, Congress has passed several amnesties for undocumented immigrants, beginning under the administration of Ronald Reagan, who gave amnesty to 3 million undocumented immigrants (some would call them illegal aliens). George H. W. Bush signed the Immigration Act of 1990, increasing legal immigration to the United States by 40 percent. In 1991, Bush signed the Armed Forces Immigration Adjustment Act, allowing

BIBLICAL INTERPRETATION FOR LAYPEOPLE AND OTHER MARTYRS   281

foreigners serving in the Armed Forces for at least twelve years to qualify for citizenship.[497] Can anything be more repressive than to deny citizenship to people who have risked their lives for the United States? Under Bill Clinton, the US Commission on Immigration Reform reduced legal immigration by 200,000 to 300,000, limiting immigration admissions level of 550,000 per year, to be divided as follows: Nuclear family immigration 400,000; skill-based immigration 100,000; and refugee resettlement 50,000, a number inadequate to fill the needs of employers in the United States.[498]

Between 10 to 11 million legal immigrants were received into the United States from 1991 to 2000. During the first five years of the 21st century, nearly 8 million people immigrated to the United States to work, almost half of whom were illegal.

But with the recession that began during the last year of George W. Bush's presidency, opposition to Hispanic immigrants increased. Since the beginning of the recovery in 2009, however, more than 1 million immigrants were given legal residence by 2011. Illegal Mexican immigrants fell from about 7 million in 2007 to 6.1 million in 2011.[499]

A 2007 Congressional Budget Office (CBO) report estimated that illegal immigrants are a net cost to state and local governments.[500] However, in 2009, a Cato Institute study found that legalization of low-skilled illegal workers in the United States would result in a net increase in US GDP of $180 billion over ten years.[501]

In June 2012, President Obama deferred the deportation of young illegal immigrants who had been brought to the United States as children, allowing 1.7 million illegal immigrants to apply for temporary residence in the United States. In 2013, illegal immigrants who could show that separation of a US spouse, child, or parent would create "extreme hardship" could apply for legal visas without first having to leave. In 2014, President

---

[497]   "S. 296 — 102nd Congress: Armed Forces Immigration Adjustment Act of 1991," *Civic Impulse*, 2016. Govtrack.com. Retrieved from https://www.govtrack.us/congress/bills/102/s296.

[498]   *NumbersUSA: For Lower Immigration levels.* https://www.numbersusa.com/content/learn/illegal-immigration/us.

[499]   *Ibid.*

[500]   http://en.wikipedia.org/wiki/Immigration_to_the_United_States.   Last modified 16 October 2015 at 22:27.

[501]   *Ibid.*

Obama announced that he would allow up to 45 percent of undocumented immigrants to legally remain in the United States.[502]

In 2013, the United States Citizenship and Immigration Services offered green cards to immigrant parents, spouses, and children of foreign-born US military personnel. Before that, relatives of military personnel, except for husbands and wives, were not allowed to remain in the United States while applying for a green card. This change in the law allows family members to avoid a ten-year separation while applying for permanent residence.[503]

The attitude of many Americans toward migrant workers has been hypocritical. Quotas have limited the number of workers so that there are not enough legal migrant workers to harvest crops. Few farmers will let their crops rot in the fields and lose their farm when they have illegal workers available. Therefore, they resort to hiring illegal workers. The workers face all kinds of risks and hardships in order to feed their impoverished families. States ignore illegal migrants as long as it is profitable for their constituency. But the minute there is a high level of unemployment in the United States, all at once they are *astonished* to find that there are illegals in the state, who all at once are seen as scavengers or parasites in America.[504]

Like many things, perceptions of illegal immigrants do not square with the reality exposed in research produced by sociologists. Recently, both legislators and members of the American public have called for increasing enforcement of existing laws with regard to illegal immigration, including, for some, building a 2,000-mile barrier along the border with Mexico.[505] In running for the Republican nomination in 2015, Donald Trump even vowed to make Mexico pay for the wall. It is no surprise that the Mexican government and citizens took offense to the statement.

One perception is that illegal immigrants, most from Mexico, siphon off American resources. However, in a 1980s study, economists overwhelmingly viewed immigration, including illegal immigration, as a

---

[502]   http://en.wikipedia.org/wiki/Immigration_to_the_United_States.   Last modified on 20 May 2011 at 18:25.

[503]   *Ibid.*

[504]   "Bush calls for changes on illegal workers." *CNN,* January 08, 2004. http://articles.cnn.com/2004-01-07/politics/bush.immigration_1_immigration-laws-illegal-immigrants-immigration-proposals?_s=PM:ALLPOLITICS.

[505]   http://en.wikipedia.org/wiki/Immigration_to_the_United_States. Last modified on 20 May 2011 at 18:25.

BIBLICAL INTERPRETATION FOR LAYPEOPLE AND OTHER MARTYRS   283

positive *for the economy*. According to the United States National Research Council (NRC), immigrants contribute as much as $10 billion to the US economy each year. The NRC report found that although immigrants caused a net loss in terms of taxes paid versus social services received, overall immigration was a net economic gain due to an increase in pay for higher-skilled workers and the lower prices for goods and services produced by immigrant labor. The US Census Bureau claims immigrants mostly do jobs Americans do not want.[506]

A second misperception is that illegal immigrants are involved in crime more than others. Studies have suggested that involvement in crime by Hispanic immigrants are *less* than that of citizens. In *Crime and Immigrant Youth*, sociologist Tony Waters found that immigrants are less likely to be arrested and incarcerated than native-born Americans.[507] A 2006 article by Migration Policy Institute found that foreign-born men had lower incarceration rates than native-born men. But because they live in a shadow world, statistics regarding illegal workers are fuzzy. What is pretty well known, however, is that illegal workers are more apt to be the *victims* of crime than the perpetrators. Because they are illegal, they do not use banks, but carry cash on them, thus being more vulnerable to robbery. And when they are robbed, they rarely report it to the authorities for fear of being deported. Additionally, when they are cheated by their employers, they have no recourse to the authorities.

In 2004, President George W. Bush said that the United States needs an immigration system that would allow illegal immigrants to get legal status as temporary workers. He would allow about 8 million illegal immigrants to obtain legal status as temporary workers, but not citizens.[508] But he argued that the 140,000 "green cards" issued each year is too low, calling on Congress to raise it in order to satisfy "realistic needs."[509] That would have been a positive step.

---

[506]   *Ibid.*

[507]   Tony Waters, "Bush calls for changes on illegal workers," *Crime and Immigrant Youth* (Thousand Oaks, CA: Sage Pub., 1999). Referred to in http://en.wikipedia.org/wiki/Immigration to the United States. Last modified 16 October 2015 at 22:27.

[508]   "Bush calls for changes on illegal workers," *CNN*, January 08, 2004, http://articles.cnn.com/2004-01-07/politics/bush.immigration_1_immigration-laws-illegal-immigrants-immigration-proposals?_s=PM:ALLPOLITICS.

[509]   *Ibid.*

He also argued that making illegal immigrants legal would make the United States more secure because America would have more control of its borders. He argued that "instead of the current situation, in which millions of people are unknown . . . law enforcement will face few problems with undocumented workers and will be better able to focus on the true threats to our nation from criminals and terrorists."[510]

Those who do not settle in the United States can go back and forth as they have in the past. Unfortunately, those who wanted to pounce on immigrants accomplished just the opposite of what they claimed they wanted. In the past, mostly male workers came to work, sent money back to their families, and when the work was over, returned home to their families. However, with the threats of being caught when they cross, they have wanted to cross the border fewer times. So a growing number have brought their families over to stay permanently. Therefore, more babies of illegals have been born in the United States, making them citizens. However, despite what earlier presidents had done, the recession that began in George W. Bush's last year in office hit Hispanic immigrants and employers of illegals hard.[511]

Do we really want to treat like some kind of low-life a person who was brought to the United States when he was a baby and is now a member of the military risking his life in Iraq or Afghanistan, a star on his high school football team, or is the president of the senior class at a major university? And if we could actually find them, do we really want to cripple the US economy by sending millions of workers and consumers back to Mexico and other nations? If not, we should look at both scripture's attitude and the personal and social realities of immigration.

Jim Wallis adds that Christians should realize that while the US-born whites' church membership is declining, growth in the church is driven by immigrants.[512] This is well documented in Robert P. Jones, CEO of Public Religion Research Institute in his recent book *The End of White Christian America*.[513]

---

[510] *Ibid.*

[511] United States Census Bureau, Department of Commerce, https://www.census.gov/main/www/ cen1990.html.

[512] Jim Wallis, *America's Original Sin: Racism, White Privilege, and the Bridge to a New America* (Grand Rapids: Brazos Press, 2016), 176–178.

[513] New York: Simon & Schuster, 2016.

Relations to Muslims

On the other hand, since the destruction of the World Trade Center on 9/11/2001, fear has resulted in Islamophobia. For despite the fact that Canada has a much more porous border with the United States, some of the fear is that terrorists will enter the United States from Latin America, especially Mexico. Unfortunately, there are politicians who will prey on our fears by vastly overstating that danger, including at the very top. It is amazing how flawed people's perceptions can be. Therefore, as Peter Berger (referred to earlier) says, faulty perceptions need to be addressed by actual facts.

Between 1985 and 2014, 3,098 Americans were killed by pseudo-Muslim[514] terrorists,[515] 2,996 of whom were killed on September 11, 2001. This is an average of almost 107 per year. However, 102 people were killed during the other 28 years, averaging 3.6 per year. During those years, an average of 49 Americans were killed by lightning.[516] During the period of time between 2005 and 2014, drunk drivers killed and averaged of 11,299.8 American.[517] The Centers for Disease Control and Prevention (CDC) estimates that more than 480,000 death annually (including deaths from second hand smoke) results from cigarette smoking.[518] To avoid being too repetitious, I refer to pages 263–265, documenting the obscene number of gun deaths in the United States. In fact, in 2013, three Americans were killed by pseudo-Muslims at the Boston Marathon. During that same year, toddlers, also documented on pages 263–265, accidentally killed their parents with guns. And an FBI study of terrorism on US soil between

---

[514] I use the term "pseudo-Muslims" because their behavior does not reflect the teachings or behavior of Muhammad. Therefore, since they do not follow the teachings of Muhammad, they blaspheme the name of Allah and are not true Muslims. I have read enough books on Muhammad, Islam, the Quran, and enough hadith to know that when Muhammad killed, it was defensive or justifiable retaliation.

[515] https://en.wikipedia.org/wiki/List_of_Islamist_terrorist_attacks.

[516] Linda Lam, "Lightning Deaths the Last 10 Years, Mapped," 22 July 2015, 12:00 AM EDT, https://weather.com/storms/severe/news/lightning-deaths-by-state-2005-2014.

[517] National Highway Traffic Safety Administration, U.S. Department of Transportation, crashstats.nhtsa.dot.gov/Api/Public/ViewPublication/812231. I did not trace back to 1985, but the statistics are stark enough to make the point.

[518] "Tobacco-Related Mortality," Centers for Disease Control and Prevention: U.S. Dept. of Health and Human Services, https://www.cdc.gov/tobacco/data_statistics/fact_sheets/fast_facts/index.htm.

1980 and 2005 concluded that 94 percent of terror acts were committed by non-Muslims.[519]

And perhaps the most duplicitous attitudes are those in Houston who hate all Muslims, but worship Hakeem Olajuwon, and those in Los Angeles who hate Muslims, but worship Kareem Abdul-Jabbar. What has been written will not change the mind of rigid ideologists. But for Christians with the integrity to realistically look at the world with the loving eyes of Christ, there should be some alteration in attitude. And if people want to address realistic fears, they will avoid smoking, drinking and driving, and possessing handguns—oh, and stay away from lightning.

The Asylum Issue

But economic issues are not the only reason people want to come to the United States. Another issue is asylum, a life-and-death issue for many, perhaps a majority of the recent applicants. The United States is obliged to recognize valid asylum claims, not only for moral reasons, but since the 1951 United Nations' Convention Relating to the Status of Refugees and its 1967 Protocol, it is an international issue. A refugee is a person outside of his own country, who, because of fear of persecution, cannot expect protection in his own nation. Signatories to the convention are obliged not to return these people who would face persecution or death if returned to their home nation. This commitment was expanded by Congress in the *Refugee Act of 1980*. The United States' Office of Refugee Resettlement (ORR) was established in the US Department of Health and Human Resources (HHS) to help refugees establish their lives in the United States. However, asylum claims are handled by the Bureau of Citizenship and Immigration Services (CIS) of the Department of Homeland Security (DHS). Asylum seekers are to appear before an immigration judge to determine the legitimacy of their claims.

Children pose a special problem. The United Nations' Convention of the Rights of the Child of 1990 was ratified by 192 nations, but did not include Somalia or the United States. However, in 2008, the United States was faced with a myriad of children from Central America (especially from Honduras, El Salvador, and Guatemala) and Mexico unaccompanied by their parents, who were fleeing for their lives. In the 2000s, because of the enormous number of murders, Honduras was called the murder capital of

---

[519] "Terrorism 2000/2005," Federal Bureau of Investigation: Dept. of Justice, https://www.fbi.gov/stats-services/publications/terrorism-2002-2005#terror_05sum.

the world. Most who survived *La Bestia* (riding on top of trains), extortion, murder, robberies, rape, kidnapping, simply crossed the Rio Grande and turned themselves in to the US Border Patrol. An Unaccompanied Refugee Minor (URM) is a person under eighteen years of age, who is not accompanied by a parent or responsible adult. The URM program is coordinated by the ORR, but is managed by two faith-based agencies, Lutheran Immigration and Refugee Service (LIRS) and the United States Conference of Catholic Bishops (USCB).[520] Children come because of forced marriages, forced labor, female genital mutilation, sex trafficking, threats of murder by gangs, and numerous other abuses of children. However, the immigration courts were overwhelmed by the number of children applying for asylum in 2008 and thereafter. This is not only a legal issue, but a moral issue. One cannot imagine anything more cruel and immoral than the radical rightwing *Breitbart News Network* referring to these vulnerable children as "invaders."[521] Maybe I'm wrong. The Trump administration decided to discourage desperate families from trying to enter the United States by a policy called "zero tolerance," punishing their children by separating them from their families.[522] Thank God there were enough moral Americans who were enraged by such cruelty that the policy was reversed.

The Death Penalty

The Old Testament is full of laws involving the death penalty and the killing of the entire male population of cities. When patriarchs ruled, they could kill anyone for anything with impunity and without any legal repercussions. If Abraham had actually killed Isaac (Gen. 22), people might not have liked it, but they could not say it was against the law. The patriarch was the law.

When an individual in a family, tribe, or clan killed someone, the patriarch would exercise "justice" and provide the execution. However, in all probability, at some point, the elders in a family or tribe rebelled against

---

[520] En.m.wikipedia_asylum_in_the_United_States.org.

[521] Aviva Chomsky, "America's Continuing order Crisis: The Real Story Behind the 'Invasion' of the Children," *Moyers*, August 26, 2014. billmoyers.com.

[522] Jeff Merkley and Christ Van Hollen, "Zero tolerance is a zero humanity policy that makes zero sense," *CNN*, 400 PM ET, Sun, 24 January 2018. cnn.com.

a particularly brutal patriarch and established some rules to limit his ability to shed blood. But feuds between families and tribes were unbridled. If someone in family A would kill someone in the family B, someone in family B, the "avenger of blood" (Num. 35; Deut. 19; Josh. 20) could retaliate against someone in family or tribe A to keep the ledger balanced. But members of family A may not be satisfied and retaliate against someone in family or tribe B. Such feuds could go on for decades. While this is speculation, it is reasonable to believe that at some point in retaliation, someone is family B, whom everyone knew was one of the nicest young boy or girl in family B was killed by an avenger of blood. So the elders in both families may have gotten together and agreed that only the specific offending person in family A should be retaliated against (Deut. 19:11–13). That would make more sense.

Laws are not just adopted out of thin air. Whether good or bad, all laws come about for a reason. Once the Israelites developed a system of law, a person could be executed for attacking his mother or father, for kidnapping, for cursing his mother or father (Exod. 2:12–17), for intentionally killing someone (Exod. 21:12), for worshipping an idol (Exod. 22:20), for allowing his aggressive bull to kill someone (Exod. 21:28–29), for committing adultery (Lev. 20:10), and for committing homosexual acts (Lev. 18:22). If a woman could not prove her virginity, she was stoned to death (Deut. 22:13–21).

As nomads, ancient Israel could not have jails. So lawbreakers were dealt with more harshly than if they were able to have jails. On the other hand, although Jesus talked about killing numerous times and used it in illustrations, he did not seem to be interested in having anyone killed at all. Although he never addressed the issue directly, his emphasis on turning the other cheek and forgiving the offending neighbor or enemy seems to indicate that he was not supportive of killing at all. And he contradicted the Mosaic Law by forgiving the woman caught in adultery (John 8:1–11).

The death penalty is a highly controversial subject. My own state of Texas performs about a third of the executions in the United States each year. Some people argue that it is a deterrent to the commission of crimes. Others argue that if it is immoral for an individual to take a human life, it is also immoral for the government to take a human life.

Although there has been at least one study that suggests a positive correlation between the death penalty and the reduction of murders, most studies of the relationship indicate no drop in homicides at all as a result

BIBLICAL INTERPRETATION FOR LAYPEOPLE AND OTHER MARTYRS 289

of publicized executions. Texas is the quintessential example. A study between 1984 and 1997 showed no evidence of deterrence in Texas, by far the state most in love with executions. Another study showed that states without capital punishment have no higher homicide rates than states that have no death penalty.[523]

Unlike the traditions of most nations prior to the adoption of the Bill of Rights, with the exception of minorities,[524] the United States has generally taken the approach that it is better to allow some guilty people to go free than to convict some innocent people. The Fourth Amendment against unreasonable searches and seizures requires a search warrant based only on probable cause and that evidence obtained illegally cannot be introduced into a criminal trial. The Fifth Amendment requires an indictment by a grand jury based on preliminary evidence, forbids double jeopardy, and does not require anyone to testify against himself, nor be deprived of life, liberty, or property without due process of law. *Miranda v. Arizona* (1966) interpreted the Fifth Amendment to require defendants to be informed of their rights to an attorney and against self-incrimination prior to interrogation by police.

Although this is abused regularly, the Sixth Amendment guarantees that the accused cannot be held for long periods of time without trial. It also says that the accused must be tried by an impartial jury, must be informed of the nature and cause of the accusation, be confronted with the witnesses against him, be allowed to have witnesses in his favor, and to have the assistance of legal defense.

The Eighth Amendment forbids the imposition of excessive bail and cruel and unusual punishments inflicted. Although this obviously included torture, exactly what "cruel or unusual punishment" meant was not specified. It has also been interpreted, among other things, to refer to the means of execution. In *Furman v. Georgia* (1972), a majority of the Supreme Court found that capital punishment itself was a violation of the amendment. Others found certain practices in capital trials to be unacceptably arbitrary, resulting in a majority decision that halted executions in the United States for four years, when *Gregg v. Georgia* (1976) ultimately found that capital punishment *was* constitutional. The Ninth Amendment protects rights not specifically enumerated by the Constitution. With so many protections

---

[523] Lauer and Lauer, *op. cit.*, 118.

[524] *Ibid.*

290   DAVID W. MELBER

for the accused, it's obvious that the framers of the Bill of Rights wanted
to make sure that the government would punish as few innocent people
as possible. However, despite all these legal protections in court, innocent
people have been convicted and executed.

One of the latest exonerations of a person convicted was the result
of deoxyribonucleic acid (DNA) testing, indicating that Clemente Javier
Aguirre-Jarquin was innocent of the 2004 murders of Cheryl Williams
and Carol Bareis for which he was sentenced to death. The number of
exonerations hit a record high in 2013, when there were eighty-seven,
eighteen of which involved DNA evidence.[525] Some occurred because
witnesses admitted they had lied or had changed their minds.

The Innocence Project (IPF)[526] has been responsible for the exoneration
of many wrongly convicted Americans, some of whom were to be executed
and others who had spent decades in prison before their innocence was
determined.

David Munchinski of Pittsburgh, Pennsylvania, and Michael Morton
of Round Rock, Texas, convicted of murder, were released after decades
behind bars because of prosecutors' misconduct by withholding evidence
proving the accused could not have committed the crimes. In the Morton
case, prosecuting attorney Ken Anderson, who hid evidence that Morton
was innocent, has been sentenced to a whole ten days in jail, a $500 fine,
and five hundred hours of community service. On top of that, the present
Williamson County DA John Bradley fought DNA testing for six years,[527]
suggesting that the record of the DAs office was more important than the
innocence or guilt of the accused.

In Illinois, Daniel Taylor was convicted of committing a crime by State
Attorney Anita Alvarez who said her office was "about always seeking
justice," even though she prosecuted Taylor in spite of knowing that police

---

[525]   Deborah Tuerkheimer, "The Changing Face of Exonerations. New DNA Testing
        Reveals Innocence of Man on Florida's Death Row and Points to Victim's Daughter
        as Likely Perpetrator," March 05, 2014. http://timeopinions.files.wordpress.
        com/2014/02/womanprison.jpg?w=480&h=   320&crop=1"
        alt="Woman in jail" title="Woman in jail"/>. (Orlando, FL; May 13, 2013).

[526]   Innocenceproject.org.

[527]   Brandi Grissom, "Williamson County DA Eyes New Prosecuting Job: Outgoing
        Williamson County District Attorney John Bradley is being considered to head
        up the state office that prosecutes crimes in state prisons and juvenile detention
        facilities," *Texas Tribune*, Oct. 19, 2012, 5:00 PM, https://www.texastribune.
        org/2012/10/19/john-bradley-eyes-new-job-prosecuting-prisoners/.

records showed that *he was under arrest elsewhere at the time of the crime*. After serving 27.5 years for a murder he did not commit, even after proof that he was innocent, William Dillon had to wait 3.5 years for the State of Texas to release him.[528]

After DNA testing revealed two wrongful convictions, Governor Mark Warner of Virginia ordered examinations of thirty-one old cases containing biological evidence. New York governor Andrew Cuomo expanded the state's DNA database in order to decrease wrongful convictions and to expose the identification and incarceration of the real perpetrators.[529] These suggest a level of integrity that *is* interested in justice.

Nationally, 19 percent of prosecutors oppose DNA testing requested by an individual in prison. Why? This kind of obstruction is prosecutorial misconduct. It might mean admitting that a mistake was made in a wrongful conviction, which to some prosecutors is worth keeping an innocent person in prison or having him executed. What kind of person prefers keeping someone in prison in order to not admit a mistake? And according to Thom Patterson, "Upwards of 10% of all death row prisoners are later exonerated for the crimes."[530]

> At a debate in the Republican primary election, Governor Rick Perry was applauded when it was announced that 234 people were executed during his tenure.[531] Something to be proud of?

> A DNA test cast doubt on the guilt of a Texas man who was executed during George W. Bush's final months as governor.[532]

---

[528] Kate Mathis, "My Experience at Innocence Project of Florida's 2016 Steppin' Out Spring Gala," June 16, 2016 at 1:00 PM, http://floridainnocence.org/content/?tag=william-dillon.

[529] Anthony Brooks, trans., "Virginia Case Review Revives DNA Debate," *Morning Edition*, National Public Radio, KUT, Austin, Jan 25, 2006. www.npr.org/templates/story/story.php?storyId=5171456.

[530] Thom Patterson, "Talk with us: America's death penalty under scrutiny," *CNN* iReport, updated Tuesday, March 4, 2014, 6:15 PM EST, http://www.cnn.com/2014/03/03/us/death-row-stories-hangout/index.html.

[531] "Texas Court Delays Execution for DNA Testing," *The Wall Street Journal*, http://blogs.wsj.com/ law/2011/11/08/texas-court-delays-execution-for-dna-testing/.

[532] Dave Mann, "DNA Tests Undermine Evidence in Texas Execution: New results show Claude Jones was put to death on flawed Evidence," *Texasoberver.org*, Thursday, November 11, 2010, at 7:57 PM CST.

A single hair had been the only piece of physical evidence linking Claude Jones to a robbery and murder at a liquor store in Point Blank, Texas, in November 1989. DNA analysis found it did not belong to Jones. He had actually been in Florida at the time, robbing banks.[533] Jones was executed in December 2000, the last person put to death during Bush's time as governor. Bush denied a reprieve, apparently because no one told him that Claude Jones was asking for a DNA test. Bush had previously shown a willingness to test DNA evidence,[534] a much more moral approach than Perry's. More than three years after Jones's execution, a witness against him reneged, saying he had been scared, and said, "I testified to what they told me to say."[535] The problem with execution is that if a person is executed and later found to be innocent, there is no way to undo the injustice, and a terrible cruelty has been done.

Gun Control

Genesis 2:7 tells us that God created humans by breathing into them the breath of life. The expression "eternal life" (*aiōnios zoē*), which is usually considered to refer to the afterlife and dealing with longevity, is not limited to the idea of duration. It also, and maybe more importantly, refers to "quality of life."[536] Life is more than existence. "People don't live by bread alone" (Deut. 8:3). That is what Jesus meant when he was recorded as saying, "I have come that they may have life, and have it to the full" (John 10:10) and talks about giving life in the present tense (John 10:28). Paul tells the Roman Christians that although they had previously been dead, they had passed from death to life in the present (Rom. 6:4.12–13).

---

[533] www.chicagotribune.com. secure-us.imrworldwide.com/cgi-bin/m?ci= us400338h&cg= 0&cc=1&ts=noscript.

[534] Steve Mills and Maurice Possley, "DNA tests sought for executed man," *Chicago Tribune*, April 19, 2005, smmills@Tribune.com and mpossley@Tribune.com.

[535] Jeff Carlton, *Associated Press*, 2014 NOLA Media Group. http://secure-us. imrworldwide.com/cgi-bin/m?ci=us-403537h&cg=0&cc=1&ts =noscript.

[536] Spiros Zodhiates, ed., *The Complete Word Study Dictionary – New Testament* (Iowa Falls, Iowa: World Bible Publishers, 1991), 107.

God even takes no pleasure in the death of the wicked, but wants them to repent and live (Ezek. 18:23). The Ten Commandments seems to list the commandments in order of importance. It begins with the relationship to God, the use of God's name in vain, and worship of God. The first nongod commandment deals with ultimate concern for the family, which for the ancient Jews was more important than life. Next is the emphasis on the sanctity of human life. "You shall not murder" (Exod. 20:13; Deut. 5:17), that is, not commit "unlawful" killing resulting in blood guilt, as opposed to warfare (1 Kings 2:5–6), capital punishment (Lev. 2:9–16), and self-defense (Exod. 22:2–3). If life is precious to God, that fact should have some implications for our use of weapons that can take life.

Have you ever wondered why it is that National Rifle Association (NRA) president Wayne LaPierre never quotes the Second Amendment but instead recites that tired old cliché "our Second Amendment rights"? After all, it is a short succinct sentence, easy to memorize. It doesn't go on and on for paragraphs like the Fifteenth Amendment. If LaPierre did quote the amendment, he would have to face the actual intent of the amendment. It says, "A well regulated Militia, being necessary to the security of a free State, the right of the people to keep and bear Arms, shall not be infringed." The amendment had to do with "collective responsibilities," not "individual rights."

When the Constitution was being considered, there was a concern among some, such as Patrick Henry and George Mason, that Article 1, Section 8, about authorizing the federal government to establish an army. Their experience with the British government made them suspicious of centralized government and its ability to marshal military power against the people. They worried that the army could be an instrument of tyranny. In the debates, Patrick Henry said, "If you give too much power to-day, you cannot retake it to-morrow . . . . It is easier to supply deficiencies of power than to take back excess of power. . . . No government can be safe without checks. . . . The militia, sir, is our ultimate safety. We can have no security without it."[537] So they wanted the states to have militias, if necessary, to stand up against tyrannical national power of the new United States government.

---

[537] "Debate in Virginia Ratifying Convention," 14 June 1788, Elliot 3:380–95, 300–402, *The Founders Constitution*, Article 1, Section 12, Clause 8 (Document 27), 1987 by the University of Chicago, published 2000, http://press-pubs.uchicago.edu/founders/.

294   DAVID W. MELBER

Second, after the bloody 1739 slave rebellion in South Carolina, southerners did not want the federal government limiting their ability to maintain militias to protect themselves from slave revolts.[538] Therefore, when the Constitutional Convention met in June 1788, the antifederalists increasingly criticized the absence of a bill of rights. James Madison and other Federalists promised that if they would adopt the Constitution, a bill of rights would be forthcoming, convincing the antifederalists to adopt it. So unless people are in the militia (National Guard, reserves), the Second Amendment did not focus on the right to own firearms. Of course, neither does it prevent the right. It simply was not an issue. So appealing to the Second Amendment carries little weight when it comes to letting individuals have all the guns they want.[539]

It is certain that militia was the intent of the Second Amendment because the Articles of Confederation, adopted on March 1, 1781, said that "every State shall always keep up a *well-regulated*[540] and disciplined militia, sufficiently armed and accoutered, and shall provide and constantly have ready for use, in public stores, a due number of field pieces and tents, and a proper quantity of arms, ammunition and camp equipage."[541] It even specified that no state (i.e., militia) shall engage in war without the consent

---

[538]   Since 1708, majority of the population of the South Carolina colony were slaves. A slave named Jemmy led the revolt on Sunday, September 9, 1739. Called the Stono Rebellion (or Cato's Rebellion), Jemmy led 20 slaves who recruited nearly 60 more who burned seven plantations and killed 22–25 whites. The South Carolina militia caught them. In the battle, 20 whites and 44 slaves were killed. Some were executed and others were sold to the West Indies. The colonists mounted the decapitated heads of the rebels on stakes along major roadways to serve as warning for other slaves not to revolt. In response to the rebellion, the South Carolina legislature passed the Negro Act of 1740 restricting slave assembly, education, and movement. They also established penalties for masters who demanded excessive work or who brutally punished slaves. Over the next two years, slave uprisings occurred independently in Georgia and South Carolina, perhaps inspired by the Stono Rebellion. http://originalpeople.org/stono-rebellion-1739-slave-revolt/. See also en.wikipedia.org/wiki/Stono_Rebellion.

[539]   *The Founders Constitution*, Article 1, Section 12, Clause 8 (Document 27), 1987 by the University of Chicago. All rights reserved. Published 2000, http://press-pubs. uchicago.edu/founders/.

[540]   Italics mine.

[541]   "Articles of Confederation: March 1, 1781," *The Avalon Project*, New Haven, CT: Lillian Goldman Law Library, Yale Law School, 2008, http://avalon.law.yale. edu/18th_century/artconf.asp.

of Congress, unless it was actually invaded by a nation or Indians.[542] The Constitution even uses the Article's words "well-regulated militia."

Third, when the Constitution was adopted, few (only about 14 percent), except those on farms and the frontier, had guns. And the guns they had were not nearly as destructive as today's weapons. Muzzle-loaded flintlock muskets, known as Brown Bess, were the most common weapon in the Revolutionary War. The average soldier could load and shoot two to three times in one minute. Therefore, the idea that the intent of the framers of the Second Amendment was for *individuals* to have multiple-shot concealable handguns and assault weapons is absolutely ludicrous. (Where are the strict constructionists on this issue?)

It is difficult to not get angry when a mass murder occurs because pundits, Congress, and the public wring their hands and say "something should be done," when everyone really *knows* what needs to be done, but do not have the will or guts to do it.

The news media drags out counselors looking for a "profile" of mass killers. They discuss felons and people with psychological disorders. The problem is that most felons are not violent, and about 1 in 17 Americans do have *serious* emotional disorders. Since 99.9 percent of them don't commit violent crimes and you only "see the signs" after the fact, background checks may prevent a few deaths, but are only a Band-Aid.

The *Houston Chronicle* bragged that in 2011, Houston had only 196 murders, down from the 269 the year before. The FBI reported 14,612 murders in the United States, a 0.7 percent decrease from the previous year. About 67 percent were killed with firearms, the rest with all other means. But here is the significant statistic: Handguns killed 6,220; rifles killed 323; shotguns killed 356; other guns (including automatic weapons) killed 97; and "type of firearms not given" killed 1,587. Although many more are killed *at one time* with assault weapons, the actual number of people killed with automatic weapons is a drop in the bucket compared to deaths by handguns. The United States has at least 47 murders per 100,000 people compared with England and Wales, which had 11 murders per 100,000; Germany 0.8 per 100,000; and France with 1.1 per 100,000. These countries do not allow the general public to own handguns and automatic weapons. Even Afghanistan has just 712-plus murders (the statistics are a little fuzzy, but still far less than the United States) or about

---

[542]   *Ibid.*

2.4 per 100,000; and Iraq had 608 plus, or about 2 murders per 100,000 in that same period of time.

Every time we have a mass murder like that at Sandy Hook Elementary School, the NRA trots out a representative who expresses "deep regret" at the death of the victims but then quotes the same cliché as if the framers of the Bill of Rights guaranteed the right of individuals to carry guns without limitations, as long as there is a fuzzy ineffectual background check. The leadership touts the needs of collectors to have handguns and automatic weapons as if their avocations are more important than the average of 8,000 lives that are lost each year. Hunting is not done with handguns or automatic weapons, but with rifles and shotguns. Collecting is fine as long as it doesn't hurt anyone. But private citizens do not *need* automatic weapons, and few need handguns. But people do need their lives.

We should be consulting sociologists. By systematically studying social issues, they point out that our perceptions are often completely contrary to reality. They give us guidance regarding how to significantly reduce murders. All we have to do is look at the European countries. They allow handguns and automatic weapons in the hands of only specific people who need them to protect the public. That is why they have so few murders. I really doubt that Americans are inherently that much more violent than Europeans. So unless people are in the militia (National Guard, reserves), *the Constitution doesn't give the right to carry guns.* The right to bear arms was to defend national security, quell insurrection, and protect against tyranny.

Insurrectionists argue that individuals should have the right to bear arms against the government. This is an important issue. I suppose it is possible for the US government to become tyrannical. During the Nixon impeachment hearings, Alexander Haig's suggestion to Nixon that he had the military to prevent being removed from office made that a possibility. Thank God Nixon resigned rather than precipitating that constitutional crisis and a possible taking of sides among generals and colonels. But the present death rate is not a matter of *what might be,* but of what is actually happening now to our nation with the unbridled use of firearms. So the question is, do we really want to do something about the enormous murder rate in the United States, or will we be satisfied to wring our hands and apply Band-Aids when surgery is needed? That is, regarding the loss of human life in the United States due to murders and accidental deaths of children with their parents' guns, what might the will of God be?

BIBLICAL INTERPRETATION FOR LAYPEOPLE AND OTHER MARTYRS   297

The argument is, if the public didn't have guns, only criminals would have guns. Of course, that is a vast overstatement since the police, the military, and certain specific individuals would have them to protect against criminals. There are criminals in European countries, which have few murders. But *criminals are not the main problem.*

The problem is that formerly law-abiding citizens *become* criminals by killing someone whom they had once liked or loved—husband, wife, brother, cousin, father, mother, friend, neighbor. And of course, there are the accidental shootings, including bizarre and tragic ones. The perception of many is that they need guns to protect themselves against others with guns. However, the reality is that for every situation in which a person protects himself, literally dozens are killed, or their children are killed, with their own guns or they accidentally kill someone else. A Tulsa woman, Christa Engles, twenty-six, was accidentally shot to death by her three-year-old with her semiautomatic handgun.[543] A three-year-old boy who removed a handgun from his mother's purse shot his father and pregnant mother with one shot in a hotel room in Albuquerque, New Mexico, while his two-year-old sister watched.[544] A mother was hospitalized after being accidentally shot with her own automatic handgun by her three-year-old in Lake Placid, New York.[545] A twenty-nine-year-old mother was fatally shot when her two-year-old son grabbed her gun from her purse in her shopping cart at a Walmart in Blackfoot, Idaho.[546]

An angry argument in Holmes County, Ohio, over a boy's chores triggered a ten-year-old boy to shoot and kill his mother. The mother had argued with her husband, from whom she was recently separated, over the

---

[543] "3-Year-Old Kills Mother With Handgun in Oklahoma," *NBC News*, 11-25-14, 10:45 AM. Updated 11-25-14, 11:19 AM, http://bit.ly.2xzOGZa; myarklamiss.com.

[544] Andreas Preuss, "3-year-old boy shoots father, pregnant mother in New Mexico," http://www.cnn.com/2015/02/01/us/new-mexico-toddler-shoots-parents/index.html.

[545] Rose Spillman, "Lake Placid mayor: 2-year-old accidentally shoots, kills his mom in Idaho Wal-Mart," *WCAX.com*, http://www.nola.com/traffic/index.ssf/2014/12/2-year-old_accidentally_kills.html, Sept. 22, 2015 5:08 PM CDT, updated Sept. 24, 2015 4:00 PM CDT.

[546] Michael Martinez and Tony Marco, "Mom fatally shot when son, 2, grabs gun from her purse in Walmart," http://www.cnn.com/2014/12/30/us/idaho-walmart-shooting-accident-mother-toddler/index.html CNN.com. Updated 3:16 PM ET, Wednesday, December 31, 2014.

boy's having the guns. The father defended his son's having the guns.[547] Many other incidents occur each year, which are not reported because no one is hit by the errant shot.

On Friday, December 14, 2012, Adam Lanza fatally shot twenty-seven people, including twenty children at Sandy Hook Elementary School in Newtown, Connecticut. The expected knee-jerk reaction of Wayne LaPierre, executive vice president and CEO of the National Rifle Association, responded, "The only thing that stops a bad guy with a gun is a good guy with a gun."[548] It is an ingenuous argument because if the bad guy had no gun, there would be no need for a good guy to have his gun. The idea that adding more guns makes us safer is as logical as saying "the more viruses we have, the healthier we will be."

Aside from that illogic, the question is, in order to make us safer, how do we know who the good guys are so that we can put guns in their hands? If we knew who the good guys were, we wouldn't have the policeman who was convicted of raping eighteen women whom he had arrested, we would not have policemen murdering unarmed teenagers who were running from them,[549] nor would we have vice principals having sex with thirteen-year-old girls.[550] Nor would we have Dr. Henry Bello, who had been accused of

---

[547] Karen Russo, "Cops Say Firewood Chore May Have Prompted Boy to Murder Mom," *ABC News*, http://abcnews.go.com/USboy-killed-mom-firewood-chore/story?id=12537130, January 4, 2011.

[548] Peter Overby, "NRA: 'Only Thing That Stops a Bad Guy with a Gun Is a Good Guy with a Gun,'" *All Things Considered, NPR*, Dec. 21, 2012, 3:00 PM ET, http://www.npr.org/2012/12/21/167824766/nra-only-thing-that-stops-a-bad-guy-with-a-gun-is-a-good-guy-with-a-gun.

[549] Bart Jansen, "'It's a problem for the nation': Former Okla. cop preyed on minority women," *USA TODAY*, 6:34 PM MST, December 11, 2015, http://www.azcentral.com/story/news/nation/2015/12/11/former-oklahoma-police-officer-found-guilty-serial-rape/77138186; Graham Rayman, "Feds probing Chicago police after cop seen on video shooting teen Laquan McDonald 16 times," *New York Daily News*, Updated Tuesday, December 8, 2015, 6:28 AM, http://www.nydailynews.com/news/national/feds-probing-chicago-police-laquan-mcdonald-killing-article-1.2457595. Audio interview can also be heard.

[550] Kevin Dolak, "Asst. Principal Accused of Having Sex With Student at Prom," *ABCNEWS.com*, https://www.bing.com/search?q=%E2%80%9Casst.+principal+accused+of+having+sex+with+student+at+prom%2C%E2%80%9D&form=EDGEAR&qs=PF&cvid=977c098af63f4580b33fad746b23e393&cc=US&setlang=en-USMarch 13, 2013. Audio interview can also be heard.

BIBLICAL INTERPRETATION FOR LAYPEOPLE AND OTHER MARTYRS   299

sexual harassment and sexual abuse by several women, open fire with an AR-15 assault rifle in the emergency room of Bronx-Lebanon Hospital, wounding seven people and killing one doctor.[551] So since most people who murder were considered "good guys" before the murder, we don't know who the "bad guys" are. Therefore, we *do not* know who the good guys are, who should have guns in their hands to stop the bad guys.

Now it is true that there are a few instances in which a good person does shoot a bad person who breaks into their homes. For example, twitchy.com points out at that a woman in New Hampshire did so.[552] However, the incidence of people being shot with their own guns accidentally or shot by people who had no criminal record are a plethora: Georta Mack, fourteen, returned home through the basement and was shot in Cincinnati, Ohio.[553] A mother in St. Cloud, Florida, shot her twenty-seven-year-old daughter, thinking she was an intruder.[554] Chelsea Jones, twenty-two, of Thomaston, Maine, was accidentally shot by her boyfriend, Dylan Grubbs, twenty-three, who was trying to sell a gun to a prospective customer.[555] A woman in Hillview, Bullitt County, Kentucky, was shot with her own 9 mm pistol, when the intruder turned the barrel on her.[556]

But even greater tragedy occurs when children three and four years old accidentally kill their parents who have handguns. But those are not the

---

[551]   Colleen long, "Doc kills 1, self in rifle spree at Bronx hospital," Associated Press report in the *Austin American-Statesman*, Saturday, July 1, 2017.

[552]   Twitchy Staff, "Attn: Obama: THIS woman was glad she had a gun (but the man who tried to rob her wasn't," *twitchy.com*, posted 4:49 PM on January 9, 2016. "A Michael Bontaites, 23, was shot in Queen City, New Hampshire by a 65-year-old woman."

[553]   John Newsome, "Police: Son, 14, shot dead by dad who says he mistook him for intruder," *CNN*, Wed., January 13, 2016, http://www.cnn.com/2016/01/12/us/father-shoots-son/index.html.

[554]   Steve Almasy and John Newsome, "Florida mother shoots daughter she thought was intruder," *CNN*, December 31, 2015, http://www.cnn.com/2015/12/30/us/florida-mother-shoots-daughter/index.html.

[555]   "Woman shot while sitting in car at Shaw's Supermarket in Bath," *WMTW News 8*, wmtw@wmtw.com, Nov. 16, 2015, 6:09.53 PM EST; updated Nov. 17, 2015, 8:50.34 PM EST.

[556]   Paige Quiggins, "Police: Woman shot with own gun during attempted home invasion in Hillview," *WDRB.com*, http://www.wdrb.com/story/23805164/woman-shot-during-attempted-home-invasion. Posted Oct. 28, 2013, 8:08 AM CDT, updated Oct. 28, 2013 4:36 PM CDT.

300   DAVID W. MELBER

most bizarre incidents. In 2015, a dog, whose name ironically is "Trigger," stepped on his owner's gun and shot her. According to the *Washington Post*, ten dogs have shot heir owners in similar fashion since 2004.[557] The list of accidents or people being killed by others intentionally *with their own guns* goes on and on. The incidence of people being accidentally shot with their own guns or shot by people who had no criminal record are a plethora. A few additional examples are listed in the footnotes. [558]

---

[557]   Christopher Ingraham, "In the past five years, at least six Americans have been shot by dogs," *Washington Post,* October 27, 2015, washingtonpost.com.

[558]   John Newsome, "Police: 14, returned home through the basement and was shot by her father in Cincinnati, Ohio," *CNN,* Wed., January 13, 2016, http://ktla.com/2016/01/12/boy-14-fatally-shot-by-dad-who-says-he-mistook-him-for-intruder-police/.

"Chelsea Jones, 22 of Thompson Maine, was accidentally shot by her boyfriend, Dylan Grubbs, 23, who was trying to sell a gun to a prospective customer," WMTW News 8, wmtw@wmtw.com, Nov. 16, 2015, 6:09.53 PM EST; updated Nov. 17, 2015, 8:50.34 PM EST, http://www.wmtw.com/article/woman-shot-while-sitting-in-car-at-shaw-s-supermarket-in-bath/2011104.

Mario Pearson, 31, shot a woman with her own gun when she aimed at him. "Woman shot with own gun by man who hired pair for sex in University City," *St. Louis Post-Dispatch*, September 23, 2015, http://www.stltoday.com/news/local/crime-and-courts/woman-shot-with-own-gun-by-man-who-hired-pair/article_aed9a632-7f45-5f2a-af17-7c49a738d1dc.html.

In Wilmington, NC, a twenty-five-year-old woman died from self-inflicted wound at BullZeye Shooting Sports Center Friday afternoon. "WPD: Woman dies after self-inflicted gunshot wound at gun range." *WCET.* http://www.k5thehometeam.com/story/30787390/wpd-woman-dies-after-self-inflicted-gunshot-wound-at-gun-range.

"Witness: Accidental shooting in Beaumont the result of a gun falling out of a purse," *12 news now,* http://myinforms.com/en/a/17855462-witness-accidental-shooting-in-beaumont-the-result-of-a-gun-falling-out-of-a-purse/ posted Oct. 19, 2015, 11:14 AM CDT. (This article is outdated and put in archives.)

A Chicago girl was accidentally shot by a male juvenile while they were playing with the gun when it went off. ("Girl, 14 Shot Dead by Boy While Playing Gun, Police Say," *abc7chicago.com*, Sunday, August 16, 2015. http://abc7chicago.com/news/girl-14-shot-dead-by-boy-while-playing-with-gun-police-say/933783/).

A twenty-nine-year-old intoxicated man accidentally shot a woman in a movie theater in Seattle (Jennifer Sullivan, "Man who accidentally shot woman in movie theater had gun permit, police say," *Seattle Times*, http://www.seattletimes.com/seattle-news/crime/renton-movie-theater-shooter-had-gun-permit-police-say/ columbian.com, published January 22, 2016, 7:20 PM.

A Michigan woman, Christina Bond, 55, of St. Joseph, shot herself adjusting the .22-caliber revolver in her bra holster (Michael Winter, "Woman accidentally kills self-adjusting bra holster," *USA Today*, usatoday.com. https://

BIBLICAL INTERPRETATION FOR LAYPEOPLE AND OTHER MARTYRS   301

For Christians, I believe it is time to ask, in this present historical period, with handguns and automatic weapons as lethal as they are, what would be Jesus's attitude toward the plethora of guns in the hands of private citizens who kill so many Americans each year?

Health Care

Jesus was big on healing. He did not withhold healing from anyone who needed it. First, rather than talk about health care in social and economic terms, it is important to acknowledge that health care is first of all a matter of life and death. Health care is measured by morbidity, which "refers to illness, symptoms, and the impairments they produce"; life expectancy, which refers to "the average number of years that individuals born in a given year can expect to live"; and the infant mortality rate, which refers to "the number of deaths of live-born infants under 1 year of age per 1,000 live births (in any given year)."[559]

Platitudinous politicians blithely assert that the United States has the best health care in the world. Of course, they would not dare refer to any specific criteria to support their assertion. Despite being the world's richest nation, UNICEF reported in 2008 that the world had thirty-seven nations with a lower infant mortality rate than the United States.[560] Private health insurance companies and the pharmaceutical industry spend massive amounts of money to prevent health care reform. A second incentive for politicians to acquiesce to powerful industries is the revolving door, "the practice of employees cycling between roles in an industry, and roles in government that influence that industry." In 2009, "three dozen former members of Congress were employed by pharmaceutical and health product industries,"[561] which gave them much larger incomes than they had received when they were in the Congress. These industries put profits above the health of people.

---

www.usatoday.com/story/news/2015/02/18/woman-kills-self-adjusting-bra-holster/23640143/, Feb. 28, 2015, 9:11 PM EST). These are just a few examples. The incidents go on and on.

[559] Linda A. Mooney, David Knox, and Caroline Schacht, *Understanding Social Problems* (Belmont, CA: Wadsworth Cengage Learning, 2011), 31.

[560] *Ibid.*

[561] *Ibid.*, 35.

The United States spends a higher portion of its gross domestic product on health care than any other nation, but ranked 37 out of 191 countries in performance. France probably provides the best overall health care.[562] In 2008, US census data determined that 15.4 percent of Americans (46.3 million people) were without health insurance. Because health care providers do not accept patients without health insurance, many individuals have to go to hospital emergency rooms, which are much more expensive than doctors' offices. Therefore, hospitals include in their charges to people with insurance the costs of serving those without insurance. It is estimated that some 45,000 Americans die prematurely each year because of a lack of health insurance. The Emergency Medical Treatment and Active Labor Act only requires that hospitals have to stabilize patients in order to release them. This point was made clear in the movie *John Q* with Denzel Washington.[563]

Other reasons for increasing health costs are the increasing number of senior citizens, people who require more health care,[564] and more expensive medical technology. The United States pays 81 percent more for brand-name prescription drugs than Canada and six western European nations, making the pharmaceutical industry one of the most profitable industries in the nation.[565] Being able to purchase medications from other nations would make capitalist competition real and greatly reduce the cost of drugs.

It is one thing to see statistics. However, this issue involves actual human beings. One outrageous escalation in price is EpiPen (epinephrine), an auto-injector by Mylan pharmaceutical company. It gained a virtual monopoly after a recall destroyed their competitor, Sanofi's Auvi-Q. "The patient now pays about 400% more for this advantage to receive a dollar's worth of the lifesaving drug: EpiPens were about $57 when Mylan acquired it. Today, it is $50 or more in the U.S. (European nations take a different approach to these things)."[566] Although the drug itself is only worth $1,

---

[562] *Ibid.*, 49–50.

[563] Nick Cassavetes, director, 2002.

[564] *Ibid.*, 53–54.

[565] *Ibid.*, 55.

[566] Emily Willingham, "Why Did Mylan Hike EpiPen prices 400% Because They Could," *Forbes*, August 21, 1016, 9:00 AM, https://www.forbes.com/forbes/welcome/?toURL=https://www.forbes.com/ sites/emilywillingham/2016/08/21/why-did-mylan-hike-epipen-prices-400-because-they-could/&refURL=https://www.bing.com/&referrer=https://www.bing.com/.

BIBLICAL INTERPRETATION FOR LAYPEOPLE AND OTHER MARTYRS   303

Mylan's profits from EpiPens made $1.2 billion in 2015, about 40 percent of Mylan's operating profits. In addition, their guidelines call for two doses if one dose fails, meaning it costs twice as much. Many parents cannot afford it for their children. The Forbes article includes heartrending statements from both parents and doctors. But now there is an authorized generic of Adrenaclick, which has been found for $142 at Walmart and Sam's Club using a coupon from Good Rx.[567] The United States is the only developed nation that does not regulate prescription drug (we spend more on drugs than any other nation).[568]

Although not all drug prices are this outrageous, an equally egregious example is pyrimethamine. In 1996, Tonya Jones had a kidney transplant that saved her life. But she got an infection that required a combination of antibiotics anchored by the antiparasite drug pyrimethamine. But Turing Pharmaceuticals increased the drug's price by 5,000 percent from $13.50 to $750 a pill. Developed more than sixty years ago, pyrimethamine is sold under the brand name Daraprim and was affordable and widely distributed. But it became available only to patients outside of a hospital via a single distributor. Physicians complained to Turing with no response. The Senate is investigating these corrupt practices. A compounding pharmacy has begun to sell pyrimethamine for $1 per pill. However, the FDA says it "does not verify the safety, or effectiveness of compounded drugs." Physicians must still rely on the expensive version of the drug if they want to prescribe drugs that meet federal quality standards. Mrs. Jones's doctors say, "We must have regulation to prohibit drug companies from severely curtailing distribution or grossly inflating prices at will."[569] They complained of the price for ninety pills. Her doctors say, "But we were left with lingering outrage at the inaccessibility of this life-saving medication. How many more vulnerable patients across the U.S. will suffer this year because of lack of access to pyrimethamine?"[570] The United States

---

[567] *Ibid.*

[568] T. Carlos Anderson, *op cit.*, 162.

[569] Leah Dickstein, MD, is a resident at the Johns Hopkins Bayview Medical Center. Rachel Kruzan, MD, is on faculty in the Department of Medicine's Division of General Internal Medicine at the Johns Hopkins University School of Medicine. Annie Antar, MD, PhD, is a fellow in the Department of Medicine's Division of Infectious Diseases at the Johns Hopkins University School of Medicine.

[570] Leah Dickstein, Rachel Kruzan, and Annie Antar, "Real cost of outrageous drug prices: What happens when a company hikes the cost of crucial medicine

is the only developed nation that does not regulate prescription drugs (we spend more than any other nation).[571]

Although pharmaceutical firms claim that their high costs have to do with research and development, the truth is that much more goes to marketing, advertising, and administration. Between 1999 and 2008, health care costs had increased by 119 percent. And because of the high cost of health care, it is difficult for American firms to compete with companies in other nations. "Health care administrative expenses in the United States per capita are six times higher than in western European nations."[572] The United States has the most bureaucratic health care system in the world because there are over 1,500 different companies, offering multiple plans, each with marketing programs and enrollment procedures, massive CEO salaries, and sales commissions. Additional costs result from people not being able to afford medicines and care, leading to worse medical conditions because of lack of prevention or early treatment, and therefore higher medical costs in the end.

As illogical as it might seem, in desperation, some people have committed crimes in order to go to prison so that they can get medical care. In managed care, primarily health maintenance organizations (HMOs), doctors report a reduced quality of care has occurred because of limitations of diagnostic tests, length of hospital stays, choice of specialists, and bonus checks to doctors for denials.[573] However, some insurance companies, including mine, have found that by emphasizing prevention, they do not have to pay out as much for their clients' medical care. I get a call every month from a nurse, who badgers me if I am not taking my medicine as I should and gives me suggestions regarding how to remember to take them.

---

by 5,000%," *USA TODAY,* Gannett Satellite Information Network, 4:40 PM ET, Dec. 27, 2015, https://www.usatoday.com/story/opinion/2015/12/27/true-cost-outrageous-drug-prices-deraprim-martin-shkreli-column/77838400/; the web site says also read this on http://usat.ly/1YKX6L3.

[571] Valerie Paris (OECD), "Why do Americans spend so much on pharmaceuticals?" *PBS News Hour,* KLRU, February 7, 2014, at 12:15 PM EDT, http://www.pbs.org/newshour/updates/americans-spend-much-pharmaceuticals/; see also T. Carlos Anderson, *op. cit.,* 162 and the FDA's explanation of his guidelines: "How FDA Evaluates Regulated Products: Drugs." U. S Food and Drug Administration: U. S. Department of Health. https://www.fda.gov/AboutFDA/Transparency/Basics/ucm269834.htm.

[572] Anderson, *op cit.,* 55.

[573] *Ibid.,* 55–57.

BIBLICAL INTERPRETATION FOR LAYPEOPLE AND OTHER MARTYRS 305

When my wife was still alive, I once said to the nurse, "I already have one wife to harass me about taking care of my health." She laughed.

The United States is the only industrialized nation in the world that does not have universal health care. Theodore Roosevelt was the first president who recommended national health care, followed by Truman, Nixon, Carter, Clinton, and Obama. A single-payer health care system would be the most efficient and inexpensive way to go, but Senator Max Baucus, chairman of the Finance Committee on health care, who received major financial support from the health insurance industry than any other Democrat, refused to allow testimony by anyone in favor of single-payer health care.[574]

Of course, other ways to reduce health care are reduction of environmental pollution, commitment to reduction of obesity, reduction of shootings, and war, which, except for the reduction of obesity, are issues having little to do directly with insurance.

The Bill and Melinda Gates Foundation "has focused on this huge, disease-ravaged, opportunity-deprived population" of southeast Africa.[575] One million people die from malaria each year.[576] But antimalarial vaccines are not profitable.[577] In 2003, the Gates Foundation "launched a project called Grand Challenges in Global Health . . . asking scientists . . . What are the biggest problems that . . . could most dramatically change the fate of the several billion people trapped in the vicious cycle of infant mortality, low life expectancy, and disease? . . . distilled them down to a list of fourteen Grand Challenges. They include the following: how to create effective single-dose vaccines that can be used soon after birth, how to prepare vaccines that do not require refrigeration, how to develop needle-free delivery systems for vaccines, how to better understand which immunological responses provide protective immunity, how to better control insects that transmit agents of disease, how to develop genetic or chemical strategy to incapacitate a disease-transmitting insect population, how to create a full range of optimal bioavailable nutrients in a single stable plant species, and how to create immunological methods that can

---

[574] *Ibid.*, 64–66.

[575] Thomas L. Friedman, *The World Is Flat: A Brief History of the Twenty-First Century* (New York: Farrar, Straus and Giroux, 2005), 378.

[576] *Ibid.*, 379.

[577] *Ibid.*

cure chronic infections . . . funding the best proposals with $250 million in cash."[578] Those are worthy objectives.

Crime and Punishment

Defining Crime

During the patriarchal period in the Old Testament, the patriarch was the law. He determined what was criminal. If Abraham had killed Isaac (Gen. 22:1–16), he would not have been labeled a criminal because he was the law. However, hundreds of years later, as we have pointed out earlier, in the Pentateuch (Five Books of Moses), criminal behavior that merited the death penalty included murder, rape, adultery, homosexuality, being a sorceress, having sexual relations with one of his father's wives, false witnesses in a capital case, kidnapping, using God's name in vain, working on the Sabbath, sacrificing to a god other than Yahweh, striking a parent, cursing a parent, and a woman not being able to prove she was a virgin (Exod. 21–22, 31, 35; Lev. 20–21, 24–26; Num. 15, 35; Deut. 13, 17, 19, 22, 24). These laws would not seem unusually cruel to the Taliban in Afghanistan in our day, but for most people, especially Westerners, many of them seem outrageously cruel and arbitrary.

Early in the life of Israel, like the Hatfields and McCoys, retaliation against *anyone* in other families or tribes satisfied honor in their honor-shame culture. However, at some point, it became reasonable to only kill the person who actually committed the offense (Deut. 24:16). Even later, it seemed reasonable to make the punishment "proportional" to fit the crime. The *lex taliones* (law of retaliation) only required a proportionate response of an eye for an eye and a tooth for a tooth rather than killing the offender (Exod. 21:23–25; Lev. 24:19–22; Deut. 19:21). But since the offended did not benefit from poking out the offenders' eyes, the law was later changed to provide compensation for the injured person (Exod. 21:22, 22:16–17; Deut. 22:29; Lev. 19:20; Exod. 21:28–32). So over time, the definition of crime and the punishment for crimes have changed.

---

[578] *Ibid.*, 360–361.

BIBLICAL INTERPRETATION FOR LAYPEOPLE AND OTHER MARTYRS   307

So what is a criminal? There was a time when people thought like Inspector Javert in *Les Miserables*,[579] that criminals were people who were born criminal. Cesare Lombroso and Guglielmo Ferrero (1893) argued that one could tell a criminal by his physical features.[580] Others argue that it is learned behavior.[581] However, in reality, people are made criminals by being labeled as such. In most cultures, murderers and rapists are defined as criminals. But so are jaywalkers and people who run red lights— misdemeanors, but crimes nevertheless. Before the laws were passed making jaywalking and running red lights crimes, they were not crimes. Please don't tell the authorities, but I have been guilty of speeding and have run red lights on numerous occasions, but have not always been caught. However, I have not always eluded the authorities. When one is stopped for speeding, he is being arrested. When he signs the "ticket," he is being released on his own recognizance rather than having to post bail to stay out of jail. That had never occurred to me before until I was "ticketed" for turning on a red light, not noticing the sign saying "No right turns on red." The police officer informed me that this was indeed an arrest, but by signing the "ticket," I would not be taken in. But later, I would have to pay the fine or appear in court to contest my commission of the "crime."

Definitions of crimes are a construct. A consistently accepted division of crimes are felonies and misdemeanors. Felonies "are serious offenses, including murder, rape, robbery, and aggravated assault; these crimes are punishable by more than a year's imprisonment or death. Misdemeanors are minor offenses, such as traffic violations, that are punishable by a fine or less than a year in jail."[582]

The sources of crime statistics in the United States is the Federal Bureau of Investigation's (FBI) Uniform Crime Report (UCR), data supplied by 17,000 federal, state, and local law enforcement agencies, which they have compiled since 1930. The information is limited by the fact that it compiles only reported crimes. A study by Kappeler, Blumberg, and Potter estimated that only 3 percent to 4 percent of crimes are actually

---

[579]   Bill August, director, Columbia Pictures, 1998, based on a novel by Victor Hugo.

[580]   Nicole Hahn Rafter and Mary Gibson, trans., *Criminal Woman, the Prostitute, and the Normal Woman* (Durham, NC: Duke University Press, 2004).

[581]   Paul B. Horton and Gerald R. Leslie, *The Sociology of Social Problems* (New York: Meredith Corporation, 1970), 154–156.

[582]   Anna Leon-Guerrero, *Social Problems: Community, Policy, and Social Action*, 5th ed. (Los Angeles: Sage Publications, 2016), 356, 37.

discovered by police. The other side of the issue is that not all crimes reported actually occurred.[583] The only crimes that are covered almost 100 percent are killings.

Another source of information is the crime index, which categorizes crimes. The other is the National Incident-Based Reporting System (NIBRS), which adds detailed offender and victim information. The FBI also releases the Crime Clock, a display of how often specific offenses are committed. Another source of data is the National Crime Victimization Survey (NCVS), published by the Bureau of Justice Statistics since 1972. Twice a year, the US Census Bureau interviews members of about 77,200 households regarding their experience with crime.[584]

Heiner points out: "Conceptions of crime and deviance vary from time to time and culture to culture."[585] During the nineteenth century, opiates were legal and popular in the United States. Although white Americans in California used opium in various forms, the Chinese smoked it. In the 1870s, laws were passed making opium *smoking* illegal.[586] Since the Chinese were needed to build the Transcontinental Railroad, which was finished in May of 1869, it seems strangely coincidental that the laws were passed against the Chinese soon after they were no longer needed for the construction of the railroad. Cocaine was part of the Coca-Cola formula until cocaine became illegal, at which time cocaine was dropped in favor of caffeine. (Caffeine is not yet illegal.) Homosexuality was defined as a crime in almost all states. But rather than a crime, the American Psychiatric Association's (APA) *Diagnostic and Statistical Manual* (DSM) defined homosexuality as a psychological disorder until 1973, when it was removed. It was a psychological disorder. And then by fiat edict, it wasn't.

Politicians, especially when they oppose defiance of a law, like to quote the saying, "We are a nation [or government] of laws, not of men." But this can be a way of focusing on "law and order" when the issue of justice

---

[583] Victor Kappeler, Mark Blumberg, and Gary Potter, *The Mythologies of Crime and Criminal Justice* (Prospect Heights, IL: Waveland Press), 2000.

[584] Leon-Guerrero, op. cit., 365–366.

[585] Robert Heiner, *Social Problems: An Introduction to Critical Constructionism*, 5th ed. (New York: Oxford University Press, 2016), 136.

[586] Patricia A. Morgan, "The Legislation of Drug Law: Economic Crisis and Social Control," J. D. Arcutt, ed., *Analyzing Deviance* (Homewood, IL: Dorsey Press, 1983), 358–371. Quoted in Robert Heiner's *Social Problems: An Introduction to Critical Constructionism*, 5th ed. (New York: Oxford University Press, 2016), 140.

may be the real issue. The Nazis also had laws, including making it illegal to harbor Jews. But there were Christians (and others) who broke the anti-Semitic laws in order to serve God. In the United States, Jim Crow laws perpetrated injustice against African Americans. In some states, marriage between blacks and whites was defined as a crime.

The passage of laws make one a criminal. Up until January 1920, August Anheuser Busch Sr. was not considered a criminal for producing alcoholic beverages. However, after that date, with the ratification of the Eighteenth Amendment, he would be considered a criminal for continuing this behavior. In December 1933, with the passage of the Twenty-First Amendment, such criminal behavior was no longer defined as criminal.

Justice and the good for society, especially the most vulnerable, is the moral issue rather than the law itself. All laws should serve justice. And sentences can also be just or unjust. In the 1980s, Judge Paul Cassell sentenced twenty-four-year-old Weldon Angelos to fifty-five years in prison for three sales of marijuana in Utah. Cassell, now retired, says he is sorry for such a punitive sentence.[587] Christopher Williams, a medical marijuana provider in Montana, faces eighty-two to eighty-five years behind bars due to mandatory minimal laws.[588] At the same time, people convicted of murder have gotten off with as little as three-year sentences.

Defining Who Are Criminals

Minorities are more likely to be stopped for no specific reason, to be searched during a traffic stop, to be arrested, to be shot, to be booked, to be prosecuted, to be convicted, and to get a longer sentence than whites for the very same crime. Racial bias and discrimination have been well documented in numerous studies: "Racial profiling is the use of race or ethnicity by law enforcement, consciously or unconsciously as a basis for judgment for criminal suspicion."[589]

---

[587] Bryon Pitts, Jackie Jesko, and Lauren Effron, "Former Federal Judge Regrets 55-Year Marijuana Sentence," *abcnews.go.com*, Feb. 18, 2015, 12:22 PM ET.

[588] Kristen Gwynne, "Ten worst sentences for marijuana-related crimes: Punishments of this sort seldom fit the offense, but these cases are especially egregious," *Salon.com*, Monday, Oct. 29, 2012, 10:54 AM CDT.

[589] Guerrero, *op. cit.*, 372; Guerino, Harrison, and Sabol (2011); Lopez and Light (2009); Carson (2014); U.S. Bureau of Justice Statistics (2008); Joseph (2000); Eith and Durose (2011).

Because of the experience of the black community, black youth (including law-abiding youth) tend to have a negative and hostile attitude toward police. In the last couple of years, numerous TV programs had shown their interviews of black parents and kids, indicating that black parents literally teach their children how to respond to police in order to not get killed, including emphasis on politeness, cooperation, and not making any quick moves.

I'm going out on a limb here because I have no data on which to base this assertion, but I believe that most Americans believe that most law enforcement personnel are honest and trying to do a good job while believing that within law enforcement agencies there are some "bad apples." Having been baptized a chief of police, having been the only nonpoliceman on the Canyon, Texas, police softball team, and having sat on a committee to evaluate applicants for the Canyon police force, I can tell you that I have known some police officers of the highest integrity and lower racial bias than the general public. I can also say that I have personally known officers who like being a policeman because it gives them the opportunity and authority to push people around. In fact, I was in a Bible class with one.

Whites trust the police and have more positive interactions with the police than do blacks, especially black youth.[590] People of all races in poor and disadvantaged neighborhoods, in general, have a lower opinion of police. But when people feel they are being treated fairly, they tend to see the police as more legitimate and comply with them.[591]

Factors Contributing to Crime

Sociologists have noted a number of factors that contribute to crime. Some of the main ones are as follows:[592]

---

[590] Guerrero, op. cit., 374–5; quoting Clive Norris, Nigel Fielding, Clark Kemp, and Jane Fielding, "Black and Blue: An Analysis of the Influence on Being Stopped by the Police," *British Journal of Sociology* 43, no. 2 (1992), 207–224, http://www.jstor.org/stable/591465.

[591] Guerrero, 375; quoting Sara E. Stoutland, "The Multiple Dimensions of Trust in Resident/Police Relations in Boston," *Journal of Research in Crime and Delinquency* 38, no. 3, 226–256. https://doi.org/10.1177/0022427801038003002.2001.

[592] Darlene R. Wright and Kevin M. Fitzpatrick deal with several of these in "Violence and Minority Youth: The Effects of Risk and Asset Factors on Fighting among African American Children and Adolescent," *Adolescence* (Summer 2006), www.questia.com.

BIBLICAL INTERPRETATION FOR LAYPEOPLE AND OTHER MARTYRS   311

1. ***Demographics.*** One is simple demographics. Since young people are overrepresented in violent and property crimes, as a large cohort becomes older and is replaced by a cohort of smaller number, the number of violence and property crimes goes down.

2. ***Poverty.*** Neighborhoods of poverty have a greater frequency and percentage of violent and property crimes. If one cannot feed his children in the legitimate economy, he will resort to illegal economy (like street drugs) or theft and robbery to be responsible for his/her loved ones. Some call neighborhoods of poverty "hot spots." One reason for crime is poverty and lack of legitimate opportunities.[593]

3. ***Single parent families.*** Teen pregnancy almost ensures poverty, and divorce tends to contribute to poverty. Also, in these families, children generally have less supervision, lack of education, and hopelessness regarding future improvement of their life in the legal world.

4. ***Abuse.*** Families that involve abuse tend to produce a higher-than-average percentage of felonious criminals.

5. ***Prison.*** John Wayne's movies often contained the concept of "paying your debt to society" and giving convicts a fresh start. Many in the social sciences fields support the concept of rehabilitation by educating and giving skills while they are in prison. However, mandatory sentencing, especially for nonviolent drug offenders, is a major reason for the increased inmate population, making up about half of all federal prisoners.[594] The long sentences often expose young people who have committed minor crimes, to hardened criminals who teach them how to be hardened criminals when they get out. In addition, the parole system in many states makes it extremely difficult to get a job and establish themselves in the legitimate economy or even find a place to live. Therefore, many must resort to crime again. The high level of recidivism, 55.1 percent within five years, shows what a failure our parole system is.[595]

---

[593] Lauer and Lauer, *op. cit.*, 101.

[594] C. Anderson, "Prison Populations challenge Already Cash-Strapped States," *News Tribune,* July 28, 2003, A7; "Punishment and Prejudice: Racial Disparities in the War on Drugs," *Human Rights Watch*, 1999. New York: Human Rights Watch, 1999; *Human Rights Watch*, "The Impact of the War on Drugs on US Incarceration," New York: Human Rights Watch, 2000.

[595] Matthew Durose, Alexander Cooper, and Synder, "Recidivism of Prisoners Released in 30 States in 2005: Patterns from 2005 to 2010," Washington DC: U.S. Department of Justice, 2014. Pew Center on the States. *State of Recidivism:*

Need for Changes

In the past, the police have been able to get away with killing people, especially minorities, without fear of accountability. However, with cell phone cameras and videos and willingness of more people to witness, recent killings have become the object of public outrage. Eric Garner, forty-seven, died by a chokehold by a Newark policeman on July 17, 2014, during an arrest for allegedly selling cigarettes illegally. Newark settled with Garner's estate for $5.9 million. Michael Brown, eighteen, unarmed, was killed on August 9, 2014, by police in Ferguson, Missouri. Ferguson police chief Thomas Jackson resigned after the Justice Department issued a scathing report on the police's treatment of minorities. On June 20, 2017, Ferguson settled on a wrongful death lawsuit. Walter Scott was killed on April 4, 2015, by police in North Charleston, South Carolina, stopped for a broken brake light. Officer Michael Slager said he feared for his life after Scott grabbed his Taser. A cellphone video showed Slager shooting Scott in the back. North Charleston settled for $6.5 million. Slager pleaded guilty of using excessive force. Freddie Gray, twenty-five, was arrested in Baltimore for having a knife in his pocket. Put in a van, he mysteriously died of severe spinal injury. On August 10, 2016, the Justice Department released an investigation, which found that the Baltimore Police Department engaged in unconstitutional practices that led to disproportionate rates of stops, searches, and arrests of African Americans.

On October 20, 2014, Laquan McDonald, seventeen, who had a three-inch knife and was on PCP, was not menacing anyone up close, but standing ten feet from the nearest person. He was shot sixteen times. The city settled with the family for $5 million, though the family had not filed a lawsuit. The city fought attempts to have the dashcam video that shows the shooting. On June 27, 2017, in addition to murder and aggravated battery with a firearm charges, three officers were indicted on felony conspiracy, official misconduct, and obstruction of justice charges for allegedly lying to investigators. On July 6, 2016, Philando Castile was killed by a St. Anthony, Minnesota, policeman during a traffic stop while reaching for his identification. His girlfriend who was with him made a live stream of the aftermath of the confrontation. St. Anthony settled for $3 million.

The Revolving Door of America's Prisons. Washington, DC: Pew Charitable Trusts, 2011, quoted in Guerrero, 378.

BIBLICAL INTERPRETATION FOR LAYPEOPLE AND OTHER MARTYRS 313

Terence Crutcher, a forty-year-old unarmed black man was killed by a Tulsa policeman on September 16, 2016.[596]

A very few policemen have been indicted for murder, some for manslaughter, some for unnecessary use of force, and various other charges. Some have been fired, some have been reprimanded, some have been disciplined, some have been forced to resign. Others have suffered no repercussions. None have been convicted of murder. Some were obviously guilty, some were probably not, some were guilty of making a bad decision. But I would like to focus on the killing of Laquan McDonald. He was not menacing and was shot sixteen times. The city fought attempts to have the dashcam video released that shows the shooting. Three officers were indicted on felony conspiracy, official misconduct, and obstruction of justice charges for allegedly lying to investigators. The officers were not guilty of the killing, but tried to cover up for a fellow officer. And this is where much of the problem occurs. Part of it is siege mentality, which is common in virtually every organization that comes under suspicion. It is known as CYA. I will not translate.

The second problem is one of relationships. Put yourself in their place and try to imagine the pressure on you. You and your partner have faced numerous dangerous situations together. Maybe he has even saved your life. He was best man in your wedding. You were godfather at his daughter's baptism. Your son is dating his daughter, and they are discussing marriage. He is your best friend. You see him kill an unarmed person, black, white, or other. He pleads with you to confirm his story that the victim had a gun or that he acted like he was going to pull a gun. You love this person. You also know that if you tell the truth, there will be numerous of your police colleagues who will resent you, maybe even take reprisals against you. Think of the level of integrity it will take to face that kind of personal and social pressure to tell the truth.

In the movie *L.A. Confidential*, the unenviable position of a policeman standing up to corruption in the police force is portrayed.[597] In the *Devil's Own*,[598] Harrison Ford is portrayed as a policeman faced with the decision

---

[596] "Controversial Police Encounters Fast Facts," *CNN Library*, updated 12:20 PM ET, Sunday, July 2 2017, http://www.cnn.com/2015/04/05/us/controversial-police-encounters-fast-facts/index.html.

[597] Curtis Hanson, director, *L.A. Confidential*, Warner Brothers, 1997. Film.

[598] *The Devil's Own*, director Alan J. Pakula, Columbia Pictures Corporation, 1997. Film.

of whether to lie about the killing of a fleeing criminal to protect his partner. He decides to retire because his conscience cannot handle the dishonesty and corruption in which he has participated. But these two examples are just movies. However, lest we think this is just movie fantasy, Francesco "Frank" Serpico was a New York Police Department (NYPD) detective who exposed corruption in the NYPD. In a sting operation, his backup officers withdrew from backing him up, allowing him to be shot by a drug dealer and then refusing to call the dispatcher for help. They would have let him die. But an elderly neighbor in the next apartment called and informed EMS that someone had been shot. An emergency crew responded, saving his life. As a result of this incident, Mayor John V. Lindsey established the Knapp Commission that investigated police corruption and, at least to some extent, changed the NYPD.[599]

Many changes need to be made in order to prevent such happenings and to make abusers accountable. Numerous police forces are, partly because of Department of Justice pressure, doing introspection and changing their culture. As I finish this book, the Texas Department of Public Safety (DPS) deputy director Robert "Duke" Bodisch has suggested hiring Eric Fritch, chair of the Department of Criminal Justice at the University of North Texas, to do an analysis of racial profiling in the DPS. The background is a study of DPS by Frank Baumgartner that found "35 percent of Texas' state troopers search minority drivers at least twice as often as they do white drivers." Comments by DPS director Steve McCraw suggest that he wants to weed out or reform those who are guilty of racial profiling.[600] If every law enforcement agency would do this and either fire them or change them, the mistrust of the police would be greatly reduced.

---

[599] https://en.wikipedia.org/wiki/Frank_Serpico. In 1973, Peter Maas wrote Serpico's biography, *Serpico: The Cop who Defied the System* (New York: The Viking Press, 1973). A movie was made based on Maas's book, directed by Sidney Lumet and starring Al Pacino. *Serpico,* Artists Entertainments Complex, Inc., 1973. Film.

[600] Sean Collins Walsh, "DPS handpicks ex-cop to study profiling," *Austin American-Statesman,* Monday, July 3, 2017, scwalsh@statesman.com. In 2011, Baumgartner did a study of data he gathered from 2000–2011 of over 20 million traffic stops in North Carolina. The study was done with UNC graduate student Derek A. Epp and PhD student Kelsey Shoub entitled "Eroding Trust, Policing Anger: How Racial Disparities in Traffic Stops Threaten Democratic Values," which is slated to be published by Cambridge University Press in the summer of 2017, unc.edu.

BIBLICAL INTERPRETATION FOR LAYPEOPLE AND OTHER MARTYRS 315

In Camden, New Jersey, police are having more face-to-face contact with the people they serve. Vidal Rivera, a black police officer, said that when he was a boy, his mother would not let him play outside because it was too dangerous. He also had a fear of the police. Beginning in 2014, the force was revamped, replacing ineffective personnel. Chief Scott Thomson ordered his officers to leave their cars and patrol on foot in order to get to know and be known by the people of the neighborhood. There was an automatic change. Although things are still not ideal since 2014 murders dropped 69% percent burglaries by 27 percent, and robberies by 33 percent. Reports of rape went up 143 percent, due partly to increased reporting (probably because of increased trust in the police) and broader definition of rape (expanded to more than just penis penetration). Crime numbers are the lowest in decades. Some two hundred surveillance cameras are placed in full view around the city, and gunshot detecting microphones are placed at certain locations so they can respond even before 911 calls come in on cell phones.

Additionally, officers are taught to slow down and *not* react so fast. It is safer for them also because they are not rushing into situations. Since 2014, police use of force has dropped 24 percent and citizens' complaints of excessive force has dropped by 49 percent. Chief Thomson says that they have made the transition from "warrior to guardian." Warrior must be used at times, but it "should not be your operating premise. That should be the anomaly. That should be the exception; not the rule."[601] And considering that the poverty rate in Camden is 40 percent, this looks like a major success.

Additionally, Jim Wallis reminds us that "it's vital to acknowledge the many good police in our communities and to recognize that our police officers do a very difficult and dangerous job. Their safety and well-being . . . is central to solving the problems that have been revealed."[602] More than 100,000 law enforcement professionals are injured each year. In 2014, 126 officers died in the line of duty, 50 firearms-related.[603]

---

[601] Hari Sreenivasan, "On the Beat," *PBS News Hour,* June 30, 2017. Judy Woodruff, anchor. TV.

[602] Jim Wallis, *America's Original Sin: Racism, White Privilege, and the Bridge to a New America* (Grand Rapids: Brazos Press, 2016), 134.

[603] *Ibid.,* 134–135.

White-Collar Crime

White-collar crime is "crime committed by a person of responsibility and high social status in the course of his occupations."[604] The FBI (1989) defined it as crimes "to obtain money, property or services; to avoid payment or loss of money or services; or to secure personal and business advantage."[605] White-collar crimes include consumer fraud, environmental offenses, insider trading in stocks, security fraud, government corruption, computer crime, and misleading advertising.[606] White-collar crimes cost taxpayers more than all other types of crime. One white-collar crime that has increased exponentially lately is cybercrime, fraud, and abuse through use of the Internet.[607] The problem is, white-collar criminals receive less severe punishments or escape punishment altogether.[608] There are many issues regarding crime and punishment in the United States that reinforce injustice and undermine the social good.

As representatives of Jesus Christ, and knowing his concern for the well-being of all people, Christians should be at the forefront of studying the information provided by disciplined studies and informing their representatives at all governmental levels of what they believe would be justice for all people whom Jesus loves.

Sex-Gender Issues

Homosexuality has recently become a major bone of contention in the United States culture. Until about the 1990s, it was not. Gays and lesbians were considered not just unnatural, but also perverted. They were privately ridiculed by those having some level of sensitivity or discretion and publicly by those who had no discretion whatsoever. They were called derogatory names, publicly harassed, sometimes beaten, and even killed. Until fairly recently, their behavior was defined as a felony in numerous

---

[604] Guerrero (2016), 370, quoting Edwin H. Sutherland, *White Collar Crime* (New York: Dryden Press, 1949), 9.

[605] Ibid., Sutherland, 3.

[606] Lauer and Lauer, *op. cit.*, 97.

[607] Guerrero, *op. cit.*, 370.

[608] Lauer and Lauer, *op. cit.*, 99.

BIBLICAL INTERPRETATION FOR LAYPEOPLE AND OTHER MARTYRS   317

states and involved stiff sentences in virtually every state. Unfortunately, the role of homosexuals in the church has been the newest issue that has split churches and resulted in the formation of new denominations. It has been the subject of study committees within denominations and discussed in Bible classes and denominational gatherings. Resolutions have been adopted regarding the role of homosexuals within the denominations. In denominations where homosexuality is absolutely "verboten" (excuse my German), the issue may not have been addressed.

As Christians, our first inclination is to find out what the Bible has to say on the issue. What we find is, in its thousands of pages, there is very little said in the Bible about homosexuality, and what is said is vague and far from clear-cut.

Biblical Evidence

Genesis 2

Although Genesis may not have been the first book of the Bible to be written down, Genesis 2, while not making specific reference to either homosexuality or heterosexuality, has a specific implication. Genesis 2:18 says, "The LORD God said, 'It is not good for the man[609] to be alone. I will make a helper suitable for him.'" There is actually no sexual reference there. The issue is companionship and compatibility. If this were not obvious enough, God brought wild animals and birds to "the Adam."[610] He gave names to livestock, birds, and wild animals, but they didn't fill the bill. So God gives Adam an anesthetic, performs the first surgery, taking a rib from Adam, and created a woman[611] (2:20–22). Boy, did he approve (2:23). Only verse 24 has what is probably a statement with sexual implications: "That is why a man[612] leaves his father and mother and is united to his wife, and they become one flesh."

When Genesis 2 was first transmitted orally and later written down, it was *probably* assumed that the heterosexual relationship between a man and a woman was the only "natural" relationship. Certainly, it is the foundational sexual relationship since without it, the human race could not

---

[609]   The term is "the Adam," a term which in Genesis 1:27 refers to "male" and "female."

[610]   Although numerous translations say "him," the Hebrew does not use the masculine pronoun "him," but "the Adam."

[611]   The term is "ishshah," which means "female."

[612]   The term is "ish," which means "male," unambiguously contrary to "Adam," which is an ambiguous term.

continue to exist. However, when one takes the historical perspective into consideration, the limited knowledge of genetics of the ancient Israelites makes that assumption completely understandable. They didn't know about testosterone and estrogen, much less the fact that both males and females have varying levels of both male and female hormones. Nor did they know about chromosomal anomalies. Not knowing of these biological influences in humans, they considered any other sexual relationship to be "unnatural."

Secondly, for them, having children was an essential purpose of sexual intercourse. Aside from someone on which to dote, and in which to take pride, children were extremely important economically. They provided a workforce for the family. As a pastoral people, they needed children to help with the tending of the sheep and goats. When they entered the land of Canaan under the leadership of Joshua and took up agriculture, they needed children to help sow, tend, and harvest the crops. Besides that, children were their social security. Children were needed to take care of the parents when they were old and could no longer take care of themselves.

The last verse of chapter 2, "Adam and his wife were both naked, and they felt no shame," has no explicit sexual implication. As will later be seen in Genesis 3, it simply has to do with shame (3:7).

Genesis 19:1–11

One text that is considered proof of the sinfulness of homosexuality is Genesis 19:1–11. In Sodom, Lot offers hospitality to two angels. Then men of the city demand that Lot turn the angels over to them to have sex with the "men." Although Lot offers his daughters to be raped instead, they demand to have intercourse with the men (angels) and threaten Lot. The men (angels) drag Lot inside and strike the aggressors blind. It is impossible to argue that this text condemns committed homosexual relationships. The real issue here is the desire to have nonconsensual sex (rape), in fact, gang rape, with the angels/men. And since such a big point is made of it in the text, the inviolability of Middle Eastern hospitality may have been equally important.

Judges 19:16–30

There is a very similar story in Judges. A Levite is taking his concubine home. His servant suggests that they stop that evening at Jebus,[613] a Jebusite

---

[613] The city will later be conquered and renamed Jerusalem.

BIBLICAL INTERPRETATION FOR LAYPEOPLE AND OTHER MARTYRS   319

city. But the master does not want to stay overnight at a Canaanite city. So they continue on and stop at Gibeah in the hill country of Benjamin, where he and his concubine are given hospitality by an old man. Like in Sodom, men of the city come to the house and demand the visitor to come out so they can have intercourse with him. Mortified by their behavior, the host offers his daughter and the concubine instead. But they insist on the man. However, the guest pushes his concubine out on the porch, where she is raped to death. The story is longer and more involved, but the men of Gibeah are punished for their behavior. Again, the real issue is not men in the story wanting a committed homosexual relation, but gang rape and violation of hospitality.

Leviticus 18:22

Leviticus 18:22 is more direct. It refers to sex between men as an "abomination," but assigns no punishment. But in verse 19, having intercourse with a woman during her menstrual period is also considered an abomination. So any man who has had intercourse with his wife during her menstrual period has committed the same "abomination" as a man who has intercourse with another man. In addition, Deuteronomy 22:5 says that a man who dresses like a woman or a woman who dresses like a man is an abomination. Therefore, if we apply these texts *as is*, we would have to conclude that a man who dresses like Lady Gaga or a woman who dresses like Batman on Halloween commits a similar offense to men who have intercourse with another man. But that is not the worst. Deuteronomy 24:1–4 says that it is abominable for a man to take back his wife whom he has divorced and who has married another man who then divorces her or has died. Although this is not a common occurrence, I venture to guess that most of us know a couple who have done that very thing. I certainly do. And without knowing the specific details of the situation, would anyone really condemn Marie Osmond for remarrying her first husband again?

Leviticus 20:13

Leviticus 20:13 is written more like a judicial law. It reads as follows: "If a man lies with a man as one lies with a woman, both of them have done what is detestable. They must be put to death; their blood will be on their own heads." Now this text seems much more direct. It seems that it *could* even include committed monogamous relationships. However, this puts it on a whole 'nother level. There are some people who take this literally enough to kill homosexuals. In their culture, it was legal and considered morally right to kill homosexuals. In our culture, it is considered murder to kill a homosexual.

But we also need to point out that in Leviticus, the law says, "If a man commits adultery with another man's wife—with the wife of his neighbor—both the adulterer and the adulteress must be put to death" (20:10). The punishment for adultery was the same as for the homosexual. I presume that some reading this text have committed adultery. If not, surely some of their siblings, parents, cousins, or friends have. According to Leviticus, homosexuals and adulterers should be treated the same. Surely there are few who would encourage the execution of whomever they know who have committed adultery. Let me also point out that the Taliban in Afghanistan still maintain and enforce similar laws.

One last point on Leviticus. Leviticus 18:3–4 says, "You must not do as they do in Egypt, where you used to live, and you must not do as they do in the land of Canaan, where I am bringing you. Do not follow their practices. You must obey my ways and be careful to follow my decrees. I am the LORD your God." It could be that aside from obvious sins like murder and robbery, some of Israel's laws were intended to set them in stark contrast to the Egyptians and Canaanites.

1 Corinthians 6:9

First Corinthians 6:9–11 says, "Do you not know that the wicked will not inherit the kingdom of God? Do not be deceived: Neither the sexually immoral nor idolaters nor adulterers nor male prostitutes nor homosexual offenders . . . will inherit the kingdom of God. And that is what some of you were." In verse 6, two words are used that may mean something regarding this issues. The Greek word *malakoi* is translated "homosexuals" in the New King James Version (NKJV), "male prostitutes" in the New International Version (NIV), "effeminate" in the New American Standard (NAS),[614] "catamites" in the Jerusalem Bible (JB), and "male prostitutes" in the New Revised Standard Version (NRSV). Mounce's lexicon defines it as follows: "soft; soft to the touch, delicate; an instrument of unnatural

---

[614] Center column note says "*effeminate by perversion.*"

lust, effeminate."[615] *The Complete Word Study Dictionary New Testament* says (the basic) meaning is "soft to the touch, spoken of clothing made of soft materials, fine texture (Matt. 11:8; Luke 7:25). Figuratively it means effeminate or a person who allows himself to be sexually abused contrary to nature."[616]

And the other word, *arsenokoitai*, is translated as "sodomites" (NKJV),[617] "homosexual offenders" (NIV), "homosexuals" (NAS), sodomites" (JB), sodomites" (NRSV). Mounce defines it as "a male engaging in same-gender sexual activity, a sodomite, pedarest."[618] The *Common English Bible* (CEB) does not even translate individual words, but simply says "both participants in same-sex intercourse."[619] Even the footnote looks like a guess. If the footnote is correct, this would reflect a common perversion in the pagan Roman Empire, whereas the concept of a committed monogamous relationship is rarely addressed. "Catamite" refers to a boy kept for homosexual practice, common among Roman citizens.[620] And of course, if male prostitutes is meant, this obviously has nothing to do with a committed relationship. *The Complete Word Study Dictionary New Testament* defines it as "a man who lies in bed with another male, a homosexual."[621] The bottom line is, there is no consistently clear understanding among translators of the meaning of these ancient Greek words, and the text provides no clear indication of addressing the issue of a committed monogamous relationship.

It should also be noted that Paul says "adulterers" will not enter the kingdom of God. I venture to say that if this is applied to adultery the way

---

[615] William D. Mounce, *The Analytical Lexicon to the Greek New Testament* (Grand Rapids: Zondervan, 1993), 307.

[616] Spiros Zodhiates, op. cit., 940

[617] Internal note says *"catamites, those submitting to homosexuals."*

[618] *Op. cit.,* 100. "Pedarest" is a misspelling of the word "pederast," which refers to "homosexual relations between a man and a boy; homosexual anal intercourse, usually with a boy or younger man as the passive partner," Wikipedia's quote of the Oxford English Dictionary, "pederasty," en.m.wikipedia.org.

[619] Footnote says, "Or *submissive and dominant male sexual partners.*"

[620] "Catamite," en.m.Wikipedia.org. The term comes from the Latin *catamitus,* which in ancient Greece and Rome was a pubescent boy used in a pederastic relationship.

[621] Zodhiates, *op. cit.,* 258.

some people like to apply it to homosexuals, then many of our loved ones will suffer the same fate as homosexuals.

1 Timothy 1:10

First Timothy 1:8–11 says, "We know that the law is good if one uses it properly. We also know the law is made not for the righteous but for lawbreakers and rebels, the ungodly and sinful, the unholy and irreligious; for those who kill their fathers or mothers, or murderers, for adulterers and perverts, for slave traders and liars and perjurers—and for whatever else is contrary to the sound doctrine that conforms to the glorious gospel of the blessed God, which he entrusted to me." The text says that the law is not made for the righteous, but for the lawless, specifying several really dastardly sins, including *"koitais,"* translated sodomites (NKJV), "homosexuals" (NAS), "perverts" (NIV), "sodomites" (NRSV), "those who immoral with women or with boys or with men" (JW). Mounce says it means "sexual intercourse, concubitus; hence, lewdness, whoredom, chambering,"[622] which are general terms and gives no specific help. *The Complete Word Study Dictionary New Testament* says it means "a lying down to rest or sleep. In the New Testament, it is a place of repose, a bed (Luke 11:7). Spoken of the marriage bed, metaphorically for marriage itself (Heb. 13:4). Cohabitation, whether lawful or unlawful . . . Also, it means seed, semen as necessary for conception."[623] Again, the generalization is not helpful, in that it does not specify exactly to what it refers.

Romans 1:18–32

In Romans 1:18–32, Paul says that God's wrath is revealed against ungodliness and wickedness. Through the creation, God had shown himself to the Gentiles. Therefore, they are without excuse when they exchanged the glory of the immortal God for images of mortal humans and animals. Paul's conclusion is that God allowed them to degrade themselves. Paul enumerates a whole array of sins, including rather benign sins that do not necessarily hurt others like envy and gossip, to serious crimes like murder, to personal sins, which only hurt the sinner, like

---

[622] *Ibid.,* 286.

[623] *Ibid.,* 872.

BIBLICAL INTERPRETATION FOR LAYPEOPLE AND OTHER MARTYRS   323

insolence, boastfulness, and foolishness. But he especially points to the fact that "their women exchanged natural intercourse for unnatural, and in the same way also the men, giving up natural intercourse with women, were consumed with passion for one another. Men committed shameless acts with men and received in their own persons the due penalty for their error" (v. 26–27 NRSV).

Now this text gets closer to the issue. First of all, it is the only one to mention both men *and* women. The implication of this text is that heterosexuality is natural and homosexuality is unnatural. But in 1 Corinthians, Paul also says, "Judge for yourselves: is it proper for a woman to pray to God with her head unveiled? Does not *nature* itself teach you that if a man wears long hair, it is degrading to him, but if a woman has long hair, it is her glory? For her hair is given to her for a covering" (11:13–16 NRSV; italics mine). He uses the same word, *physis* (nature, natural), in both passages. Like homosexuality, Paul considered it unnatural for women to pray with her head uncovered. Now what he considered to be natural and unnatural in 1 Corinthians was purely a cultural *more*.[624] When I was a boy, women wore hats to church, thinking that they were fulfilling what Paul considered to be natural, when what he was actually talking about was headscarves. Women no longer do this, even though Paul considered it an important necessity.

So this makes one wonder if what he considered "unnatural" in Romans was also a cultural belief, which few of us believe today. Few of us would consider first-century hairstyles to determine what is natural or unnatural. Or I wonder if Paul was thinking like many people do, of these homosexual practices as being done by promiscuous perverts who live degraded lives, as was so common in the Roman Empire. I also wonder whether he ever stopped to think about the issue of people of the same sex living in a long-term loving monogamous committed relationship.

The Failure of Popular Perception

Very often, the assumption is that people make a personal choice to be homosexual, to live what they consider to be a perverted lifestyle. But first of all, one must ask how much sense does it make to believe a person would

---

[624] Mores are "'strong' norms that specify normal behavior and constitute demands, not just expectations" (Alex Thio, *Sociology: An Introduction* [New York: Harper & Row Publishers, 1989], 76) and "violators of such norms will be severely punished" (57).

choose a lifestyle that he/she knows will be despised, that will set themselves up for ridicule, physical attacks, and maybe even death?

I can remember that when I was young, I thought that way. It never occurred to me to wonder why anyone would choose to be persecuted. But my thinking began to change some forty years ago when I read an article in *Amarillo Globe-News* entitled something like "He's a Boy, or Is She?" It related stories of individuals with both male and female primary sex organs and secondary sex characteristics. It was long ago, and I do not remember whether it specified the possible reasons or not. However, in recent decades, at least some reasons have been discovered.

Recently, the male/female binary construct (i.e., boy-girl only) as the only natural order of things has been questioned. And with the binary sexual construct, certain gender roles have previously been assumed. Mollenkott points out, "The binary gender construct has dictated that real males must be naturally be drawn to those attitudes, behaviors, and roles any given society considers 'masculine,' including sexual attractions to females only. And real females must be naturally drawn to those attitudes, behaviors, and roles any given society considers 'feminine,' including sexual attraction to males only."[625] It is assumed that the way things are is the way they *ought* to be.[626] Theologically, it is called the "order of creation, the will of God, unchangeable and beyond question."[627]

When I was in high school, there was one boy that everyone "knew" was a "queer." I don't know if he was or not. I don't know that he was ever threatened, but everyone (*maybe* even I) made fun of him, thinking of him as a pervert. When I worked as a social worker at the Texas Department of Human Resources in Amarillo, I had a colleague who, I was told, acknowledged being homosexual. However, he was such a nice guy I could not see him as a "pervert." And on top of this, the *Amarillo Globe-News* article referred to earlier, chronicling births of children with both male and female sex organs, made it impossible to maintain my previous way of thinking. For me, the binary construct and homosexuality as a *conscious choice* and a perversion began to break down. Over time, research has shown that the

---

[625] Virginia Ramey Mollenkott, *Omnigender: A Trans-religious Approach* (Cleveland: Pilgrim Press, 2007), 2.

[626] See the concept of "Reification" in Peter L. Berger and Thomas Luckmann, *The Social Construction of Reality: A Treatise in the Sociology of Knowledge* (New York: Anchor Books, 1966), 89–92, 186, 187.

[627] Mollenkott, 2007, *op. cit.*, 2.

problem with the binary construct is that there are so many exceptions that the binary construct does not work.[628] Scientific evidence indicates that masculine and feminine gender identity is far more dependent on social learning than on genetic makeup.[629]

About 1 in 100 births shows some anomaly in sex differentiation, and about 1 in 2,000 is different enough to raise the question of whether the newborn is actually a girl or a boy.[630] As many as 4 percent of all births are intersexual—babies with indeterminate genitals or with both male and female genitals, sometimes internal and difficult to discover.[631] Some people with apparently normal male bodies sense themselves as female, some people with female bodies sense themselves to be male, and these people may decide to cross-dress permanently and use hormonal and/or surgical means to become or "pass" as the gender they feel themselves to be.[632]

Another contradiction to the idea that gender roles are absolute is that around the world, "societies vary radically in their understanding of what constitutes "masculinity" and "femininity.""[633] Because of her observations of the role of girls in Samoa, Margaret Mead concluded that gender roles are dictated more by the local culture than by nature. In 1932, she studied three tribes in Papua New Guinea, doing pioneering work on gender consciousness, exploring whether temperamental differences between the sexes were culturally determined or whether they were innate. She found major differences between the tribes. Among the Arapesh, the temperament for both males and females was generally gentle, responsive, and cooperative, which in the West has traditionally been considered female gender characteristics. Among the Mundugumor (now Biwat), both males and females tended to be violent and aggressive, seeking power and position, which in the West is generally considered male roles. But among the Tchambuli (now Chambri), male and female temperaments were completely different from each other, generally reflecting role reversal

---

[628]   *Ibid.*, 2.

[629]   Mollenkott, 1977, *op. cit.*, 76.

[630]   Mollenkott, 2007, *op. cit.*, 2; quoting Cheryl Chase, "Hermaphrodites and Attitude: Mapping the Emergence of Intense Activism" in *Transgender Studies Reader*, ed. Susan Stryker and Stephen Whittle (New York: Routledge, 2006), 300.

[631]   *Ibid.*, 2–3, quoting Martine Aliana Rothblatt, *The Apartheid of Sex: A Manifesto on the Freedom of Gender* (New York: Crown, 1995), 9.

[632]   *Ibid.*, 3.

[633]   *Ibid.*, Mollenkott, 1977, 62.

from Western gender stereotypes of that time. The women were dominant, impersonal, and were the providers and emotionally independent. Women were the sole economic providers, doing the fishing and traveling to do the trading. Although a patrilineal culture, neither party loses full control in the marriage situation. Women work with male family members to choose a man for marriage in which there is no bride price. The men were also wary of what the women could possibly give to a sorcerer to put a hex on them.[634]

The main exceptions to the binary construct are *intersexual* or *hermaphrodite* individuals who are "those with medically established physical or hormonal attributes of both male and female gender."[635] A *transsexual* is a person who is interested in permanently changing gender through hormones or surgery. A *transvestite* or *cross-dresser* is a person involved in cross-dressing and cross-living, but does not have hormonal therapy or genital surgery. An androgyne is a person who takes on the characteristics of both or neither gender roles.[636]

There are several biological reasons for these abnormalities:

1. ***Androgen Insensitivity Syndrome* (AIS), or *Testicular Feminization Syndrome*** is an inherited genetic defect of the X chromosome in which the body's cells cannot respond to androgen. A baby born with AIS has genitals that appear to be female, with "undescended or partially descended testes" in the abdominal cavity. S/he will later develop breast growth, but has no womb and will not menstruate or be able to bear children.

2. ***Partial Androgen Insensitivity Syndrome*** is a condition that usually results in "ambiguous genitals"—large clitoris or small penis—and may be the cause of infertility in some men.

3. ***Progestin-Induced Virilization*** is caused by prenatal exposure to the drug progestin or other external androgens. People with a XX

---

[634] Margaret Mead, *Coming of Age in Samoa: A Psychological Study of Primitive Youth for Western Civilization* (New York: Will Morrow & Co, 1928); *Sex and Temperament: In Three Primitive Societies* (New York: HarperCollins Publishers), 1935.

[635] Mollenkott, 1977, *op. cit.*, 43.

[636] Mollenkott, 2008, 44, quoting Giana E. Israel and Dr. Donald E. Traver II. *Transgender Care Recommended Guidelines, Practical Information, and Personal accounts* (Philadelphia: Temple University Press, 1997), 43.

BIBLICAL INTERPRETATION FOR LAYPEOPLE AND OTHER MARTYRS   327

(female) karyotype[637] affected in utero by virilizing hormones may range from "a female with a large clitoris" to a "male with no testes."

4. ***Congenital Adrenal Hyperplasia*** virilizes XX people (considered female) in utero. In this abnormality, the adrenal glands produce a hormone that has a masculinizing effect. Despite having XX chromosomes, after puberty, virtually complete bodily masculinization occurs.[638]

5. ***Klinefelter Syndrome*** is a situation in which the individual, instead of inheriting a single X chromosome from its mother and a single Y from its father, inherit an extra X chromosome from either father or mother. Their chromosomal pattern could be XX with an extra Y chromosome or an XY with an extra X chromosome. They are generally defined as female, but are "pragmatically male."[639] They may not develop facial or body hair, a deep voice or heavy muscles in puberty, nor produce sperm. Some develop breast growth. Physicians usually recommend that Klinefelter men take testosterone all their lives, but many do not like the side effects of taking testosterone and do not take it or reduce the dosage.

However, sex hormones, especially testosterone or estrogen, are needed for strong bones, and not taking them can result in osteoporosis (brittle bones). One woman seemed to be a normal girl at birth, but at twelve, her clitoris began to enlarge into a penis.[640]

Genetic sex (the organization of sex chromosomes) is not a sure test of true sex since about 1 person in every 500 had karyotype[641] other than XX or XY. About one in 1,000 women has three X chromosomes, some even having four plus two Y chromosomes. The sex chromosomes cause anatomical sex streaks[642] and which determine the differentiation of

---

[637]   A karyotype is the number and occurrence of chromosomes in the nucleus of the eukarystic cell.

[638]   *Ibid.*, 48–50.

[639]   *Ibid.*, 50, quoting Sally Cross, "Intersexuality and Scripture," *Theology and Sexuality* 6, no. 11 (September 1999), 67.

[640]   *Ibid.*, p. 50–51.

[641]   The number and appearance of chromosomes in the nucleus of a eukaryotic or membrane-enclosed cell.

[642]   Wikipedia, s.v. "gonadal dysgenesis," "a form of aplasia in which the ovary is replaced by functionless tissue."

328   DAVID W. MELBER

external genitalia into male, female, or intermediate (intersexual). All told, over seventy syndromes have been discovered.[643] So considering the fact that babies are created with abnormalities that confuses what sex they are, Mollenkott asks, "Why assume that any person would willfully seek out discrimination and suffering? And even if they did, wouldn't compassion be a more appropriate response than judgementalism?"[644]

"My assumption," she continues, "is that ethics, medicine, and theology should begin with the facts of the Creator's work, respecting that work as worthy, instead of telling people that they must adapt themselves to a humanly constructed set of abstractions."[645]

The Bible was written by human beings, who are a product of their culture. In no other letter does Paul struggle with the difficulty of distinguishing between morality and opinion, between Gospel and culture, than in 1 Corinthians (11:3–16, 14:33–35). He shows vestige of his socialization in both the patriarchal Jewish culture and Greek culture. [646] Mollenkott points out that "having argued for female head-covering because the woman came from the man, Paul suddenly admits: 'In the Lord, however, woman is not independent of man, nor is man independent of woman . . . .' (v. 11 NIV)."[647] Mollenkott further points out that everyone approaches any written text with certain expectations "and those expectations govern what we are able to see in what we are reading."[648] Paul appeals to social customs of rabbinic Judaism: "Judge for yourselves: Is it proper for a woman to pray to God with her head uncovered? Does not the very nature of things teach you that if a man has long hair, it is a disgrace to him, but that if a woman has long hair, it is her glory? . . . we have no other practice—nor did the churches of God" (1 Cor. 11:13–16).[649] It is important for us to distinguish between what is "for one age" and what is "for all time."[650] Therefore, it is time we reassess our

---

[643]   *Ibid.*, 46–48.

[644]   *Ibid.*, 44.

[645]   *Ibid.*, 46.

[646]   Mollenkott, 1977, *op. cit.*, 95.

[647]   *Ibid.*, 98.

[648]   Mollenkott, 1988, *op. cit.*, 64–65.

[649]   *Ibid.*, 98.

[650]   Mollenkott, 1977, 91.

BIBLICAL INTERPRETATION FOR LAYPEOPLE AND OTHER MARTYRS   329

understanding of, and our treatment of, those who do not fit neatly into the traditional binary gender role. The Gospel of Jesus Christ demands it.

Racism

I had not planned to have a section on race. I knew it was important, but the book had already gone a hundred pages more than I had planned. Things seemed to be getting out of control. Plus, I had spent numerous pages on the treatment of immigrants (see pp. 251–252). But I made the mistake of checking out Alice Walker's *In Search of Our Mothers' Gardens* at the Presbyterian seminary in Austin to find a quote. However, I began to read and could not put it down. So I bought a copy.

Scriptural Direction

The stories she related caused me to search the scriptures. Genesis 1 says that God created humankind, both male and female, in the image of God. All human beings are all over 95 percent the same genetically. Skin colors developed in different climates.

Over and over, followers of God say that God shows no partiality (Exod. 23:3; Job 32:21; Acts 10:34; Rom. 2:11, 10;12; 1 Cor. 12:13; Gal. 2:6; 1 Peter 1:17; Eph. 6:9; James 2:9). Jesus healed the daughter of a Canaanite woman, saying her faith was great (Matt. 15:22–28) and healed the Syrophoenician woman's daughter (Mark 7:25–30). He praised the Samaritan leper for being the only one of the ten to come back and thank him for their healing (Luke 17:12–19). He ministered to the Samaritan woman at Jacob's well even though "Jews do not associate with Samaritans" (John 4:9). He commissioned his disciples to make disciples of all the nations (Matt. 28:19). At Pentecost, there were people from "every nation under heaven" (Acts 2:5; hyperbole), many of whom responded to Peter's proclamation. Philip baptized the Ethiopian eunuch (Acts 8:27ff). Jesus even identifies with the alien in Matthew 25, saying, "I was a stranger (*xenos*)[651] and you invited me in (25:35)." So according to Jesus, *racist attacks are attacks on him.* Peter said that although it was unlawful for a Jew to associate with a foreigner, God

---

[651] This Greek word is the term from which we get our term xenophobia, "fear of foreigners."

330   DAVID W. MELBER

has shown him that he should not call any man unholy or unclean whom
God had called clean (Acts 10:28).

Now regarding black people per se, there is little in the Bible. Since
most African Americans came from the western coast of Africa, in a sense,
neither the Old Testament nor Jesus ever spoke about them. However, the
terms in the Bible referring the black people is a bit loose. Ethiopia was
a word used by the Greeks and Romans for the Hebrew name Cush in
the Old Testament, which originally referred to the southern part of the
Egyptian empire and perhaps in a limited sense referred to the empire of
Meroë, at the convergence of the White and Blue Nile.

Cush was a southern enemy of Egypt, and Pi-ankhi of Cush conquered
Egypt and established the twenty-fifth dynasty of Egyptian rulers (716–656
BCE). With the fall of Jerusalem, some Jews were exiled to Cush (Isa. 11:1;
Zeph. 3:10).[652] Aaron and Miriam showed their prejudice by criticizing
Moses for marrying an Ethiopian woman (Num. 12:1). Ethiopia per se
is generally only referred to as a nation with Egypt in war against Israel
(2 Chron. 12:3; Zeph. 2:12). However, Ebed-melech the Ethiopian saved
Jeremiah's life (Jer. 38:7ff). The beautiful bride in the Song of Solomon
was black (1:5–6).

However, by carefully cherry-picking Genesis 9, ideologists have
claimed that the "curse of Ham" justified every kind abuse of the black race
(v. 25).[653] The basis of our attitude as Christians toward other races is the
same as mentioned earlier in detail—care of the "stranger" (Exod. 22:21
and numerous others). About a hundred Old Testament passages say to love
the stranger and sojourner (Lev. 19:18, 34; Deut. 6:5; 10:12, 19). Further,
the promise to Abraham, Isaac, and Jacob is that their descendants will
be a blessing to "all the nations of the earth" (Genesis 26:4). This promise
is reiterated throughout the Old Testament (e.g., Isaiah 11:10, 42:1, 49:6,
66:19). When Paul claims that in Christ, there is neither Jew nor Greek,
slave nor free, male nor female (Gal. 3:28), he was protesting exclusion of
Gentiles, women, and slaves (or anyone) in the people of God.

---

[652]   Thomas Briscoe, s.v. "Cush," *Holman Bible Dictionary*, gen. ed. Trent C. Butler
        (Nashville: Holman Bible Publishers, 1991), 324.

[653]   Dealt with earlier on pp. 64, 192.

BIBLICAL INTERPRETATION FOR LAYPEOPLE AND OTHER MARTYRS 331

Black People in America

The first black people in the Americas came 8,000 to 10,000 year ago, or earlier. They were not Africans, but Asian Australian. Generations have been amazed by the "Negroid" features of the Olmec heads in Mexico. Recently, South American discoveries have provided other indications.[654] The first black whose name we know is Juan Garrido, a free African from Angola, a member of Ponce de León's exploration of Florida as early as 1513. The first that we know much about is Estevanico, a Moroccan slave of Andrés Dorantes de Carranza on the Pánfilo de Narváez expedition of 1527 to colonize Florida. By 1828, only eighty members of the expedition survived. Led by Álvar Núñez Cabeza de Vaca, the devastated party tried to cross the Gulf of Mexico, but were shipwrecked. Only four survived, including Estevanico and de Vaca, landing at Galveston Island, where they were enslaved. They escaped to the Texas coast, where Estevanico was treated with respect as a healer. They later escaped to Mexico.[655]

Blacks were introduced in 1619 to Jamestown in the Virginia Colony as indentured servants for seven years. But by 1641, the law was changed, making the indentured servants into slaves, who could be treated as chattel.[656] I don't need to relate the history of slavery, Reconstruction, Black Codes, segregation, Jim Crow laws, degradation, and unrequited murder of black people in America.[657] But as I read the accounts of the life of Alice Walker and others that she recounted, it did not surprise me that one of my students at Pflugerville High School once said to me, "I hate all white people." It is a wonder that there are not more like him. Maybe there are, and we just don't know it. Of course, I tried to tell him that *his* attitude was the same as the Ku Klux Klan who hate all black people. But then,

---

[654] Stefan Anitei, "The First Americans Were Black! Very Similar to Australian Aborigines," *SOFTPEDIA NEWS*, Aug. 31, 2007, 18:46 GMT, http://news.softpedia.com/news/The-First-Inhabitants-of-the-Americans-Were-Black-64307.shtml.

[655] https://en.wikipedia.org/wiki/Estevanico#North_American_explorer.

[656] http://www.history.com/topics/black-history/slavery.

[657] "During the time of Jim Crow laws, and *at least* 3,440 black men, women, and children were lynched—publicly murdered by white mobs," Wallis, *op. cit.*, 78. David Pilgrim, "What Was Jim Crow?" Jim Crow Museum, Ferris State University, September 2000, htpp://ferris.edu/jimcrow/what.htm.

the KKK hadn't suffered the oppression to which black people have been subjected. Unfortunately, my student's behavior in school make it almost certain that he would, despite his level of intelligence, probably live a life of miserable poverty or end up in prison.

Reading Walker's book caused my mind to be flooded with images from my youth. When I was about four, my dad delivered bread for Mellow Toast bakery. His route was in East Austin. Sometimes I accompanied him. All of his clients that I can remember were black or Hispanic. I barely remember the black owner of a mom-and-pop grocery who "made over me" and reached into that ice-cold container for a Coke for me. I remembered "Zene" Harris (I learned only recently that his real name was "Ernest"), who worked for Christian Jahnke, my cousin Sonny's father-in-law, who worked so hard, yet lived in relatively squalid conditions (I say relatively because he and his family were treated by the Jahnkes much better than many blacks I had seen). I remembered picking cotton with "coloreds" on my grandpa Melber's farm.

I thought about the "Coloreds Only" signs over a bucket with a ladle with a water fountain for whites next to it. I chuckle when I think about McCallum High School's integration in 1955. When we learned that the first black male student was going to compete in cross-country and track, we assumed that with him we were going to kick some serious butt. Kenneth worked hard, but burst our racial stereotype by turning out to be a mediocre athlete. I thought of the seminary students I had known (including my roommate, Sam Coleman), who had graduated from Concordia College, Selma, Alabama, and the fracas over Sam's being in my wedding. Even though I addressed the issue in sermons in the late 1960s, I thought about how little I had done to fight segregation and racism compared to what some people thought I had done. I thought about the indignities my racially mixed son, Stephen, suffered at the hands of parents of some of his playmates. I thought about how I was a Shirley Chisholm delegate to the Democratic precinct primary in 1972, not because I thought she could win (or even be nominated), but because she was saying what I believed needed to be said. I thought about how, when I supported Jesse Jackson seriously in the 1984 primaries, one of my students in Shepherd, Texas, middle school, assured me that no black man would ever be elected president. I thought about how far we had come, electing a black president.

BIBLICAL INTERPRETATION FOR LAYPEOPLE AND OTHER MARTYRS 333

Limitations of Our Progress

But then there was Sandra Bland (Waller County, Texas), Freddie Gray (Baltimore), Michael Brown (Ferguson, Missouri), Walter Scott (North Charleston), Jermane Reid (Bridgeton, New Jersey), Tamir Rice (Cleveland), Ezell Ford (Florence, California), Eric Garner (New York), and Dontre Hamilton (Milwaukee), who died in police custody under mysterious conditions and the demonstrations in response to these incidents. And in response to the Black Lives Matter movement, I have actually heard Christians call it a racist movement, as if they shouldn't be upset over these circumstances. Recently, another white student has sued the University of Texas, claiming reverse discrimination because of affirmative action.[658] Affirmative action has always been practiced, only before the late twentieth century, it was practiced in favor of whites. If we practice affirmative action for minorities for two hundred years, it may be that we will arrive at parity and it will no longer be needed.

As I finish this book, we have experienced the awful tragedy when a large group of white supremacists, Neo-Nazis, KKK members, and white nationalists held a hate rally in Charlottesville, Virginia; was met by a counterprotest; and a hate-group member plowed his vehicle into a crowd, killing one young woman and injuring numerous others. In his book *America's Original Sin*, Jim Wallis says, "But racism lingers far more pervasively in implicit and convert ways in American institution and culture, in often unconscious attitudes, and in the very structure of our society."[659]

Even as we elected an African American president, racism was unleashed against him in the "birthers' movement," stirring up doubts about Obama's parentage and citizenship. And just as egregious were the intentional lies that referred to him as a Muslim despite the fact that he was more outspoken about his faith than any recent president other than Jimmy Carter.

I have documented the fact that there are some racists among policemen (p. 277–282) and won't say more except that the Department of Justice found racist jokes by Ferguson policemen on emails, including jokes about

---

[658] Regents of the University of California v. Bakke, 438 U. S. 265 (1978), Hopwood v. the University of Texas, 48 F.3d 932 (5ᵗʰ Cir. 1996), Grutter V. Bollinger, 539 U.S. 306 (2003), and Fisher v. University of Texas, 570 U.S. ___ (2013).

[659] Wallis, *op. cit.*, xv–xvi.

the president and first lady.[660] Could anyone really argue that there was a group of racist policemen within that department who need to be fired?

The United States was built by white Americans by enslaving one people, the use and abuse of another group (Hispanics), and the almost total annihilation of another people (Native Americans). And what makes it so hurtful to me is that it was done, in most cases, by Christians. Wallis further points out that "white people in the United States have benefited from the structures of racism, whether or no they have ever committed a racist act, uttered a racist word, or had a racist thought (as unlikely as that is)."[661]

It is not mere coincidence that black drivers are 31 percent more likely to be pulled over than whites, are more than twice as likely to be subject to police searches, are nearly twice as likely to not be given any reason for the traffic stop.[662] They are about three times more likely to be arrested, comprise 14 percent of drug users, but are 37 percent of those arrested for drug offenses.[663] They are held 10 percent longer for the same crimes.[664] Now 60 percent of people in prison are people of color. Black men are 6 times more likely to be incarcerated than whites, Hispanics are 2.5 times

---

[660] Mark Berman, "The Seven Racist E-Mails the Justice Department Highlighted I its Report on Ferguson Police," *Washington Post*, March 4, http://www.washingtonpost.com/news/post-nation/wp/2015/03/04/th -seven-racist-e-mails-the-justice-department-highlighted-in-its-report-on-ferguson-police/. Although I could not find this citation of Wallis, I did find numerous reports by other news agencies, including Mark Berman, "The seven racist e-mails the Justice Department highlighted in its report on Ferguson police," March 4, 2015, https://www.washingtonpost.com/news/post-nation/wp/2015/03/04/the-seven-racist-e-mails-the-justice-department-highlighted-in-its-report-on-ferguson-police/?po stshare=1971425516292622&utm_term=.26f03bfda5ad.

    The department reported that a November 2008 email said Obama would not be president very long because "What black man holds a steady job for four years." An April 2011 email depicted Obama as a chimp. An October 2011 email included a photo of a group of bare-chested women dancing with the caption "Michelle Obama's High School Reunion." An email on December 2011 included jokes that are based on offensive stereotypes about Muslims.

[661] Wallis, *op. cit.*, 49.

[662] *Ibid.*, 138. Christopher Ingraham, "You Really Can Get Pulled Over for Driving While Black, Federal Statistics Show," *Washington Post*, September 9, 2014, http://www.washingtpnpost.come/blogs/ wonkblog/wp/2014/09/09/you-really-canget-pulled-over-for-driving-while-black-federal-statistics-show/.

[663] Wallis, *op. cit.*, 138.

[664] *Ibid.*, 139.

BIBLICAL INTERPRETATION FOR LAYPEOPLE AND OTHER MARTYRS   335

more likely. And 1 in 3 African American men will be imprisoned at some point in their lifetime, whereas 2 in 6 Latino men and 1 in 17 white men.[665]

Overcoming Racism

The more overt expressions of racism are usually condemned by most Americans. Still, it is difficult to overcome such engrained social structures—but necessary. Most people are not even aware of their prejudice and certainly not aware of how they have benefitted from the social structures. Wallis points out that biases can be changed by "exposure to different facts, realities, and situations, and especially, getting to know and understand real people who can change our stereotypes and biases about them."[666] Earlier in the book, I pointed out how, although sociologists cannot give us moral guidance, they can give us accurate information regarding social issues (pp. 106, 191–193, 257, 293–294).

For the most part, white Christians, even the ones who are aware of the unfairness of the situation, have chosen to be comfortable rather than prophetic. But "racism negates the reason for which Christ died—the reconciling work of the cross, first of God and then to one another."[667] Israel's prophets called them to repent and renounce their detestable practices!" (Ezek. 14:6, 33:11; Isa. 45:22, 55:7; Joel 2:12–13; Isa. 1:16–17). John the Baptist did the same (Matt. 3:7–10; Luke 3:8–14). And we have already spoken about Jesus's proclamations and behavior.

Wallis says, "When the church 'refuses to face the stern reality of sin,' it will have no credibility when it talks about its faith, forgiveness, and salvation."[668] Repentance only comes when the sin is acknowledged. But repentance means more than just saying "I'm sorry." It is a complete change of direction, "a new and better direction."[669] Christ's forgiveness can free us from the burden of racism and enable us to live in harmony with Him and the Father and "all God's children." May God give Christians the gumption to support such attempts at equal opportunity. What I have

---

[665] *Ibid.*

[666] *Ibid.*, 86.

[667] *Ibid.*, 54.

[668] *Ibid.*, 64.

[669] *Ibid.*, xxiii.

just said regarding African Americans goes to a large extent regarding Hispanics and an even greater degree regarding Native Americans.

One would hope that Christians would respond because of the Gospel. However, it should also be pointed out that in about thirty years, the majority of Americans will be descended from Africans, Asians, and Latin Americans.[670] That is already the case in Los Angeles, New York, San Francisco, Dallas, Chicago, Boston, Milwaukee, and in the states of California, Texas, New Mexico, Hawaii, and in Washington DC.[671] For those not motivated by the Gospel, it is important to change racist attitudes, behaviors, and structures to prevent retaliation. May God grant it.

We Will Go Wrong, But . . .

Because Christians are not simply the new persons in Christ, we still have the taint of the Old Adam (original sin), which includes selfishness, ignorance, reality avoidance, and self-deception; we will still fall short of "the image of God." Paul said of himself, "I don't know what I'm doing, because I don't do what I want to do. Instead, I do the thing that I hate" (Rom. 7:15). Let's be honest and clear about that. For God to love us, we do not depend on getting it right every time. Even when we have the highest motivation, we may make a mess.

Christian sociologist Berger and others argue that "sociology is . . . an *attempt to understand*[672]. . . . by clearing away collective illusions."[673] But as much as I have touted the use of research to tell us what the real situations are rather than relying on faulty perceptions, science, while better than perceptions, is not perfect either. Berger is very clear on the fact that "science can never provide moral guidelines for action."[674] It can only attempt to provide accurate information.

Second, when sociologists or historians predict the future, they never know exactly what the outcome will be. Their predictions must always be

---

[670] *Ibid.*, 38.

[671] *Ibid.*, 189.

[672] Berger, 1963, *op. cit.*, 4.

[673] Ibid., 6.

[674] Berger and Kellner, 1981, *op. cit.*, 12.

in terms of "if . . . then."[675] Max Weber called the ethics of responsibility "an ethics that derives its criteria for action from a calculus of probable consequences rather than from absolute principles"[676] Therefore, we cannot arrogantly presume that even our best efforts with the best information is a foolproof assurance of positive outcome.

One should always look for unintended consequences also. For example, an unintended consequence of the Prohibition Amendment was the growth of organized crime, the consequence of built-in obsolescence in the American automotive industry that allowed German and Japanese cars to usurp the market in the United States, and the enhancement of the medical profession that enabled Americans to live longer, putting a major burden on the cost of health care in America.

Also, Karl Marx's social analysis was right on point. But his prognostications for the future were faulty because he was ignorant of the power of original sin. Original sin is not a behavior, but a human condition, one dimension of which we might loosely call selfishness. Marx was, to some extent, locked into the belief of nineteenth-century liberalism that believed that if you educate people to the truth, they will buy it and act accordingly. He was not aware of the fact that part of original sin was the fact that vested interests can suppress the truth from others and repress the truth from even themselves. While St. Paul wrestled with the issue of "I do not understand myself, because the good that I want to do, I do not do, but the evil that I do not want to do, I so" (Rom. 7:19–21), Freud explained it by his concept of "defense mechanisms," including "rationalization" and "repression."

And C. Wright Mills showed how the misuse of the structural-functionalist view of sociology can be used as ideology to support the status quo.[677] Berger and Kellner also point out how sociology *can* be usurped by the "technocrat" and the "ideologist" whose deductions a priori can proceed to find what he intended to find[678]—but that is a subject for another time. It should never be used as justifications for suffering and injustice in the world.[679]

---

[675] *Ibid.*, 147.

[676] *Ibid.*, 75.

[677] *Ibid.*, 134.

[678] *Ibid.*, 122–145

[679] *Ibid.*, 145.

A person's conclusion is often dependent on his apriority (nothing prior), which is his foundational belief. To illustrate: There was a man named George who thought he was dead. His wife took him to psychologists, psychiatrists, philosophers, until he came to a philosopher who thought he could convince George that he was actually alive.

"George, dead men don't bleed, do they?"

"No," answered George.

"Then if I stuck you and you bled, that would mean you are not dead, right?"

"Right," answered George.

Then the philosopher quickly produced a pin and pricked George, who began to bleed. George looked at the blood and then the philosopher.

"Doc," he said, "I want to thank you for showing me how wrong I have been all along. I have been under this delusion for a long time. Now you have convinced me . . . dead men do bleed."

The philosopher's problem was that he assumed George's basic belief was that dead men don't bleed, whereas his apriority, the belief through which he interpreted other phenomena, was that *he was dead.*

Because as God's children, we live under forgiveness and are freed from the curse of the law. With freedom from that burden, God pushes us back into the world with confidence that we can continue to do our best to "serve Him in everlasting innocence, righteousness, and blessedness."[680]

Christians believe the Bible records "the story of God's action in history for the salvation of fallen humankind and the completion of God's intentions for creation."[681] In applying the Bible to present-day situations, many of which are extremely complicated, one can never have all the information needed. We should seriously try to get as much information as he can so that he can make a decision that reflects the will of God. But even with the best intentions and as much information about the reality of the situation as we can get, we can still make wrong decisions.

Berger and Kellner point out that "an individual possessed of absolute certainty with regard to his own perceptions and values . . . would then proceed to seek explanations as to why these other people are so blind to what to him are obvious truth."[682] We must be honest enough to

---

[680] Martin Luther, *The Small Catechism*, "The Third Article," bookofconcord.org.

[681] Grenz, *op. cit.*, 164.

[682] Berger and Kellner, *op. cit.*, 57.

BIBLICAL INTERPRETATION FOR LAYPEOPLE AND OTHER MARTYRS   339

acknowledge that our knowledge is partial and, based on new information, modify or change our beliefs about a given issue. That takes faith.

Berger and Kellner point out that any science, including sociology, can only provide information and "can never provide moral guidelines for action."[683] But (and this is a big but) it does affect ethics "precisely because it makes the ethicist aware of the empirical relativity of moral beliefs. . . . [and] increases awareness of the consequences."[684]

Another unintended consequence: In the 1970s, during the Biafran rebellion in Nigeria, each night on the Huntley-Brinkley Report, I would see children in Nigerian hospitals with distended stomachs, skin and bones, and hollow eyes. In my compassion for those children, I was responsible for getting Christians to contribute thousands of dollars to send food and medicine to care for them. After the war was over, a study showed that some of the medicine and food did get to the children, but much of it actually got to the rebels. And the planes were also carrying arms to the rebels. So the war may have gone on longer because of my involvement and more children may have died than would have been the case if I had kept my big nose out of it. That is a load of guilt that is hard to bear.

Faith is the abandonment of false securities, including dogmatic definitions that supposedly defend the Bible, and letting God's message speak to us. "The statement 'I am freed from sins' is not a dogmatic [statement], but an existential one,"[685] a personal life's experience. Rudolph Bultmann is so right when he says, "We are not speaking of an idea of God but of the living god in whose hands our time lies."[686]

But our relationship to God is not based on our always being right or having a squeaky-clean motivation, but on the grace of God that gives us the Spirit to attempt to do God's will. And because of God's forgiveness, when we falter, when we make the wrong decision, God picks us up, dusts us off, pats us on the butt, and sends us back out into the world to try again to do God's will. Therefore, as Luther said, we can "sin boldly" and continue to try to do God's will unafraid.

---

[683]   *Ibid.*, 12.

[684]   *Ibid.*, 83.

[685]   Bultmann 1958, 76f.

[686]   *Ibid.*, 78.

CONCLUSION

According to Stanley Grenz in his book, *A Primer on Postmodernism*, the gospel of today must have four characteristics, which he describes with four seventy-five-cent words: post-individualistic, postnationalistic, postdualistic, and postnoeticentric.

By post-individualistic, he means that contrary to the modernist world, in which the individual was center stage, the postmodernist world is a world in which community is the emphasis, in which the focus is not the radical individualism, which only asks, "What do I get out of it?" but "How am I responsible before God for care of others?" He says that if we are to make an impact in the world, Christians had better "live out the gospel in wholesome, authentic, and healing relationships . . . seek[ing] to draw others to Christ by embodying that gospel in the fellowship they share."[687]

For Grentz, postrationalistic means while valuing "reason," the postmodern child of God goes beyond the cognitive and values "mystery," which is a reality that "transcends human reason. Faith must not be just fixated propositions."[688] And yet he recognized the truth of Peter Berger's and Thomas Luckmann's insight, namely, that our understanding does not occur in a vacuum, for our ideas are influenced by our life's experience,

---

[687]   Grenz, *op. cit.*, 164.

[688]   *Ibid.*, 169–170.

342   DAVID W. MELBER

which "shapes our understanding of our encounters with God . . . that are propositional in nature."[689] That is, they can be expressed.

For Grentz, postdualistic means that rather than seeing the person as dualistic body and soul, he is seen as a unified whole in which the Gospel we proclaim, like that of Jesus, is not merely "pie in the sky," but expresses care for the whole person here and now.

Finally, Grenz says that the world of the Christians' gospel must be a postnoeticentric gospel. That is, in the life of sanctification, in the life of a Christian (1 Cor. 8:1), faith is relevant "for every dimension of life," with our behavior having purpose that does not come from within ourselves, but from God's resources within us, the Holy Spirit. Since our behavior is shaped by what we believe about God and the meaning of the Gospel, to be Christ's disciples, we not only proclaim the good news, but we also embody what it means to be Christian in every aspect of our lives.[690]

So how do we do that? The Holy Spirit works through God's revolutionary word in scripture. In order to know God's will for us in this life, it is a life-and-death issue that we search the scriptures "so that the man of God may be thoroughly equipped for every good work" (2 Tim. 3:17). And we should not be surprised if we experience opposition in living out the Gospel because some recipients of the Gospel were threatened by the revolutionary nature of Paul and Silas who were accused of "turning the world upside down" (Acts 17:6).

The title of this book is *Biblical Interpretation for Laypeople and Other Martyrs: A Sane Study in Hermeneutics for Contemporary Life.* The question is, why do people have difficulty interpreting the Bible? The first reason, of course, is biblical illiteracy. One can't understand a book he does not read. So part of the solution is turning off the television or the internet and becoming acquainted with the contents of the book.

In earlier chapters, we reviewed personal, historical, and cultural factors that interfere with our openness to understanding the scriptures. We also said that reading the Bible is not just to know something about an important piece of literature. Something is to happen to us. Micah put it this way:

> He has showed you, O man, what is good.
> And what does the LORD require of you?

---

[689]   *Ibid.*, 170.

[690]   *Ibid.*, 172–174.

BIBLICAL INTERPRETATION FOR LAYPEOPLE AND OTHER MARTYRS 343

> To act justly and to love mercy
> and to walk humbly with your God (6:8).

That is exactly what is reflected in Jesus's ministry. At Nazareth, he proclaimed that his ministry was the fulfillment of Isaiah 61:1–2:

> The Spirit of the LORD is on me,
> > because he has anointed me
> > to preach good news to the poor.
> He has sent me to proclaim freedom for the prisoners
> > and recovery of sight for the blind,
> > to release the oppressed, to proclaim the year of the
> LORD's favor.[691]

Is that not what he wants done? Then is that not our ministry also? Paul put it another way: "All this is from God, who reconciled us to himself through Christ and gave us the ministry of reconciliation: that God was reconciling the world to himself in Christ, not counting men's sins against them. And he has committed to us the message of reconciliation. We are, therefore, Christ's ambassadors, as though God were making his appeal through us. We implore you on Christ's behalf: Be reconciled to God" (2 Cor. 5:18–20).[692] In Philippians 2, Paul calls on us to have the self-sacrificing "mind of Christ" (5–11). Our ministry is what we do as His people as a response to his love for us. It is my fervent prayer that this little book will, in some way, help facilitate our doing a better job of being what we were created to be. *Sola deo Gloria!*

---

691   "The year of the Lord's favor" is reference to Leviticus 25:8–55, when every fifty years, indentured servants were freed, debts were canceled, and ancestral property was returned to the original family.

692   I used this text in my sermon upon the death of Martin Luther King Jr. because his message was one of true reconciliation, challenging the phony peace that existed under segregation as long as fear prevented African Americans from demanding justice.

APPENDIX A:
THE TOOLS

Concordance

Young, Robert. *Analytical Concordance to the Bible.* Grand Rapids: Wm. B. Eerdmans Publishing Company. Based on the KJV wording. Very helpful to those who memorized verses in the KJV or RSV. It gives the English word, the meaning of the word, the Greek or Hebrew word, and the transliteration. In the meantime, Young's concordances have been made in other versions.

Dictionaries

Achtemeier, Paul J., ed. *The HarperCollins Bible Dictionary.* San Francisco: HarperSanFrancisco, 1996. Excellent resource.

Butler, Trent C., ed. *Holman Bible Dictionary.* Nashville: Holman Bible Publishers, 1991. Many articles are excellent, but some betray strong bias and poor scholarship to support that bias.

Douglas, J. D., ed. *The New Bible Dictionary.* Grand Rapids: Wm. B. Eerdmans Publishing Co., 1962. Excellent resource. Some material dated because of recent archeological discoveries.

Grentz, Stanley J. *A Primer on Postmodernism*. Grand Rapids: 1996.

Metzger, Bruce M. and Michael D. Coogan (Ed). *The Oxford Companion to the Bible*. Oxford University Press, New York, 1993. Good basic source. But no pictures or illustrations.

Sakenfeld, Katharine Doob, (Ed). *New Interpreter's Dictionary of the Bible* (5 volumes). Nashville: Abingdon Press, 2009. Excellent resource, but expensive.

Commentaries

Ackroyd, Peter, James Barr, Bernhard W. Anderson, and James L. Mays. *The Old Testament Library*. Louisville: Westminster Press, 1974.

Fee, Gordon D., ed. *The New International Commentary on the New Testament*. Grand Rapids: William B. Eerdmans Publishing Company, 1990. Really technical stuff including Greek and Hebrew. They are usually put in notes at the bottom. Greek and Hebrew words are translated in body of commentary.

Gibson, John C. L., ed. *The Daily Study Bible Series*. Philadelphia: Westminster Press, 1986.

Harrisville, Roy A., Jack Dean Kingsbury, and Gerhard A. Krodel, eds. *Augsburg Commentary on the New Testament*. Minneapolis: Augsburg Publishing House, 1986. Good basic commentary. Greek and Hebrew transliterated. Helpful for those who do not know Greek and Hebrew.

Henry, Matthew Hubbard, David A., and Glenn W. Barker. *Word Biblical Commentary*. 53 vols. Waco, Texas: Word Books, Publishers, 1987. Fine commentary. May be difficult at times. However, most of that is put in a separate "Notes" section. Expensive. Sometimes wordy and technical.

Keck, Leander, ed. *The New Interpreter's Bible*. Nashville: Abingdon Press, 1994. Eventually, will be 12 volumes. Exposition after exegesis. NIV and NRSV in parallel texts.

Malina, Bruce J. and Richard L. Rohrbaugh. *Social Science Commentary on the Synoptic Gospels*. Fortress Press, Minneapolis, 1992. Focuses on the cultural milieu and is quite helpful in that way. Aside from that, there is not much help.

Mays, James L., ed. *Harper's Bible Commentary*. San Francisco: Harper & Row, Publishers, 1988. Good basic one-volume commentary (1,328 pages). Greek and Hebrew transliterated. Includes the Apocrypha.

Mays, James Luther, ed. *Interpretation: A Bible Commentary for Teaching and Preaching*. John Knox Press.

Von Rad, Gerhard. *The Message of the Prophets*. Harper, San Francisco, 1967.

Bible Atlases

Kraeling, Emil C. *Rand McNally Bible Atlas*. New York: Rand McNally & Company, 1956.

Gardner, Joseph L., ed. *Reader's Digest Atlas of the Bible: An Illustrated Guide to the Holy Land*. *Pleasantville*, New York: The Reader's Digest Association, Inc., 1981.

Wright, George Ernest and Floyd Foxwell Albright, eds. *The Westminster Historical Atlas to the Bible*. Revised edition. Philadelphia: The Westminster Press, 1956.

Contemporary and Near Contemporary Writings

Eusebius. *The Ecclesiastical History of Eusebius Pamphilus*. Grand Rapids: Baker Book House, 1962.

Gaster, Theodor H., trans. *The Dead Sea Scriptures*. Garden City, New York: Doubleday & Company, 1964.

Heidel, Alexander. *The Gilgamesh Epic*. University of Chicago Press, 1946. Babylonian flood story.

————. *The Babylonian Genesis*. University of Chicago Press, 1965. Babylonia creation story.

Josephus, Flavius. *Josephus: Complete Works*. Grand Rapids: Kregel Publications, 1963. History of the Jews written by a younger contemporary of Jesus.

Lightfoot, J. B., trans. and ed. *The Apostolic Fathers*. Grand Rapids: Baker Book House, 1962. Writings by church fathers after the New Testament church, including books that some early Christians thought should be included in the canon.

Lost Books of the Bible and the Forgotten Books of Eden. The World Publishing Co., Cleveland, 1926.

Robinson, James M., ed. *The Nag Hammadi Library in English*. San Francisco: HarperSanFrancisco, 1988. Includes many of the writings unearthed in southern Egypt in 1945, including the famous Gospel of Thomas.

Barnstone, Willis. *The Other Bible*. San Francisco: HarperSanFrancisco, 1984. Includes Jewish pseudepigrapha, Christian apocrypha, Gnostic writings (including the famous Gospel of Thomas), numerous apocalyptic writings, and some of the Dead Sea Scrolls. Some overlap with the Nag Hammadi Library, the Lost Books, and the Dead Sea Scriptures.

Hermeneutics

Braaten, Carl E. and Robert W. Jensen, eds. *Reclaiming the Bible for the Church.* Grand Rapids: William B. Eerdmans Publishing Company, 1995.

Frye, Northrop. *The Great Code: The Bible and Literature.* San Diego: Harcourt Brace Jovanovich, 1982.

Grant, Robert M., with David Tracy. *A Short History of the Interpretation of the Bible.* Minneapolis: Fortress Press, 1984.

Mayer, Herbert T. *Interpreting the Holy Scriptures.* Concordia Publishing House, St. Louis, 1967.

McKim, Donald K. *The Bible in Theology and Preaching: How Preachers Use Scripture.* Nashville: Abingdon Press, 1985.

Mickelson, A. Berkeley. *Interpreting the Bible.* Eerdmans, Grand Rapids, 1963.

Von Hofmann, J. C. K. *Interpreting the Bible.* Augsburg, Minneapolis, 1959.

Von Rad, Gerhard. *The Message of the Prophets.* San Francisco: HarperSanFrancisco, 1965.

Westermann, Claus. *A Thousand Years and a Day.* Fortress Press, 1957.

Historical Background

Bright, John. *The Kingdom of God: The Biblical Concept and Its Meaning for the Church.* Nashville: Abingdon Press, 1953.

Milton, John P. *God's Covenant of Blessing.* Madison, Wisconsin: Straus Publishing Co., 1965.

Russell, D. S. *Between the Testaments.* Philadelphia: Fortress, 1965.

Historical Novels

Eldad, Israel and Moshe Aumann. *Chronicles.* 2 vols. Jerusalem: Reubeni Foundation, 1954, 1967.

Melber, David W. *The Making of a Messiah: Influences on Jesus' Childhood and Youth.* San Diego, California: Aventine Press, 2008.

Michener, James A. *The Source.* Fawcett Publishers, Inc. Greenwich, Connecticut: Fawcett Publishers, 1965.

Rice, Anne. *Christ the Lord: Out of Egypt.* New York: Random House, 2005. Edited by Alan Richardson. *A Theological Word Book of the Bible.* New York: Macmillan Company, 1950.

Isagogics

Boadt, Lawrence. *Reading the Old Testament: An Introduction*. Paulist Press, NY, 1984.

Hunter, Archibald M. *Introduction the New Testament*. Philadelphia: Westminster Press, 1957.

Key, Howard; Franklin W. Young; and Karlfriend Froehlich. *Understanding the New Testament*. Englewood Cliffs, New Jersey: Prentice-Hall, 1973.

Van der Woude, A. S., gen ed. *The World of the Old Testament*. Eerdmans Pub. Co., Grand Rapids, 1989.

Borg, Marcus J. *Meeting Jesus Again for the First Time: The Historical Jesus & the Heart of Contemporary Faith*. San Francisco: HarperSanFrancisco, 1994.

Bultmann, Rudolf. *Jesus and the Word*. New York: Charles Scribner's Sons, 1934.

————. *Jesus Christ and Mythology*. New York: Charles Scribner's Sons, 1958.

Fiorenza, Elisabeth Schussler. *Jesus Miriam's Child Sophia's Prophet: Critical Issues in Feminist Christology*. New York: Continuum, 1995.

Johnson, Luke Timothy. *The Real Jesus: The Misguided Quest for the Historical Jesus and the Truth and Traditional Gospels*. San Francisco: HarperSanFrancisco, 1996.

Tracy, David. *Blessed Rage for Order: The New Pluralism in Theology*. Chicago: The University of Chicago Press, 1996.

Parallels

Throckmorton, Burton H., Jr., ed. *Gospel Parallels: A Synopsis of the First Three Gospels*. New York: Thomas Nelson & Sons, 1957. Most study Bibles, while not including the wording side by side, lines up the references in parallel.

Translations (English)

Barker, Kenneth, ed. *The NIV Study Bible*. Grand Rapids: Zondervan Publishing House, 1985. Concordance, topic reference, center column reference, and footnotes on texts.

Coleman, Lyman, Dietrich R. Gruen, Gary G. Christopherson, William F. Culter, Mary H. Naegeli, Lance Pierson, Denny Rydberg. *The Serendipity Bible for Study Groups*. Zondervan Bible Publishers, 1988. Designed for study groups. Has many illustrations and reflections for discussion—some excellent, some not so good.

Hoerber, Robert G., ed. *Concordia Self-Study Bible: New International Version*. St. Louis: Concordia Publishing House, 1984.

Metzger, Bruce M. and Roland E. Murphy, eds. *The New Oxford Annotated Bible with the Apocryphal/Deuterocanonical Books*. New Revised Standard Version. New York: Oxford University Press, 1994. Excellent resource. Good translation and commentary at the bottom of the page, discussion of Bible Study, nice little concordance, and good maps.

The Holy Bible: Contemporary English Version. New York: American Bible Society, 1995.

The Holy Bible: King James Version. Almost every major publishing house that produces any kind of theological writing publishes a KJV. Some also have good reference and study resource. Although the common language of 1611 sounds flowery and beautiful to some people today, it is hard for most people to understand. And the text is based on a very late manuscript and is not as accurate as any of the newer versions.

The Holy Bible: Revised Standard Version. New York: Thomas Nelson & Sons, 1952–1959.

Jerusalem Bible. New York: Doubleday & Company, 1966. *Good News Bible: The Bible in Today's English Version*. New York: American Bible Society, 1976.

The Hebrew-Greek Key Study Bible. New American Standard. Chattanooga, 1984.

Word Study Book

Richardson, Alan, ed. *A Theological Word Book of the Bible*. New York: Macmillan Company, 1950.

Nave, Orville J. *Nave's Topical Bible: A Digest of the Holy Scriptures*. Hendrickson Publishers. Very helpful in studying topics.

Zodhiates, Spiros, ed. *The Complete Word Study Dictionary: New Testament*. Iowa Falls, Iowa: Word Bible Publishers, Inc., 1992.

APPENDIX B:
DEFINITIONS

The first two or three times that I taught this lesson, there was no historical background chapter, and "definitions" were in the second or third chapter. However, I found that I often had to spend time explaining or defining terms before I could go on, so it seemed necessary to begin by defining terms. I could have put them in a glossary, but I don't believe it would be helpful to have to turn to the glossary every time a term comes up. Some of the defined terms may not be in the study itself, but will probably come up at some point in the discussions.

Autograph. The original text written by the author. It would be the specific original manuscript of Mark Twain's *The Adventures of Huckleberry Finn* or the original letter that Paul wrote to the Thessalonian or Corinthian congregation. We have no autographs of any original writing of a biblical book or letter. All we have are copies of the original. I'm not sure we would know if an autograph of a book of the Bible were found. But the very thought of it is exciting and intriguing.

351

Canon. A canon is a group of texts that are accepted by the Jews and/or the church as being "Holy Scripture."

Codex. A codex is a bound volume fastened together at the edge with a protective cover. This is a text in book form. Codices (plural form) came into common use in about AD second century.

Cuneiform. Cuneiform is a wet clay tablets on which wedge-shaped script is written with a stylus (sharp stick of metal object).

Exegesis. Exegesis is the process of interpreting a specific text.

Hermeneutics. Hermeneutics is the art and science of interpretation. It is a basic method of interpretation.

Hieroglyphics (sacred writings). A hieroglyphic is a pictorial symbol to express the things they represent. Later used to express syllables or specific sounds.

Homiletics. The art of applying the text to present situations. Preaching and teaching are example of homiletics at the point that we ask "what does this mean to me?" or "how does this apply to my life?"

Isagogics. Isagogics is the study of who wrote a text, time and place of writing, to whom it was written, the reason for writing, and its basic divisions. When you see a book called *Introduction to the Old Testament* or *Introduction to the New Testament*, it is usually an isagogical book.

Ostraca. Ostraca are strips of stone or potsherds with inscriptions written on in ink.

Papyrus. A papyrus is a scroll written on reeds that grow in the Nile. Papyrus is the word from which "paper" is derived.

Paraphrase. Paraphrase is a restatement of a text giving the meaning in another form. I don't know if the following story is true, but it makes a good illustration. I have been told that when the first missionaries to the Eskimos wanted to tell the story of the lost sheep, since there was no word

BIBLICAL INTERPRETATION FOR LAYPEOPLE AND OTHER MARTYRS   353

in the Eskimo language for "sheep," and since they had no idea of what a sheep might be, a paraphrase had to be manufactured. The story goes that the word for "seal pup" was used so that they got some idea of what a sheep is. But of course, something was lost in that modification. A biblical example of a paraphrase is when the original text uses the expression "the circumcised." There may be some who do not have enough background to know that this is a reference to "Jews." Therefore, if the term "Jews" is used, the sense or the meaning is communicated even though, strictly speaking, the exact term is not used. This is becoming a common practice in modern versions of the Bible.

Parchment. A parchment is a leather or animal skin on which script is written.

Scroll. A scroll is a roll of papyrus or parchment on which text is written.

Septuagint. The Septuagint is the first Greek translation of the Hebrew Old Testament and certain other books. Like many immigrant groups, the second- and third-generation Jews in Alexandria, Egypt, were losing their Hebrew language. They were learning Greek, and their children were not able to read the Hebrew Bible. So (according to Josephus) the king of Egypt, Ptolemy II Philadelphus, had a Greek translation made as a favor to the Jews. However, in the process, some writings were added that were not in the Hebrew Old Testament. These additional books are included in the Roman Catholic Bible. They are referred to as "Deuterocanonical" by the Catholic Church and "Apocrypha" by Protestant Churches. The Septuagint is often designated by the Roman numeral "LXX."

Translation. The rendering of a text of one language into another language. The Old Testament was written in Hebrew and Aramaic. The New Testament was written in Greek. Most of us do not read those languages, so we have to depend on the translation that someone or some group made of the text into English.

Transliteration. The rendering the words of one language in the lettering of another language. The Greek word for "brother" is ἀδελφός. But if we read only English, we must transliterate the word into English.

"Adelphos" is the way this word is usually transliterated into English. The Hebrew word pisc, usually translated "peace" is transliterated "shalom." That gives us some idea of the way the word is pronounced. Since very few languages have all the exact same sounds, very often the best you can do is get close to the pronunciation.

Version. A version is a translation. Although not the first one, the King James Version of the English Bible is the best-known translation. Now, however, a plethora of translations exist—the New English Bible, the Jerusalem Bible, the Revised Standard Version, the New Revised Standard Version, the English Version (*Good News for Modern Man*), New International Version, etc. There are many others, usually called by the old alphabet soup: KJV, NEB, JB, RSV, NRSV, TEV, NIV, etc. While it is nice to have versions that now speak modern English that is more understandable to us, it also can be confusing as to which one to use. And it makes learning passages by memory very difficult.

BIBLIOGRAPHY

"3-Year-Old Kills Mother With Handgun in Oklahoma," *NBC News*. <http://bit. ly.2xzOGZa>; <myarklamiss.com>, updated 11-25-14, 11:19 AM.

Achtemeier, Paul J., ed. *The HarperCollins Bible Dictionary*. San Francisco: HarperSanFrancisco, 1996. Print.

Ackroyd, Peter, James Barr, Bernhard W. Anderson, and James L. Mays. *The Old Testament Library*. Louisville: Westminster Press, 1974. Print.

Aland, Kurt et al., eds. *The Greek New Testament*. Philadelphia: American Bible Society, 1966. Print.

Aland, Barbara, Kurt Aland, Johannes Karavidopoulos, Carlo M. Martini, and Bruce Metzger, eds. (4th revision editors). *The Greek New Testament*. Stuttgart, Germany: Deutsche Bibelgesellshaft, 1993. Print.

"Alexander the Great." *History.com*. <www.history.com/topics/ancient-history/ alexander-the-great>.

Almasy, Steve and John Newsome. "Florida mother shoots daughter she thought was intruder." *CNN.com*. December 31, 2015. <http://www.cnn. com/2015/12/30/us/florida-mother-shoots-daughter/index.html>.

Alternet, Kristen Gwynne. "Ten worst sentences for marijuana-related crimes: Punishments of this sort seldom fit the offense, but these cases are especially egregious." *Salon.com*. Monday, Oct. 29, 2012, 10:54 AM CDT.<http://www.salon.com/2012/10/29/ten_worst_sentences _for_marijuana_related_crimes/.

Andreae, James et al. "Formula of Concord." *The Book of Concord: The Confessions of the Evangelical Lutheran Church.* Translated and edited by G. Tappert. St. Louis: Concordia Publishing House, 1959. Print.

Anderson, C. "Prison Populations challenge Already Cash-Strapped States." *News Tribune.* July 28, 2003, p. A7; "Punishment and Prejudice: Racial Disparities in the War on Drugs," *Human Rights Watch,* 1999. New York: Human Rights Watch, 1999; *Human Rights Watch,* "The Impact of the War on Drugs on US Incarceration," New York: Human Rights Watch, 2000. Print.

Anderson, T. Carlos. *Just a Little Bit More: The Culture of Excess and the Fate of the Common Good.* Austin, Texas: Blue Ocotillo Publishing, 2014. Print.

Articles of Confederation: March 1, 1781. New Haven, CT: Lillian Goldman Law Library, Yale University, 2008. <avalon.law.yale.edu/18th_century/artconf.asp>.

Associated Press. "2-year-old accidentally shoots, kills his mom in Idaho Wal-Mart." <www.nola.com/traffic/index.ssf/2014/12/2-year-old_accidentally_kills.html>, Sept. 22, 2015, 5:08 PM CDT. Updated Sept. 24, 2015 4:00 PM CDT.

August, Bill, director. *Les Miserables.* Columbia Pictures, 1998. Film.

Barker, Kenneth, ed. *The NIV Study Bible.* Grand Rapids: Zondervan, 1985. Print.

Barnabas. "Epistle." *The Ante-Nicene Fathers.* vol. 1. Edited by Alexander Roberts and James Donaldson. Grand Rapids: Eerdmans, 1981. Print.

Barnhart, Clarence L. and Robert K. Barnhart, eds. *The World Book Dictionary.* Chicago: World Book-Childcraft, 1982. Print.

Barnstone, Willis. *The Other Bible.* San Francisco: HarperSanFrancisco, 1984. Print.

Berger, Peter L. *A Rumor of Angels: Modern Society and the Rediscovery of the Supernatural.* New York: Anchor Books/Doubleday, 1970. Print.

————. *Invitation to Sociology: A Humanistic Perspective.* Garden City, New York: Anchor Books/Doubleday, 1963. Print.

————. *The Noise of Solemn Assemblies.* Garden City, NY: Doubleday, 1961. Print.

Berger, Peter L. and Hansfried Kellner. *Sociology Reinterpreted: An Essay on Method and Vocation.* Garden City, New York: Anchor Press, 1981. Print.

Berger, Peter L. and Thomas Luckmann. *The Social Construction of Reality: A Treatise in the Sociology of Knowledge.* Anchor Books, 1966. Print.

Bible Education Center. <Reading.hopeinchampaign.com>. Blog.

Bishop, Don. "Woman on balcony shot by man with gun downstairs." *KRMG.* <krmg.com>.

Boadt, Lawrence. *Reading the Old Testament: An Introduction.* NY: Paulist Press, 1984. Print.

Books of Eden. The World Publishing Co., Cleveland, 1926. Print.

Borg, Marcus J. *Evolution of the Word: The New Testament in the Order the Books Were Written.* NY: HarperCollins, 2012. Print.

————. *The God We Never Knew: Beyond Dogmatic Religion to a More Authentic Contemporary Faith.* San Francisco: HarperSanFrancisco, 1998. Print.

————. *Meeting Jesus Again for the First Time: The Historical Jesus & the Heart of Contemporary Faith.* San Francisco: HarperSanFrancisco, 1994. Print.

Boring, M. Eugene. "Names of God in the New Testament," *HarperCollins Bible Dictionary.* Edited by Paul J. Achtemeier. San Francisco: HarperSanFrancisco, 1996. Print.

Braaten, Carl E. and Robert W. Jensen, eds. *Reclaiming the Bible for the Church.* Grand Rapids: Eerdmans, 1995. Print.

Bratcher, Dennis. "Community and Testimony." *Cultural Influence in Biblical Studies.* <http://www.crivoice.org/historyculture.html>.

Bright, John. *The Kingdom of God: The Biblical Concept and Its Meaning for the Church.* Nashville: Abingdon Press, 1953. Print.

Brinkerhoff, David B. and Lynn K. White. *Sociology.* St. Paul: West Publishing Company, 1991. Print.

Brooks, Anthony, trans. "Virginia Case Review Revives DNA Debate," Morning Edition, National Public Radio, KUT, Austin, Jan 25, 2006. <www.npr.org/templates/story/story. php?storyId=5171456>.

Bryan, William Jennings. *Bryan's "Cross of Gold" Speech: Mesmerizing the Masses.* <historymatters.com>.

Bultmann, Rudolf. *Jesus and the Word.* New York: Charles Scribner's Sons, 1934. Print.

————. *Jesus Christ and Mythology.* New York: Charles Scribner's Sons, 1958. Print.

————. "New Testament and Mythology." *Kerygma and Myth: A Theological Debate.* London: SPCK, 1953. Print.

"Bush calls for changes on illegal workers." <http://articles.cnn.com/2004-01-07/politics/bush.immigration_1_immigration-laws-illegal-immigrants-immigration-proposals?_s=PM:ALLPOLITICS>, January 08, 2004.

Butler, Trent C., ed. *Holman Bible Dictionary.* Nashville: Holman, 1991. Print.

Carlton, Jeff. *The Associated Press.* 2014 NOLA Media Group. <http://secure-us. imrworldwide. com/cgi-bin/m?ci=us403537h&cg=0&cc=1&ts= noscript>."Cat10.

"Chernobyl: Consequences of the Catastrophe for People and the Environment." *Annals of the New York Academy of Science* 1181 (December 2009). <nyas.org>. Retrieved 15 March 2011.

Childs, Brevard S. *A Biblical Theology of the Old and New Testaments: Theological Reflections on the Christian Bible.* Minneapolis: Fortress Press, 1993. Print.

Chomsky, Marvin, John Erman, David Greene, and Gilbert Moses, eds. 7-part series. David L. Wolper Productions, Warner Bros., 1977. TV.

Citizens United v. Federal Election Commission, 558 U.S. 310 (2010).

Clement. "First Epistle of Clement to the Corinthians" XIII (p. 8); XL. *The Ante-Nicene Fathers,* Grand Rapids: Eerdmans, 1981. Print.

<climate.nasa.gov/causes/>, last updated: Oct. 29, 2015.<climate.nasa.gov/causes/>.

Coggins, Richard. "The Book of Ezra." *The HarperCollins Bible Dictionary.* Gen. ed. Paul J. Achtemeier. San Francisco: HarperSanFrancisco, 1996. Print.

Coleman, Lyman et al. *The Serendipity Bible for Study Groups.* Grand Rapids: Zondervan, 1988. Print.

<Com/quote/quotes/m/martinluth390143.html>.Updated 3:16 PM ET, Wed., Dec. 31, 2014.

Cone, James. *Black Theology and Black Power.* NY: Seabury, 1969. Print.

"Controversial Police Encounters Fast Facts." *CNN Library.* Updated 12:20 PM ET, Sunday, July 2 2017. <http://www.cnn.com/2015/04/05/us/controversial-police-encounters-fastfacts/index. html>.

Cook, John, Naomi Oreskes, et al. "Consensus on consensus: a synthesis of consensus estimates on human-caused global warming." *Environmental Research Letters.* Published 13 April 2016 IOP Publishing Ltd, http://iopscience.iop.org/article/10.1088/1748-9326/11/4/048002/meta.

Corley, Matt. "Hagee Says Hurricane Katrina Struck New Orleans Because It Was 'Planning a Sinful' 'Homosexual Rally." *ThinkProgress.* April 23, 2008.<https://thinkprogress.org/ hagee-says-hurricane-katrina-struck-new-orleans-because-it-was-planning-a-sinful-homosexual-rally-55b392a04322>.

Costner, Kevin, dir. *Dances With Wolves.* Tig Productions, 1990. Film.

Craddock, Fred B. *Interpretation: A Bible Commentary for Teaching and Preaching—Luke.* Ed. James Luther Mays. Louisville: John Knox Press, 1990. Print.

Culpepper, R. Alan. *The New Interpreter's Bible—Luke-John (Vol. X).* Edited by Leander E. Keck. Nashville: Abingdon, 1995. Print.

"Cuneiform script." *History of Writing.* <en.m.wikipedia.org>.

Cunningham, Lawrence S. "The Latter-Day Saints, Church of Jesus Christ." *The HarperCollins Dictionary of Religion.* Edited by Jonathan Z. Smith. San Francisco: HarperSanFrancisco, 1995. Print.

Dabla-Norris et al. *Causes and Consequences of Income Inequality: A Global Perspective.* International Monetary Fund, June 25, 2015.

"'Das Elektroauto': Opel Ampera- impresses with electrifying high-tech." *Automotive World.* <Automotiveworld.com>.

Davidson, Benjamin. *The Analytical Hebrew and Chaldee Lexicon.* Peabody, MA: Hendrickson Publishers, 1981. Print.

Dearman, J. Andrew. *Religion & Culture in Ancient Israel.* Peabody, MA: Hendrickson Publishers, 1992. Print.

"Debate in Virginia Ratifying Convention." *The Founders Constitution.* Article 1, Section 12, Clause 8 (Document 27). Chicago: The University of Chicago. <http://press-pubs.uchicago.edu/founders/>,14 June 1788, Elliot 3:380-95, 300-402.

Dickstein, Leah, Rachel Kruzan, and Annie Antar. "Real cost of outrageous drug prices: What happens when a company hikes the cost of crucial medicine by 5,000%," *USA TODAY,* Gannett Satellite Information Network, 4:40 PM ET Dec. 27, 2015.<https://www. usatoday.com/story/ opinion/2015/12/27/true-cost-outrageous-drug-prices-deraprim-martin-shkreli-column/77838400/; the web site says also read this on http://usat.ly/1YKX6L3>.

Dixon, A. C., ed. *The Fundamentals: A Testimony to the Truth.* Los Angeles: Bible Institute of Los Angeles, 1915. Print.

Dolak, Kevin. "Asst. Principal Accused of Having Sex With Student at Prom." *ABCNEWS.com.*
https://www.bing.com/search?q=%E2%80%9Casst.+principal+accused+of+having+sex+with+student+at+prom%2C%E2%80%9D&form=EDGEAR&qs=PF&cvid=977e098af63f4580b33fad746b23e393&cc=US&setlang=en-US. March 13, 2013.

Douglas, J. D., ed. *The New Bible Dictionary.* Grand Rapids: Eerdmans, 1962. Print.

Dred Scott v. Sandford, 60 U.S. 393 (1857).

Durden, Tyler. "Fukushima Five Years Later: 'The Fuel Rods Melted Through Containment And Nobody Knows Where They Are Now.'" <zerohedge.com>, 3/11/2016; 23:27.

Durose, Matthew, Alexander Cooper, and Synder. "Recidivism of Prisoners Released in 30 States in 2005: Patterns from 2005 to 2010." Washington DC: U.S. Department of Justice, 2014.

Eastwood, Clint, dir. *The Outlaw Josie Wales.* Warner Brothers. 1976. Film.

Edin, Kathryn J. and H. Luke Shaefer. "Ronald Reagan's 'welfare queen' myth: How the Gipper kickstarted the war on the working poor." <salon.com>. Sunday, Sept. 27, 2015, 10:59 AM CDT.

Eldad, Israel and Moshe Aumann. *Chronicles.* 2 vols. Jerusalem: Reubeni Foundation, 1954, 1967. Print.

"Enchiridion: The Small Catechism of Dr. Martin Luther for Ordinary Pastors and Preachers." *The Book of Concord: The Confessions of the Evangelical Lutheran Church.* Theodore G. Tappert, translator and editor. St. Louis: Concordia, 1959. Print.

Engelbrecht, Edward A. "Luther's Threefold Use of the Law." *Concordia Theological Quarterly* 75:1–2 (January/April 2011), referring to Martin Luther, *Luthers Werke: Kritische Gesamtausgabe [Scriften]*, 65 vols. (Weimar: H. Böhlau, 1883–1993) 10:I:456-457; 26:17. Print.

<En.m.wikipedia.org/wiki/Papyrus>.

<en.wikipedia.org/wiki/Erin_Brockovich>, last edited on 23 May 2017, at 12:50.

<en.wikipedia.org/wiki/File:Population_curve.svg>.

<en.wikipedia.org/wiki/Global_Warming#Scientific_discussion>.

<en.wikipedia.org/wiki/Immigration_to_the_United_States>. Last modified 16 October 2015, at 22:27.

<en.wikipedia.org/wiki/John_Wayne>. Last modified on 28 July 2016. at 07:07 am.

<en.wikipedia.org/wiki/Second_Great_Awakening>, last modified on 18 July 2016, at 18:46.

<En.m.wikipedia.org/wiki/The_Fundamentals>.

<en.wikipedia.org/w/index.php!title=Trickle-down_economics&oldid=713856282>. Last modified on 6 April 2016, at 05:42.

<En.wikipedia.org/wiki/John_Wayne>, last modified Nov. 2, 2015 at 15:31.

<en.wikipedia.org/wiki/The_Conqueror>, last modified on 5 March 2016, at 17:06.

<en.wikipedia.org/w/index.php?title=Flood_myth&oldid=607582294>. Last modified on 8 May 2014 at 04:39.

<en.wikipedia.org/w/index.php?title=Idiom&oldid=727716105>. Last modified June 30, 2016, at 20:21.

<en.wikipedia.org/w/index.php?title=Modern_Hebrew_verb_conjugation&oldid=727096289>. Last modified on 26 June 2016, at 17:05.

<en.wikipedia.org/wiki/Womanist_theology>. Modified on 25 July 2011 at 03:11.

<en.wikipedia.org/wiki/Stono_Rebellion>.

Eusebius. *The Ecclesiastical History of Eusebius Pamphilus.* Grand Rapids: Baker Book House, 1962. Print.

Ewert, David and Bruce M. Metzger. "Texts, Versions, Manuscripts, Editions." *HarperCollins Bible Dictionary.* Edited by Paul J. Achtemeier. San Francisco: HarperSanFrancisco, 1996. Print.

Fee, Gordon D., ed. *The New International Commentary on the New Testament.* Grand Rapids: Eerdmans, 1990. Print.

Fearnside, W. Ward and William B. Holther. *Fallacy: The Counterfeit of Argument.* Englewood Cliffs, NJ, 1959. Print.

"Fifty Years of Honda in America." July 7, 2009. http://www.automobilemag. com/news/fifty-years-of-honda-history/>.

Fiorenza, Elisabeth Schussler. *Jesus Miriam's Child Sophia's Prophet: Critical Issues in Feminist Christology.* New York: Continuum, 1995. Print.

"First Epistle of Clement to the Corinthians." *The Ante-Nicene Fathers*, XIII. Grand Rapids, Michigan: Eerdmans, 1981. Print.

Ford, John, dir. *3 Godfathers* (also known as *Three Godfathers*). Argosy Pictures, 1948. Film.

Ford, John, ed. *The Searchers.* Warner Brothers, 1956. Film.

Founders Constitution, The. Article 1, Section 12, Clause 8 (Document 27). Chicago: University of Chicago, 2000. <press-pubs.uchicago.edu/founders/>.

Fox, Douglas. "The Crisis on the Ice," *National Geographic* 232, no. 1 (July 2017), 32. Magazine.

Fretheim, Terence. "The Book of Genesis." *The New Interpreter's Bible.* vol. 1. Edited by Leander E. Keck. Nashville: Abingdon, 1994. Print.

Friedman, Thomas L. *The World is Flat: A Brief History of the Twenty-First Century.* New York: Farr, Straus and Giroux, 2005. Print.

————. *Hot, Flat, and Crowded: Why We Need a Green Revolution—And How It Can Renew America.* NY: Farrar, Straus and Giroux, 2008. Print.

"From Scroll to Codex." http://courses.educ.ubc.ca/etec540/July03/batchelorj/ researchtopic/>.

Fruchtenbaum, Arnold G. *Midrash/Pesher and Hermeneutics.* Ariel Ministries.<file:///C:/Users/ David-PC/Documents/Writings/Biblical%20 Interp%20for%20Laypeople/2009-ChaferConf-Fruchtenbaum-Paper.pdf>.

Frye, Northrop. *The Great Code: The Bible and Literature.* San Diego: Harcourt Brace Jovanovich, 1982. Print.

Fundamentals, The: A Testimony to the Truth. A. C. Dixon, ed. Bible Institute of Los Angeles. En.m.wikipedia.org/wiki/The_Fundamentals.

"G. Stanley Hall." emergingadulthood.umwblogs.org; psyking.net.

Galbraith, John Kenneth. "Recession Economics." *New York Review of Books* 29, no. 1 (February 4, 1982). Print.

Ganim, Sara and Linh Tran. "How tap water became toxic in Flint, Michigan." *CNN.* January 13, 2016, 10:53 AM ET. CNN.com.

Gardner, Joseph L., ed. *Reader's Digest Atlas of the Bible: An Illustrated Guide to the Holy Land.* Pleasantville, NY: The Reader's Digest, 1981. Print.

Geza, Vermes. *The Complete Dead Sea Scrolls in English*. New York: Pelican Books, 1997. Print.

Giangreco, D. M., and Kathryn Moore. *Dear Harry: Truman's Mailroom, 1945-1953*, quoted in <https://en.wikipedia.org/w/index. php!title=Trickledown_economics&oldid=713856282>. Last modified on 6 April 2016, at 05:42.

Gibson, John C. L., ed. *The Daily Study Bible Series*. Philadelphia: Westminster Press, 1986. Print.

"Girl, 14 Shot Dead By Boy While Playing Gun, Police Say." abc7chicago. com>,Sunday, August 16, 2015. http://abc7chicago.com/news/girl-14-shot-dead-by-boy-while-playing-with-gun police-say/933783/>.

"Global Climate Change Impacts in the United States." IPCC Fourth Assessment Report, 2007 United States Global Change Research Program. Cambridge, Mass. University Press, 2009. climate.nasa.gov/causes/.

Global Climate Change and Carbon Dioxide Lesson – Earth & Environmental Science – Teacher Version (with answers).<sos.noaa.gov/_media/cms/sosx/ climate_change_and_carbon _dioxide_ lesson_teacher.pdf. http://nsl. caltech.edu/home/>.

"Global Climate Change: Vital Signs of the Planet." *NASA*. http://climate.nasa. gov/causes/>. Last updated October 29, 2015.

Gore, Al, dir. *An Inconvenient Truth*. Davis Guggenheim. Paramount Classics, 2006. Movie.

"Gospel of Thomas." *The Nag Hammadi Library in English*. Edited by James E. Robinson. San Francisco: HarperSanFrancisco, 1988. Print.

Grant, Robert M., with David Tracy. *A Short History of the Interpretation of the Bible*. Minneapolis: Fortress Press, 1984. Print.

Green, Joel B., gen. ed. *The CEB Study Bible with Apocrypha*. Nashville: Common English Bible, 2013. Print.

Grenz, Stanley J. *A Primer on Postmodernism*. Grand Rapids Eerdmans, 1996. Print.

Grissom, Brandi. "Williamson County DA Eyes New Prosecuting Job: Outgoing Williamson County District Attorney John Bradley is being considered to head up the state office that prosecutes crimes in state prisons and juvenile detention facilities." *Texas Tribune*. Oct. 19, 2012, 5:00 PM. https://www.texastribune.org/2012/10/19/ john-bradley-eyes-new-job-prosecuting-prisoners/.

Guggenheim, Davis, dir. *Alliance for Climate Protection, Climate Reality Project, Natural Resources Defense Council, National Wildlife Federation,* and *Stop Global Warming*. Paramount Classics, 2006. Print.

Gwynne, Kristen. Alternet. "Ten worst sentences for marijuana-related crimes: Punishments of this sort seldom fit the offense, but these cases are especially egregious." Salon.com. Monday, Oct. 29, 2012, 10:54 AM CDT.

Hamilton, Adam. *Making Sense of the Bible: Rediscovering the Power of Scripture Today.* New York: HarperCollins, 2014. Print.

Hanson, Curtis, dir. *L.A. Confidential.* Warner Brothers, 1997. Film.

Harrington, Daniel. "Introduction to the Canon." *New Interpreter's Bible.* vol. 1. Edited by Leander E. Keck. Nashville: Abingdon, 1994. Print.

———. "Introduction to the New Interpreter's Bible." *New Interpreter's Bible.* vol. 1. Edited by Leander E. Keck. Nashville: Abingdon, 1994. Print.

Harrisville, Roy A., Jack Dean Kingsbury, and Gerhard A. Krodel, eds. *Augsburg Commentary on the New Testament.* Minneapolis: Augsburg, 1986. Print.

Harrisville, Roy A., and Walter Sundberg. *The Bible in Modern Culture: Baruch Spinoza to Brevard Childs.* Grand Rapids: Eerdmans, 2002. Print.

Hatch, Nathan O. *The Democratization of American Christianity.* New Haven, CT: Yale University Press, 1989. Print.

"Heblish-Hebrew lessons: Day 36," <Iclnet.org>; Yaron, free-hebrew.com, Sept. 2, 2010.

Hebrew-Greek Key Study Bible. Chattanooga: New American Standard. 1984. Print.

Heiner, Robert. *Social Problems: An Introduction to Critical Constructionism.* 5th ed. New York: Oxford University Press, 2016. Print.

Henry, Matthew Hubbard et al. *Word Biblical Commentary.* 53 vols. Waco, Texas: Word Books, Publishers, 1987. Print.

Henslin, James M. *Introducing Sociology: Selected Readings.* NY: Free Press, 1975. Print. <Hermeneutics.kulikorskyonline.net>.

Hill, George Roy, dir. *Hawaii.* Metro-Goldwyn-Mayer Studios Inc., 1966. Film.

Hoerber, Robert G., ed. *Concordia Self-Study Bible: New International Version.* St. Louis: Concordia, 1984. Print.

Holy Bible: Contemporary English Version, The. New York: American Bible Society, 1995. Print.

Hooper, Russell. *Two Big Things You Didn't Know About Oil Subsidies.* http://www. policymic. com/articles/73903/two-big-things-you-didn-t-know-about-oil-subsidies. November 20, 2013.

Horton, Paul B. and Gerald R. Leslie. *The Sociology of Social Problems.* New York: Meredith Corporation, 1970. Print.

"How FDA Evaluates Regulated Products: Drugs." US Food and Drug Administration: US Department of Health.<https://www.fda.gov/AboutFDA/Transparency/Basics/ ucm269834.htm>.

<http://climate.nasa.gov/causes/; the panel's full Summary for Policymakers report is online at http://www.ipcc.ch/pdf/assessment-report/ar4/syr/ar4_syr_spm.pdf>.

<http://climate.nasa.gov/causes/>. Last updated October 29, 2015.

<http://en.wikipedia.org/wiki/File:Population_curve.svg>.

<http://en.wikipedia.org/w/index.php?title=Flood_myth&oldid=607582294>. Last modified on 8 May 2014 at 04:39.

<http://en.wikipedia.org/wiki/Global_Warming#Scientific_discussion>.

<http://en.wikipedia.org/wiki/Global_Warming#Scientific_discussion>.

<http://en.wikipedia.org/wiki/Immigration_to_the_United_States>. Last modified 16 October 2015, at 22:27.

<http://en.wikipedia.org/wiki/Immigration_to_the_United_States>. Last modified on 20 May 2011 at 18:25.

<http://en.wikipedia.org/wiki/Womanist_theology>. Modified on 25 July 2011 at 03:11.

<http://originalpeople.org/stono-rebellion-1739-slave-revolt/>.

<http://patrioticmillionaires.org/>.

<http://www.automobilemag.com/news/fifty-years-of-honda-history>/.

<http://www.ipcc.ch/pdf/assessment-report/ar4/syr/ar4_syr_spm.pd>f.

<http://www.sourcewatch.org/index.php/SourceWatch>.

<http://www.ucsusa.org/global_warming#.VjZzrbSFNyQ>.

<https://climate.nasa.gov/scientific-consensus/>.

<https://en.wikipedia.org/wiki/Erin_Brockovich>. Last edited on 23 May 2017 at 12:50.

<https://en.wikipedia.org/wiki/Frank_Serpico>.

<https://en.wikipedia.org/wiki/List_of_Islamist_terrorist_attacks.

<https://en.wikipedia.org/wiki/Love_Canal>, last edited on 18 June 2017, at 21:40.

<https://en.wikipedia.org/w/index.php!title=Trickle-<down_economics&oldid=713856282>. Last modified on 6 April 2016, at 05:42.

<https://public.wmo.int/en/media/press-release/wmo-confirms-2016-hottest-year-record-about-11°c-above-pre-industrial-era>.

https://www.census.gov/popclock/>.

Huxley, Aldus. *Jesting Pilate: A Diary of a Journey.* New York: George H. Doran, 1926. Print.

Ignatius. "The Epistle of Ignatius to the Philadelphians." *The Ante-Nicene Fathers.* vol. 1. Edited by Alexander Roberts and James Donaldson. Grand Rapids: Eerdmans, 1981. Print.

————. "The Epistle of Ignatius to the Smyrnaeans," VII. *The Ante-Nicene Fathers.* vol. 1. Edited by Alexander Roberts and James Donaldson. Grand Rapids: Eerdmans, 1981.

"Immigration Adjustment Act of 1991." Civic Impulse. (2016). Govtrack.com, S. 296 — 102nd Congress: Armed Forces Retrieved from <https://www.govtrack.us/congress/ bills/102/s296>.

Imagine the Universe. National Aeronautics and Space Administration: Goddard Space Flight Center. <imagine.gsfc.nasa.gov/docs/ask_astro/answers/980403a.html>.

<Innocenceproject.org>.

Jansen, Bart. "It's a problem for the nation': Former Okla. cop preyed on Minority women," *USA TODAY,* <www.azcentral.com/story/news/nation/2015/12/11/former-oklahoma-police-officer-found-guilty-serial-rape/77138186>, 6:34 p.m. MST December 11, 2015.

Jerusalem Bible. New York: Doubleday & Company, 1966. Print. July 30 2015, 6:09 p.m.

Johnson, Luke Timothy. *The Real Jesus: The Misguided Quest for the Historical Jesus and the Truth and Traditional Gospels.* San Francisco: HarperSanFrancisco, 1996. Print.

Joint science academies' statement: Global response to climate change. http://nationalacademies. org/onpi/06072005.pdf.

Jones, Robert P. *The End of White Christian America.* New York: Simon & Schuster, 2016. Print.

Josephus, Flavius. "Antiquity of the Jews: Flavius Josephus Against Apion" (Book I, 8). *Josephus: Complete Works.* Grand Rapids: Kregel, 1963. Print.

Justin Martyr. "The First Apology of Justin," LXVII, 3. *The Ante-Nicene Fathers.* vol. 1. Edited by Alexander Roberts and James Donaldson. Grand Rapids: Eerdmans, 1981. Print.

Kaiser, Walter C. Jr. and Moises Silva. *Introduction to Biblical Hermeneutics: The Search for Meaning.* Grand Rapids: Zondervan, 2007. Print.

Kappeler, Victor, Mark Blumberg, and Gary Potter. *The Mythologies of Crime and Criminal Justice.* Prospect Heights, IL: Waveland Press, 2000. Print.

Keck, Leander E. "Introduction to the New Interpreters' Bible." *New Interpreters' Bible.* vol. 1. Edited by Leander E. Keck. Nashville: Abingdon, 1994. Print.

King, Martin Luther, Jr. (n.d.). BrainyQuote.com. <http://www.brainyquote>, July 7, 2016,

Key, Howard et al. *Understanding the New Testament.* Englewood Cliffs, New Jersey: Prentice-Hall, 1973. Print.

Kittelson, James M. *Luther the Reformer: The Story of the Man and His Career.* Minneapolis: Augsburg Publishing House, 1986. Print.

Kraeling, Emil C. *Rand McNally Bible Atlas.* New York: Rand McNally, 1956. Print.

Kramer, Stanley, dir. *The Defiant Ones.* United Artists, Sept. 24, 1988. Movie.

"LG Chem sees GM selling over 30,000 Bolt electric vehicles next year," *Reuters.* Oct. 18 2016, 4:22 AM. <Businessinsider.com>.

La Santa Sede. <http://w2.vatican.va/content/francesco/en/apost-exhortations/documents/papa-francesco_esortazione-ap_20131124_evangelii-gaudium.htmo#No_to_an_economy_of_ exclusion>.

Lam, Linda. *Lightning Deaths the Last 10 Years, Mapped.* July 22, 2015, 12:00 AM EDT. <https://weather.com/storms/severe/news/lightning-deaths-by-state-2005-2014>.

Lauer, Robert H. and Jeanette C. Lauer. *Social Problems and the Quality of Life.* Boston: McGraw-Hill, 2008. Print.

Leon-Guerrero, Anna. *Social Problems: Community, Policy, and Social Action.* 5th ed. Los Angeles: Sage Publications, 2016. Print.

Levison, Barry, dir. *Wag the Dog.* Baltimore Pictures TriBeCa Productions, 1997. Movie.

Lightfoot, J. B., trans. and ed. *The Apostolic Fathers.* Grand Rapids: Baker Book House, 1962. Print.

Lindsey, Hal. *The Late Great Planet Earth.* Grand Rapids: Zondervan, 1970. Print.

Lindsey, Rebecca. "Collapse of the Larsen-B Ice Shelf." January 31, 2002. <https://www.earthobservatory.nasa.gov/Features/WorldOfChange/larsenb.php>.

Liston, Robert A. *Why We Think as We Do.* New York: Franklin Watts, 1977. Print.

Long, Colleen. "Doc kills 1, self in rifle spree at Bronx hospital." Associated Press report in the *Austin American-Statesman*, Saturday, July 1, 2017. Newspaper.

Lost Books of the Bible and the Forgotten Books of Eden, The. Cleveland: World Pub. Co., 1926. Print.

Luther, Martin. "Enchiridion: The Small Catechism of Dr. Martin Luther for Ordinary Pastors and Preachers." *The Book of Concord: The Confessions of the Evangelical Lutheran Church.* Edited and translated by Theodore G. Tappert. St. Louis, MO: Concordia Publishing House, 1959. Print.

———. *The Bondage of the Will.* Trs. J. I. Packer & O.R. Johnston. Grand Rapids: Fleming H. Revell, 1957. Print.

Luther, Martin. "The Third Article," *The Small Catechism.* Translated by Michael Martinez and Tony Marco. bookofconcord.org.

Maas, Peter. *Serpico: The Cop Who Defied the System.* New York: Viking Press, 1973. Print.

Maher, Bill. *Real Time with Bill Maher.* HBO. TV.

Malina, Bruce J. and Richard L. Rohrbaugh. *Social Science Commentary on the Synoptic Gospels.* Minneapolis: Fortress Press, 1992. Print.

Malthus, Thomas Robert. *An Essay on the Principles of Population.* 4th ed. London: J. Johnson, 1807. Print.

Mann, Dave. "DNA Tests Undermine Evidence in Texas Execution: New results show Claude Jones was put to death on flawed Evidence." Texasoberver.org. Thursday, Nov. 11, 2010 at 7:57 PM CST.

Martin, Richard C. "Jesus Christ." *The HarperCollins Dictionary of Religion.* Edited by Jonathan Z. Smith. San Francisco: HarperSanFrancisco, 1995. Print.

Martin, W. J. *The New Bible Dictionary.* Org. Ed. J. D. Douglas. Grand Rapids: Eerdmans, 1962. Print.

Martin, Richard C. "Jesus Christ." *The HarperCollins Dictionary of Religion.* Edited by Jonathan Z. Smith. San Francisco: HarperSanFrancisco, 1995. Print.

Martinez, Michael and Tony Marco. "Mom fatally shot when son, 2, grabs gun from her purse in Walmart," <http://www.cnn.com/2014/12/30/us/idaho-walmart-shooting-accident-mother-toddler/index.html> CNN.com. Updated 3:16 PM ET, Wed December 31, 2014.

Marty, Martin. *The Hidden Discipline.* St. Louis: Concordia Publishing, 1962. Print.

Mathis, Kate. "My Experience at Innocence Project of Florida's 2016 Steppin' Out Spring Gala." June 16, 2016 @ 1:00 PM. <http://floridainnocence.org/content/?tag=william-dillon>.

Mayer, Herbert T. *Interpreting the Holy Scriptures.* St. Louis: Concordia, 1967. Print.

Mays, James L., ed. *Harper's Bible Commentary.* San Francisco: Harper & Row, 1988. Print.

Mays, James Luther, ed. *Interpretation: A Bible Commentary for Teaching and Preaching.* John Knox Press, 1988. Print.

McCarter, Kyle P., Jr. *The HarperCollins Bible Dictionary.* s.v. "writing." Gen. Ed. Paul J. Achtemeier. San Francisco: HarperSanFrancisco. 1996. Print.

McConn, J. Clinton, Jr. "The Book of Psalms." *The New Interpreter's Bible.* Edited by Leander Keck. Nashville: Abingdon Press, 1996. Print.

McKim, Donald K. *The Bible in Theology and Preaching: How Preachers Use Scripture.* Nashville: Abingdon Press, 1985. Print.

McLuhan, Marshall. *The Mechanical Bride: Folklore Man.* New York: McGraw-Hill, 1964. Print.

———. *The Medium is the Message: The Inventory of Effects.* New York: Random House, 1967. Print.

———. *Understanding Media: The Extensions of Man.* New York: McGraw-Hill, 1964. Print.

Mead, Margaret. *Coming of Age in Samoa: A Psychological Study of Primitive Youth for Western Civilization.* New York: Will Morrow & Co, 1928. Print.

———. *Sex and Temperament: In Three Primitive Societies:* New York: HarperCollins Publishers, 1935. Print.

Melber, David W. *The Making of a Messiah: Influences on Jesus' Childhood and Youth.* San Diego: Aventine Press, 2011. Print.

Metzger, Bruce M., and Michael D. Coogan, eds. *The Oxford Companion to the Bible.* NY: Oxford Univ. Press, 1993. Print.

Mickelson, A. Berkeley. *Interpreting the Bible.* Grand Rapids: Eerdmans, 1963. Print.

Mills, Steve, and Maurice Possley. *DNA Tests Sought for Executed Man.* April 19, 2005. <smmills@Tribune.com> and <possley@Tribune.com>.

Milton, John P. *God's Covenant of Blessing.* Madison, Wisconsin: Straus Publishing Co., 1965. Print.

Michener, James A. *The Source.* Greenwich, CT: Fawcett Publishers, 1965. Print.

"Modern Hebrew verb conjugation,"<https://en.wikipedia.org/w/index.php?title=Modern_ Hebrew_verb_conjugation&oldid=727096289>, last modified on 26 June 2016, at 17:05.

Mollenkott, Virginia Ramery. *Omnigender: A Trans-religious Approach.* Cleveland: The Pilgrim Press, 2007. Print.

———. *The Divine Feminine: The Biblical Imagery of God as Female.* New York: Crossroad Publishing Co., 1988. Print.

———. *Women, Men, & the Bible.* Nashville: Abingdon, 1977. Print.

Mooney, Linda A. et al. *Understanding Social Problems.* Belmont, CA: Wadsworth Cengage Learning, 2011. Print.

Mott Stephen C. *HarperCollins Bible Dictionary.* s.v. "poor." Gen. Ed. Paul J. Achtemeier. San Francisco: HarperSanFrancisco, 1996. Print.

Morgan, Patricia A. "The Legislation of Drug Law: Economic Crisis and Social Control." Edited by J. D. Arcutt. *Analyzing Deviance.* Homewood, IL: Dorsey Press, 1983. Print.

Mounce, William D. *The Lexicon to the Greek New Testament.* Grand Rapids: Zondervan, 1993. Print.

Muilenburg, James. *The Interpreter's Bible.* Gen. Ed. George Buttrick. Nashville: Abingdon Press, 1956. Print.

BIBLICAL INTERPRETATION FOR LAYPEOPLE AND OTHER MARTYRS   369

Murphy, Roland E. *The HarperCollins Bible Dictionary.* s.v. "The Bible," Ed. Paul J. Achtemeier. San Francisco: HarperSanFrancisco, 1996. Print.

"Nate Lewis Leads US Energy Innovation Hub at Caltech." *The Planning Report: Insider's Guide to Planning & Infrastructure, August 7, 2013.*<https://www.verdexchange. org/news/nate-lewis-leads-us-energy-innovation-hub-caltech>.

National Center for Children in Poverty. Columbia University.<http://www.nccp. org/topics/child poverty.html>.

National Highway Traffic Safety Administration, U.S. Department of Transportation. <crashstats.nhtsa.dot.gov/Api/Public/ ViewPublication/812231>.

Nave, Orville J. *Nave's Topical Bible: A Digest of the Holy Scriptures.* Hendrickson Publishers (n.d.). Print.

Neubeck, Kenneth J. *Social Problems: A Critical Approach.* New York: McGraw-Hill, 1991. Print.

Neusner, Jacob. *What Is Midrash?* Philadelphia, PA: Fortress Press, 1987.

Newsome, John. "Police: Son, 14, shot dead by dad who says he mistook him for intruder." *CNN,* Wed., January 13, 2016. <Cnn.com>. <http://www.cnn. com/2016/01/12/us/father-shoots-son/index.html>.

Nida, Eugene A. *God's Word in Man's Language.* New York: Harper, 1952. Print.

————. Oral Presentation, Concordia Theological Seminary, Springfield, IL, 1963 or 1964. (n.d).

———— and Charles R. Taber. *The Theory and Practice of Translation.* Leiden, Netherlands: E. J. Brill, 1969. Print.

———— and William D. Reyburn. *Meaning Across Cultures* (American Society of Missiology Series, No. 4). Maryknoll, New York: Orbis Books, 1961. Print.

NumbersUSA: For Lower Immigration levels. <https://www.numbersusa.com/content/ learn/illegal -immigration/us>.

O'Brien, J Randall. *Holman Bible Dictionary.* s.v. "Rahab." Gen. Ed. Trent C. Butler. Nashville: Holman, 1991. Print.

Oreskes, Naomi. "The Scientific Consensus on Climate Change." *Science* 306, no. 5702 (December 2004), 1686. doi: 10.1126/science.1103618. *IPCC Fourth Assessment Report, 2007.* "Global Climate Change Impacts in the United States," United States Global Change Research Program,Cambridge University Press, 2009. <http://climate.nasa.gov/causes/>.

<originalpeople.org/stono-rebellion-1739-slave-revolt/>.

Overby, Peter. "NRA: 'Only Thing That Stops A Bad Guy With A Gun Is A Good Guy With A Gun'," *All Things Considered, NPR,* Dec 21,

20123:00 PM ET. <http://www.npr.org/2012/12/21/ 167824766/ nra-only-thing-that-stops-a-bad-guy-with-a-gun-is-a-good-guy-with-a-gun>.

Pakula, Alan J., dir. *The Devil's Own*. Columbia Pictures Corporation, 1997. Film.

Paris, Valerie (OECD). "Why Do Americans Spend So Much on Pharmaceuticals?" *PBS News Hour*. KLRU. February 7, 2014, at 12:15 PM EDT. <http://www.pbs. org/newshour/updates/ americans-spend-much-pharmaceuticals/>.

"Pastor of Hermas, The." *The Ante-Nicene Fathers*. vol. 2. Alexander Roberts and James Donaldson, Eds. Grand Rapids: Eerdmans, 1979. Print.

Patterson, Thom. "Talk with Us: America's Death Penalty under Scrutiny." *CNN* iReport. Updated Tuesday, March 4, 2014, 6:15 PM EST. <http://www.cnn.com/2014/03/03/ us/death-row-stories hangout/index. html>.<patrioticmillionaires.org/>.

Pew Center on the States. *State of Recidivism: The Revolving Door of America's Prisons*. Washington, DC: Pew Charitable Trusts, 2011.

Perdue, Leo G. "Names of God in the Old Testament." *HarperCollins Bible Dictionary*. Ed. Paul J. Achtemeier. San Francisco: HarperSanFrancisco, 1995. Print.

Phillips, J. B. *Your God Is Too Small*. New York: Macmillan, 1961. Print.

Philo. *Allegory of the Jewish Law*, I, 31–32.<http://www.earlyjewishwritings.com/ text /philo/book2.html>.

Pitts, Bryon et al. "Former Federal Judge Regrets 55-Year Marijuana Sentence."<abcnews.go. com>. Feb. 18, 2015, 12:22 PM ET.

Plato. *The Republic*. *The Gutenberg Project*. Translated by Benjamin Jowett. <www. gutenberg.com>. May 22, 2008 [EBook #150].

Plato. *The Republic*. Translated by J. Harwood. *Great Books of the Western World*. vol. 7. Editor in Chief Robert Maynard Hutchins. Chicago: Encyclopaedia Britannica. Print.

Popovich, Nadja, John Schwartz, and Tatiana Schlossberg. "How Americans Think About Climate Change, in Six Maps." *New York Times*. March 21, 2017. Newspaper. <https://www.nytimes.com/ interactive/2017/03/21/climate/ how-americans-think-about-climate-change-in-six-maps.html>.

Population Pyramids of the World from 1950 to 2100: State of Palestine.<http://www. populationpyramid.net/state-of-palestine/2001/>.

Poverty and Justice Bible, The. Contemporary English Version. New York: American Bible Society, 2008. Print.

Presley, Elvis. "In the Ghetto." RCA Victor. April 1969. Record.

Preuss, Andreas. "3-year-old boy shoots father, pregnant mother in New Mexico." <http://www.cnn.com/2015/02/01/us/new-mexico-toddler-shoots-parents/index.html>.

Quiggins Paige. "Police: Woman shot with own gun during attempted home invasion in Hillview." <*WDRB.com*>, posted Oct. 28, 2013, 8:08 AM CDT, updated Oct. 28, 2013 4:36 PM CDT.

Rafter, Nicole Hahn, and Mary Gibson, trans. *Criminal Woman, the Prostitute, and the Normal Woman*. Durham, NC: Duke University Press, 2004. Print.

Rayman, Graham. "Feds probing Chicago police after cop seen on video shooting teen Laquan McDonald 16 times." *NEW YORK DAILY NEWS*,<www.nydailynews.com/news/ national/ feds-probing-chicago-police-laquan-mcdonald-killing-article-1.2457595>.

Reuters. "LG Chem sees GM selling over 30,000 Bolt electric vehicles next year," Oct. 18 2016, 4:22 AM. <*Businessinsider.com*>. News Agency.

Rice, Anne. *Christ the Lord: Out of Egypt*. New York: Random House, 2005. Print.

Richardson, Alan, ed. *A Theological Word Book of the Bible*. New York: Macmillan, 1950. Print.

Robinson, James M., ed. *The Nag Hammadi Library in English*. San Francisco: HarperSanFrancisco, 1988. Print.

Russo, Karen. "Cops Say Firewood Chore May Have Prompted Boy to Murder Mom".<abcnews.go.com/USboy-killed-mom-firewood-chore/ story?id=12537130>. January 4, 2011.

Russell, D. S. *Between the Testaments*. Philadelphia: Fortress, 1965. Print.

Schiffman, Lawrence H. "Jubilees, Book of," *The HarperCollins Bible Dictionary*. Gen. Ed. Paul J. Achtemeier. San Francisco: HarperSanFrancisco, 1996. Print.

"S. 296 — 102nd Congress: Armed Forces Immigration Adjustment Act of 1991," *Civic Impulse*, 2016. Govtrack.com. Retrieved from <https://www.govtrack. us/congress/bills/102/s296>.

St. Clement. "First Epistle of Clement to the Corinthians." *The Ante-Nicene Fathers*. vol. 1. Edited by Alexander Roberts and James Donaldson. Grand Rapids: Eerdmans, 1981. Print.

Sanders, E. P. *The Historical Figure of Jesus*. New York: New York: Penguin Press, 1993. Print.

Sanders, James A., and Astrid Beck. "The Leningrad Codex: Rediscovering the Oldest Complete Hebrew Bible," *Bible Review*, Vol. XIII, Number 4, Aug 1997. Print.

Sauer, Alfred von Rohr. "Problems of Messianic Interpretation." *Concordia Theological Monthly*. St. Louis: Concordia, 1962. Print.

Schiffman, Lawrence H. "Jubilees, Book of." *The HarperCollins Bible Dictionary*. Gen. Ed. Paul J. Achtemeier. San Francisco: HarperSanFrancisco, 1996. Print.

"Scroll and Codex." <http://penelope.uchicago.edu/~grout/encyclopaedia_romana/scroll/ scrollcodex.html#anchor171306>.

"Scroll versus the Codex, The." <http://www.biblewheel.com/Canon/Scroll_vs_Codex.ph>.

"Second Great Awakening." <En.m.wickipedia.org>.

Segal, Peter, dir. *Naked Gun 3 1/3: The Final Insult.* Paramount Pictures, 1994. Film.

Septuagint Version of the Old Testament and Apocrypha, London: Bangster. Print.

Simpson, Cuthbert A. "The Book of Genesis." *The Interpreter's Bible.* vol. 1. George Buttrick (Gen. Ed). Nashville: Abingdon Press, 1956.

Slack, Megan. *Five Reasons to Repeal Subsidies for Oil Companies.* <http://www.whitehouse.gov/blog/2012/03/29/repeal-subsidies-oil-companies>. March 29, 2012, 11:57 AM EDT.

Smith, Gary. "Levirate Law, Levirate Marriage," *Holman Bible Dictionary.* Gen. Ed. Trent C. Butler. Nashville: Holman, 1991. Print.

Smith, Ryan. "Pat Robertson: Haiti 'Cursed' After 'Pact to the Devil.'" CBSNEWS.com, Jan. 13, 2010, 1:58 pm. <http://www.cbsnews.com/news/pat-robertson-haiti-cursed-after-pact-to-the-devil/>.

Soderbergh, Steven, dir. *Erin Brockovich,* Universal Pictures 2000. Film.

Spillman, Rose. "Lake Placid mayor: 2-year-old accidentally shoots, kills his mom in Idaho Wal-Mart." WCAX.com <http://www.nola.com/traffic/index.ssf/2014/12/2-year-old_accidentally_kills.html>, Sept 22, 2015 5:08 PM CDT, Updated Sept. 24, 2015 4:00 PM CDT.

Sreenivasan, Hari. "On the Beat." *PBS News Hour.* June 30, 2017. Judy Woodruff, anchor. Television.

Stewart, Heather. "Wealth doesn't trickle down – it just floods offshore, research reveals." *The Guardian* (London).<https://www.theguardian.com/business/2012/jul/21/ offshore-wealth-global-economy-tax-havens>, July 21, 2012. Retrieved August 6, 2012.

Storti, Craig. *The Art of Crossing Cultures.* Yarmouth, Maine: Intercultural Press, 1990. Print.

Streisand, Barbara, dir. *Yentl.* MGM, 1983. Film.

Sullivan, Jennifer. "Man who accidentally shot woman in movie theater had gun permit, police say." *The Seattle Times,* <columbian.com>, published January 22, 2016, 7:20 PM.

Swansea University. "The one trillion ton iceberg: Larsen C Ice Shelf rift finally breaks through." *ScienceDaily,* 12 July 2017. <www.sciencedaily.com/releases/2017/07/170712110527.htm>.

BIBLICAL INTERPRETATION FOR LAYPEOPLE AND OTHER MARTYRS   373

Swiggum, Harley. *The Bethel Series* Madison, WI: Adult Christian Education Foundation, 1960. Print.

Tenny, Merrill C. *The New Testament: An Historical and Analytic Survey.* Grand Rapids: Eerdmans, 1953. Print.

"Terrorism 2000/2005." Federal Bureau of Investigation: Dept. of Justice.<https://www.fbi.gov/ stats-services/publications/terrorism-2002-2005#terror_05sum.

"Tesla Model 3 to roll off the line Friday." *Austin American-Statesman.* Tuesday, July 4, 2017, B5. Print.

"Texas Court Delays Execution For DNA Testing." *The Wall Street Journal.*<http://blogs.wsj. com/law/2011/11/08/texas-court-delays-execution-for-dna-testing/>. on November 14, 2010 at 12:30 PM.

www.chicagotribune.com.   secure-us.imrworldwide.com/cgi-bin/m?ci=us400338h&cg= 0&cc=1&ts=noscript.

The Septuagint of the Old Testament and Apocrypha with an English Translation of with Various Readings and Critical Notes. London: Samuel Bagster and Sons. Print.

Thio, Alex. *Sociology: An Introduction.* New York: Harper & Row, 1989. Print.

"The first Volkswagen Beetle in America looked like this." *Autoweek.* January 29, 2014. <http://autoweek.com/article/car-news/first-volkswagen-beetle-america-looked>.

The Founders Constitution. Article 1, Section 12, Clause 8 (Document 27), 1987 by the University of Chicago. All rights reserved. Published 2000. <http://press-pubs.uchicago.edu/founders/>.

"Three Mile Island Accident." <en.wikipedia.org/wiki/Three_Mile_Island_accident>, last edited on 7 June 2017, at 02:46.

Thom Hartmann Show. July 30, 2015, 6:09 PM. http://www.thomhartmann. comTelevision.

Throckmorton, Burton H., Jr., ed. *Gospel Parallels: A Synopsis of the First Three Gospels.* New York: Thomas Nelson & Sons, 1957. Print.

<timeopinions.files.wordpress.com/2014/02/woman-prison. jpg?w=480&h=320&crop= 1" alt="Woman in jail" title="Woman in jail"/>. (Orlando, FL; May 13, 2013).

"Tobacco-Related Mortality." Centers for Disease Control and Prevention: U.S. Dept. of Health and Human Services.<https://www.cdc.gov/tobacco/data_statistics/fact_sheets/fast_facts/ index.htm>.

Torah, Prophets, and Writings. The Hebrew Old Testament. The British and Foreign Bible Society, Israel, 1962. Print.

Trible, Phyllis. *Texts of Terror.* Minneapolis: Fortress Press, 1984. Print.

"Trickle Down." Perot campaign ad. (n.p.).

Tucker, Gene M. *The New Interpreter's Bible—The Book of Isaiah 1-39 (Vol. VI)*. Ed. Leander E. Keck. Nashville: Abingdon, 2001. Print.

Tuerkheimer, Deborah. *The Changing Face of Exonerations. New DNA Testing Reveals Innocence of Man on Florida's Death Row and Points to Victim's Daughter as Likely Perpetrator.* <http://timeopinions.files.wordpress.com/2014/02/woman-prison.jpg?w=480&h=320&# 038;crop=1" alt="Woman in jail" title="Woman in jail"/>. Orlando, FL; May 13, 2013). March 05, 2014.

———. *The Changing Face of Exonerations. New DNA Testing Reveals Innocence of Man on Florida's Death Row and Points to Victim's Daughter as Likely Perpetrator.*<https://www.innocenceproject.org/new-dna-testing-reveals-innocence-of-man-on-floridas-death-row-and-points-to-victims-daughter-as-likely-perpetrator/March 05, 2014>.

Twitchy Staff. "Attn: Obama: THIS woman was glad she had a gun (but the man who tried to rob her wasn't." *twitchy.com*. Posted 4:49 pm on January 9, 2016. <http://twitchy.com/dougp-3137/2016/01/09/attn-obama-this-woman-was-glad-she-had-a-gun-but-the-man-who-tried-to-rob-her-wasnt/> posted 4:49 pm on January 9, 2016.

Union of Concerned Scientists: Science for a healthy planet and safer world.<http://www. ucsusa.org/global_warming#.VjZzrbSFNyQ>.

United Nations Framework Convention on Climate Change.<http://unfccc.int/paris_agreement/ items/9485.php>.

United States Census Bureau, Department of Commerce.<https://www.census.gov/main/www/cen 1990.html>.

US Population in Millions: 1940 to 2050. Census.gov.

Van der Woude, A. S., gen. ed. *World of the Old Testament, The*. Grand Rapids: Eerdmans, 1989. Print.

"Volvo to go electric and ditch gas-only vehicles." *Austin American-Statesman*. Thursday, July 6, 2017. Print.

Von Hofmann, J. C. K. *Interpreting the Bible*. Augsburg, Minneapolis, 1959. Print.

Von Rad, Gerhard. *The Message of the Prophets*. San Francisco: HarperSanFrancisco, 1965. Print.

<w2.vatican.va/content/francesco/en/apost-exhortations/documents/papa-francesco_esortazione-ap_20131124_evangelii-gaudium.htmo#No_to_an_economy_of_exclusion>.

Walker, Alice. *In Search of Our Mother's Gardens: Womanist Prose*. San Diego: Harcourt, 1983. Print.

Wallis, Jim. *America's Original Sin: Racism, White Privilege, and the Bridge to a New America*. Grand Rapids: Brazos Press, 2016. Print.

Walsh, Sean Collins. "DPS handpicks ex-cop to study profiling," *Austin American-Statesman*, Monday, July 3, 2017. <scwalsh@statesman.com>.

Waters, Tony. "Bush calls for changes on illegal workers." *Crime and Immigrant Youth.* Thousand Oaks, CA: Sage Publications, 1999. <http://en.wikipedia.org/wiki/Immigration_to_the_United _States>, last modified 16 October 2015, at 22:27.

WCET Staff. "WPD: Woman dies after self-inflicted gunshot wound at gun range." WCET. <http://www.k5thehometeam.com/story/30787390/wpd-woman-dies-after-self-inflicted-gunshot-wound-at-gun-range>. Dec. 18, 2015, 2:18 PM CST.

Weis, Don, dir. *The Affairs of Doby Gillis.* MGM, 1953. Film.

Williams, Timothy. "Iraqi Journalist Who threw Shoes at Bush Was tortured in Jail, His Brother Says," <nytines.com>, <http://www.nytimes.com/2008/12/22/world/middleeast/22iraq.html>, Dec. 21, 2008.

Willingham, Emily. "Why Did Mylan Hike EpiPen prices 400%? Because They Could," *Forbes,* August 21, 1016, 9:00 A.M.<https://www.forbes.com/forbes/welcome/?toURL=https://www. forbes.com/sites/emilywillingham/2016/08/21/why-did-mylan-hike-epipen-prices-400-because-they-could/&refURL=https://www.bing.com/&referrer=https://www.bing.com/>. Magazine.

Winter, Michael. "Woman accidentally kills self-adjusting bra holster." *USA Today,*usatoday.com, <https://www.usatoday.com/story/news/2015/02/18/woman-kills-self-adjusting-bra-holster/23640143/>, Feb. 28, 2015, 9:11 p.m. EST.

Westermann, Claus. *A Thousand Years and a Day.* Fortress Press, 1957. Print.

Wiseman, D. J. "writing," *The New Bible Dictionary.* Org. Ed. J. D. Douglas. Grand Rapids: Eerdmans.

"Witness: Accidental shooting in Beaumont the result of a gun falling out of a purse." <12newsnow.com>, posted Oct. 19, 2015 11:14 AM CDT. (This article outdated and put in archives *WMO confirms 2016 as hottest year on record, about 1.1°C above pre-industrial era.* World Meteorological Organization. <https://public.wmo.int/en/media/press-release/wmo-confirms-2016-hottest-year-record-about-11°c-above-pre-industrial-era>.

"Woman shot while sitting in car at Shaw's Supermarket in Bath." *WMTW News 8,*<wmtw@ wmtw.com>, Nov. 16, 2015, 6:09.53 PM EST; Updated Nov. 17, 2015, 8:50.34 PM EST.

"Woman shot with own gun by man who hired pair for sex in University City" *St. Louis Post-Dispatch,* September 23, 2015, <http://www.stltoday.com/news/

local/crime-and-courts/woman-shot-with-own-gun-by-man-who-hired-pair/article_aed9a632-7f45-5f2a-af17-7c49a738d1dc.html>.

Woodruff, Judy, anchor. *PBS News Hour.* Wednesday, May 29, 1917. PBS.org, News Hour Productions. Television.

Woodruff, Judy, anchor. *PBS News Hour.* Wednesday, May 31, 1917. PBS.org, News Hour Productions. Television.

Worldometers. http://www.worldometers.info/world-population/.

"WPD: Woman dies after self-inflicted gunshot wound at gun range." *WCET.* <http://www.k5thehometeam.com/story/30787390/wpd-woman-dies-after-self-inflicted-gunshot-wound-at-gun-range>.

Wright, Darlene R. and Kevin M. Fitzpatrick deal with several of these in "Violence and Minority Youth: The Effects of Risk and Asset Factors on Fighting among African American Children and Adolescent," *Adolescence,* Summer 2006. <www.questia.com>.

Wright, N. T. *The New Testament and the Peoples of God.* Minneapolis: Fortress Press, 1992. Print.

————. *The New Interpreter's Bible – The Letter to the Romans.* Vol. X. Ed. Leander E. Keck. Nashville: Abingdon, 2002. Print.

<wsj.com/law/2011/11/08/texas-court-delays-execution-for-dna-testing/>. Blog

Wyrick, Steve. "Leviathan," *Holman Bible Dictionary.* Gen. Ed. Trent C. Butler. Nashville: Holman, 1991. Print.

<www.biblegateway.com>.

<www.chicagotribune.com. secure-us.imrworldwide.com/cgi-bin/m?ci=us-400338h&cg=0&cc=1&ts=noscript>.

<www.cnn.com/2014/03/03/us/death-row-stories-hangout/index.html>.

<www.earlyjewishwritings.com/text/philo/book2.html>.

<www.historyworld.net/wrldhis/PlainTextHistories.asp?historyid=ab33>.

<www.numbersusa.com/content/learn/illegal-immigration/us. kvue.com>, Nov. 8, 2013, 3:44pm.

<www.textweek.com>.

<www.ucsusa.org/global_warming#.VjZzrbSFNyQ>.

<www.worldometers.info/world-population/>.

Young, Robert. *Analytical Concordance to the Bible.* Grand Rapids: Eerdmans (n.d). Print.

Zodhiates, Spiros, ed. *The Complete Word Study Dictionary: New Testament.* Iowa Falls, IA: Word Bible Publishers, 1992. Print.